The LIFE and TRAVELS
of JOHN BARTRAM

The·
Botanist.

The LIFE and TRAVELS of JOHN BARTRAM:

From Lake Ontario to the River St. John

Edmund Berkeley
and
Dorothy Smith Berkeley

A Florida State University Book
University Presses of Florida
Tallahassee

University Presses of Florida is the central agency for scholarly publishing of the State of Florida's university system. Its offices are located at 15 NW 15th Street, Gainesville, FL 32603. Works published by University Presses of Florida are evaluated and selected for publication by a faculty editorial committee of any one of Florida's nine public universities: Florida A&M (Tallahassee), Florida Atlantic University (Boca Raton), Florida International University (Miami), Florida State University (Tallahassee), University of Central Florida (Orlando), University of Florida (Gainesville), University of North Florida (Jacksonville), University of South Florida (Tampa), University of West Florida (Pensacola).

Library of Congress Cataloging in Publication Data

Berkeley, Edmund.
   The life and travels of John Bartram: from Lake
Ontario to the River St. John.

   "A Florida State University book."
   Bibliography: p.
   Includes index.
   1. Bartram, John, 1699–1777. 2. Botanists—
Pennsylvania—Biography. 3. Botany—United States—
History. I. Berkeley, Dorothy Smith. II. Title.
QK31.B3B47   581'.092'4 [B]   81–4083
ISBN 0–8130–0700–3   AACR2

Typography by Graphic Composition
Athens, Georgia

Printed in U.S.A.

Acknowledgments

THE beginning of our study of John Bartram is
difficult to pinpoint, but it certainly goes back
to the period when we were doing research toward a biography of
his friend John Clayton in the early 1960s. In the interim we have
been involved with two other friends of Bartram, Alexander Garden and John Mitchell. During these years so many people have
generously assisted us that it is hazardous to attempt to thank
them all. We are deeply indebted to the manuscript librarians and
their assistants of a great many libraries, and we have tried to express our appreciation to them individually. It is, nonetheless, a
pleasure to thank them collectively for all that they do to make our
writing possible.

We have been extremely fortunate in our study of Bartram to
have been able to build on a foundation of years of hard work by
other people, whose writings, both published and unpublished,
have been of the greatest assistance to us. We feel particularly indebted to Carlotta Herring-Browne, William Darlington, Ernest
Earnest, Joseph Ewan, Francis Harper, Francis D. West, and Edward E. Wildman.

We were cordially encouraged to undertake a biography of
Bartram by Emily Read Cheston and Joseph B. Townsend, Jr., of
the John Bartram Association, and we have made extensive use of
their valuable manuscript materials on deposit at the American
Philosophical Society. At the fine library of this brainchild of John
Bartram, Whitfield J. Bell, Jr., Murphy D. Smith, Carl F. Miller,
and other members of the staff have been remarkably patient and
cheerful over the years and have helped in innumerable ways.

It has always been a privilege to work in the splendid manuscript collections of the Historical Society of Pennsylvania. Their Bartram Papers have been indispensable to us in this study. The manuscript collections and the fine rare book section of the Library Company of Philadelphia were of special interest to us. We were greatly helped by Edwin Wolf, II, Lillian Tonkin, and Edward A. Hughes, Jr. Ruth E. Brown and Martha T. Pilling of the Academy of Natural Sciences gave thoughtful assistance. We also enjoyed a visit to the Friends' Historical Library of Swarthmore College, where the director, J. William Frost, and his staff were most gracious.

Many pleasant hours were spent at the Chester County Historical Society, where Dorothy B. Lapp and Conrad Wilson, a Bartram descendant, were very cordial and helpful. Among many things discovered there, a small note made in 1917 concerning a Common Place Book of William Bartram started us on a treasure hunt of many months' correspondence which eventually led us to the present owner, a Bartram descendant, Frances Kaighn Robinson. We are very much indebted to her and to her parents, Mr. and Mrs. George S. Kaighn, for all their help and for making it possible for us to examine this little-known book.

A visit to the Hunt Institute for Botanical Documentation of Carnegie-Mellon University started inauspiciously when we were snowbound on the Pennsylvania Turnpike for thirty-seven hours, but it was worth it to have the pleasure of working there. We only resented the curtailment of our research time. A great many people did everything they could to compensate. We should like to thank particularly Theodore W. Bossert, Bernadette G. Callery, Anita T. Karg, Abby Levine, Mary Jo Lilly, Denise M. Pearson, and Merry W. Ziegler.

George W. White of the University of Illinois was generous with good geological advice for nongeologists. He has not, however, seen anything that we have written on the subject and must not be blamed for any errors we may have made. Paul P. Hoffman of the North Carolina Division of Archives and History went far beyond the call of duty in assisting us with information concerning early eighteenth-century Indian warfare in Carolina. Wanda S. Campbell of the Bladen County North Carolina Historical Society was very helpful with information concerning the North Carolina Bartrams. So, too, was Mary Bartram Robeson Hunter, of Charlottesville, Virginia, a descendant of Colonel William Bartram of Ashwood. The late E. Milby Burton, Charleston, South Carolina, generously sent us information and a booklet.

Our research concerning Bartram and his friends has required three summers of work abroad, during which we have worked in manuscript collections in England, Ireland, Scotland, Wales, Denmark, the Netherlands, and Sweden. We are greatly indebted to manuscript librarians in all of these countries for their generous assistance. As she has done so often in the past, Phyllis I. Edwards of the British Museum (Natural History) helped us time and again. It is difficult to thank her adequately. We were also assisted by Alwyne Wheeler of the Zoology Department of the museum, and we appreciate his help. The Curator-Librarian of the Royal Society of Arts, D. G. C. Allan, has assisted us numerous times, and we once more thank him.

Attempts to learn something of the Bartram family from Derbyshire records involved many people. We are very much indebted to Lesley J. Webster, Friends House Library, London; Joan Sinar, County Archivist, Matlock, Derbyshire; Helen Forde, London; Mrs. F. M. Wilkins-Jones and C. Weir, Nottinghamshire County Council; Denis Stuart, University of Keele; Victor Burch, Clerk of the Staffordshire Monthly Meeting; Norman W. Tildesley, Willenhall, West Midlands.

It is a pleasure to recognize the great assistance of that unique institution the Biohistorisch Instituut der Rijkuniversiteit at Utrecht. We are deeply indebted to Miss H. de Vries and W. D. Margadant of their staff for a great deal of important help. The librarian of the manuscript department of the Royal Swedish Academy of Sciences, Christer Wijkstrom, was exceedingly gracious, sending copies of several Bartram letters from their collection.

The staff of the Interlibrary Loan Section of the Alderman Library, University of Virginia, has made it possible for us to study many materials which we should not have been able to see without a great deal more travel than we were free to undertake. For all of the work that they have done on our behalf we are very grateful. Angelika S. Powell, of the Slavic Section of the library, very kindly translated Russian letters for us, which we appreciated greatly. It has also been a privilege to make extensive use of other divisions of that fine library, especially the Rare Book and the Manuscript departments, and it is a pleasure to express our thanks.

Space limitation does not permit us to detail the help given by a number of other people but we must, at least, say thank you again to: Elizabeth Alexander, University of Florida; Bernita L. Anderson, Libraries of the Gray Herbarium and Arnold Arboretum; G. E. Bentley, Princeton University Library; Dana G. Beyer, Pennsylvania Historical and Museum Commission, Harrisburg; Herbert Cahoon, The Pierpont Morgan Library; Ward J. Childs, Department of Records, City of Philadelphia; Doris E. Cook, The Connecticut Historical Society, Hartford; Ruth Corry, Georgia Department of Archives and History, Atlanta; Alan R. Eager, Royal Dublin Society; Carla M. Fass, Universiteits-Bibliotheek, Amsterdam; Malcolm Freiberg, Massachusetts Historical Society; J. Gandy, Royal Commission on Historical Manuscripts, London; Lawrence Gardiner, *The Catskill Quarterly*; James Gregory, the New York Historical Society; Marilyn S. Horbund, the Long Island Historical Society, Brooklyn; Lisabeth M. Holloway, College of Physicians of Philadelphia; E. L. Inabinett, University of South Carolina; William F. Johnstone, The Pennsylvania State University; William L. Joyce, American Antiquarian Society; James Lawton, Boston Public Library; Helmut T. Lehman, The Lutheran Theological Seminary at Philadelphia; Kenneth A. Lohf, Butler Library, Columbia University; Roy N. Lokken, East Carolina University; Helen Weir McHenry, Gladwyne, Pennsylvania; Harriet McLoome, Huntington Library and Art Gallery; Jean R. McNiece, The New York Public Library; Charles W. Mann, The Pennsylvania State University; Paul Maloney, Bryn Mawr, Pennsylvania; Archie Motley, Chicago Historical Society; Theodore O'Grady, Linnean Society of London; A. Payne, Department of Manuscripts, The British Museum; Mrs. Charles A. Potter, Essex Institute; Mary B. Prior, The South Carolina Historical Society; Mary Wolcott Quereau, Philadelphia; E. W. Quinn, The John Crear Library, Chicago; Lyman W. Riley, The Charles Patterson van Pelt Library, University of Pennsylvania; Mrs. Charles W. Rita, Philadelphia; J. Albert Robbins, Indiana University; N. H. Robinson, The Royal Society of London; George C. Rogers, Jr., University of South Carolina; Virginia Rugheimer, Charleston Library Society, South Carolina; Richard W. Ryan, Ohio University Library, Athens; Martha Slotten, Dickinson College; Alan Smith, Salford Public Libraries, Salford, England; Susan B. Tate, University of Georgia Libraries, Athens; David R. Taylor, Havelock, North Carolina; Frank Taylor, The John Rylands University Library of Manchester, England; Robert A. Tibbetts, The Ohio State University, Columbus; Elizabeth B. Trittle, Haverford College; and Carolyn A. Wallace, University of North Carolina Library, Chapel Hill.

We are grateful for the courtesy of all of the following who have kindly given permission to quote from manuscripts in their collections:

The Academy of Natural Sciences of Philadelphia
The British Library, London
The Earl of Derby
The Historical Society of Pennsylvania
The New-York Historical Society
The Pierpont Morgan Library
The Royal Society of London
The Royal Society of Arts
The Trustees of the Boston Public Library
The Trustees of the British Museum (Natural History)
Universitetsbiblioteket Uppsala
Yale University Library

All maps, all line drawings of plants and people, and the drawing of the governor's house in St. Augustine are by Dorothy Smith Berkeley.

E. B.
D. S. B.

This biography is respectfully dedicated to the memory of Francis Harper, meticulous scholar, whose long study of John and William Bartram made him the recognized and respected authority concerning them and set a high standard for others to try to follow.

Contents

List of Illustrations   xiii

Introduction   xv

One. From Derbyshire to Darby   1

Two. Peter Collinson and His Friends   18

Three. The Education of a Botanist   35

Four. New Travels, New Friends, and a Growing
    Reputation   50

Five. Experimental Botany   61

Six. "For the Encouragement of Mr. John Bartram"   77

Seven. A Journey to the Headquarters of the Five
    Indian Nations   91

Eight. Of Science and Philosophy   112

Nine. The International Scientific Circle   126

Ten. A Companion for His Travels   148

Eleven. Affairs of Family and of Conscience   167

Twelve. To the Carolinas at Last   186

Thirteen. To Carolina Again   202

Fourteen. "His Majesty's Botanist for North
    America"   221

Fifteen. On to Florida   236

Sixteen. The River St. John   255

Seventeen. New Honors for a Scientist   272

Eighteen. "Like Newton, in Simple Facts he saw
   Great Principles"   293

Appendixes

   1. Will of Richard Bartram   305

   2. Indian Physick, from *Poor Richard's Almanac*   306

   3. The Salt-Marsh Muscle   306

   4. List of Seeds in Bartram's Five-Guinea Box   308

   5. "Our spring red maple"   310

   6. Lists of Bartram's Customers   311

   7. List of Some of Bartram's Geological Specimens   318

   8. Observations on Geographical Distribution of
      Plants   320

   9. Letter of Disownment to Bartram   322

Notes   325

Literature Cited   359

Index   369

List of Illustrations

Map, from Lake Ontario to the River St. John   xvi

Residence of John Bartram   12

"The botanist"   14

"The old corner cupboard"   16

Breintnall's leaf prints   20

Peter Collinson   23

Sir Hans Sloane   24

Illustrations from Mark Catesby, *Natural History*   27–31

Carolus Linnaeus   38

Map, trip to the Great Cedar Swamp in 1736   40

Illustration of cicada from *Philosophical Transactions*   42

Map, trip up the Schuylkill River   44

Map, trip to Maryland and Virginia in 1738   47

Ginseng (*Panax quinquefolium* L.)   52

Dr. John Fothergill   54

John Custis   56

Colonel William Byrd II   58

Sweet gum (*Liquidambar styraciflua* L.)   62

Campion (*Lychnis*)   64

Dr. Cadwallader Colden   67

Great laurel (*Rhododendron maximum* L.)   69

Shooting star (*Dodecatheon meadia* L.)   71

Bartramia   73

The Reverend George Whitefield   80

"Departure for New York"   84

Map, trip to Onondago and Oswego   93

Cucumber tree (*Magnolia acuminata* L.)   97

Bartram's drawing of the town of Oswego   102

Benjamin Franklin   116

Peter Kalm   132

Bartram's drawing of the Chesapeake Bay river
    system   144–45

William Bartram   152

Illustration of ruffed grouse from *Philosophical
    Transactions*   154

Jared Eliot   165

Moses Bartram   170

Bartram's drawing of his house and garden   181

Travels in the Carolinas   188

"Tipitiwichet sensative" (*Dionaea muscipula* Ellis)   212

St. John de Crèvecoeur   222

Travels in Georgia   239

Franklinia alatamaha, Marsh.   246

Governor's house, St. Augustine, Florida   251

Travels in East Florida   257

"The old chimney-corner"   286

Letter of disownment   323

Introduction

A FULL and adequate biography of John Bartram has long been a desideratum," wrote Francis Harper in the introduction to his annotated edition of Bartram's "Diary of a Journey Through the Carolinas, Georgia, and Florida" in 1942. Since no one was so well qualified to undertake one as Harper himself, many expected that he would ultimately do so. Having long been involved with Bartram's friends, we were no exception. With Dr. Harper's untimely death, we felt impelled to undertake what we had expected he would do.

The limited group of North American botanists in the middle third of the eighteenth century—John Clayton, Alexander Garden, John Mitchell, and Cadwallader Colden—were all Bartram's personal friends. All had benefited from a more formal education than Bartram had, but none left a more permanent record of influence on the history of American and European botany. He was by far the most colorful of them, and none of them exceeded him in scientific acumen. Bartram's botanical explorations involved travel from northern New York to Florida and west to Pittsburgh, a far wider area than that covered by any of his contemporaries or predecessors.

Much of what has been written about Bartram has been brief or sketchy, and some of it is inaccurate. Surprisingly, among the latter must be included the account of his son, William, whose "Some Account of the Late Mr. John Bartram" in its first sentence confuses John's grandfather, John, with his great-grandfather, Richard, and in the second paragraph gives the botanist's father the name John instead of William. We hope that we have not perpetuated any similar errors.

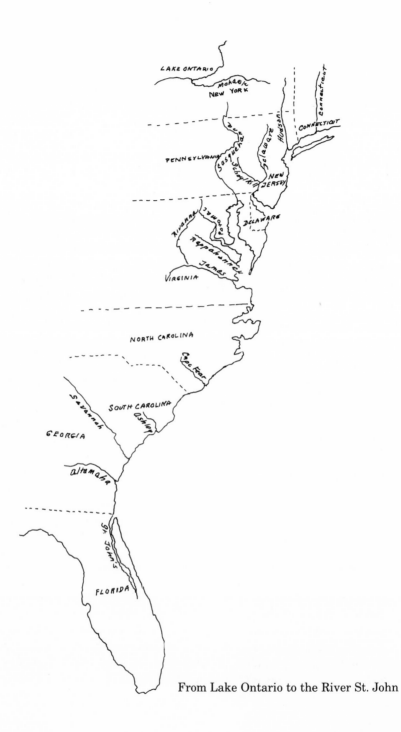

LAKE ONTARIO

Mohawk
NEW YORK

Connecticut

Hudson

CONNECTICUT

Susquehanna

Delaware

PENNSYLVANIA

Schuylkill

NEW JERSEY

Potomac

DELAWARE

Rivanna

Rappahannock

James

VIRGINIA

NORTH CAROLINA

Cape Fear

Savannah

SOUTH CAROLINA

Ashley

GEORGIA

Altamaha

St. Johns

FLORIDA

From Lake Ontario to the River St. John

ONE

From Derbyshire
to Darby

O N COLD winter evenings, when the farm chores had been completed, young John Bartram and his brother James enjoyed sitting around the fireplace, listening to their grandmother telling of her early life in England. It was of Compton and Clifton, parts of the parish of Ashbourne, in Derbyshire, that she spoke. Not only had she and their grandfather, John, made their home at Compton, but so had the boys' great-grandfather, Richard, a fellmonger, and his father before him.[1] Compton is in that mountainous part of Derbyshire known as "The Peak." This is limestone country, and Mrs. Bartram spoke of caves, sinkholes, springs, and waterfalls, of fine land for cultivation in the valleys and of excellent pastures for cattle and sheep in the uplands. At first the boys wondered why anyone would leave such a country to undertake a long and hazardous voyage to a strange land, to clear the virgin forest, and to build a new home. Their grandmother explained that the reason for their migration was related to the peaceful Meetinghouse where they worshipped every First Day. She reminded her grandsons that the Society of Friends was still very young and that the Bartrams and many of their neighbors had been closely associated with its beginnings.

Mrs. Bartram proudly told her grandsons that it had been in Derbyshire that the first recorded meeting of the Society of Friends was held, although the society had begun earlier in a few other counties.[2] It was in Derbyshire that the first active center of the sect had become established in 1647. George Fox had been imprisoned there for a year in 1650–51, and it was upon his release from prison that his triumphal ministry began to gather momentum. In these early days of the society there could be no established places for worship so meetings were held in private homes. It took courage to become a Friend, Mrs. Bartram told her grandsons, for many were persecuted, placed in the stocks, thrown into ponds by mobs, and even imprisoned. Members of the Bartram family were among those who shared in the Derbyshire "sufferings," as they came to be known.

Meetings were held at the home of the boys' great-grandmother, Mary Bartram, until authorities stormed into her house and broke up a meeting in 1663. In that same year her son, John, the boys' grandfather, had been ordered to appear before the bishop's court at Wirksworth and, in the following year, he had been imprisoned.[3] In 1668 both he and his mother were in difficulties for "absence from the publick worship."[4] But they were not to be intimidated. When Mary died in 1672, she left in her will ten shillings for the relief of poor Friends in the county.[5] In 1675 her son, "John Bartram of Compton, was prosecuted in the Ecclesiastical Court, at the Suit of Thomas Godread, Vicar there, for Tithes or Easter-Offerings, and was committed to prison on a Significavit, by Warrant from two Justices of the Peace."[6] He was released this time after twelve days.

John and James were impressed by their grandmother's account of the rapid increase of converts to the Society of Friends that soon caused the "Children of Light" to become a serious problem for the Church of England. A solution for both the church and the society had been found when Charles II made a large grant of North American land to William Penn, a Friend, in payment of a debt owed to his father. Penn's offer of land in Pennsylvania, at forty shillings per 100 acres, with the promise of religious freedom, had been eagerly accepted by thousands of harassed and threatened Quakers.

In the fall of 1681 a group of ships sailed from England for Philadelphia, soon to be followed by many others. They were to bring more people to Pennsylvania in three years than had reached New York in fifty. Within two years some ninety ships brought over 7,000 people to Philadelphia.[7] Among them were John and Elizabeth Bartram and their four children: John, Isaac, William (the boys' father), and Mary.[8] Mrs. Bartram shuddered as she described to the boys that wretched voyage and the primitive conditions they

had found at Philadelphia. Makeshift housing there was so inadequate that some people were living in caves dug in the ground.

The Bartrams were not among those who had purchased land
from Penn before sailing. They joined a small group of eight families, three of which, the Bonsalls, the Cartlidges, and the Hoods,
were also from Derbyshire. They settled in a community west of
Philadelphia, which was part of Chester County, and they gave it
the name of Darby in 1683.[9] For Mrs. Bartram it had been a great
relief to find that this was no wilderness. Both Dutch and Swedish
settlers were already there, the latter having arrived as early as
1638. Land had been cleared and small farms developed. The
Swedes were cordial to the exhausted travelers, and even the Indians were friendly (the earlier settlers had purchased land from
them and had avoided antagonizing them). The Friends were able
to establish themselves comfortably sooner than they had expected.
Many of them had brought the tools of their trades with them from
England, including a complete sawmill.

A second daughter, the boys' Aunt Elizabeth, had been added
to the Bartram family in 1684.[10] It was not until the following year
that they had been able to buy the three hundred acres on the west
side of Darby Creek on which they lived and which was now a prosperous farm.[11] John Bartram had quickly established himself as
one of the leaders of the new community. He had been active in the
organization of Darby Meeting and the construction of a meetinghouse.[12] He served on petty juries, grand juries, and coroner's in-
quests. He held office as supervisor of highways, as an appraiser of
estates, and as a constable.[13] His interest in public affairs extended
beyond Darby as well, and he represented Chester County in the
thirty-four-member Pennsylvania Assembly in 1689.[14]

There were many changes in the Bartram family during the
next few years. The eldest son, John, died unmarried in 1692. Four
years later Mary married John Woods, whose family had arrived at
Darby with the Bartrams.[15] Soon afterward William had become
engaged to Elizah, daughter of James and Elizabeth Chambers
Hunt. James Hunt had been a prosperous linen weaver in Kent. He
had come to Philadelphia in 1684 with a patent from Penn for
1,000 acres. He had acquired three tracts of land in the region that
the Swedish settlers had called Kingsessing (a name derived from
an Indian word meaning bog-meadow), southwest of Philadelphia

on the west bank of the Schuylkill River.[16] William and Elizah
Hunt were married on the "3rd. mo. 22, 1696" at Darby Meetinghouse.[17] William's father had conveyed to him 100 of his original
300 acres, and William had purchased an adjoining fifty from Daniel Hibbet (Hibberd).[18] On the first of June of the following year
John Bartram had conveyed the remaining 200 acres of his farm to
his second son, Isaac, giving him his entire "estate both real and
personal to wit lands and plantation with buildings orchards and
all other appurtenances Chattles Cattles Depts Implements of
Household and Household Stuff of what kind quality or condition
they may be in."[19] Bartram died three months later, on 1 September
1697.[20]

John Bartram, the future botanist, was born to Elizah and
William on 23 May 1699.[21] William, like his father, was active in
community affairs and is recorded as having served on coroners' in-
quests and grand juries and in other such public capacities.[22] A second son of the William Bartrams was born 6 October 1701 and was
named James for his maternal grandfather. Elizah failed to recover
from her confinement and died two weeks later.[23] Thus, young John
and James had been left to the care of other members of the family,
particularly their grandmother Bartram.

John was a delicate child, often suffering from indigestion and
heartburn. For these ailments he was dosed with a mixture of
chalk, saccharin, cinnamon water, and the dregs of bentonite,
which usually helped him. He was inclined to be timid and was
particularly fearful of thunderstorms. Soon after a storm broke,
John was apt to be found sitting motionless in the house, praying
for protection. When the storm had passed he would say prayers of
thanksgiving. This "slavish fear" of lightning, as he later called it,
remained with him for much of his life even though he told himself
that very few people were killed by lightning. There were other
things of which he was afraid and, as an adult, he described himself
as having been "Naturaly one of the fearfull Mortals from my Infancy."[24]

When John was old enough to attend school he did not have
far to walk. The schoolhouse was a short distance down the Springfield road, which crossed the Bartrams' land. It had been built on
land originally owned by John Bethel, whose farm adjoined that of
the Bartrams. The Friends had established compulsory education
in 1692. The first schoolmaster appointed for Darby School was

Benjamin Clift, who served from 1692 until 1707. He received the munificent salary of twelve pounds a year for twelve months' work, with two weeks' vacation. There were probably additional compensating factors, such as room and board, but they do not seem to have been a matter of record. Clift taught John for three or four years, but nothing is known of his qualifications or those of his successor.[25]

Quaker schools, like other schools of that day, brooked no nonsense in imparting knowledge to the children in their charge. Not only was there a twelve-month session, but school met for an eight-hour day, five days a week, and for four hours on Saturday. Little information is available concerning the number of years of required attendance, but it is likely that children finished schooling by their twelfth year. Even so, with such a concentrated program their training was probably equivalent to that of the average high school graduate today.[26] The curriculum was eminently practical: reading, writing, and "casting accounts." The textbooks usually included George Fox's *Primers* and his *Instruction for Right Spelling*, printed in Philadelphia in 1702. This last was not confined to orthography but covered reading and writing as well. Other books that John may have studied were *The Young Clerk's Tutor*, *A Short Introduction to Grammar,* and *Elements of Geometry*. The school library was furnished exclusively with religious works. Bartram has been generally regarded as a largely self-educated man. By European standards this is no doubt true, but by colonial ones he received the average education of children whose parents were not wealthy. He received the basic tools with which to work and then his native intelligence took over.[27] Even in childhood he had an interest in scientific subjects. By the time he was twelve this interest was strongly developed, but he was handicapped by having few science books and no one who could instruct him. "Physick" and surgery were his favorites. Since medicine then depended heavily on plant drugs, he naturally developed a fascination with "Botanicks." He may have received some elementary instruction in botany since George Fox urged that all Quaker schools provide instruction concerning plants. Penn, too, had stressed the importance of training in natural history.[28]

On 5 September 1705 the boys' Aunt Elizabeth and John Cartlidge declared to the Meeting their intention to marry and received approval.[29] At about the same time their father was considering a second marriage. He was courting Elizabeth, daughter of the Bartrams' next-door neighbors, the William Smiths. The Bartrams and the Smiths had both bought land from Thomas Brassey on the same day in 1685. William Bartram and Elizabeth declared their intentions of marriage on 3 September 1707 and were married on 1 October.[30] Although both families had been active in the organization of Darby Meeting and its subsequent proceedings, some difficulty arose concerning the marriage. William Smith was declared "out of unity" with the Meeting on 2 February 1708 and William Bartram was so declared on 2 June.[31]

William's standing with Darby Meeting did not prevent him from being elected to represent Chester County in the Provincial Assembly in 1708. His brother Isaac died on 7 March 1708, leaving the family place to his mother for her lifetime and to his nephew John upon her death. William was named as his brother's executor.[32] It might be expected that he would now have become his mother's sole support in running the family farm and that he would have had little time for anything else. Instead, he left his mother, eight-year-old John, six-year-old James, and his pregnant wife and went to Carolina to look for land.

After a time William returned to Philadelphia, pleased with the land that he had found. He informed his family that he intended to move to Carolina to live. Two tracts of land on Bogue Sound, near the mouth of the White Oak River, had been surveyed for him on 22 December 1709. The land lay east of present-day Swansboro, Carteret County, then Bath County. One tract contained 500 acres and a second, adjoining it, 340.[33] There had been some Friends in this part of North Carolina since 1665. William told his family of the conditions that he had found there among the 1,500 inhabitants of Bath County. The town of Bath had twelve houses and a population of sixty. He may or may not have told his family of the incessant jockeying for control of the government between the Friends and the adherents of the Church of England. He probably did not dwell upon the very strained relations existing between the white settlers and the Indians. There had been good reason for bitterness on the part of the latter. Their hunting grounds were being overrun. Traders cheated them. Some of their land had been purchased, but much had simply been taken. Still worse, many Indians had been seized and sold as slaves. This practice had become sufficiently prevalent to justify Pennsylvania's banning of the importation of Indian slaves. To make this inflammable situation worse, the Indians were being sold both rum and weapons with ammunition.[34]

William was advised to make a will before leaving Philadelphia permanently. In it he wrote: "I William Bartram of Darby in the County of Chester and provence of Pensilvania Yeoman, being now about to remove myself, wife and youngest child from these parts into Carolina there to dwell but calling to mind the many dangers & difficulties too frequently attending Travelers as well as the uncertainty of all things here & well knowing that it is appointed for all men to dye do make & ordain this my last will & Testament my uncle Benj. Chambers & my father in law William Smith & Joseph Harvey of Ridley . . . to be executors thereof."[35] The youngest child to whom William referred was not James but the boys' half-sister, Elizabeth, born 10 February 1709/10.[36] William's executors were directed to sell his land in Pennsylvania and pay his debts whether he lived or died. Should he survive, he would later direct them what to do with any remaining balance. Should he die, it was to be equally divided between his sons, John and James, who were left behind. William's land consisted of 450 acres, and his principal debt was one of £37 owed to James Hunt, father of his first wife.

John's father and stepmother arrived safely in Carolina, and not long afterward a son, William, was born on 3 June 1711.[37] Other settlers were arriving in the region. Some, like William, were moving south from other colonies, but the majority were Swiss and German immigrants brought over by Baron von Graffenreid.[38] William's land lay twenty miles beyond that of most of the other Friends, many of whom had advised him against settling that far away.[39] Eventually word reached Philadelphia of horrors in Carolina, but it was a long time before the Bartrams learned all of the grim details. On 22 September 1711 Indians attacked throughout the area. William was killed, and Elizabeth and her two small children were taken prisoner.[40] They were more fortunate than many. Christopher Gale reported to the governor of South Carolina that "Women were laid upon the house floor and great stakes driven through their bodies; from others, big with child, the infants were ripped out and hung from trees."[41]

Elizabeth and her children were taken to "Hancock's Fort," so-called from the name of the Tuscarora chief, west of New Bern.

They and others captured would serve as hostages against a retaliatory attack by the whites. At the fort they found Baron von Graffenreid, already a prisoner. He and John Lawson, the Proprietory's surveyor, had been captured together. Lawson had been burned at the stake, but von Graffenreid was being held for ransom. He was later released and reported that some five hundred Indians had been assembled for the attack. He had been forced to watch with horror their preparations and the return of the warriors with captives and scalps.[42]

Elizabeth and her fellow captives were certain that an attempt would be made to rescue them but feared what might happen when the fort was attacked. They felt less certain when first weeks and then months passed with no sign of help. It was not until six months after their capture that rescue was attempted by a party of whites and friendly Indians, led by Colonel John Barnwell of South Carolina. Hancock's men went out of the fort to meet them but were driven back. When the water supply gave out in the fort, the Indians sent white women out to get it, threatening torture of their children if they failed to return. When Barnwell continued the siege, an eight-year-old girl was killed within hearing of the attackers. A mother of five children was then sent to inform Barnwell that unless he withdrew, all hostages would be killed and the Indians would fight to the last man. Barnwell was forced to negotiate a truce but succeeded in rescuing the women and children.[43]

Elizabeth and her children returned to Philadelphia late in 1712. William's will was proved there on 17 January 1712/13.[44] His Carolina land was sold in March of the following year to Daniel Richardson, Recorder of Bath County, for £5, William's title having lapsed when he failed to complete payments.[45] William's executors, William Smith and Benjamin Chambers, discovered that the burden which William had laid upon them was not light. Since there were minor children involved, the administration of the estate came under the jurisdiction of the Orphans' Court at Chester, and settlement could not be made until John and James reached twenty-one years of age. The executors had disposed of William's Pennsylvania land as he had directed, selling 150 acres to William Smith, Jr., on 24 November 1711 for £120 and the remaining 300 acres to Vincent Caldwell for £150. When the estate was finally settled a number of the charges against it were for expenses incurred by the executors in traveling to meetings of the court.[46]

There had been difficulties over the auditing of their accounts in 1718, and new auditors had been appointed.[47] John Bartram signed his release of the executors in January 1720/21, receiving £35 as did James upon his majority. Their stepmother received £71, half of the estate.[48]

John, now "a tall thin Spare" young man, was courting young Mary Maris of Chester Meeting. Mary was the daughter of Richard and Elizabeth Hayes Maris. Her grandfather, George Maris, having been both fined and imprisoned for holding meetings of Friends in his home, had left Grafton Flyford, Worcestershire, for Philadelphia in 1683. He had settled in Springfield township, Chester County, quickly assuming a position of leadership there as a county justice, a member of the assembly, and a member of the Provincial Council. He represented Chester County in the assembly from 1684 to 1688, being replaced in 1689 by John Bartram, the immigrant.[49] On 6 February 1722/23 John Bartram formally proposed marriage with Mary before Chester Meeting. The proposal was approved and they were married there on 25 April.[50]

John's grandmother had been in failing health at the time of his wedding and she died on 14 July.[51] He felt her loss acutely, for he had been closely associated with her for far longer than he had with either of his parents. Upon her death he received clear title to the farm. For years "Widow Bartram" had paid the taxes due on the farm, but now they were paid by John; they varied between seven and nine shillings per year. John and Mary lived very comfortably. He had inherited a two-hundred-acre farm, its buildings, livestock, orchards, and equipment—no small legacy. He had lived there all his life and was an excellent farmer. Furthermore, he had inherited from the estates of his father and his maternal grandmother almost £100, a substantial sum at a time when cash was often scarce.[52]

Richard, John and Mary's first child, was born on 24 March 1723/24, and a second son, Isaac, arrived nineteen months later, on 17 November. That same year John's brother, James, married Mary's sister, Elizabeth. When Mary died in 1727, Elizabeth and James named their daughter, born 12 November, for her. A second tragic loss for John occurred with the death of Richard before his fourth birthday.[53]

In September 1728 John Bartram purchased additional property. Frederick Schopenhausen owed £50 to Christopher Lynmoyer and, to settle the debt, a tract of 112.5 acres in Kingsessing township, on the west side of the Schuylkill, was sold to Bartram at a sheriff's sale for £45.[54] The land had once belonged to Peter Peterson Yocum, one of the early Swedish settlers arriving prior to Penn's grant. On it stood a small two-story house with but one room on each floor. It was large enough for John for a time, and he had plans for enlarging it. There was a good apple orchard, and he soon constructed a cider mill near the river behind the house. He also built a story-and-a-half outbuilding of stone on the north side of the house. This served a variety of purposes and later came to be known as the "Seed House."[55]

Two years after Mary's death, John was again engaged to marry. He and Ann Mendenhall declared their intentions before several Concord Monthly Meetings in 1729.[56] Ann was the daughter of Benjamin Mendenhall, a wheelwright who had come to Pennsylvania from Mildenhall, in Suffolk, about 1686.[57] At the meeting on 10 October, "John Bartram taking the said Ann Mendenhall by the hand did in a solemn manner openly declare that he took her . . . to be his wife promising with the Lord's assistance to be unto her a loving and faithful husband. . . ." She made reciprocal vows, and both signed the marriage certificate. It was a joyous occasion with fifty-eight witnesses, including, in addition to the Bartrams and the Mendenhalls, many of the Marshall family. Mary Hunt, John's aunt, had married Abraham Marshall. John's brother, James, was present, and so was his half-sister, Elizabeth, now nineteen.[58]

John wasted little time in enlarging the house at Kingsessing. If he was not already an experienced stonemason, he soon became one. He had to quarry the stone before any building could begin, and before that he had to make or have made crowbars and wedges. He found that the iron swept off the hearth and discarded by forgemen at a nearby foundry was ideal for his purposes. It cost him nothing and was tempered like steel. Both the quarrying operation and the hauling and setting of the rock were strenuous and sometimes dangerous operations for a young man who had been a delicate child.[59] The Bartrams' home, still standing, solid and comfortable, is witness to John's methodical and careful workmanship. It is built on a slope overlooking the Schuylkill. Bartram cut the gray stone in long, smooth rectangles, which he laid one upon another to form two stories. The front door he flanked by a single window on the left and two on the right, with similar windows above. The back of the house faced the 400-yard sweep of the river. For each room on the first floor he made a door to the outside.[60] Inside, the great thickness of the stone yielded deep window sills. Virgin timber provided wide floorboards. In the living room, Bartram constructed a closet over the fireplace which he later used for drying seeds. For the hearth he found interesting stones in which were embedded fossils. The lintel above an attic window he inscribed in Greek: "God Save." Beneath it he engraved, "John Ann Bartram 1731." A London correspondent wrote to him a few years later, "I have heard of thy house, and thy great art and industry in building it. It makes me long to see it, and the builder."[61]

Around the front and sides of the house and extending southeast down the slope at the back, John gradually developed a large garden which came, in time, to include about six acres.[62] The development and improvement of his garden and farm occupied much of his time throughout the remainder of his life. The farm was ideally located from a marketing standpoint, having a good road nearby, and it was close to a ferry over the river. John had definite ideas about the care and improvement of land but was willing to experiment. Ultimately, his fields yielded twenty-eight to thirty-six bushels of wheat to the acre, and oats, flax, and corn did equally well. He credited this, in part, to his planting of red clover every fourth year and in part to his system of fertilizing. He experimented with lucerne or alfalfa (*Medicago sativa*). This did well if kept free of weeds but otherwise dwindled away. Common red and white clover could compete with weeds, thus requiring less labor, and hence were more profitable. He piped water from a spring to a reservoir into which he dumped horse manure and wood ashes. He used this water to irrigate his meadows and also spread manure, barn fodder, old hay, and straw on the land. As a result he harvested fine crops of hay where little had grown formerly but cinquefoil and other weeds. While his neighbors mowed but a short ton of hay per acre he was able to produce more than twice that amount.[63]

When other chores failed to keep him busy, John set about draining the swampy areas near the river. Dissatisfied with what he was able to accomplish alone, he promoted a cooperative venture with the owners of adjacent land. Exactly when this project began is not known. Bartram and the others formed the "Company of the Southern District of Kingsessing Meadows" and undertook the construction of dikes, floodgates, and ditches for the reclamation of the

Residence of John Bartram built by him in 1730 (reproduced from William Darlington's *Memorials of John Bartram and Humphry Marshall*)

swamplands. This enterprise was later incorporated (1795) and has been said to have been the "first incorporated drainage district in America," resulting in the reclamation of several thousand acres.[64]

In traveling about, Bartram realized that the seemingly endless supply of timber in this new country was rapidly diminishing as a result of the clearing of the land for fields and the need for wood for buildings, fences, and fuel. As one of the earliest conservationists, he advocated reforestation as an adjunct to farming. Specifically, he urged the planting of red cedar and wrote an essay on the subject which was published in 1749 as a preface to Benjamin Franklin's *Poor Richard Improved*. Bartram was impressed by the durability of cedar wood and by its many uses. It would grow rapidly even on worn-out land. Seed for a nursery could be easily obtained, and large numbers of trees could be grown along fence rows and on land not otherwise useful. The farmer who could plant 100 trees per year would eventually be able to harvest £40's worth of posts per year, "a fine yearly profit, considering we lose so little ground from tillage, and the trouble and expense of raising them is but little."

Wherever he went, Bartram was a keen observer of farming practices and ready to adapt those that he considered valuable to his own use. He was a great conservationist in land usage and was impressed by the Indians' custom of fertilizing their fields with oyster shells. He recognized the value of "green sand marls" (containing potassium) seventy years before Edmund Ruffin discovered it. He was well aware of the proper reclamation methods for salt-marsh lands. He observed that the bottomlands along the rivers often lost their richness when cultivated. The river would wash away the disturbed topsoil, depositing sand in its stead. He was concerned when he discovered how rapidly erosion could take place on hillside pastures. Interested in the ecological influence of soil on plants, he determined that the baffling fertility of some lands was entirely due to the presence of limestone. He was the "first in Pennsylvania to make what may be considered a soil survey."[65]

As might be expected of such an enthusiastic farmer, Bartram soon found 112 acres to be insufficient and added to his Kingsessing holdings. Apparently he leased the old family place at Darby, for his half-brother William paid the taxes on it for at least two years, 1730–32.[66] On 8 April 1738 John purchased 142 acres of land with several buildings from Andrew Jonason for £283, some of which he

"The botanist," from Howard Pyle, "Bartram and his garden"

paid for in cash and some in mortgage bonds. The tract had earlier included a stone quarry, but this had been leased for 999 years to a ship's carpenter, Humphrey Jones. Bartram, in turn, leased the quarry from Jones.[67] He bought additional land as well and sold some. At about the same time as the Jonason purchase, he bought sixty acres from Andrew Souplis for £175. He also sold thirty-three acres to Nathan Gibson for £120. Part of that sold was Souplis land, and part was the land he had bought earlier from the Yocum family.[68] Still later he purchased three lots in Philadelphia on the west side of New Market Street and the south side of Margaretta (now Produce) Street, on which he built houses.[69] He even bought some cedar swampland in Jersey.[70] Thus, he not only inherited substantial property but added to it considerably.

John and Ann soon had need of the larger house. Five-year-old Isaac was joined by a tribe of half-brothers and sisters. James was born 25 June 1730, followed by Moses (13 August 1732), Elizabeth (27 October 1734, who died in infancy), Mary (21 November 1736), twins, Elizabeth and William (9 April 1739), Ann (24 August 1741), John (24 October 1743), and Benjamin (6 September 1748).[71] John, and probably Ann too, had rather precise ideas concerning the proper rearing of children. Some were due to the Quaker influence, but others were certainly his own. He objected to babies being "swathed up not quite so tight as an Egyptian mummy" soon after birth and cited the Indians with their fine physiques produced without excessive clothing. He objected to too much rich and spicy food and to forcing a child to overeat. He believed that this sort of thing led to catching colds, indigestion, and nervous disorders. He disapproved of the bribing of children to ensure their good behavior or of "frightening them by telling them that such and such big bear will catch them if they Dont Doe as they Bod them," both of which practices he thought had long-range effects on the child's personality. He thought that "parents by their foolish proceedings looseth much of their authority over their children and often their love too."[72]

His ideas were not all negative. On the contrary, he believed that parents should not "let a good Deed pass without praise nor a bad one without Rebuke" and that this policy should be applied very early in infancy. By the age of four or five the child should be informed "in a solid yet pleasant manner of the power, majesty & mercy of God & ye Dependency we have upon him." This was a time

"The old corner cupboard," from Howard Pyle, "Bartram
and his garden"

to impress upon the child the "ill effects of Lying, Cheating, and using bad words or Sausy Expressions" and "the benefit and advantage of a pious life." He had found his method to be "much better than all ye whiping thumping boxing and scolding & I know not what that is commonly used by parents." He believed that parents often earned the loss of affection and respect, and even the hatred, of their children by letting them have their own way most of the time and then suddenly trying to restrain them. If punishment could not be avoided, then it should be "adequat to the fault committed" and should be rendered with a "Stearn Countenance which hath more effect on some Children than either words or blows." Also the children should be taught to respect each other as well as their parents.[73]

By the time children reached the age of twelve or fourteen the parents must "have a Continual watch over them; their minds then begin to open, their understanding to expand." This was the time to take them along as one went about one's business, that they might meet their parents' friends and associates and learn about public affairs, and a time for parents to avoid associates who might lead them astray. "Between the ages of 16 and 20 is the time to instruct him into Natural Phylosophy & the Wisdom of God manifest in the Creation." Children should "behave in moderation to your servants," being neither condescending nor "Hail fellow well met," but pleasant and dignified and earning their respect, "for the good character of a young man or woman by a good servant is taken a Pretty Deal of notice of."[74]

Bartram's theories of child rearing are difficult to quarrel with, and he had reason to believe that they were sound. He raised a large family in an era of extremely high child mortality, losing only two of eleven children. Of the nine who survived, all demonstrated the principles of character that he had sought to instill. Only one seems to have really troubled him from time to time, and he ultimately reflected much credit upon his upbringing.

TWO

Peter Collinson and
His Friends

THE BUSY life that Bartram led as he developed his new farm and helped to raise his
growing family left little time for recreation or casual visits to the
city. He did occasionally go to Philadelphia for necessities, and
he made acquaintances there, some of whom were to become life-
long friends. Among them was Joseph Breintnall (d. 1746), whose
Quaker family had come to Philadelphia from Derbyshire. He was
a merchant and "a copyer of deeds for the scriveners, a good
natur'd, friendly, middle-ag'd man, a great lover of poetry, reading
all he could meet with, and writing some that was tolerable. . . ."[1]
In 1733 he was absorbed in the fascinating hobby of making leaf
impressions, an ancient craft, dating back at least to Leonardo da
Vinci's time. Leaves of ferns, grasses, herbs, trees, and shrubs were
smeared with printer's ink and then pressed firmly on absorbent
paper, producing delicately beautiful and accurate reproductions.

Bartram provided considerable assistance to Breintnall when
the latter visited his farm to collect leaves, and he took Breintnall
specimens when he went to Philadelphia. In June 1733 Dr. Samuel
Chew (1693–1743), a Maryland physician who had moved to Philadelphia the previous year, brought the traveler M. Aubrey de la
Mottraye to call on Breintnall and to see his impressions. The
Frenchman admired them greatly and was very much pleased to
receive a set of them. At about the same time Breintnall sent a set
to his London correspondent, Peter Collinson (1694–1768).[2]

Collinson was a woolen draper engaged in commerce with the
colonies. He was a Quaker and had a number of other correspondents at Philadelphia. He was a rabidly enthusiastic gardener,

with a passion for collecting plants from abroad that might thrive in his garden at Peckham, in Surrey. The nature of his business put him in frequent contact with ship captains and others in the mercantile world, and he made the most of every connection to obtain seeds, bulbs, or plants from abroad. He was an active leader of a great movement of enthusiasm for gardening then gathering momentum in England. When William and Mary arrived in England in 1689 they brought along the continental interest in exotic plants such as those European merchants had been importing from distant places. Gardening had become popular and fashionable among those in England who could afford such hobbies. Collinson had a wide acquaintance among the nobility and gentry, especially those who shared his botanic interests. He found botany a great social asset and, being a cheerful extrovert and an excellent conversationalist, he was frequently invited by members of the nobility to spend several days at their country estates. He thoroughly enjoyed these social occasions and gave much advice on the planting of his hosts' gardens.[3]

In spite of all his enthusiasm, Collinson had become increasingly frustrated by the difficulties of obtaining any appreciable number of the vast array of unknown plants that he felt sure could be found in North America. Many people promised to look for them, but distressingly few plants actually arrived. By 1733 he had become convinced that it was useless to rely on the promises of friends. He wanted to find someone in North America who would act as a collector for him in a less casual manner, someone with whom he could exchange favors and who would have something to gain from helping him. He sought advice on the matter from Dr. Chew, who unhesitatingly recommended John Bartram. In the short time that Chew had known Bartram he had been impressed by his great knowledge of the local flora and his interest in it. Some years later Collinson commented that Chew had certainly been correct when he wrote that Bartram let nothing escape him.[4]

Seldom, if ever, has there been a more opportune introduction of two individuals than that of Bartram and Collinson. The association then begun became a close working relationship profoundly influencing the lives of both men. They never met, since neither would leave his native land, yet it is doubtful that either ever had a more devoted friend. Their correspondence began in 1733, but the earliest surviving letter was written by Bartram on 17 July 1734.

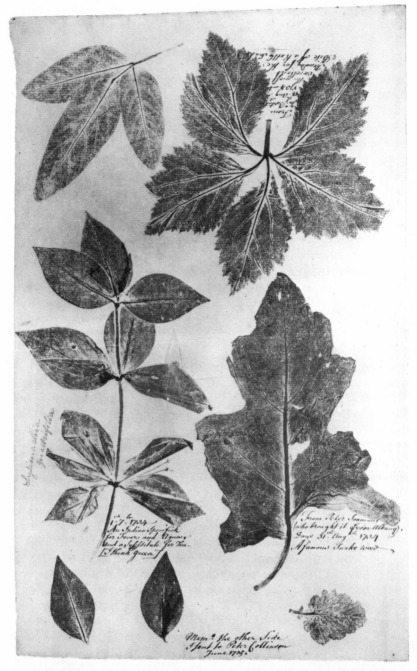

Joseph Breintnall's leaf prints. The one at the upper right is "From Jno. Bartram 18th Aug. 1734—the most excellent Remedy for the Bite of a Rattlesnake" (courtesy Library Company of Philadelphia).

It described not a plant but the dissection of the mouth of a rattle-snake that Bartram had killed near Germantown, concentrating particularly on clusters of small teeth at the base of each poison fang. Bartram correctly speculated that the function of these teeth must be to replace the main fangs, if these were injured. Collinson was so impressed by Bartram's account that he read it to his fellow members of the Royal Society of London, and it was published in their *Philosophical Transactions*. This was Bartram's first published writing, and he was highly gratified.[5]

The Royal Society of London had been founded in 1660 and had been granted a charter by Charles II in 1662. Its founding and royal recognition proved to be a major landmark in the history of science. The society was firmly committed from its inception to the philosophy of Francis Bacon, a complete departure from the authoritarian Aristotelian philosophy that had so long prevailed. From its beginning the society concerned itself with a great range of subjects. It sought to make itself widely known and to attract the assistance and cooperation of people in other parts of the world. One of its first acts had been to appoint a Committee for Foreign Correspondence, emphasizing communication with British overseas colonies in particular. At the time Bartram's paper was read the Royal Society had established itself as the world's foremost scientific society, and its influence was worldwide.[6]

The president of the society in 1733 was Sir Hans Sloane (1660–1753), a doctor who had spent some time in the West Indies. Upon his return he had written the two-volume *Voyage to the Islands*, published in 1707 and 1725, dealing with the natural history of Jamaica and nearby islands.[7] A greater impetus to English curiosity had been the return home of Mark Catesby (1682?–1749). He had spent seven years in Virginia and had later been sent to Carolina and the Bahamas by a group of patrons for the specific purpose of studying the natural history there. He had exhibited the first part of his great *Natural History of Carolina, Florida and the Bahama Islands* to the society in 1729. His beautiful illustrations had done much to stimulate further interest in the plants and animals of North America.[8]

By January 1734/35 Collinson was writing lengthy letters at frequent intervals in reply to equally lengthy ones from Bartram, a practice which they continued with little interruption for thirty-five years. Within two years they had progressed from "Friend John

Bartram" and "Mr. Collinson" to "John" and "Peter." In one of his early letters Bartram sought Collinson's help in obtaining suitable botany books from which he might study the science. He had not had much success in Philadelphia but thought that there must be good ones available in London. Collinson was frustrated too: "Indeed I am at a loss which to recommend, for, as I have observed, a complete history of plants is not to be found in any author. For the present I am persuaded the gentlemen of the Library Company, at my request, will indulge thee the liberty, when thee comes to town, to peruse their botanical books: there is Miller's *Dictionary*, and some others."[9]

Bartram was disappointed not to be able to obtain a suitable book, but the suggestion that he might be able to use those of the Library Company was welcome. Breintnall was the secretary of the company, which had its beginnings with Benjamin Franklin's Junto, an informal discussion group. The members had first pooled all the books that they could spare to form a common library. This had proved inadequate so they had sold subscriptions, each subscriber paying an annual fee.[10] The money was sent to Collinson, who not only purchased their books and had them shipped in 1732 but continued to do so for more than thirty years without charge to them. He also made gifts to the library, one of which was Philip Miller's *Gardener's Dictionary*, which he had mentioned to Bartram. Miller (1691–1771) was in charge of the Chelsea Physic Garden, the finest botanical garden in England. The members of the Library Company were very glad to oblige Collinson by welcoming Bartram to the library. This was not quite such a privilege as it sounded as Bartram discovered when he wanted to borrow a book. Breintnall told him he would have to make a deposit equal to the book's value and pay sixpence a week rent.[11]

Collinson's 20 January 1734/35 letter was a very long one and typical of the many that were to follow. He discussed a number of plants that Bartram had mentioned, indicating which ones he would particularly like to have: "Please to remember those Solomon's Seals, that escaped thee last year. . . . Pray send a root or two of Joseph Breintnall's Snake-root." Breintnall had indicated common names for the leaf prints he had sent. Having mentioned at least twenty plants that he would very much like to have, Collinson hastened to add: "I only barely mention these plants; not that I expect thee to send them. I don't expect or desire them, but as they happen to be found accidentally: and what is not to be met with one year, may be another." He begged Bartram "not to neglect thy more material affairs to oblige me" but in the next sentence suggested that a great many plants could be packed in a box two feet square and stowed under a ship captain's bed![12]

Collinson had already sent seeds to Bartram by an earlier ship. Among these were hard-shelled almonds from his garden and soft-shelled ones from Portugal. He now sent detailed instructions for making a fine almond pie. He had also sent vine cuttings and some of "the great Neapolitan Medlar" (*Mespilus germanica*), a small tree with fruit resembling the crab apple.[13] Clearly, this was to be a fair exchange whereby each would have his garden enriched by the choicest items the other could provide. Collinson's contributions to the exchange soon gave it a truly international character. Not long after sending the medlars he sent some "Spanish Nuts," "a Lebanon Cone," and seed of the "China Aster." He described the last as "the noblest and finest plant thee ever saw, of that tribe. It was sent per the Jesuits from China to France; from thence to us: it is an annual."[14] A week later he wrote again, sending "sixty-nine sorts of curious seeds" which he had obtained from Miller as well as several sorts which he had collected.[15] All of these were soon followed by green and brown cole (kale) from Germany.[16] To these was added the "double flowering China or India pink," sent from

Peter Collinson (1694–1768)

France. Collinson hoped that this great collection of seeds would convince Bartram of his good intentions. He pointed out that the English plants grew at scattered locations outside of London and were not easy for him to obtain. "If I lived, as thou does, always in the country, I should do more. . . ." He could not neglect his business affairs to seek seeds for Bartam and Bartram must not neglect his to serve him.[17]

It was Collinson's original proposal that Bartram should send any seeds he could of common plants, giving both a number and a common name. This Bartram did in 1733; some germinated in Collinson's garden in 1734, others lay dormant until sprouting in 1735, and some never germinated. By 1735 Collinson had a new idea. He sent two quires of brown paper and one of "whited-brown." These were to be used in pressing herbarium specimens. Whenever Bartram sent any seeds he was to send with them a good herbarium specimen of the plant. Even better, he was to send two specimens. Collinson would get them identified by the "most knowing botanists" and then would return one to Bartram. He believed that this would improve Bartram's botanical knowledge more than books would.[18] Living plants were being sent by Bartram as well as seeds and herbarium specimens. A collection sent late in 1734 delighted Collinson. In June of the following year he reported to Bartram that he had six species of ferns, many quite different from the English varieties. There were both the true and false Solomon's seals,

Sir Hans Sloane (1660–1753)

dittany (*Cunila origanoides* [L.] Britt.), goldenrod, skunk weed, Indian turnip (an *Arisaema*), honeysuckle, and many others.[19]

Very early in their correspondence Collinson made it plain to Bartram that, while his principal interest was in plants, all aspects of natural history appealed to him. Having received a box of insects from Bartram in 1735, Collinson sent detailed instructions for the catching and preserving of butterflies, a project for Bartram's little boys, for which he promised to reward them. He did not intend to engage Bartram in butterfly collection except as he might come across them by chance.[20] As Collinson received the various shipments of butterflies he carefully preserved them between sheets of glass, where they were much admired by his friends. Some were a little torn, and he requested duplicates, urging Bartram always to walk with a box or two in his pocket.[21] Later Bartram sent cocoons rather than the butterflies, which traveled with less damage but were unpredictable. The suspense added to Collinson's pleasure but perhaps not as much to his collection.[22]

The bright hues of North American birds contrasted with the sober colors of English birds, so they and their nests were equally acceptable to Collinson. One of his friends wanted the Bartram children to send a pair of redbirds, which he hoped to acclimate and eventually integrate into the English bird population.[23] Unfortunately, cardinals did not travel well unless there was someone to feed them daily, and ship captains seldom had time for this. Bartram sent a hummingbird's nest, complete with eggs. This proved to be something of a mistake for Collinson's friends then wanted them, and hummingbirds' nests were not easily found. To the request for birds' nests, Collinson added requests for those of wasps, bees, and hornets. He also desired fossils, and Bartram sent him some. He had found these marine specimens on a Pocono ridge where there was a large deposit. Collinson was interested to learn that they were found more than 100 miles from the sea. Later Bartram found others in the Catskills at least 150 miles from the coast. Collinson wanted terrapins and shells of freshwater shellfish and snails, telling his friend, "My inclination and fondness to natural productions of all kinds is agreeable to the old proverb: Like the parson's barn,—refuses nothing."[24]

Bartram's first shipment of terrapins was unlucky, for those that did not die were stolen by the sailors. In August 1737 he sent the eggs instead, for which Collinson thanked him: "I shall now tell thee something which very much pleased me, and will surprise thee. The box of turtle eggs (which was an ingenious thought of thine to send) on the day I brought it from on board ship, being the 20th of October, I took off the lid, having a mind to see the eggs, and on peeping about I saw a little head just above ground, and while I was looking, I saw the ground move in a place or two more. In short, in the space of three or four hours, eight tortoises were hatched. It was very well worth observing, how artfully they disengaged themselves from the shell, and then with their forefeet scratched their eyes open. They have had many visitors, such a thing never happening, I dare say, in England before."[25]

Requests for information from Collinson covered a wide range. In January 1739 he referred Bartram to a dissertation on the deer and moose of North America in the *Philosophical Transactions* of the Royal Society and asked for any information that Bartram might be able to add to the account. He would like very much to obtain the scalp and horns of a buck fallow deer if Bartram could procure them.[26] He inquired about another American animal with which he had some personal acquaintance, which he called the *Monack*. This was our groundhog or woodchuck (*Marmota monax*). A friend had sent him one from Maryland, and he had found it most attractive. He had given it to Sir Hans Sloane, in whose house it ran about as tamely as a cat.[27] Perhaps Bartram put it in the same category with another American varmint much admired by Collinson, the opossum. Collinson took Bartram sternly to task for his unreasoning prejudice against this animal, which was attracting a great deal of attention in England. Collinson had handled and played with a female with three young and could find nothing objectionable about them. English scientists had previously known only placental mammals and were fascinated by their first marsupial.[28]

American snakes were exciting to English scientists and became the subject of controversy. Not long after Bartram sent Collinson his description of the rattlesnake's mouth, Collinson sent him a paper concerning the bite of the rattlesnake and asked his opinion of it. He admired Bartram's courage in plant collecting in the woods at the risk of being bitten, confessing that he would only do so on horseback. Collinson, Sloane, and other friends were debating the question of how the rattlesnake seized its prey. Sloane

From Mark Catesby, *Natural History*, vol. II, p. 115: "*Magnolia flore alba, folio majore . . .* " and "*Formica villosa coccinea*, Velvet ant": "Specimens of this Tree were first sent me in the year 1736, by my worthy friend, *John Clayton*, Esq; of *Virginia*, and from the only Tree known in that Country; since which, Mr. *Bartram* of *Pensylvania* has discovered many of them growing on the North branch of Susquehannah River; some of them were above an hundred feet in height. The wood has a fine grain, very tough, and of an orange colour. The Indians make bowls of the wood."

From Mark Catesby, *Natural History*, vol. II, p. 117: "*Chamaerhodo-dendrons, lauri-folio semper virens . . .*": "Several of these young Trees have been sent from *Pensylvania* by Mr. *Bartram*, who first discovered them there; but they have not yet produced any blossoms here; and though they have been planted some years, they make but slow progress in their growth, and seem to be one of those *American* plants that do not affect our soil or climate. . . ." "*Chamaedaphne semper virens*": "This shrub is a native of *Pensylvania*, and produced its blossoms at Peckham, in *September* 1743, and several succeeding years."

From Mark Catesby, *Natural History*, vol. II, p. 104: "*Vespa ichneumon tri-
pilis*" and "*Rhus glabra*, sumach": "This odd Fly was a native of *Pensylvania*, and was sent from thence to Mr. *Collinson*, amongst many other remarkable Insects, by Mr. *John Bartram*."

From Mark Catesby, *Natural History*, vol. II, p. 101: *"Meadia"* and *"Urogallus minor fuscus"*: "It flowered in Mr. *Collinson's* garden at *Peckham*, in September 1744, from seeds sent him by Mr. *Bartram*, who gathered them from beyond the Apalachian mountains, which lie parallel with *Virginia*. The seeds were contained in a long membranous *capsula*, which opens into four parts, and discharges its very small seeds."

From Mark Catesby, *Natural History*, vol. II, p. 72: "The Lady's Slipper of
Pensylvania, *Cypripedium calceolus*, L." and "*Rana maxima Americana
acquatica*": "This curious Helleborine was sent from *Pensylvania*, by Mr.
John Bartram, who, by his industry and inclination to the searches into
Nature, has discovered and sent over a great many new productions, both
animal and vegetable. This plant flowered in Mr. *Collinson's* garden, in
April, 1738."

believed that the snake struck first and then waited for the poison to take effect before swallowing the animal. Breintnall and Dr. Christopher Witt (1675–1763) of Philadelphia contended that the snake charmed its victim into its mouth. Bartram was urged to make observations to settle the debate. He had no difficulty in disagreeing with Sloane for he knew of many cases in which a rattlesnake had been interrupted in the process of swallowing a rodent and the released animal had run away unharmed. He was less sure about the ability of the snake to charm. Many people of his acquaintance believed it, but he had no personal experience on which to report. He promised to be alert for an opportunity to observe rattlesnake behavior.[29]

While Collinson had long sought seeds from abroad, he had a special reason for wanting them in quantity in 1734. No small or casual collection would fill his needs. In 1731 the eighteen-year-old Robert James, Baron Petre (1713–42), had been elected a Fellow of the Royal Society. The young man was extremely interested in horticulture. Botanically inclined members found him most congenial, especially Peter Collinson, who became his devoted friend. When Petre married in 1732 he took up residence at Thorndon Hall, near Brentwood, in Essex. He had ambitious plans for extensive changes at his new home, and he could well afford to carry them out. He wanted new formal gardens, windbreaks of trees, restoration of the tree-lined drive, improvement of the park, and particularly forestation of the barren area around the park.[30] Twenty-four sixty-foot elms, two feet through the trunk, were moved from his former home to extend the driveway planting at Thorndon Hall.[31] To carry out his plans further he would require a large number of trees, and he wanted as much diversity as possible. The first thing he proposed was to establish forest nurseries and begin acquiring tree seeds in quantity. It was in this connection that Petre sought Collinson's assistance.

Bartram's first collecting for Collinson was purely to oblige a fellow Quaker, with promise of a mutual exchange. When the latter proposed that Bartram collect forest tree seeds in 1734, he told him that he intended to share them with a friend and hoped to obtain a present for John. He was as good as his word and in 1735 sent a calico gown for Ann and cloth for a suit for Bartram as a joint gift from his noble friend and himself. Always cautious where finances were involved, he warned Bartram to tell no one how they obtained the clothing: "There may be some, with you, may think they deserve something of that nature."[32] He then sent a very large order for forest tree seeds for his friend the same year. Bartram was able to collect them, and they reached England in the winter of 1735–36. The shipment was impressive, including sixteen species in quantities such as 3,000 black walnuts, a peck and three-quarters of dogwood berries, 3,200 swamp Spanish acorns, and two pecks of red cedar berries. Collinson at last revealed the friend to be Lord Petre. He took it upon himself to decide what Petre should pay Bartram and credited John with £18:13s:3d.[33]

Bartram then proposed that he be paid a regular annual allowance for traveling and collecting. This would make it easier for him to devote the time required and to pay his expenses. Lord Petre approved the suggestion enthusiastically and agreed to pay ten guineas per year. Collinson thought that he could interest some other people. He soon persuaded Charles Lennox, the second Duke of Richmond (1701–50), to contribute five guineas and Philip Miller to do the same.[34] This put Bartram's seed collecting on a businesslike basis, but Collinson's cautions to Bartram about discussing gifts were repeated with regard to subscriptions.

Collinson and Bartram had another mutual friend in Philadelphia, the above-mentioned Dr. Witt. He had been born in Wiltshire, England, coming to Philadelphia in 1704. He had settled at Germantown, where he developed a very successful practice as both a physician and a surgeon. He had a large garden in which he grew native plants, and he was cordial and helpful to Bartram. Witt was interested in such things as Rosicrucian philosophy and "the casting of nativities," which Bartram viewed with considerable skepticism.[35] He was frequently mentioned in the Bartram-Collinson correspondence and often to their considerable amusement, although both held him in affectionate regard. In 1738 Collinson asked Bartram to visit Witt's garden and check on a curious plant bearing a pod shaped like an acorn which had baffled the doctor. Bartram found it to be a common goldenrod with an "excresence which some flying insect had darted & laid her egs therein which was hatched when ye doctor made his superficial observation who had rather believe allmost anything than be at ye pains of accurate examinations."[36] Collinson had arrived at a comparable conclusion and was pleased to have his views vindicated.[37]

Once Collinson decided that the doctor was too cunning for

Bartram. Witt had talked Bartram out of some choice lady's slippers, on the grounds that they were too dry to ship to Collinson. To prevent such an accident in the future, Collinson suggested that Bartram make use of a device that he employed. He should take large ox bladders, cut off the necks, and fill them with plants. They could then be watered, tied up, and hung from his saddle, and the plants would keep fresh for days. Any modern plant collector will recognize this as the eighteenth-century version of the plastic bag. Collinson had no intention of being outwitted and hastened to advise Bartram not to let his favorite lady's slippers escape. He already had a yellow one thriving well in his garden but wanted the other sorts.[38]

In the fall of 1735 Bartram heard of an unusual tree in Jersey and rode there to procure seed of it. Collinson applauded his initiative and willingness to go to so much trouble to oblige his English friends. He did not know the plant, but when the seeds had germinated the mystery was solved. It was a lotus, or nettle-leaved tree.[39] Known today as the hackberry (*Celtis occidentalis*), it was thought to have been introduced into England by the younger John Tradescant in the seventeenth century.[40] Another journey took Bartram to the mountains, where he found a great variety of plants, most of which were quite different from those around Philadelphia. His account of 3 November of this expedition excited Collinson and whetted his appetite for more travels by his American agent. He found Bartram's suggestion that he search out the source of the Schuylkill River an excellent idea.[41] Bartram did not wait for his English patrons' decision on this before traveling again, this time to the Rattlesnake Mountains in the spring of 1736.[42]

THREE

The Education of
a Botanist

O N 19 June 1736 James Logan (1674–1751) forwarded to Bartram a letter from Collinson
and volunteered to lend him a publication that Collinson had sent
to Logan earlier. He had meant to offer it when Bartram had visited him.[1] Logan, an able scientist, was Philadelphia's foremost
scholar and a very wealthy man. He had come to Pennsylvania as
Penn's secretary and had remained as his deputy when Penn returned to England. In the years that followed, Logan had held
many important posts, including president of the Council and chief
justice. His estate, Stenton, was four miles from Philadelphia, a
handsome brick house surrounded by a beautiful park complete
with an orangery. Logan had been crippled by a fall in 1728, but in
spite of this handicap he had recently completed experiments demonstrating the method of sexual reproduction in maize. His scientific interests were not confined to botany, and his superb library
covered many fields.[2]

Although Logan had seen Bartram only twice he had found
him to be "a botanist by nature" who knew the name of every plant
that he encountered. To assist Bartram's studies, Logan gave him a
"microscope" and helped him to acquire a knowledge of Latin sufficient for reading botanical books, whose plant descriptions were
customarily in that language. He lent Bartram William Salmon's
Botanologia, but this was of little use in identifying North American plants. Logan therefore asked Collinson to obtain a copy of the
herbal of John Parkinson (1567–1650), which did describe some.[3]
Collinson was properly impressed by Logan's generosity and took
care that John would be. He urged Bartram to call now and then to

inquire after Logan's health. Collinson was always concerned that Bartram might fail to make a proper impression on people of importance, an entirely unjustified concern and one that seems never to have bothered his friend at all. In fact, Bartram commented that "James Logan is possesed of learning & knowledge beyond any in our province or perhaps our neibors yet he hath but a measure of it & some times I can see as far into a milstone as he unless he puts on his spectacles."[4]

Collinson may have been unusually sensitive concerning Logan, for the latter, knowing nothing of the remuneration that Bartram was receiving, had been sharply critical of Peter for exploiting John:

> Pray procure for me a good Parkinson's Herbal; and I shall make a present of it to a person thou valuest, and who is worthy of a heavier purse than fortune has hitherto allowed him; and I cannot but admire that you who have them should be so narrow to those you know well deserve to be considered, in another manner. Bartram has a genius perfectly well turned for botany and the productions of nature; but he has a family that depend wholly on his daily labour, spent on a poor narrow spot of ground, that will scarce keep them above the want of the necessaries of life. You, therefore, are robbing them while you take up one hour of his time without making a proper compensation for it. Both thyself, at the head of so much business, and thy noble friend, and friends, should know this; no man in these parts is so capable of serving you, and none can better deserve encouragement, or worse bear the loss of his time without a consideration.

This was pretty frank criticism, rather typical of Quakers of that period, but apparently did not give offense. Logan hastened to add that he had heard no complaints from Bartram and knew his circumstances only from what other people had told him.[5] Bartram later convinced him that his affairs were not quite so difficult as Logan had pictured them.

The publication that Collinson had sent to Logan, and that Logan lent to Bartram, was Linnaeus' *Systema Naturae*, which had been published in December 1735. Bartram was among the first botanists to try out the sexual system of Carolus Linnaeus (1707–78), the great Swedish botanist. Logan explained it to Bartram as follows: "His method in the Vegetables is altogether new, for he takes all of his distinctions from the *stamina* and the *styles*, the first of which he calls husbands and the other wives. He ranges them, therefore, under those of 1 husband, 2, 3, 4, 5, 6, 7, 8, 9, 10, 12, 20, and then of many husbands. He further distinguishes by the styles, and has many heads, under which he reduces all known plants. The performance is very curious and at this time worth thy notice."[6] The system proposed by the youthful Linnaeus was a highly artificial one, as he well knew, and it has not withstood the test of time. It was, however, a relatively easy system for a beginner in botanical studies to use since it involved primarily the counting of stamens and styles.

Logan's assistance and patient tutoring of Bartram were not entirely disinterested. Linnaeus had asked Logan to carry out studies of pollen structure for use in determining species. Although Logan had carried out his own corn experiments, he had little time for such things and "little competency in Botany," so he turned to Bartram to perform the studies requested by Linnaeus.[7] Bartram plugged away at floral anatomy whenever time permitted. Candlelight and low magnification were no help when dissecting small flowers and, before long, he asked Collinson if he could obtain a microscope with greater magnifying power. Collinson replied that Logan, who was well versed in optics, could explain to Bartram why it was not possible to make a glass capable of magnifying as much as he wanted.[8]

On 19 August 1737, a year after Logan had started Bartram using the Linnean tables, his pupil sent him a report on the floral anatomy of a variety of flowers: "Germander blew flowered hath one forked stile & four apices which touch ye top of ye stile at ye discharg of ye farina. Succory is a double flower compounded of many single petals ye botom of which incloseth 4 stamina & apices which closely embraceth one forked stile which riseth higher than ye apices." Bartram's descriptions were accompanied by rough sketches of "the farina as it appeared magnified by ye fourth magnifier." He added a brief note: "kind friend I here give thee some account of ye farina as I observed it at ye time when ye Apices opened & discharged it   I observed all these flowers at several states of perfection with what judgment & ingenuity I was capable of   I believe it is near right but if thee sees mistakes I hope thee

will consider that I am at ye best but A learning   pray excuse my
freedom   So in Consideration of thy many favours & ye kind instruction I remain thy sincere friend."[9] Logan was pleased and impressed by Bartram's progress and forwarded the results of the investigation to Linnaeus.

Collinson had reservations about Bartram's new interest, and
it was his turn to protest the distraction of Bartram from the serious business of earning a living. He wrote Bartram that he thought
it an interesting amusement for those who could afford the time
but not for Bartram and Collinson.[10] Collinson's concern for Bartram's well-being was doubtless genuine, but he was undoubtedly
concerned that his friend might be distracted from the collecting of
seeds and plants for shipment to England. This activity was beginning to take Bartram further afield, and Collinson was excited by
the reports of these trips and already making plans for further exploration by his friend. English botanists at this time were debating the distinctions between American red cedars (*Juniperus virginiana* L.) and white cedars (*Chamaecyparis thyoides* [L.] BSP),
and Collinson asked Bartram to send specimens of each.[11] This
seemed a simple request but involved Bartram in a strenuous trip
and a great deal of work. There were plenty of red cedars on his
own land, but the nearest white cedars were in the Jersey swamps.

Carolus Linnaeus (1707–78)

To obtain specimens of these required a journey of perhaps 150 miles. He persuaded a man who owned some of this land to guide him to a spot where the trees might be found.

In the late spring of 1736 the two men crossed the Delaware River into Jersey and rode southeast. They left behind the settlements along the river and eventually came to a region of great sand dunes. Interspersed among these dunes, small streams had created boggy areas congested with shrubs and difficult to pass through. Bartram and his guide finally reached the great Cedar Swamp near the source of the Egg Harbor River, a large acreage with an almost pure stand of white cedar. Where the land was a little drier "Silver Laurel or Bay Maple, Holly & Sarsifras" were to be found and, on small ridges, some pines. Cedars, two inches in diameter, might reach twenty feet in height, and others, two feet in diameter, reached eighty to a hundred feet. Some of them stood knee-deep in water, and their roots lent a reddish color to the water (which was, however, sweet to drink). Great masses of ferns grew at the bases of many of the trees. Since there were few limbs beneath the top canopy, Bartram found it necessary to cut down a tree in order to obtain specimens. Collinson was always delighted to make a contribution toward the settlement of any scientific question and hastened to send the specimens to John Jacob Dillenius (1687–1747), who held the chair of botany at Oxford. He told the professor that he could now correct Ray and other botanists.[12]

There was a zoological question troubling Collinson as well, and again he shared his problem with Bartram. He inquired whether or not Bartram knew anything about a certain species of locust that returned every fifteenth year. He had been informed of one such in New England.[13] Bartram was well ahead of him, as he often was. He had heard of the reports made from New England by Paul Dudley (1676–1751), and he had made careful observations of his own. When he replied to Collinson he sent specimens and twigs with eggs and an excellent account of the life cycle of the cicada, more detailed than the accounts to be found in many present-day zoology textbooks.[14]

Dudley had sent an "Account of the Locusts in New England" and specimens to the Royal Society in 1733. He indicated that he had begun his studies of the insect in 1716 but had decided to wait for another seventeen years before reporting them to the society— surely some sort of record for scientific persistence and restraint.

He had first observed the locusts in 1699 and thus could report his observations for three seventeen-year periods. Like others before him and since, he was confused by the use of the same common names for different insects and thought our cicada (*Magicicada septemdecem*) to be comparable, if not identical, to the locusts that had plagued Egypt since biblical times (*Locusta migratoria*). Sloane was not confused and promptly tried to set Dudley straight on this point by sending him a specimen of an Italian cicada, but Dudley still insisted that these were identical with the Egyptian locusts. He admitted his mistake only when the society sent him an Egyptian locust.[15] Dudley's confusion on this point is easier to understand than his insistence that the adult insect arose within minutes from the egg without metamorphosis. Bartram held no such

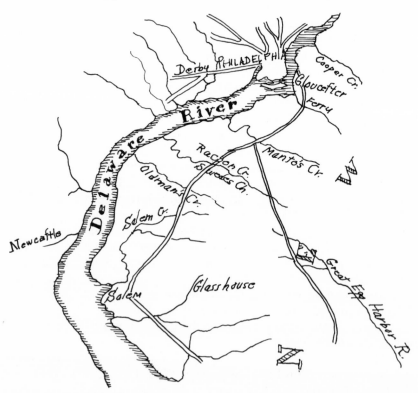

Trip to the Great Cedar Swamp near the source of Egg Harbor River in 1736 (adapted from map by Thomas Kitchin, 1777)

notion. He was not sure how the larvae reached the ground from the trees, but he was fully aware that the insect underwent a long period of growth deep in the ground before its final emergence to molt in the open air. He had also observed that the adults, unlike those of Egypt, seemed to eat little or nothing.

Collinson was delighted with Bartram's account of the cicada. On 10 December 1737 he read it to the Fellows of the Royal Society, who not only enjoyed it but were much impressed by how little escaped Bartram's notice.[16] Collinson hoped that Bartram might make further observations; still confused, he thought that the winged cicada later became a grasshopper or a locust. This notion of the cicada's metamorphosis into a grasshopper seems particularly surprising in view of Sloane's clear understanding of the distinction between a locust and a cicada, for Collinson and Sir Hans were close friends as well as associates in the Royal Society. Bartram was gratified to learn how well his observations had been received, writing Peter: "I am very thankful to thee, and the Royal Society, for taking so much notice of my poor performances. It is a great encouragement for me to continue my observations of natural phenomena."[17]

Bartram did continue his investigation of the life cycle of the cicada and reported his findings from time to time. In 1749 he sent Collinson another detailed account of daily observations as the insects emerged from the ground, enlarging on his earlier account. To this he added observations made by his son, Moses, on the depositing of eggs by the female in a stick held in his hands. This, too, was read to the Royal Society.[18] Finally, Collinson prepared an article for the society entitled "Some Observations on the Cicada of North America, Collected by Mr. Peter Collinson, F.R.S.," which appeared in the *Philosophical Transactions* for 1764, with a very nice illustration of specimens that Bartram had sent to him. The article mentions Bartram only once, yet almost the entire essay is composed of loosely paraphrased commentaries from his letters.[19]

While Bartram was on the subject of periodic appearances of organisms in great numbers, he commented to Collinson on their broad ecological implications. Certain caterpillars which seemed to appear in hordes every twenty years attacked the oaks particularly. They stripped the trees of every green leaf, often killing the trees. There was a periodic abundance of bears near Philadelphia, which Bartram thought might be caused by an acorn shortage in regions

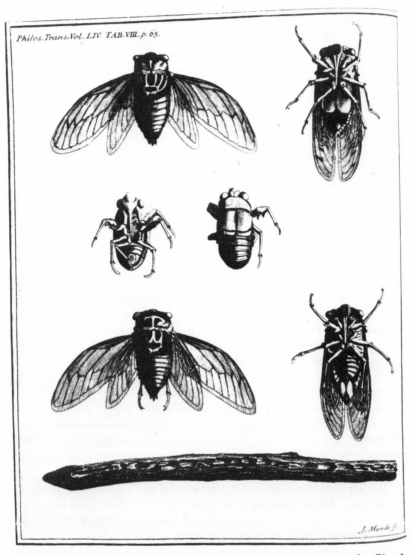

Illustration for Peter Collinson's article "Some Observations on the Cicada of North America," *Philosophical Transactions of the Royal Society* 54 (1764):65

where the caterpillars had attacked the oak trees. This, in turn, reminded him of the extraordinary numbers of passenger pigeons that had appeared about ten years earlier. He again attributed the numbers to probable scarcity of acorns. From all of these observations he drew some interesting conclusions:

> I shall now beg leave to make some Remarks on these Observations, as first the wonderfull order and Ballance that is maintain'd between ye vegetable and Animal Oeconomy, that the Animal should not be too numerous to be supported by the Vegetable, nor the Vegetable Productions be lost for want of gathering by the animal.
> Secondly the surprizing Instinct these Creatures are endowed with, that leave their natural Habitations to travel such a long way after their Food, and return back again to breed. Thirdly it persuades me to think that there must be very great Forests and a Fertil Country to the Westward, that can maintain and support so many Millions of Pigeons (besides other Animals). For it is observed the Pigeons always frequent the most fruitfull part of the Country: there being the greatest variety of Vegetables produced for their Support.[20]

Bartram had a special interest in the behavior and reproduction of insects. He often sent Collinson and his friends specimens not only of insects but of their nests and included interesting accounts of his observations. In 1738 he wrote that he had been studying beetles for the past two years but was not yet ready to communicate his findings.[21] He did comment on the presence of parasites on the beetles. Again in November 1742 he remarked on experiments he had made concerning the composition of hornets' nests. He had noticed a difference between the material of the cells and that of the outside of the nest. He was sure that the latter was made from wood, and he found that it burned like paper. By contrast, the cell material, when burned, behaved like animal substances such as silk. He concluded that this material was produced by the hornet as silk is by the worm.[22]

Both Collinson and Lord Petre considered themselves fortunate to have found a dependable plant collector in Pennsylvania. Lord Petre had not only approved Bartram's suggestion that he be paid a regular annual sum, but he liked his idea of exploring the watershed of the Schuylkill to its source. Collinson gave detailed advice to Bartram on how he should equip himself for the expedition. Three horses would be required, one each for himself and a servant and a third to serve as a packhorse. The servant's horse and the packhorse should be furnished with large panniers covered with waterproof skins for the protection of specimens. It was understood that he might not be able to complete the exploration in a month or two and might even require several expeditions over a

Trip up the Schuylkill River in 1736 (adapted from Thomas Kitchin's map of the *Seat of War in the Environs of Philadelphia*, 1777). See *A Book of Old Maps*, edited by Emerson D. Fite and Archibald Freeman, p. 264.

period of years. Collinson and Petre sent a compass complete with a sundial to enable Bartram to tell the time. The compass would enable him to observe and record the course of the river. Paper was included for the preservation of specimens. They wanted him to keep a daily journal of his trip and suggested what sorts of seeds they wanted as well as some they did not.[23]

Bartram was much amused by Collinson's idea of a well-equipped expedition. He was delighted to go, but one good horse for himself was all that he required, and his saddlebags would have to hold whatever he collected. In the early fall of 1736 he set out, riding more or less northwestward, following the course of the Schuylkill through present-day Norristown, Valley Forge, Potts-town, and Reading to its source in the Blue Mountains near Tusca-rora State Park. Little escaped his keen eyes along the way, and he filled his plant press with specimens as he went: gentians, asters, cardinal flowers, goldenrod, and birches. He found the abundance of rhododendron impressive. Nowhere but on the banks of this river had he seen this plant, although he had heard that it grew beyond the Blue Mountains along the Delaware River. Here it grew five feet tall, but as he went further the riverbanks grew drier, sandier, and poorer, and the stunted plants stood but two feet high. He found a cave and explored it briefly. He saw or heard a panther or mountain lion and reflected on tales that he had heard of their fol-lowing and attacking men on horseback, but he was not greatly concerned.[24]

When he returned home he had ridden nearly 300 miles, and his saddlebags were bulging with his collections. He completed his journal and map and packed them with all of his specimens for shipment to England. Lord Petre and Collinson pored over his jour-nal, tracing his route on the map he had drawn, which they thought "prettily done." In fact, they were so impressed that they planned to show it to a London mapmaker to help him more accu-rately depict the Schuylkill's course as well as the Blue Mountains, since this was probably the first mapping of them.[25] Bartram's apologies for the roughness of his journal were brushed aside with the comment that "It contains many Curious remarks and obser-vations in nature, and very pertinently and well expressed; needs no apology for the natural way of expressing thyself; is more ac-ceptable, clear & intelligible than a fine set of words and phrases."[26]

Collinson and Petre did have some questions they would like

to have answered. They wanted to know the length of the Schuylkill and more details about the cave that Bartram had explored.
They wondered if he had brought home living plants as well as
dried specimens of the rare plants that he had found. If not, they
hoped that he would do so in the future.[27] Collinson collected live
plants when he traveled about England, and he told Bartram his
method of keeping them alive until he got home. He took them up
with soil around the roots and wrapped them first in moss and then
in paper before putting them into his saddlebags. At night, he loos-
ened the branches and placed the moss and roots in a bowl of water.
He was able to keep them fresh for several weeks of traveling. Bartram could plant them in his garden as a future source of seeds or
of further descriptions and could also take them up and ship them
later if desired. He added that Bartram's journey to the Blue Mountains showed that he was not easily discouraged by the danger of
Indians.[28] Among many plants and seeds which Bartram sent to
Collinson from this expedition were bulbs of a lily or "martagon"
(*Lilium superbum* L., or Turk's-cap lily). In July 1738 Collinson
wrote that it was near flowering, was five and a half feet high, and
would have fifteen flowers.[29]

In 1737 Collinson became irritated by Bartram's suggestion
that he was not adequately remunerated for his work. He felt that
the £21 sterling which Bartram was being paid would amount to
more than £40 in American currency and should be more than adequate. If Bartram could not afford to do it for this amount, he had
only to say so and the arrangement would be given up.[30] One might
have thought that this would be the end of their harmonious relationship but not at all. Bartram did not drop the subject but supported his position in a letter of May 1738:

> In thy letter of December 20th, thee supposes me to spend
> five or six weeks in collections for you, and that ten pounds
> will defray all my annual expenses: but I assure thee, I spend
> more than twice that time, annually; and ten pounds will
> not, at a moderate expense, defray my charges abroad—be-
> side my neglect of business at home, in fallowing, harvest
> and seed time.
>
> Indeed, I was more than two weeks' time in gathering the
> small acorns of the Willow-leafed Oak, which are very scarce,
> and falling with the leaves,—so that daily I had to rake up

the leaves and shake the acorns out, before they were de-
voured by the squirrels and hogs; and I reckoned it good luck
if I could gather twenty under one tree—and hardly one in
twenty bore any. Yet I don't begrudge my labour; but would
do anything reasonable to serve you. But by the sequel of thy
letter, you are not sensible of the fourth part of the pains I
take to oblige you.

He then turned to other matters but could not end his letter without a further note: "Now, my kind and generous friend, I shall return thee my hearty thanks for thy care and pains which thee hath
taken, and the many good offices thee hath done for me; and further, if thee finds any expressions in my letter a little out of the
way, thee will not take it in the wrong sense. I assure thee, I bear
thee a great deal of good-will; or if thee thinks I am too short and

Trip to Virginia in 1738 (adapted from reproduction of map of Dr. John
Mitchell, 1755). See *A Book of Old Maps*, edited by Emerson D. Fite and
Archibald Freeman.

imperfect in explaining any subject, which I give thee any account
of, pray let me know, and I will satisfy thee according to the best of
my knowledge; for I love plain dealing."[31]

Over the years one or the other would occasionally point out
to his friend that he had no idea how hard he worked to please him,
but it never became a matter of serious offense. Although Bartram
never thought that he was adequately paid for the work he did, he
was frequently slow to spend what he had earned. Collinson would
chide him for failing to write what to purchase. Most items requested by Bartram, such as glass and nails, were easily obtain-
able. Occasionally, his requests were a real nuisance to Collinson.
The narrow binding that Bartram had ordered in 1736 was not to
be found, so Collinson had had it specially made. When he went to
pick it up, it was unsatisfactory, and he had to find another man to
make it.[32] Some items were not for personal or even family use.
Bartram frequently wanted things that he hoped to sell for a profit.
In February 1737/38 Collinson sent two pounds of sewing silk, less
than Bartram had ordered because he thought current silk prices
too high.[33] Collinson thought to protect Bartram as much as possible in this respect and even exercised a sort of veto power over
Bartram's suggestions, which he considered to be too frivolous for
one in his station in life: "The magic lantern is a contrivance to
make sport with ignorant people. There is nothing extraordinary
in it; so not worth thy further inquirey."[34] When Bartram expressed
a wish for the *Elémens de Botanique* of Joseph Pitton de Tournefort
(1656–1708), Collinson reported that the three volumes were too
expensive, particularly since Bartram already had those of Miller
and Parkinson: "Remember Solomon's advice; in reading books,
there is no end."[35] To which Bartram replied, "I take thy advice
about books very kindly,—although I love reading dearly: and I believe, if Solomon had loved women less, and books more, he would
have been a wiser and happier man than he was."[36]

At times Bartram had problems selling the goods that Collinson sent him and long delays in obtaining his money. It was difficult to determine which goods might be profitable. If he guessed
incorrectly, it resulted in his money being tied up in slow-selling
merchandise. In 1738 he suggested that Collinson send his payments in kegs of half-pence, which were double in value in this
country. If this could be done safely, Bartram thought that the
pence could be sent in "small parcels that ye law will not take

hould of. . . ."[37] He thought that the prohibitions against export of
gold and silver from England might apply to copper, but Collinson
saw nothing wrong with it. In February 1738/39 he shipped £10
worth of half-pence, which arrived just in time to pay the interest
on Bartram's mortgage.[38] The scheme was so successful that additional monies were transferred thus from time to time.

The armchair travelers in England were happy to encourage
Bartram to extend his travels. In the spring of 1737 he had gone to
Conestoga, where his aunt, Elizabeth Cornish (the widow Cartlidge), lived, and then on a short trip to the Jerseys and to Kent
County, Maryland.[39] Now his patrons suggested that his next trip
should take him south through the three lower counties (now Delaware). In characteristic fashion Collinson was able to suggest several friends in the region who might prove helpful. He sent letters
of introduction to Colonel James Hollyday and George Robbins.[40]
When the crops had been harvested and Bartram thought seeds
should be ripe, he rode south along the Delaware to the Eastern
Shore of Maryland and Virginia, all the way to Cape Charles,
where he turned north along the Chesapeake Bay. His first visit
was to the Robbinses at Peach Blossom on the Choptank River.
From there he rode north to Readbourne, home of Colonel Hollyday
on the Chester River. Reaching home he was delighted to find that
he had discovered more new plants than he had on any previous
journey. Some seeds were immature, and Collinson suggested that,
in the future, Bartram should carry a plant press of two boards so
that he might at least bring back specimens even if the seeds were
unripe.[41] In spite of the unripe seeds and some that he had lost in
Virginia, he was able to ship Collinson two boxes of seeds and two
of plants.[42]

FOUR

New Travels, New Friends, and a Growing Reputation

B ARTRAM'S seed-collecting trips were, of necessity, made in the fall of the year, but he managed to make expeditions at other times for plant collecting. In late May of 1738 he crossed the Susquehannah River and spent some time collecting on the southwest side with the assistance of a guide familiar with the local terrain.[1] While looking for plants along the river they found a large rattlesnake. Remembering Collinson's admonitions, Bartram stared long and hard at the snake's eyes. He was unable to detect any emanations from them or any effect whatever upon himself. Hoping to observe the snake's discharge of venom, he poked it a number of times with a stick but found it uncooperative. He objected strongly to unnecessary killing of animals so left the snake in peace.

After one day with his guide Bartram continued alone, riding southeast along the river. About midafternoon he arrived at the house where he expected to spend the night. He turned his horse loose in the pasture and walked toward the river, about two miles away, to see what he could find before dark. It was a very hot afternoon so he left his coat and jacket, but he carried the compass that Collinson had sent him. This had now become his constant companion on trips. Preoccupied with searching for plants, he failed to notice gathering clouds until thunder and lightning called his attention to the weather too late for him to turn back. He hastily sought an overhanging rock for shelter but lost his footing and rolled to the bottom of a steep slope. Here he was soon greeted by "unhospitable salutations & churlish compliments by way of ye north wind blowing." In spite of his fear of lightning, he was soon more con-

50

cerned about the cold. He could think of but one solution as he again sought shelter under the rock: "i puled off my trousers from my breeches & put one arm in one leging & ye other arm in ye other so ye back part of my trousers hung down my back & I kept reasonably warm during ye shower; but if a Mohameton had spied me there he might have taken me for a hermit or pagan."

From his eyrie high above the river Bartram had a fine view of the stream. He was interested to see how much more rapidly it flowed here among the rocks than it did upstream, where it was much wider. He had been pleased to find nearly a hundred papaw trees along the river but disappointed to find no fruit. He had previously sent papaw flowers to Mark Catesby and had promised to send fruit later. A new plant which interested Bartram was a "different kind of sumach of prodigious sizes near 25 feet high & 8 to 10 inches diameter in two years shoots it will grow 15 foot high   ye first shoots is covered with down very much like a bucks horn while it is tender." Both the staghorn sumac and the papaws were being gradually crowded out by trees of more permanent growth: locust, linden, mulberry, sycamore, and ash. Bartram recognized this ecological phenomenon of natural succession and thought that it had begun when Marylanders had driven the Indians from their cleared fields along the river. The abandoned land had first produced papaw and sumac, and these were later being replaced by other trees.

Bartram's most exciting discovery on this trip was not the staghorn sumac but another plant that soon attracted attention in scientific circles in several widely separated parts of the world. Dr. John Kearsley (1684–1772), a wealthy Philadelphia physician, had given him a drawing of a plant which he hoped Bartram might find,[2] and here along the Susquehannah he came across it, "ye ginsang exactly agreable acording to ye best description & ye famous root for ye cure of plurisie." Ginseng (*Panax quinquefolium* L.) had, and still has today, something of an international reputation as a panacea. An Asiatic species had long been extensively used in Chinese medicine. Dr. Kearsley was skeptical concerning its medicinal virtues but was curious to know whether or not there was an American species. Bartram was a little surprised by the publicity given his discovery. Benjamin Franklin promptly announced in the *Pennsylvania Gazette* of 27 July: "We have the pleasure of acquainting the World, that the famous Chinese or Tartarian Plant, called Gin seng, is now discovered in this Province near Susquehannah: From whence several whole Plants with a Quantity of the Root, have been lately sent to Town, and it appears to agree most exactly with the Description given of it in Chambers's Dictionary and Père du Haldé's Account of China. The Virtues ascrib'd to this Plant are wonderful. . . ."[3]

Collinson, too, was excited when he received specimens of these plants from Bartram. He promptly informed the Royal Society: "The Ginseng, a Root so celebrated for its virtues in China that it is exchanged for its weight in Gold, is this year discovered by John Bartram, who has sent over these two specimens of their Roots, Leaves and Seed Vessel of the North American Ginseng."[4] Bartram included ginseng among some plant specimens that he sent to Antoine de Jussieu (1686–1758), a botanist at the Jardin du Roi at Paris. These were delivered personally by Dr. Thomas Bond (1712–84), a Philadelphia physician. Jussieu told Bond that ginseng was now common in Paris, having been brought from Canada, and was held in no esteem.[5]

Word of Bartram's discovery continued to spread. Dr. John Frederick Gronovius (1690–1760), botanist of Leiden, wrote to Linnaeus in Sweden that the ginseng that had been found in Pennsylvania was similar to that which Sloane had received from China.[6] Collinson, meanwhile, conceived a great bonanza for Bartram. He sent some ginseng roots to China. If they sold well, Bartram might develop a profitable trade. In the meantime he should sow the seed and establish a crop.[7] One might expect that Bartram would have

Ginseng (*Panax quinquefolium* L.)

eagerly pursued such glittering prospects. On the contrary, he said that Collinson had a higher opinion of ginseng than it deserved. More to the point, the few plants that Bartram had moved to his garden had failed to thrive, and, if the plant were easily cultivated, the Chinese would have done so long ago.[8]

Dr. Bond, who had delivered Bartram's plants to Jussieu, had gone to Paris by way of London in September 1738. Bartram had burdened the long-suffering young doctor with boxes of snake eggs, turtle eggs, and insects for Collinson and jars of papaw flowers and fruit for Catesby.[9] Bond was soon adding to Bartram's reputation abroad. Dr. John Fothergill (1712–80) of London wrote to Israel Pemberton of Philadelphia thanking him for a box of seeds packed by Bartram and delivered by Dr. Bond. Bond had described Bartram as an "extraordinary Genius." Fothergill promised to mention Bartram and his discovery of ginseng to the botany professor at the University of Edinburgh, Dr. Charles Alston (1683–1760).[10]

When Bartram had returned from his seed-collecting trip to Cape Charles the previous fall, he had planned that his expedition in the autumn of 1738 should take him down the western shore of Chesapeake Bay. Collinson and Lord Petre had readily agreed and had started giving him advice well in advance of his going. Collinson sent some fine drugget cloth with explicit instructions: "One thing I must desire of thee, and do insist that thee oblige me therein: that thou make up that drugget clothes, to go to Virginia in, and not appear to disgrace thyself or me; for though I should not esteem thee the less, to come to me in what dress thou will,—yet these Virginians are a very gentle, well-dressed people—and look, perhaps, more at a man's outside than inside. For these and other reasons, pray go very clean, neat, and hansomely dressed, to Virginia. Never mind thy clothes: I will send more another year."[11]

Collinson mentioned plants that he hoped Bartram might find, including more ginseng and the "umbrella tree" (*Magnolia tripetala* L.). Bartram had suggested that he go south along the bay, through the more settled portions of Virginia, and return through the Shenandoah Valley, west of the Blue Ridge Mountains. Collinson agreed that he was more likely to find new plants in the western part of Virginia and would not have to carry them as great a distance as if he went there first.[12] He took the added precaution of writing to the friends for whom he had given introductory letters to Bartram, advising them of his friend's coming. A long letter to

John Custis (1678–1750) of Williamsburg urged him not to be startled by Bartram's appearance, claiming that his conversation would compensate for it. Such warning did not perturb Custis at all. He replied that nothing suited him better than "down right plainness."[13]

Since Bartram had planned to leave home on 25 September he did not let the fact that it was raining change his plans.[14] Had he known that it would continue to pour for the next three days he might well have delayed. He was fortunate in having comfortable places to spend the night, thanks to Collinson's introductions, but after hours of riding in the rain he fulfilled Collinson's worst fears for his appearance. Nevertheless, he was cordially received at the homes of Philip Thomas on West River,[15] Richard Hall in Calvert County,[16] Dr. Alexander Hamilton at Annapolis, and William Maudait near the north branch of the Potomac River. Having crossed the Potomac four miles below the falls, he continued on to the Rappahannock and Pianketank, finally reaching the home of John Clayton at Gloucester Court House.

Visiting Clayton had been one of Bartram's prime objectives, for no other man in America had more in common with him. Clayton (1694–1773) had been born in England and educated there. He had joined his father, attorney general of Virginia, some time prior to 1720, in which year the younger Clayton became clerk of court for Gloucester County. He had developed a great interest in the plants of Virginia and had sought the help of Catesby, then in Lon-

Dr. John Fothergill (1712–80)

don, in identifying them. Catesby had been a family friend during his seven years in Virginia but, being more an artist and zoologist than a botanist, had introduced Clayton to Dr. Gronovius, to whom Catesby forwarded Clayton's specimens. As early as 1735, Gronovius was receiving large numbers of plants from Clayton. These were studied not only by Gronovius but by his friend Linnaeus during the latter's three years in Holland. Shortly before Bartram's visit, Clayton had compiled "A Catalogue of Plants, Fruits, and Trees Native to Virginia" and had sent it to Gronovius in appreciation of his assistance in identifying a number of them.[17]

It was a bitter disappointment to Bartram to find that Clayton was away from home. Clayton had gone to the mountains to investigate some land and was not expected back for some days. His family persuaded Bartram to spend the night and showed him Clayton's garden. Bartram found it very interesting, although it lacked many of the English and continental plants commonly found in Philadelphia gardens. He was more interested in the native plants and begged a root of Hercules'-club (*Aralia spinosa* L.) before he left for Williamsburg. This plant grew so well in Bartram's garden that he was able to send specimens to friends in England twenty years later.[18] Throughout much of his long ride across Maryland and Virginia, Bartram the conservationist was shocked to see everywhere evidence of poor farming practices. Many of the fields had been worn out by continuous planting of corn and tobacco and had been largely abandoned. Pastures had miserably poor grass, scarcely enough to keep the cattle alive. Here and there were large estates where better farming practices were followed and the labor of many slaves enabled the owners to live in considerable luxury and style.[19]

Late in the afternoon Bartram arrived at the home of Custis on Francis Street in Williamsburg. It was a fine brick house, built some twenty years previously, on a four-acre lot referred to as "Custis Square." Custis had planted holly and cedar trees around the perimeter of his yard and developed an excellent garden.[20] A native Virginian educated in England, he was an extremely wealthy man, owning some 15,000 acres of land. One of his plantations, Queen's Creek, adjoined Williamsburg and encompassed 2,330 acres. He had been a member of the council since 1727. Custis and Bartram, having many interests in common, were instantly congenial despite the differences in their ages and backgrounds. Custis found

Bartram the "most takeing facetious man" that he had "ever met with and never was so much delighted with A stranger" in his whole life.[21] Bartram felt that he had never received such "extraordinary Civility & respect" from a stranger.

On the morning following his arrival Bartram called on Lieutenant Governor William Gooch and presented a letter of introduction given to him by his own governor. Gooch received him warmly and offered to recommend him to various people. They conversed for an hour, and Gooch invited Bartram to dine with him the following day. During his visit Bartram met John Blair, president of The College of William and Mary, and Dr. John Tennent (c.1700–1748), to whom he had a letter of introduction from London. Tennent was the author of *Every Man His Own Doctor*, which Bartram had read and enjoyed. Franklin had published a Philadelphia edition, as well as extracts from Tennent's *Essay on Pleurisy*, printed at Williamsburg in 1736.[22] Tennent had just returned from London, where he had hoped to obtain the endorsement of the Royal Society for the virtues of Seneca snakeroot (*Polygala senega* L.) as a cure for pleurisy and other lung infections. He was not in a very kindly mood toward the society at the moment, for they had not been impressed by his remedy. He still had hopes of convincing them of its efficacy and planned a second trip to London.[23] Bartram, always interested in medicinal plants, queried the doctor not only about snakeroot but also Indian physic (*Gillenia*), which Tennent

John Custis (1678–1750)

advocated strongly. He gave Bartram a liberal supply of it and advised the proper dosage.[24] Bartram enjoyed discussing his London correspondents with someone who had recently seen them.

Bartram spent two nights and a day with Custis, the only break in travel that he had made since leaving home. Custis could not show him his plantation since he had just "crawld out of the grave," as he put it. Bartram rode out to Queen's Creek and did some collecting as well as admiring the best agricultural methods he had seen since leaving home. Custis raised cattle, sheep, hogs, corn, wheat, and tobacco with the labor of seventy-seven slaves. His fields were well fenced and ditched, and he alternated fine stands of red clover with other crops. Custis was able to show Bartram his garden, in which he took much pride and pleasure. It was not at its best since it had been injured first by a severe winter and then by a very dry summer. There were many English and European plants collected over a number of years: silver and gilded hollies, fine yews, roses, Persian lilacs, Cornish cherries, Arabian jasmine, and many bulbs, all enclosed by an edging of Dutch boxwood. Bartram was particularly interested in the young horse-chestnut trees, grown from seed sent by Collinson. He had tried to raise them from Collinson's seeds without success.[25]

Custis urged Bartram to linger for several days, but his guest felt that he could not do so if he was to reach home approximately when he had planned. He rode up the north side of the James River to Westover, the home of Colonel William Byrd (1674–1744), who had married Mrs. Custis's sister. Again Bartram found a man who shared his intense interest in natural history. Byrd, a member of the House of Burgesses, was, like Custis, a very wealthy man. He had inherited 26,000 acres of land and two fine homes from his father and had added to these holdings extensively. He had been educated in England, where he spent fifteen years, and was admitted to the English bar. He was one of the few American Fellows of the Royal Society of London, having been elected at the age of twenty-two. He had both a personal acquaintance and a correspondence with Sir Hans Sloane and other society members and had presented them with both an opossum and a rattlesnake in 1697.[26]

Westover, often called a "Georgian masterpiece," was certainly one of the most handsome houses in the colony. Byrd showed Bartram his excellent library, comparable to that of Logan in Philadelphia. Next morning they inspected his fine garden. It was enclosed by a brick wall, its entrance adorned with eagles and mono-grammed gates. Inside there were brick walks connecting sections of the garden: flower beds, vegetable plots, fruit trees, and grape arbors. The beds were bordered with dwarf boxwood, accented by clumps of larger boxwood at the corners. There was even a green-house containing orange trees in fruit. The thirty-nine-year-old Bartram and the sixty-four-year-old Byrd found other areas of shared interest beside their gardens. Both were keenly interested in medicine and frequently prescribed for neighbors, friends, and servants. Byrd shared Tennent's enthusiasm for Seneca snakeroot and had provided Tennent with an introduction to the Royal Soci-ety. Byrd had sent Indian physic to England as early as 1707 and was an ardent believer in the efficacy of ginseng. He had found the latter valuable while serving as one of the commissioners ap-pointed to survey and establish the dividing line between Virginia and North Carolina. He reported that he had chewed a piece of gin-seng root as he tramped along and that "This kept up my Spirits, and made me trip away as nimbly in my half Jack Boots as younger men cou'd in their Shoes." He had corresponded about the virtues of ginseng with Catesby, Collinson, and Sloane. Byrd contended

Colonel William Byrd II
(1674–1744)

that the earth had never produced a finer plant for man's use, insisting that it benefited man in all manner of ways without "those naughty effects that might make Men troublesome and impertinent to their poor wives."[27]

Byrd was still acquiring land and thought that Bartram might help him to find buyers for some of it at Philadelphia. He had, in the previous year, surveyed and begun to advertise lots in "a town called Richmond," a few miles further up James River.[28] In addition, he had acquired title to 100,000 acres of land on the Roanoke River which he hoped to sell, and he gave Bartram a sales brochure describing it. Byrd was willing to sell land at £3 per acre and had already interested some Swiss and German settlers. He hoped that Bartram would circulate the brochure among friends at Philadelphia.[29]

Byrd gave Bartram a letter for his friend William Randolph (1681–1742) of Tuckahoe, where Bartram spent the next night. The following day he continued up the James to Dungeness, west of Byrd's proposed town of Richmond. This was the home of William Randolph's relative Isham Randolph (1685–1742). Bartram had been handed along from one wealthy Virginian to another. Isham was a merchant as well as a farmer and represented Goochland County in the assembly.[30] He went well beyond the dictates of mere courtesy in receiving Bartram. He insisted that Bartram rest his horse and provided one of his own for his guest. He took time from his own affairs to ride with Bartram the next day and showed him a cave on the bank of the James and other local curiosities. Bartram was curious about the cave and crawled through it for some ninety feet. The two men later crossed the river to see some trees that puzzled Randolph. They were new to Bartram, but he later identified them as arborvitae (*Thuja occidentalis* L.) and recommended them to both Byrd and Custis for their gardens. Near the arborvitae trees Bartram found another new plant, which proved to be a "Leather-bark or Mezeron" (*Dirca palustris* L.). Two such discoveries made Bartram's day.

Randolph had enjoyed Bartram's company so much that he rode with him twelve miles along his way and sent a servant, Cornelius, to guide him. Bartram was touched by so much kindness, finding Randolph "a man of great humanity."[31] Cornelius and Bartram had started late in the day, so they camped that night before riding on to the home of Bartram's next host. The latter was never identified, but his location and Bartram's few comments suggest that he was Isham Randolph's son-in-law, Peter Jefferson. Bartram rose early next morning and was abroad before daybreak. He climbed the nearby small Southwest Mountain and watched a beautiful sunrise illuminate the valley between it and the Blue Ridge to the west. He returned in time for breakfast with his host and then rode west toward the mountains. He crossed the Blue Ridge at Wood's Gap and enjoyed the magnificent prospect both east and west as he rested his horse on the mountaintop. He did not expect such hospitality as he had enjoyed in eastern Virginia when he left the mountain and felt almost sad to be saying "adieu to all ye pleasant entertainment of Virginia and conversations."[32]

Bartram made his way down the mountain into the great Shenandoah Valley and turned northward toward home. This being limestone country, he found a considerable change in the flora and many plants to investigate. He was deeply affected by the beauty and unique qualities of the "Valley of Virginia" and determined to come again with more time to collect. He continued northward to the Potomac and the Susquehanna and reached home on 26 October. He had been away for five weeks and estimated that he had ridden 1,100 miles. It had been a strenuous trip but a very satisfying one. He had seen a great deal of interest and felt sure that he would return. He had made some new friends who had promised to correspond with him and whose conversation had stimulated his own thinking.

FIVE

Experimental Botany

IN 1739 Bartram became an experimental botanist. He became involved in a botanical debate
that had been going on for some time and made a small contribution toward its settlement. Rudolf Camerarius (1665–1721), professor of medicine at Tübingen, had performed experiments in the
1690s demonstrating the functions of the stamens and pistils of
flowers; but his findings had not been fully accepted, and botanists
were still arguing the pros and cons of sexual reproduction in
plants in the eighteenth century. In 1717 Thomas Fairchild reported in England that he had successfully crossed a carnation
with a pink. Both Paul Dudley and Cotton Mather in this country
had made observations on hybridization in Indian corn. When Bartram began making studies of floral anatomy and plant pollen for
Logan and Linnaeus, he became familiar with Logan's demonstration of the necessity for pollination in the development of the fruit
(grain) in Indian corn. Logan had stressed that what he had found
to be true of maize did not necessarily hold true for other species of
plants.[1]

Collinson had written to Bartram in May 1738 asking him to
collect flowers of sweet gum (*Liquidambar*).[2] Gronovius had urgently requested them for Linnaeus in a letter which Collinson had
forwarded to Logan. Bartram had seen this letter just before he left
for Williamsburg and promised to be diligent in his observation on
the flower.[3] He was surprised to find that no one had studied it before but supposed that it was because the tree seldom flowered before it became quite tall. He was as good as his word, and by July
1740 Gronovius was able to inform Linnaeus that "that most accu-

rate observer of plants in Pennsylvania reported 'it hath male and female distinct upon the same sprig: the male consists of a spike of mossy buttons, being constituted of a cluster of Apices upon slender stamina: the female is the lowermost upon a long footstalk.'"[4]

At about the same time that Bartram was studying these trees with distinct male and female flowers on the same plant, his attention was attracted to some plants that had male and female flowers on separate plants. For several years he had been interested in some *Lychnis* (campion) plants in his garden which bore "flesh-colored" (an eighteenth-century term for pale red) flowers, although he had planted only seeds of white-flowered and red-flowered *Lychnis* sent him from England. He suspected that the flesh-colored plants were hybrids of the red and white and thought that he might be able to prove it. He took advantage of an opportunity to test his hypothesis and at the same time to confirm that of Camerarius and others concerning the necessity of male pollen or farina. One plant of the white-flowered *Lychnis*, bearing female flowers, bloomed two weeks ahead of the other plants. The only plant

Sweet gum (*Liquid-ambar styraciflua* L.)

near it bearing male flowers was a red-flowered plant ten yards away. Fruit capsules on the white-flowered plant filled with good seed, and when they were ripe Bartram gathered them. He kept them separate from capsules formed by the same plant after white-flowered male plants were blooming. He gathered the late capsules also and later planted seeds from both. He reasoned that seed from the first capsules "must partake of ye nature & color of ye red one or else we should be pusled to reconcile ye hypothesis of receiving of male & female parts."

As he had expected, the first-formed seeds produced only plants with flesh-colored flowers, intermediate between red and white, while the seed from the later-formed capsules produced only pure white flowers. Manifestly, the male flowers had contributed to the formation of the plant embryo in the seeds. This was emphasized still further when Bartram gave a single female *Lychnis* plant to Dr. Witt. This flowered well in his garden where no other campions were growing. It produced fruit capsules, but they were entirely lacking in seeds. From all these observations, Bartram concluded that "it appears that ye male parts of Vegitables is really necessary to vegitation."[5]

In addition to reporting the results of his experiments to Collinson, Bartram wrote to William Byrd on the subject:

I have this spring made several microscopical observations upon ye malle and femall parts in vegetables to oblige some ingenius botanists in Leyden, who requested that favour of mee which I hope I have performed to their satisfaction and as a mechanical demonstration of ye certainty of this hypothesis of ye different sex in all plants that hath come under my notice. I can't find that any vegetable hath power to produce perfect seed able to propagate without ye conjunction of malle seed any more than animals and by a good microscope ye malle and femall organs is as plainly discovered. I have made several Successful experiments of joyning several species of ye same genus whereby I have obtained curious mixed Colours in flowers never known before but this requires an accurate observation and judgment to know ye precise time when ye femall organs is disposed to receive ye masculin seed and likewise when it is by ye masculin organs fully perfected for ejection. I hope by these practical observations to open a

gate into a very large field of experimental knowledge which
if judiciously improved may be a considerable addition to ye
beauty of ye florists garden.[6]

Collinson wrote to Bartram in July 1740 thanking him for his
April letter concerning his "curious and entertaining" experiments
and telling him about Fairchild's hybrids.[7] Whether or not Bartram
had previously known of these is not clear. Although his interest in
hybrids continued, Bartram's experimentation was sporadic. Many
years later, in 1760, he told Collinson, "I have now united double to
upright larkspur & they have produced not only a monstrous but a
gigantick monster of a flower upon ye top of ye central shoot   it is
in form & magnitude like ye double Nigela   Above 30 petals com-
pose ye lower part of ye flower & is blew & measures one inch &
half in diameter like ye double larkspur   ye midle part is composed
of above 80 petals delicately striped purple & white spread horizon-
tally upon ye other   ye other or uper course is composed of 40 petals standing more upright & darker purple   Another plant stood
just by it which had such a like flower but hanged perpendicular &
two common flowers growed out of ye oposite side of ye stalk. Both
these plants had many curious common flowers growing on several

Campion (*Lychnis*)

branches under them."[8] Bartram had produced double larkspur, which Collinson was eager to have, but the plants produced no seed.[9]

In the summer of 1737 Bartram received a copy of Miller's *Dictionary* as a gift from Dillenius, who had been identifying Bartram's plants for Collinson and receiving some of Bartram's seeds. Dillenius had sent the *Dictionary*, at Collinson's suggestion, to express his appreciation for the seeds.[10] Bartram reciprocated by sending in Collinson's care a quire of plants, and a direct correspondence between Bartram and Dillenius was begun.[11] The professor desired information concerning a number of plants, and Bartram answered his queries as best he could.[12] Dillenius sent paper for plant specimens, writing paper, and seeds of medicinal plants.[13] He also sent a plate of mosses which had been collected by William Vernon in Maryland, hoping that Bartram would find the same species in Pennsylvania.[14] These were unfortunately sent back to England by mistake and returned to Philadelphia too late for Bartram to collect the desired plants that year.[15] He became increasingly interested in mosses: "Before Doctor Dillenius gave me a hint of it, I took no particular notice of mosses, but looked upon them as a cow looks at a pair of new barn doors; yet now he is pleased to say, I have made a good progress in that branch of botany, which really is a very curious part of vegetation."[16]

Previous to this period, Bartram had collected a few mosses for Dillenius at Collinson's request, but now he concentrated on such collecting and sent a great many. On 10 June 1740 Collinson urged Bartram to special effort as Dillenius was deferring completion of his book until he should receive shipments from Bartram, Clayton, and Dr. John Mitchell (1711–68), a Virginia physician.[17] Bartram had already sent a large collection which Dillenius declared had outdone those of all his other correspondents.[18] The book mentioned was Dillenius' famous *Historia Muscorum*, which was published in 1741. He sent Bartram one of the 250 copies printed, wherein Bartram read: *"Polytrichum acaulon capillaceum* The dwarf leaf'd Polytrichum with cylindrical heads from John Bartram of Pennsylvania. Gathered on Jersey side at the Minisinks at the upper Inhabitants on Delaware."[19] Unfortunately, most of the mosses that Bartram had sent were identified only as having come from Pennsylvania.

Dillenius did not limit his interest in plants to the mosses. He asked Bartram to inquire about the "cornelian Chery with a big leaf" when he went to Virginia. Bartram was unable to gather any information concerning it and hazarded a guess that it might be either a sour or a black gum.[20] The other plant specimens that Bartram sent to Dillenius bore notes, as did his mosses, concerning the situation in which he had found them. There was the false hellebore (*Veratrum viride* Ait.), which grew "in moist places." He had found a similar but rare plant in the mountains, but since it bloomed in August he was always too busy on the farm to collect the seed. A *Lycopodium* was usually dry but became "moist & springy" in damp weather; the "Rein deer Moss" he had found growing in sand in a Jersey desert; "Old Man Beard Moss" was growing on a high oak in Virginia; "*Porella permata*" was found on a tidal rock in Pennsylvania; a *Lychenoides* was discovered on a laurel in the mountains "toward Susquehanna," and a package containing a mixture of mosses and lichens he thought he remembered gathering on the ground at the root of an old oak.[21]

When his plant lists arrived from Collinson in the summer of 1739, Bartram found the names abbreviated and many lacking, for Dillenius had not been well enough to identify all of them.[22] Bartram, wondering if the professor was tired of this extra burden, suggested that he might identify the plants himself if only Collinson would lend him the books.[23] Instead, Collinson recruited Gronovius in Dillenius' place.[24] Such an arrangement was far more satisfactory, since Gronovius had been working with Clayton's American plants. He had just published Clayton's "Catalogue," without the author's permission, as *Flora Virginica*, Part I, and immediately sent Bartram a copy. Nothing could have delighted him more or could have been more useful. He wrote to Collinson, "I am certainly pleased with doctor gronovius present whereby I have been informed what kind of plants my brother Claton hath discovered & how far to ye northward Mountains he hath travailed as well as my friends ingenious observations upon them & ye good order which he hath digested them in pray return my hearty thanks to him & desire him from me to use much freedom with me as to let me know what he desires wherein I can oblige him. . . ." This arrangement benefited not only Gronovius and Bartram but Collinson as well. The doctor returned the specimens mounted on "fine white Paper" looking "as beautiful as so many pictures," an art for which Collinson had neither the time nor the skill.[25]

In October 1740 Collinson excitedly informed Bartram, "I can tell thee in the next edition of Virginia plants, thee will see *Bartramia.*"[26] Collinson was determined that Bartram's work and discoveries should be commemorated by "a species of eternity" as his own contributions to botany had been honored by the naming of *Collinsonia* and Clayton's by *Claytonia*. Collinson was disappointed to find no genus *Bartramia* in Part II of the *Flora Virginica* when it appeared in 1743. Early in the new year, Collinson approached Linnaeus, who had shared in many of the parcels of Bartram's seeds: "For his great pains and industry pray find out a new genus, and name it *Bartramia.*" Collinson then wrote to Bartram that he had urged both Gronovius and Linnaeus "not to forget the pains and travel of indefatigable John Bartram,—but stick a feather in his cap, who is as deserving as the rest." A year later, when there was still no action from Sweden, Collinson attempted a more subtle approach. He wrote to Linnaeus that he was glad to know that he was corresponding with Bartram and Dr. Cadwallader Colden (1688–1776), surveyor-general of New York, adding that "Those two gentlemen are much obliged to you for the honour that you intend them." By August 1746 subtlety was dropped and Collinson suggested outright that Linnaeus name the "new and rare plant," of which he was sending a specimen, *Bartramia* if a new genus. This was the charming shooting star (*Dodecatheon meadia* L.),

Dr. Cadwallader Colden
(1688–1776)

which Bartram had found in Virginia.[27] In the meantime, Gronovius wrote Bartram that indeed Linnaeus was naming two new
genera *Bartramia* and *Coldenia*.[28] Bartram was unfamiliar with his
namesake, a plant native to Florida.[29]

A parcel of West Indian plants and seeds arrived in the spring
of 1739. It had been sent to Bartram by Dr. J. Slingsby Cressy of
Antigua, a friend of William Graham, an acquaintance of Bartram
who kept a tavern in Chester County. Bartram was "exceedingly
pleased" to have a correspondent with a taste for botany in the
American tropics. He and Cressy exchanged great numbers of
plants and seeds, but they found it frustrating. Those tropical
plants that did not mature seed within six months were useless in
Philadelphia. The "indian shot" (*Canna indica* L.) did perform in a
highly satisfactory manner for Bartram, growing to a height of four
feet and producing a fine scarlet flower, but it was one of the few
that prospered. Plants from the temperate zone failed in Antigua.
Both men were disappointed, and their correspondence and exchange were discontinued.[30]

Reports that Bartram's seeds and plants were being cultivated
successfully elsewhere cheered him. Many of his plants were now
flowering in Collinson's garden: an Atamasco lily, a spirea, a yellow
lady's slipper, two other kinds of lilies, a pale blue *Lychnis*, a dwarf
honeysuckle, and a fringed orchis.[31] It was in this garden that
Catesby found many of his models for the handsome illustrations
in the second volume of his *Natural History*. Of the North American plants the majority had come from Bartram, and Catesby often
acknowledged his indebtedness to him. There was the skunk cabbage: "The introduction of this most curious Plant with innumerable others, is owing to the indefatigable attachment of Mr. *Collinson*, who, in the year 1735, received it from *Pensilvania*, and in the
spring following it displayed itself in this manner at Peckham."
There was the yellow lady's slipper and another "sent from *Pensylvania*, by Mr. *John Bartram*, who, by his industry and inclination
to the searches into Nature, has discovered and sent over a great
many new productions, both animal and vegetable. This plant flowered in Mr. *Collinson's* garden, in *April*, 1738." There was the
mountain laurel, long known in England, where it had always been
a problem, for none of the plants flourished until Bartram sent
some from Pennsylvania, where the climate was similar. Collinson

gave Catesby some of the plants, which finally bloomed in his Fulham garden in 1741.[32]

As Catesby proceeded with his monumental work many questions arose concerning both flora and fauna. After having pestered Collinson to query Bartram on various points, he decided that a direct correspondence would be far more satisfactory. He was encouraged in this when Bartram sent him three plants in one of Collinson's boxes, so he wrote to him on 29 November 1739 and proposed an exchange. Bartram would send, with his shipments to Collinson, as many as possible of the plants or animals requested by Catesby. In return, Catesby would send him each year a part of his *Natural History*, consisting of twenty plates with their descriptions. He promised not to ask for too much, knowing how busy Bartram was from reading his letters to Collinson.[33] Catesby indicated the types of plants he desired, but when a box arrived for him along with the shipment to Collinson in February 1740/41 he was disappointed that there was no letter from Bartram and that the plants were not those he had mentioned. When he thanked Bartram he sent a copy of his previous letter, afraid that the Spaniards might have seized the ship on which it was sent. He also sent the first part of his book, confessing that it was a smaller version of the one that Bartram had seen at Thomas Penn's.[34]

Meantime, Catesby's original letter had finally reached Bartram, and he replied enthusiastically on 22 March:

The reading of thy acceptable letter incited in me the different passions of joy, in receiving a letter of friendship and re-

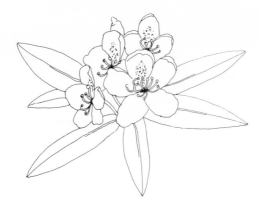

Great laurel
(*Rhododendron
maximum* L.)

quest from one so much esteemed, and sorrow in considering what time we have lost when we might have obliged each other. Its a pity thee had not wrote to me ten years ago. I should by this time have furnished thee with many different species of plants, and, perhaps some animals; but the time past can't be recalled, therefore, pray, write often to me and inform me in every particular what thee wishes of me, and wherein I can oblige thee: for when I am traveling on the mountains, or in the valleys, the most desolate, craggy dismal places I can find, where no mortal ever trod, I chiefly search out. Not that I naturally delight in such solitudes, but entirely to observe the wonderful productions in nature. . . . I am exceedingly pleased with thy proposals, and shall do what I can, conveniently, to comply with them. I have a great value for thy books, and esteem them as an excellent performance, and an ornament for the finest library in the world.[35]

Catesby wanted more details concerning the rhododendron that Bartram had found on the banks of the Schuylkill in 1736. Collinson had despaired of raising it from seed and in 1737 had asked Bartram to transplant a lot of them to his garden and to ship half a dozen at a time.[36] This was done, and the following year Collinson was able to report that the plants promised well.[37] They grew but did not bloom, and in 1741 Catesby desired to paint the rhododendron. However, he was at a loss for the exact figure, shape, and color of the flowers. First Bartram had said they were a pale red or blush color but later described them as being studded with green spots. Bartram volunteered to draw or even paint the flowers, and Collinson urged him to do so. One single flower would be sufficient.[38] So successfully did Bartram comply that Catesby was able to draw a "tolerable figure of it."[39] In November 1742 Bartram shipped plants that Catesby wanted, but the latter still often went to Peckham to paint flowers.[40] When the shooting star, raised from seed collected by Bartram in the Shenandoah Valley, bloomed in September 1744, Catesby was there to paint it. There were also lilies to be pictured, and another mountain laurel, and the ginseng, which finally flowered and was drawn for posterity in 1746.[41]

Catesby inquired about numerous animals as well as plants. He, too, was curious about the *Monax* or groundhog of Pennsylvania. It is surprising that he had not seen this animal frequently in

Virginia and the Carolinas, but he may have thought that of Pennsylvania to be different. He had omitted describing the bird "that at night calls *Whipper Will*, and sometimes, *Whip Will's widow*," and he wanted a specimen. He desired a house swallow and its nest.[42] Bartram sent a nest of the chimney swift but was unable to send any whippoorwills in spite of hiring several persons to try to shoot them.[43] Catesby's specimens and description of this bird are credited to Clayton. Both the latter and Bartram commented on the resemblance between it and the nighthawk. Bartram wrote "if thay be not ye same thing thay are much alike. I have often found their nests which is a little concave on ye bare ground in which they lay large speckled eggs." He even offered to paint a sketch of them if Catesby would but send the colors.[44]

Having now seen most of the *Natural History*, Bartram realized that many birds of the northern colonies were quite different and sent Catesby a list: gray and white owls, a large kite, both gray and white herons, cormorants, woodcocks, pheasants, crows, ducks, and a number of small birds.[45] Planning a trip along the seacoast in the summer of 1742, he thought that he might be able to collect

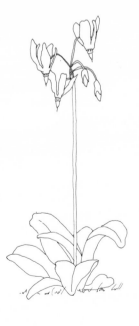

Shooting star (*Dode-catheon meadia* L.)

some birds for Catesby "by the charms of sulphur, nitre and lead."[46] Catesby was anxious to acquire any birds that Bartram could send and advised him to dry them gradually in the oven and cover them with tobacco dust to preserve them during shipment.[47] There were several kinds of snakes, fish, and turtles that Bartram had not seen in the books, nor had Catesby pictured a six-inch red lizard.[48] In June 1743 Bartram sent a large blackbird similar to the purple jackdaw that Catesby had drawn but with far finer colors.[49] Two of the insect specimens sent by Bartram appeared in the later numbers of the *Natural History*: a *Sphex caerulea* [L.] and an *Ichneumon* "sent amongst other remarkable Insects, by Mr. John Bartram."[50] Catesby acknowledged his indebtedness by listing Bartram's name as one of the "Encouragers of this work."[51]

Unfortunately, the correspondence which had begun so enthusiastically was doomed by the fortunes of war. The War of Jenkins' Ear, which began in 1739, had broadened into the War of the Austrian Succession. English and American ships were being sunk by the French as well as by the Spaniards. Not only were the plants that Catesby sent to Pennsylvania lost, but so were the 1744 and 1745 cargoes that Bartram had sent to him. Catesby did receive several letters from Bartram and was able to keep up with his travels through Collinson, but when he wrote in April 1746 he had to confess that he was in Bartram's debt as far as letters went. He had become discouraged by their ill luck and had failed to write for two years. Now he asked Bartram to accept a bird book as a peace offering.[52] Bartram received another letter from Catesby in October,[53] but by then even Collinson was becoming cautious. In March 1747 he advised Bartram to send no unusual or rare plants until the war was over.[54]

In July 1741 Bartram had initiated a correspondence with a letter addressed to "Desired Friend, Sir Hans Sloane." He wrote, "My good, faithful friend Peter Collinson, in his last letter to me, that I received, acquainted me that thee desired I would send thee some petrified representations of Sea Shells. Accordingly, I have sent thee a few, which I gathered toward the northward. . . . I hope these few things may meet with thy acceptance, so as to introduce a further correspondence; which if they do; pray be so kind to favour me with a letter containing instructions what kind of Particular Curiosities will be most agreeable."[55]

Sir Hans replied in January, thanking Bartram not only for

"Shells and Petrifactions" but also for a triangular arrowhead of "white chrystal, or spar; the like of which, in green jasper, I have had from Tierra del Fuego, on the south side of the Straits of Magellan. The Indian instrument you sent, was the head of a hatchet, made of a sort of jasper. This, fitted to a handle, was made use of by the Indians of Jamaica, and several parts of the West Indies, for making their canoes, before they were taught the use of iron and steel." Sloane was so pleased that he asked Collinson what he should send to Bartram. Collinson suggested that Sir Hans's *A Voyage to the Islands* would be a very welcome gift. Sir Hans sent it along with the letter saying that he would be glad to have seeds and samples of plants for his plant collections and asked how he might best serve Bartram.[56] Sloane was then eighty-three years old but was still adding to his famous collections. Unfortunately, when the ship that was bringing Sir Hans's letter and books finally reached Philadelphia, it had "left the captain asleep in Neptune's bosom: and now, such a mortal sickness is on board that she is ordered to ride quarantine below the town. No goods can be got off." Bartram waited impatiently for the quarantine to be lifted.[57]

When Bartram replied to Sloane in November, he changed his form of address to "Respected Friend" and expressed his deep appreciation for the present of Sir Hans's book. His gratitude went beyond words for he sent *"first* . . . a quire of paper filled with dry specimens of plants, numbered, so that if thee wants any more of any sort there, or any more particular remarks on any of them, please to mention it to each number. *Secondly*, I have sent thee a box of insects, with thy name at large on ye box, numbered, and a paper with my remarks to each number. *Thirdly*, I have sent thee a

Bartramia

collection of curious stones figured with Sea Shells, and some other curiosities, which, if they should many of them prove new and acceptable, I shall be well pleased." Finally, he offered to send Sloane "an Indian Tobacco Pipe of stone," which had been dug from an old Indian grave, if he did not already have one.[58]

There were more than thirty insects in the collection Bartram sent: bumblebees, wasps, borers, locusts, hornets, "tumble turds," and a louse from a female hawk. The notes that accompanied them were most informative. Bartram described their feeding and breeding habits. He enclosed samples of some of the nests and, in one case, described the pollen placed in the cells for the larvae. He had carefully examined it under a microscope and found that it came from male squashes and gourds. He had burrowed in his cornfield, attempting to dig up one type of bee, but the holes were too small for him to follow. His sons had dug another species out of his stone wall. He drew a small diagram of the three-inch preliminary nest that hornets make before they "all forsake this little habitation & pitcheth upon a suitable Branch of a tree or under ye roof of an out house for to build A City." To the quire of specimens of flowering plants that he sent Sir Hans, he added a collection of mosses.[59]

All of this correspondence passed through Collinson's hands, and he thoroughly enjoyed the promotion of it. He even added a few items that Bartram had sent to him which he thought would please Sir Hans. From time to time he suggested to Bartram things that he might send: "for Sir Hans, with thy account, will wonderfully please him," or, he informed John, "I showed them to Sir Hans. He was much pleased." Another time he wrote, "Today I breakfasted with Sir Hans. He always inquires after thee." All of this was most gratifying to Bartram. In May 1743 he told Collinson, "I am very thankful to my good friend Sir Hans Sloane, for his fine present of five guineas. Being he hath so generously bestowed it upon me, I desire thee would send me a silver can, or cup, as big and good as thee can get for that sum, which I or mine may keep to entertain our friends withal, in remembrance of my noble benefactor."[60]

If either Collinson or Sloane was startled by this request they did not say so but added to Bartram's pleasure in the gift by having the large and handsome cup engraved "The Gift of S. Hans Sloane Bart to his Frd   John Bartram Anno 1742." In due course the cup arrived, and Bartram, delighted by it, hastened to inform Sir Hans: "I have received thy kind present of a silver cup, and am well pleased that thy name is engraved upon it at large, so that when my friends drink out of it, they may see who was my benefactor."[61] The cup was a source of pride to him throughout his life. He continued to send anything that he thought might please Sir Hans and promised him to "use all reasonable endeavours to oblige thee with any curiosity that is in my power to procure. However, in the meantime, thee hath fully engaged—by thy many favours and kindnesses—the respect, with the hearty love and good will of thy sincere friend, John Bartram."[62]

Sloane's largess did not stop with the cup. In April of 1743 he asked Bartram for a catalogue of his botanical books, which the latter was more than happy to send:

Indeed it is soon done, I have so few of them on Natural History, which I love dearly to read. The first authors I read, were SALMON, CULPEPPER, and TURNER. These James Logan gave me to read. Doctor DILLENIUS sent me MILLER's Dictionary, and his own book of Mosses. Lord Petre sent me MILLER's Second Part, and the second book of TURNER's complete Herbal; and thee kindly obliged me with thy History of Jamaica. Our friend PETER sent me them fine books of Nature Delineated. Catesby sent me his books of Birds, and some books of Physic and Surgery, which was my chief study in my youthful years. I have heard of PETIVER's fine collections of Plants and Animals, which thee published; nay, I am well acquainted with his nephew, Captain GLENTWORTH, who lived with his Uncle PETIVER. He tells me he used to change, spread, and dry his uncle's specimens, and carried many curiosities between thee and his uncle.[63]

Bartram's not-too-subtle hint paid off. Sloane wrote him that he was sending "all Mr. Petiver's Works which are very Scarce and may be useful to you and have added the Natural History of Ireland, Etmullen Abridged in English, Herman's Paradisus Batavus, & Selius's account of the Timber Worms that eats the Ships, which I perceive you may have not and which may be Diverting & instructive to you who love such Things. . . ."[64]

Although Bartram's letter of thanks to Sloane for these welcome additions to his library does not seem to have survived, his delight is not difficult to imagine. He did not always like the books he received and, on at least one occasion, was frank enough to say so. In March 1741/42 Collinson, who had once teased him about loving books too much, sent him Robert Barclay's *Apology* (London, 1676), the undisputed textbook for the Quakers for many generations. Collinson added the comment that it was intended to "replenish thy inward man."[65] To which Bartram replied thanking him but adding that "It answers thy advice much better than if thee had sent me one of Natural History, or Botany, which I should have spent ten times the hours in reading of, while I might have laboured for the maintenance of my family. Indeed, I have little respect to *apologies* and disputes about the ceremonial parts of religion, which often introduce animosities, confusion, and disorders in the mind. . . ."[66]

When Bartram returned from Virginia in 1738 he thought that he might attempt a long northern trip the following fall. In July of the next year he was still making plans for such a trip when he wrote to Dr. Alexander Colhoun, surgeon of the garrison at New York, who had recently visited him. Bartram thought that he might collect through the Jerseys, visit Colhoun at New York, and continue on to Albany in late September. He asked Colhoun about the distance from New York to Albany and the extent of settlement in between. In the meantime he made a trip up the Delaware to collect white pine seed beyond the Blue Mountains. Unfortunately, his favorite mare was stolen and he had to rent a horse to ride home. Soon afterward he cut his foot badly and was confined to bed for a month. He was forced to forget long trips in 1739.[67]

SIX

"For the Encouragement of Mr. John Bartram"

I N EARLY September 1740 Bartram saddled a horse and rode northward toward the "lakie Hills" beyond Reading. When he climbed them the next morning, he was able to see all the way to the "great Blew or Paiqualian mountains," across a lovely valley twenty to thirty miles wide. He could see the western branch of the Delaware, the Lehigh River, extending diagonally across the valley to the mountains forty miles distant from the northeast branch. He crossed the western branch and rode to within a few miles of the mountains and then followed the valley to the northeast. He admired the fine land and was particularly interested to see the improvements being made on the 5,000-acre Whitefield tract.[1]

The Reverend George Whitefield (1714–70) had arrived in Philadelphia about a year earlier. An Oxford graduate and a Methodist minister, he had brought with him a vast array of goods donated in England. These were to be sold for the support of the Georgia orphanage and school, which he had established near Savannah in 1738. While in Philadelphia he had preached to great crowds almost hypnotized by his eloquence despite the fact that he sometimes referred to his listeners as "half beasts and half devils." Franklin had been tremendously impressed by the clergyman and had tried to interest him in moving his orphanage to Philadelphia. He contributed to the Georgia project and reported Whitefield's travels and sermons in the *Pennsylvania Gazette*. Although he did not succeed in persuading Whitefield to move the orphanage, the minister did buy the 5,000-acre Pennsylvania tract for a Negro school.[2]

Bartram did not share his friend's enthusiasm for Whitefield, perhaps because he had been less exposed to Whitefield's eloquence. Bartram had, however, heard enough about him and his ideas to have strong views on the subject. When Collinson inquired what Whitefield planned to do with his Pennsylvania land,[3] Bartram replied:

> . . . he proposed to bring as many as would make a township of his friends from England I suppose he designs them to be such favorites as was elected before thay was born or begot or before ye foundations of ye worlds was laid & then when thay get up into heaven thay are to witness against us at ye great day of Judgment when our bodies must rise again after they have wonderfully disolved & transformed in elemental & vegitable & often animal species & some of thair bretherin talks of being Judges: (I suppose then thay will send us reprobates hundreds and thousands if not Millions to hell) nay one of them tould his auditorys he would sit at ye right hand of ye father to Judge them (but surely first he must heave ye sun out of his seat:—enough of this wish it were better) ye great stone house that was begun but I know not when it will be finished is to teach young negroes a year I know not what then return them to thair masters if thay was elected so long ago what need he to trouble his head about them if thay was damned what signifieth his tutoring however this we may be sure he will teach them to think themselves as good or better than thair masters & too good for servants[4]

Bartram's account amused Collinson, who replied with equal irreverence that Whitefield "has, for some time made no noise here; which I presume is on account of a rich wife, he has lately got,—which may spoil his spiritual exercises for the Creature must be minded and gratified else his bedfellow may quote the Apostle paul on Him and from the Scripture can bring cue that Husband should give a Wife her due."[5]

After viewing the Whitefield tract, Bartram followed a rough Indian trail away from the valley toward the mountains. Neither Indians nor whites were to be seen. At the foot of the mountain he found groves of pines and one of a spruce or fir, but when he climbed several he found that they had shed their seed. The terrain became extremely rocky, and he was amazed to see both birches and pines growing out of crevices which seemed too small for anything but ferns. He made his way almost to the gap through which the Delaware flowed through the mountains but did so with great difficulty "by wandering passages between ye rocks so steep I could hardly lead my mare up. this pasage is about a mile of where ye river runs thorow but there is no pasing near ye river side." On the north side of the water gap he descended into rich lowlands along the Delaware, extending along both sides of the river. The lands were well watered by creeks "tumbling down ye mountains in glistening cascades." He found the land to be settled for over forty miles beyond the Blue Mountains. He swam his mare three times across the stream where it was about 150 yards wide, in order to explore both sides. Ten miles beyond the mountains he found mostly good land on the Jersey side but very steep and barren land on the Pennsylvania side, where there were "strange representations of snails & scalop shels with other curiosities." He collected some of these fossils and was sure that he could have found many more if he had had time. The rocks disintegrated in the winter cold, and fossils were washed free by spring rains.

On his return trip Bartram recrossed the mountains on the Jersey side of the Delaware. As he descended he saw a great pile of rock which he was told marked the grave of an Indian king. He was sorely tempted to pull it apart "to search what antiquities I could find laid with this royal body but was afraid of disturbing ye Indians nearby." Later he explored a cave, "ye mouth of which began toward ye top of a limestone hill & descended down until I came to a pond of clear water." He decided that he had dawdled long enough and set out for home as fast as he could travel. Bartram sent Collinson a journal of his trip, a map of the region, a drawing of the cave, and sundry seeds, nests, fossils, and other curiosities that he had collected on this trip and several others to Jersey. He suggested that if he were sent some watercolors, he could improve on his drawings of plants by showing proper colors of flowers. Collinson was so gratified that he promptly sent Bartram four volumes on natural history, and Lord Petre sent him books by Tournefort.[6]

The winter of 1740–41 was one of the most severe ever known at Philadelphia. Ice froze so thickly on the Schuylkill that it could support the weight of horses. Ships could neither leave the port nor enter it. Communications to and from Europe were delayed, and it was not until the middle of May that Bartram received letters from Collinson, dated from October to April.[7] Collinson and Petre were optimistic that Bartram might stay healthy and be able to make the long-planned trip to New York this year. With this in mind, Collinson sent a letter of introduction to a man Bartram must certainly meet, Dr. Cadwallader Colden. Collinson was sure that Colden could advise Bartram about many things, but particularly about the location of the balm of gilead firs (*Abies balsamea* L.) which Collinson coveted. As usual, he also wrote to Colden advising him to expect Bartram. Colden replied that he would be delighted to offer any assistance he could.[8] He was a Scot, although born in Ireland. He had graduated from the University of Edinburgh and then studied medicine in London. His first American practice had been in Philadelphia, where he had settled in 1710. In 1718 he had been persuaded by Robert Hunter, governor of New York, to move there. He was appointed surveyor-general in 1720, and the following year he became a member of the council on which he served for twenty years. He had largely given up his medical practice but maintained a keen interest in medical matters and in science generally.[9]

On 20 May 1741 Bartram left home on his New York trip. His first stop was at Trenton, across the Delaware in Jersey. Here he called on Lewis Morris (1671–1746), a fellow Quaker.[10] Morris had large landholdings in New York and had rented a farm called Kingsbury, near Trenton, when he became governor in 1738. Bartram was warmly welcomed not only by Morris but by his son,

The Reverend George Whitefield
(1714–70)

Chief Justice Robert Hunter Morris (1700–1764), and a daughter.[11] All three had scientific interests and gave Bartram what assistance they could. The daughter brought out some curious nuts which had been sent to them from Oswego, New York. Robert Morris gave him a letter to a New York friend who might be helpful. The governor showed him his library, of which he was justifiably proud. Bartram thought it the finest that he had seen "except for Col. Byrd's & but little short of that." It was here that Bartram first saw Sloane's *Natural History of Jamaica.* The governor did not give Bartram a letter to a particular person but instead a general letter to magistrates and others in responsible positions, requesting that they assist him in any way possible.

When Bartram left Trenton he headed for the "highlands." Crossing these hills between the Delaware and Hudson rivers, he found many small ponds and one five miles long. There, sixty miles from the ocean, he found sea shells "in a sort of loam or rotten stone," and among the foothills he found great caches of them. He circled around the end of the Shongo Mountains, a continuation of the Blue Mountains, and soon afterward he came to the home of Peter Bayard, not very far from New York City. It was an imposing country house, a quarter of a mile from the road. On one side lay a wood and on the other fine vegetable and flower gardens. Locust trees in full bloom perfumed the air along the walk. Bartram's host supplied him with letters to Francis Salisbury at Catskill and other friends along the way.[12] Bartram's next stop was at Coldengham, where he was disappointed to find that Colden had gone to New England.[13] Bartram continued up the Hudson to Salisbury's home, built in 1705 on land that his father had purchased from the Indians.[14] Salisbury told him exactly where he could find the balm of gilead firs.[15] To get there would not be easy. Morris had warned Bartram that the Catskills were a mile high. While Bartram thought that they were considerably less than that, he conceded that they were the highest mountains that he had seen. Naturally, the firs that he wanted grew near the top of the mountains.

As he had been promised, Bartram found the climbing difficult. High rock walls frequently blocked his path and he had to detour. Thick brush made progress difficult, but Bartram was an old hand at this sort of thing and not easily discouraged. He finally reached the top and found the trees that he wanted. They were fine specimens, some as much as a foot in diameter and sixty feet high.

It was not the proper season for collecting seed, but he did fill some bladders with the clear resin that formed "blisters" on the trunks and branches. He was so busy examining other plants in the area that he suddenly realized that it was nearing sunset. A little worried about getting off the mountain before dark, as he later wrote, he "made what hast I could carefully down by runing & sliping & tumbling & yet it was so dark before I reached ye bottom that I could hardly see ye branches or rocks before I run against them." Near the foot of the mountain he found a man who agreed to gather a bushel of the fir cones at the proper time and deliver them to Salisbury. Bartram paid the man ten shillings for doing so and returned to Salisbury's home for the night. His host promised that when the cones were delivered he would see that they were shipped to Derick Skiller's at Brunswick, in Jersey, who would forward them to Philadelphia.[16] Bartram was particularly concerned about this, not only because of all the effort that had gone into the trip but because he knew Collinson would question his having gone at a season when seeds would not be ripe.

When Bartram left Salisbury's, he did not head south but continued to the Mohawk River, turning downstream. Coming to the falls, he was so impressed he had to pause long enough to make a drawing. At Albany he made the acquaintance of several of Bayard's friends who "shewed much Civility" to him, but he did not linger long. Before departing, he promised his hosts that he would send them some curious seeds when he reached home.[17] On his homeward trip, a stream that he was fording proved much deeper than he had expected. He, his horse, and his specimens were soaked, and his notes were obliterated.[18] At home, Bartram made up parcels to send to those who had received him so hospitably. To Bayard, he sent double and breeding tulips, hyacinths, and narcissus.[19]

As fall approached, Bartram worried about the fir cones for which he had paid. They did not arrive, and he began to make inquiries. Eventually he learned that the man he had paid had failed to deliver them. Salisbury, knowing how anxious Bartram was to obtain them, had sent his own man to collect cones, but he returned empty-handed, saying that birds had eaten all of the seeds. Bartram was disgusted and decided he would have to plan a trip to New England for the following year.[20] He did not travel far again until fall, for his family and his farm needed his attention. A new daughter, Ann, arrived soon after his return from New York. In order to prepare seed shipments for England, Holland, Sweden, and the Jardin du Roi at Paris, he made three short trips to the mountains of East Jersey, to Great Egg Harbor, and to Cape May for the berries of myrtle and both red and white cedar. All seeds were scarce, and he had to cut down two white cedars in addition to climbing many others in order to get enough. He collected as many seeds as he could and packed his boxes for shipment to London: a box for the Duke of Norfolk and one for the Duke of Richmond; a box for Lord Petre and another for Philip Miller; one for Collinson and Catesby; a box of insects for Catesby and a mud-daubers' nest for Sir Hans. By candlelight and on Sundays he had completed his journal of his New York trip and sent it, with his sketch of the falls of the Mohawk.

Collinson was impressed when he received these in March 1741/42, especially by the drawing: "I was really both delighted and surprised to see it so naturally done,—and at the ingenuity of the performance. Upon my word, Friend John, I can't help admiring thy abilities, in so many instances. I shall be sparing to say what more I think. A man of thy prudence will place this to a right account, to encourage thee to proceed gently in these curious things, which belong to a man of leisure, and not to a man of business. The main chance must be minded. Many an ingenious man has lost himself for want of this regard." In spite of all this pious advice, Collinson displayed the drawing to Sir Hans and other friends who were very complimentary.[21] Collinson was less cautious in his praise when he wrote to Colden: "He really Surprised Mee with a Beautiful Draught on a Sheet of paper of the falls of Mohocks River wch He took when he was there with a Perticular account of It and also a Mapp of His own Makeing of Hudsons River Delaware Katskil & the bay which takes in the provinces of New York, Jerseys, Pensilvania, Maryld. & Virginia for He has travelled all over these Countrys."[22]

By 1741 Bartram had been collecting for Lord Petre for six years. Of all of his patrons at this time, Petre was certainly the most ambitious. The great nursery beds were sown wholesale with Bartram's tree seeds, where Collinson found that the oak, hackberry, and sweet gum seeds germinated the first year. It took longer for the seeds of the tulip poplar, the sassafras, the sugar maple, and the white cedar.[23] Petre's order for tree seeds had continued to be

"Departure for New York," from Howard Pyle, "Bartram and his garden"

huge. In January 1738/39 he asked Collinson to order red cedar berries, "a bushel or two in glasses" from Bartram, with appropriate payment over and above the annual subscription. Two years later, after remarking to Collinson that "our frd. John is not to be complained of this time," he asked him to tell Bartram that he could not send "too much of the Ld. Weymouth's Pine."[24] The extent of Petre's nurseries, which included other seedlings besides those of Bartram, can be gauged by the fact that Petre planted forty thousand trees in 1741/42.[25] Flowering shrub and tree seeds and plants were also supplied by Bartram: Judas trees, service trees, chokecherries, cockspur thorns, laurels, magnolias, and dogwoods. In September 1737 Lord Petre had visited his cousin, the Duke of Norfolk, who had begun to reforest Worksop Manor. Petre designed plans for planting the whole estate, and it was not long before Bartram was supplying seeds for Norfolk, who joined the small group paying an annual subscription.[26]

When Collinson wrote to Bartram on 1 September 1741, he described Petre's Thorndon Hall, picturing for Bartram the changes he was helping to make in the English landscape:

The trees and shrubs raised from thy first seeds are grown to great maturity. Last year Lord Petre planted out about ten thousand Americans, which, being at the same time mixed with about twenty thousand Europeans, and some Asians, make a very beautiful appearance:—great art and skill being shown in consulting every one's particular growth, and the well blending the variety of greens. Dark green being a great foil to lighter ones, and bluish green to yellow ones, and those trees that have their bark and back of their leaves of white, or silver, make a beautiful contrast with the others.

The whole is planted in thickets and clumps, and with these mixtures are perfectly picturesque, and have a delightful effect. This will just give thee a faint idea of the method Lord Petre plants in, which has not been so happily executed by any: and, indeed, they want the materials, whilst his lordship has them in plenty.

His nursery being fully stocked with flowering shrubs, of all sorts that can be procured,—with these, he borders the outskirts of all his plantations: and he continues, annually, raising from seed, and layering, bedding, grafting—that

twenty thousand trees are hardly to be missed out of his nurseries.

When I walk amongst them, one cannot well help thinking
he is in North American thickets, there are such quantities.
But to be at his table, one would think South America was
really there—to see a servant come in every day with ten or
a dozen Pine Apples—as much as he can carry. I am lately
come from thence, quite cloyed with them.[27]

Both Collinson and Logan had warned Bartram about the
danger that collecting seeds and plants might take more of his time
than he could afford. No one was more aware of this than Bartram
himself, and each year the demands on his time became greater. He
also had to forego many things of a scientific nature that he would
have liked to do, and which needed to be done, simply because he
could not take the time from his family responsibilities. Early in
1742 some of his friends thought that they might have found a solution to the problem. A notice appeared in Franklin's *Pennsylvania Gazette* on 17 March, explaining their proposal:

A copy of the Subscription Paper, for the Encouragement of
Mr. John Bartram, promised in our last.

Botany, or the Science of Herbs and Plants, has always
been accounted in every Country, as well by the Illiterate as
by the Learned, an useful Study and Labour to Mankind, as
it has furnished them with Cures for many Diseases, and
their Gardens, Groves and Fields with rare and pleasant
Fruits, Flowers, Aromaticks, Shades and Hedges.

And as the Wildernesses, Mountains and Swamps in
America, abound with a variety of Simples and Trees, whose
Virtues and proper Uses are yet unknown to Physicians and
curious Persons both here and in Europe; it should be esteem'd fortunate, and a general Benefit, if a Man could be
found sufficiently skilful and hardy, who would undertake, as
far as in his Power, a compleat Discovery of such Herbs,
Roots, Shrubs and Trees, as are of the Native Growth of
America, and not described in Herbals or other Books.

And as John Bartram has had a Propensity to Botanicks
from his Infancy, and to the Productions of Nature in general,
and is an accurate Observator; well known in Pennsylvania,

where he was born and resides, to be a Person fitted for this
Employment; acquainted with Vegetables and Fossils, and
Books treating of them; of great Industry and Temperance,
and of unquestionable Veracity; and has by many Ships sent
over to some of the Members of the Royal Society in London,
at their Request, Plants, Seeds and Specimens, as were new
and unknown to them (and received by them as Curiosities)
in order to be farther discovered and made useful by the
Learned and Ingenious there, who have yearly return'd him
Names for them, and Accounts of some of their Virtues; we
the Subscribers, to induce and enable him wholly to spend
his Time and exert himself in these Employments, have proposed an annual Contribution for his Encouragement; with
which he being made acquainted, and it agreeing with his be-
nevolent Temper, he has promised some of us, that if it appears by what shall be subscribed, that he can maintain himself and Family, and defray the Expences he must sometimes
unavoidably be at in long Journies for Guides and Assistance,
he will without delay dispose his Affairs at Home, and undertake what is desired of him; and that his Searches after Vegetables and Fossils, shall be throughout the Governments of
New-York, the Jerseys, Pennsylvania and Maryland; and that
whatsoever he meets with worthy of Notice, in the Places and
Things before mentioned, and in the Form, Situation and
Produce of Mountains, Lakes, Springs, Grottoes, Rivers, &c.
he will describe and yearly communicate to the Subscribers
in the best Manner he can.

We the Subscribers, do therefore severally promise, for Us,
our Heirs, Executors and Administrators, to pay him yearly
the Sums annex'd to our Names for three Years next ensuing,
he for so long time industriously employing himself in the
Premises.

N.B. *Subscriptions are taken in at the Post-Office in Philadelphia. Near £20 a Year is already subscribed.*

Bartram was naturally very gratified by the proposed subscription. He mentioned it to several correspondents, to one of
whom he sent a copy of the proposal and commented: "Many of my
friends both in Jersey & pensilvania hath proposed a method to engage me devote my life chiefly to ye observation of natural produc-

tions & curious inquiries of ye formation & qualities of ye vegitable animal mineral & fosils with perticular descriptions of every curiosity that comes under my observation with a exact map draught or picture in ye four provincial governments. . . ."[28] In spite of Franklin's optimism, Bartram had doubts of the success of such a venture almost from the beginning. In the severe winter of 1740/41, farmers had lost great numbers of cattle, merchants had lost ships at sea, and money was scarce. Six months before Franklin's newspaper appeal, Bartram was convinced that there would be too few subscribers. He was correct in this assumption, for nothing came of the proposal. Meanwhile, he continued to make scientific observations as best he could without a subsidy. He sent Collinson a mole and promised a "Natural history of them." Their activities transported him with "rage and admiration."[29] He sent observations concerning chimney swifts, cliff swallows, and martins and promised specimens of turtles.[30]

Collinson had been enthusiastic over Franklin's proposal, for he foresaw the day when Bartram's present English customers might be completely supplied or there might be other problems. This premonition was realized when the thirty-year-old Lord Petre contracted smallpox and died 2 July 1742. Collinson wrote to Bartram, "I have lost my friend—my brother. The man I loved, and was dearer to me than all men, is no more. I could fill this sheet, and many more: but Oh! my anxiety of mind is so great that I can hardly write. . . ."[31] Lord Petre's widow was left with four small children. By his will he had directed that the nursery trees be sold. The plants were inventoried at 219,925. Collinson and the children's guardian helped Lady Petre to sell much of the nursery stock to the dukes of Norfolk, Bedford, and Richmond, the Earl of Lincoln, and others. Thus it was "that the eighth Baron Petre's importation of plant material and trees from John Bartram helped to reforest Essex, Sussex, Surrey, Bedfordshire, and Nottinghamshire in the mid-eighteenth century."[32]

A few months before Lord Petre's death Collinson had sent orders which again included balm of gilead fir seeds, so Bartram once more headed for the Catskills. He hoped to collect many seeds other than those of the firs, especially hemlocks, maples, and hickories. This trip proved to be a "happy journey," for he found Colden at home. Bartram thought him "one of the most facetious, agreeable Gentlemen" that he had ever met with.[33] Colden was pleased and astonished by Bartram's breadth of knowledge. Their conversation ranged from plants to Indians to mutual friends overseas. Bartram was interested in Colden's bush squash, which was unknown in Philadelphia. He wanted some seed and suggested that Collinson would, too. Colden wanted Bartram to inquire about Maryland ipecacuana, which he had seen only in Clayton's *Flora Virginica*.[34] When Bartram departed for the Catskills, Mrs. Colden supplied him with a great hamper of food. She was so generous and the food was so good that Bartram even saved a bit to take home to his wife so that Ann might see how delicately they fared in the north. At Catskill he hired a guide to assist him but found it a poor investment. He was "no man of curiosity so consequently was soon weary" of tramping the woods.[35]

In spite of his guide's lack of interest, Bartram found what he had come for. He collected a fine parcel of balm of gilead fir seeds "gathered at ye right time just when thay began to dry & shed."[36] He found many other things as well, especially a wide variety of trees and shrubs: pines, birches, Newfoundland spruce, quicken trees (mountain ash), cherry, viburnum, and dwarf yew.[37] "A comical species of Lycopodium" caught his eye, and he gathered some for Dillenius but unfortunately lost it before he got home.[38] There was little animal life. At the lake on the summit of the mountain he saw five-inch ash-colored "lizards" (salamanders), with golden spots on their sides. He heard tales of some unusual animals, one the size of a medium-sized dog but resembling a small lion, and another creature called a tiger. He gave little credence to such tales for he thought that the Indians had lived here long enough to have eradicated such game, if it had ever existed. He stopped at Coldengham again on his return trip and left two boxes of specimens there to be forwarded in care of William Allen, John Penn's father-in-law, at Philadelphia. When Bartram received them, he returned one box filled with black walnuts for Colden, with instructions for planting them.[39]

In July 1742 Bartram had planned to make an expedition to some part of the territory of the Five Indian Nations following his return from the Catskills. He had engaged Conrad Weiser (1696–1768) to go with him up the branches of the Susquehanna. Weiser was the provincial interpreter for Pennsylvania. He had been raised among the New York Iroquois and adopted by the Mohawks, and he not only spoke their language but was familiar with their customs. His great sympathy and understanding for the Indians were invaluable in his mediations between them and the Pennsylvanians. Bartram was disappointed to learn that, during his absence, Weiser had been engaged by a Maryland gentleman to treat with the Indians, so his plans were disrupted.[40] Not only was he unable to visit the Five Nations, but he did not get far up the Susquehanna alone collecting seeds. He became quite ill with a digestive upset and had to turn back. He obtained temporary relief through his favorite remedy, two teaspoons of Madeira wine in a pint of water with "a hot burning crust" added, but the ailment continued and he had to go home. He was slow to recover and gave up thoughts of traveling for a time with the exception of two brief trips to Egg Harbor in late October and early November.[41]

In the interim he started a lively correspondence with Colden about a variety of subjects ranging from the treatment of cancer with *Phytolacca*, which Colden advocated, to the hibernation of bears.[42] Colden soon interested Bartram in another possible trip. This was one planned by Captain John Rutherford, a son of Sir John Rutherford, who had come to New York to command an independent company. Colden had suggested Bartram as a companion for Rutherford, who wished to explore some of the hinterlands. In May 1742/43 the captain "with several Gentlemen of ye Chiefest distinction in Philadelphia" called on Bartram, who was much taken with the young man.[43] He was disappointed when Rutherford was ordered back to England and had to cancel his travel plans.

SEVEN

A Journey to the Headquarters
of the Five Indian Nations

A LTHOUGH Rutherford's proposed trip had not materialized, another one had. Bartram outlined it in a letter to Colden in June 1743: "I am now providing for a Journey up Susquehanna with our interpreter in order to introduce A Peaceable understanding between ye Virginians & ye five nations we suppose ye meeting will be in ye Onondagues Country: I suppose not far from your fort Oswego we are to set out in a week or two."[1] There had been a clash between white settlers in western Virginia and an Iroquois hunting party in the fall of 1742, and rumors of possible war in Virginia had alarmed the Pennsylvanians. The governor of Pennsylvania had sent Weiser to Shamokin in January with assurances of friendship to the Iroquois representatives there, urging them not to become involved in the warfare. Now the Virginia governor was sending presents of belts and strings of wampum to them to convey the same message.[2]

The much desired trip into this rather awesome and little known Indian territory had at last become a reality for Bartram. The greater part of it was a land of virgin forests undisturbed by the white man. The Iroquois were joined together in the confederation of the Five Nations (actually six, including the Tuscaroras). They controlled an immense area stretching from the Laurentian Mountains in Canada, through the Thousand Islands, all the way to the Susquehanna. Colden had written a history of the Five Nations, published in 1727, and Bartram was familiar with it.[3] In spite of his family's experience with Indian savagery, Bartram was eager to see this comparatively unexplored land. He had confidence in Weiser's ability to guarantee a safe journey, as he was held in great affection by the Indians. There was a third member of the party, Lewis Evans (c. 1700–1756), a Welshman who had come to Philadelphia about 1736 and soon joined Franklin's circle of friends. A surveyor and draughtsman, he was responsible for the 1738 map of the "famous Walking Purchase." Now he was anxious to collect data on the area to the north since he was planning a map of the Middle Colonies.[4]

It was blisteringly hot on 3 July when Evans and Bartram left Kingsessing to join Weiser at his home, but a new road made it easier for the horses. It went over the Flying Hills, named for the large number of wild turkeys that flew from them to the Tulpehocken Valley below.[5] This valley had been settled by "High-Dutchers" (German immigrants), and there were fine plantations there. They reached Weiser's home, west of Reading, near Womeldorf, the next evening. Early on 5 July the three men set out on their journey.[6]

Their first objective was the Indian settlement at Shamokin (now Sunbury), where the east and west branches of the Susquehanna join. Four days of clambering up steep ridges, sliding down stony paths, and slogging through swamps finally brought them there. Bartram, alert for any new plant or animal, saw nothing of great moment. Oak and chestnut dominated the "middling land," white pine, white oak, and poplar the lowlands, and spruce the swampy ground. He did see a monster *Scutellaria* (skullcap) two feet high. On one ridge they killed a large rattlesnake, which had been infuriated by the attacks of an Indian dog. Bartram was interested to note the reflection of light from the scales of the live snake and the dullness of the scales when the snake was dead. As they had begun to climb the first ridge, Lewis had carefully made observations with level and sextant, and he continued to do so throughout the journey. None of the three travelers got much sleep on the trip. The first night was made miserable by gnats when they camped near a creek. The next night they moved and rebuilt an old "Indian Cabin," hoping to avoid the fleas that commonly infested them. They did not rebuild very well for rain kept them awake. They were more than ready for a restful night when they reached the hill above Shamokin on 8 July. The slope was so steep they had to dismount in order to help the packhorse down, holding it back by both its head and its tail.

The Delawares' "town" of Shamokin was a bit disillusioning,

Trip to Onondago and Oswego (adapted from Lewis Evans' *Map of the Middle British Colonies in North America, 1755*)

consisting of but eight cabins along the river. Bartram thought it an excellent strategic location for the growth of a town of importance as the gateway to a flourishing trade down the Ohio to the Mississippi. He wished that the English government was more interested in exploring the sources of the rivers running to the west. He thought that LaSalle had been well justified in warning the Count de Frontenac concerning the inevitable competition between the English and the French for trade on the Mississippi. Bartram spent the night in a trader's cabin and once again had problems. This time he was awakened by an Indian calling to the trader and his squaw, who were sleeping in another part of the cabin, "whether together or no" he did not ask. The Indian wanted rum, which the squaw provided, whereupon he and some friends became madly convivial. They danced about their fires singing lustily for the remainder of the night and well into next day. Bartram began to appreciate the virtues of traveling alone. As he listened to the performance outside, he reflected on the comparative effect of alcohol consumption on the behavior of Indians and whites. The former seemed to moderate the effect by violent activity, while the latter tended to relax under the influence and fall asleep.

Evans and Bartram were so exhausted the next morning that they took their blankets to a nearby hill after breakfast and slept soundly for three hours and then brought their journals up to date. Feeling a little better by afternoon, they borrowed a canoe and explored the western branch of the river. They found no curiosities but had a fine time swimming in water so clear that a pin could have been seen on the bottom. That night Bartram tried a new tactic. He fashioned a hammock by hanging his blanket between two trees. Again he was frustrated; having no blanket to keep him warm he was kept awake by a cold northwest wind.

A week after they had left home, Bartram and his friends left Shamokin for the long trip to Oswego. There would be no more settlements at which to rest. Their party had been increased by two guides, Shickellamy, chief of Shamokin's Delawares, and his son. Bartram felt that "We had many advantages from the company of these guides, [who] were perfectly acquainted with that part of the country, and being of the Six Nations, they were both a credit and protection; and also, as we went to accomodate the differences and allay the Heart-burnings that had been raised by a late skirmish on the back of *Virginia*, between some of these nations and the *En-*

glish, we could not but derive a confidence from the company of a chief."

On the first day they followed the west branch of the river for a time, fording it at a large island nearly two miles long and a quarter mile wide. They noted several cabins at the lower end of the island. Soon after leaving the river they came to a spring, the last one they were to see until they neared Onondago. They continued through rich low ground to a fine meadow. From there their way "lay through an old *Indian* field of excellent soil, where there had been a town, the principal footsteps of which" were peach trees, plums, and some "excellent grapes." Continuing through low ground much of the day, they passed a place where Shickellamy had formerly lived. Later they passed through a gap in the mountains and camped for the night.

They awoke at daybreak to rain beginning to fall. Their guides demonstrated an ingenious way to provide shelter with the bark of a tree: "They cut the tree round through the bark near the root, and make the like incision above 7 feet above it; these horizontal ones are joined by a perpendicular cut, on each side of which they loosen the bark from the wood." They used a sharpened pole to pry loose the bark and then suspended it on forked sticks stuck in the ground with poles laid across them. This provided very adequate shelter from the rain. When it stopped, the weather still looked threatening, so they decided to stay where they were, feasting on venison which the guides had shot.

By the following day, 12 July, the weather had improved, and they continued on their generally northward course. When they met eight mounted "Shawanese Indians" from the Ohio, they all sat down in the shade for a smoke. Weiser knew these men were chiefs and took pains to explain his mission to them. They were very pleased and complimented him highly for all of his efforts, past and present, in preserving peace between the Indians and the whites.

That night they camped not far from the hunting cabin of two Indians with a squaw and child, who invited Shickellamy, his son, and Weiser to dine with them. According to custom, the guests must completely consume all put before them or burn it. Weiser, as a traveler, would be served double portions. Since he felt ill, he exercised the privilege of appointing a proxy and asked Bartram to be his substitute. Bartram made a noble effort but could not complete his share so asked Evans to assist him. Even then they had difficulty, and Evans committed the faux pas of tossing bones to the dog. Bartram noted that "tho' hungry Dogs are generally nimble, the Indian more nimble, laid hold of it first and committed it to the fire, religiously covering it over with hot ashes. This seems to be a kind of offering, perhaps first fruits to the Almighty power to crave future success in the approaching hunting season, and was celebrated with as much decency and more silence than many superstitious ceremonies." Bartram was impressed and compared this and other Indian customs with some Christian practices: "The bigotry of the popish missionaries tempts them to compass sea and land to teach their Proselites what they call the Christian religion."

Their Indian hosts of the previous evening repaid the visit the following morning and talked for half an hour before the travelers resumed their journey, with the Indians accompanying them part of the way. Bartram and his friends continued on their course, following valleys as much as possible and crossing hills when they must. There were fine white pines, spruce, oaks, poplars, chestnuts, and even ginseng, which Bartram had often seen on this trip. They killed two young deer and another rattlesnake. The next day, the fourteenth, took them through an area where the mountains "often clos'd on one side," along a stream whose flow was strong enough "to turn two mills." The Indians tried their hand at spearing trout with sharp sticks but had no luck. In the afternoon they crossed some bottomland in which they found a "Licking Pond." Tracks indicated that it had been visited that morning by a great elk. Bartram noted that such licking ponds are common, "some of black sulphureous mud, some of pale clay." Elk and deer, finding something salty in the ground, might enlarge the licking area to cover as much as half an acre.

Days of travel passed, alternating from the higher land of oak and hickory through forests of chestnut, linden, ash, sugar maples, birch, and the great magnolia, to lowlands "perpetually shaded and for the most part wet," haven of rotten trees and yellow wasps, and then again into spruce jungles. Sometimes they traveled through more open vales, lovely with maidenhair, *Panax*, and "christophoriana" (*Actaea*). One day they found a hillside covered with stones suitable for whetstones, one of which Bartram carried home, where he found it excellent for sharpening scythes, knives, and chisels.

Another day they came to a spot where Indians had been "apawpawing." Bartram had seen other such places in his travels. A sort of wigwam was constructed in which a conjurer placed himself. It was covered with blankets, and hot stones were placed inside. "After all this the priest must cry aloud and agitate his body after the most violent manner, till nature has almost lost all her faculties, before the stubborn spirit will become visible to him, which they say is generally in the shape of some bird. There is usually a stake drove into the ground about four foot high and painted. I suppose this they design for the *winged airy Being* to perch upon, while he reveals to the invocant what he has taken so much pains to know." One night Bartram discovered another manifestation of the Indians' spiritual feelings. Always a light sleeper on such expeditions, he was awakened by singing: "One of the *Indians* who had so generously feasted us, sung in a solemn harmonious manner for seven or eight minutes, very different from the common *Indian* tune; from whence I conjectured it to be a hymn to the great spirit, as they express it." He asked Weiser later what was the significance of the hymn, but neither he nor Evans had heard it. Bartram was acquiring a new appreciation of the Indians and their customs.

On the afternoon of the sixteenth they approached Tohicon, lying between the Cayuga and one of its branches, and were welcomed by the continuous beating of a drum "after the *English* manner" as they dismounted and unsaddled their horses. The townhouse that they entered was about thirty feet long, the finest of any that Bartram had seen: "The *Indians* cut long grass and laid it on the floor for us to sit or lie on; several of them came and sat down and smoked their pipes, one of which was six foot long, the head

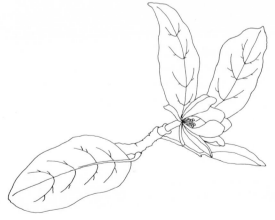

Cucumber tree (*Magnolia acuminata* L.)

of stone, the stem a reed. After which they brought victuals in the usual manner."

When Bartram and his party left the Tohicon hospitality, they crossed a neck of land to the east branch of the Susquehanna and traveled up this stream through a valley. At midday they found an Indian preparing to dine on an eel that he had roasted in front of a fire. Bartram was intrigued by the way in which the eel had been secured between the two halves of a split stick to keep it flat and then roasted by sticking one end of the stick in the ground close to a fire. The Indian generously presented them with the eel, all that he had to eat, and they reciprocated by giving him some of their food.

On the morning of the eighteenth Weiser sent an Indian with a string of wampum ahead to Onondago to announce their coming. Messengers would be sent to inform "the several nations" so that they might send deputies to meet them as soon as possible. Bartram found that "this town serves the Five Nations as *Baden* does the thirteen cantons of *Switzerland*, with this difference, that *Onondago* is at the same time the capital of a canton." The party still had three days of riding ahead. On the nineteenth they saw a great number of passenger pigeons roosting in the trees of a rich woodland. After their noonday meal on the twentieth they came to the branch of the Susquehanna nearest to Onondago, on the banks of which Bartram found gale or bog myrtle. They were told that a remarkable discovery had been made on a hill to the left. An Indian hunter had there met a young squaw who said that she had come from heaven to "provide sustenance for the poor Indians." If he would return in twelve months he would find food. The hunter did so and found corn, squash, and tobacco.

Traveling was not without its difficulties. Bartram was much troubled by gnats. On one occasion these were so bad that he had to forego writing in his journal because they bit his hands so cruelly. On the night of the twentieth they were sleeping soundly when an unexpected thunderstorm caught them in darkness without shelter. They improvised with their blankets and coats but got pretty well soaked. By this time Bartram could sleep through almost anything. As he noted in his journal, he "waked a little after midnight and found our fire almost out, so I got the hatchet and felled a few saplings, which I laid on and made a rousing fire, tho' it rained stoutly; and laying down once more, I slept all night."

Toward midday on the twenty-first they approached an Indian village some four miles from Onondago. As they neared it they observed many sugar maples, which the Indians had tapped, and both plum and apple trees. Many of the latter were full of young fruit. Bartram was amused to see that "The *Indians* had set long bushes all round the trees at a little distance, I suppose to keep the small children from stealing the fruit before they were ripe." Their arrival at the village created something of a sensation. Everyone turned out to gaze upon them. Children climbed to the roofs of cabins to get a better view of the strangers. Food for their dinner was produced and, while their horses grazed, they ate and rested. A messenger was sent ahead to Onondago to announce their imminent arrival. Soon afterward they followed, descending into the fine valley where the town was situated.

They rode up to the council house, where the chiefs had assembled to greet them. This they did "with a grave chearful complaisance, according to their custom." The chiefs were extremely pleased to see these visitors who had come so far. Weiser told Tocanontie, the "black Prince of Onondago," that "It was enough to kill a Man to come such a Long & bad Road over Hills, Rocks, Old Trees, and Rivers, and to fight through a Cloud of Vermine, and all kinds of Poison'd Worms and creeping things. . . ."[7] They were shown to the quarters that they were to occupy, the two end apartments of the large council house, where rush mats had been laid for the visitors. Their guides were located near them. The bark-covered house was immense, eighty by seventeen feet, with a six-foot passageway down the center. The five-foot apartments on each side were raised a foot above the passage. A modicum of privacy was provided by boards or bark separating the cubicles. Holes in the roof drew out smoke from the individual fireplaces. The town consisted of about forty cabins spread out for nearly three miles along both sides of the river. Many of the cabins seemed to house two families, and they tended to be well separated, though sometimes in groups of four or five. There were gardens of peas, corn, and squash. The town had been much larger before it was almost destroyed by the French under Frontenac, as Bartram recalled from Colden's *History*.

Bartram and his friends had just gotten to sleep in their unaccustomed surroundings when John was awakened. He and Weiser were sleeping next to the passageway, so he poked Weiser and asked: "What was that noise?" Before Weiser was awake enough to reply, Shickellamy called from nearby:

"Lie still, John." This startled Bartram as much as the noise had done, for he had never "heard him speak so much plain English before." They were then treated to the most bizarre event of this strange trip—a weird apparition, which Bartram described:

> We were entertained by a comical fellow, disguised in as odd a dress as *Indian* folly could invent. He had on a clumsy vizard of wood colour'd black, with a nose 4 or 5 inches long, a grining mouth set awry, furnished with long teeth, round the eyes circles of bright brass, surrounded by a larger circle of white paint; from his forehead hung long tresses of buffaloes hair, and from the catch part of his head ropes made of plated husks of *Indian* corn. I cannot recollect the whole of his dress, but that it was equally uncouth. He carried in one hand a large staff, in the other a calabash with small stones in it for a rattle, and this he rubbed up and down his staff; he would sometimes hold up his head and make a hideous noise like the braying of an ass.

The "jack-pudding," as Bartram called him, continued to dance about their fire, which was built up by a boy who came with him, until he had "tired himself, which was some time after he had well tired us." In the course of his gyrations the performer held out his hand frequently for gifts of tobacco. When he finally departed they once more attempted sleep but were awakened before morning when serenaded by "a drunken *Squaw* coming into the cabin, frequently complimenting us and singing."

Neither Bartram nor Evans had any responsibility in connection with the Indian conference, so they occupied themselves seeing as much of the area as they could. The first day was rainy, and they were tired enough to be glad of it and stuck close to the cabin. The next day the weather had improved, so they hired a guide to take them five miles down river to a salt spring. Here they found a "kind of sandy beach" of several acres near the river. The Indians dug holes two feet deep, which would fill with water. They then filled kettles and boiled the water over fires until only salt remained. An

Indian family was there at the time. The squaw was tending the fire while her sons fished, and her "husband was basking himself on the sand under the bushes." Bartram and Evans filled a gallon keg with water which they took back to the cabin and boiled. They were surprised to obtain nearly a pound of salt. Bartram decided that there must be a deposit of fossil salt somewhere nearby which would account for the brine. Some of the brine had evaporated on the bushes, and they glittered in the sun like snow.

On their third day the two white men became more adventurous. They hired a guide for sixteen shillings to go with them to Oswego, a small trading post on Lake Ontario. They were anxious to see it and hoped that they could obtain provisions there for the return journey. Oswego had been established by New York in the hope of gaining control of Indian trade on the five great lakes and increasing Indian dependence on the British. Bartram, Evans, and their guide walked to Onondago Lake, near which they had collected brine, and then embarked in an Indian birchbark canoe. They crossed the lake in about two hours, and Bartram reported that they "went down the river a mile N., big enough to carry a large boat, if the trees fallen into it were but carried away. This brought us to the river from the *Cayuga* country, near 100 yards wide, very still, and so deep we could see no bottom, the land on both sides very rich and low to within a mile of the *Oneido* river, where the river began to run swift and the bottom became visible, tho at good depth. At three o'clock we came to the last mention'd river, down which the Albany trader[s] come to Oswego." Soon they began to encounter rapids, and eventually a ten-foot-high waterfall barred their further passage. They hauled their canoe out of the river and tramped for about a mile downstream to a small Indian settlement of four or five cabins, where their guide had relatives who made them welcome, providing them with boiled corn and watermelon. These Indians earned a living by fishing and by assisting the traders in carrying their boats and goods around the falls.

That night while Bartram and Evans slept the Indians were fishing. Next morning Bartram noticed one of the canoes with a piece of bark placed across it and covered with sand and gravel on which a fire had been made. He assumed that the fire had served not only to attract the fish but to enable the fishermen to see how

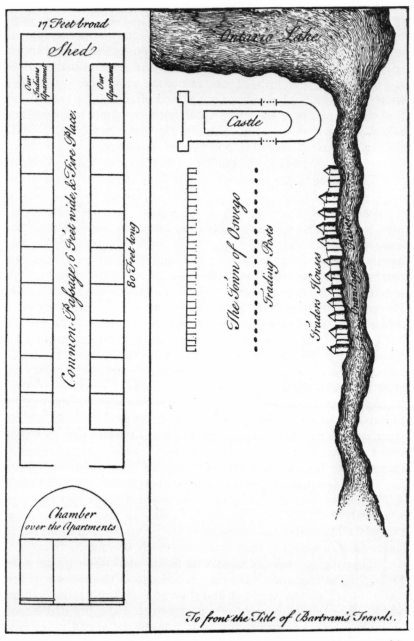

The following labels appear within the drawing:

17 Feet broad

Shed

Our Indians Apartment

Our Apartment

Common Passage, 6 Feet wide, & Fire Place.

80 Feet long

Ontario Lake

Castle

The Town of Oswego

Trading Posts

Traders Houses

Chamber over the Apartments

To front the Title of Bartram's Travels.

Adapted from Bartram's drawing of the town of Oswego, title page to his *Observations* to spear them. Their spears were "long slender shafts, eighteen or twenty feet long, pointed at the end with iron." The efficiency of these weapons was demonstrated by their catch, which included "some stout eels and a great fish two feet long." The travelers entered a canoe belonging to the village in high hopes of being paddled to Oswego. They were somewhat chagrined when they were landed on the opposite shore of the river with a twelve-mile tramp ahead. Having no other choice, they shouldered their gear and set out. Most of the day's hike was within sight of the river, which was swift and filled with rapids most of the way.

About noon they arrived at the "fort or trading castle" on the point where the river enters Lake Ontario. This was a stone building with a stone wall twenty feet high and 120 paces around. Bartram was so impressed by the softness of the stone that he could not resist carving his name on it with his knife. In addition to the fort there were some seventy log houses, as Bartram later related:

> . . . of which one half are in a row near the river, the other half opposite to them. On the other side of a fair were two streets divided by a row of posts in the midst, where each *Indian* has his house to lay his goods, and where any of the traders may traffick with him. This is surely an excellent regulation for preventing the traders from imposing on the *Indians*, a practise they have been formerly too much guilty of, and which has frequently involved the *English* colonies in difficulties and constantly tended to depreciate us in the esteem of the natives. Who can scarcely be blamed for judging a nation by the behavior of those with whom they have the most intercourse, a judgment I am sorry to confess that has (till lately) tended much to the making them in favour rather of the French than English. I speak of private persons, not of the respective government.

It was the practice of the commanding officer of the fort to maintain a watch on the lake for the approach of Indian canoes with goods and to have them met and brought directly to the castle. Thus the Indians avoided the dishonest trader who would have intercepted them, offered them rum, and then cheated them.

Bartram was very favorably impressed not only by what was being done to maintain goodwill and trade with the Indians but by

the immense potential of the Great Lakes for "English navigation."
He recognized the barriers presented by Niagara Falls and Sault
Ste. Marie, but "a vessel of considerable burthen may sail from the
hither end of the *Erie* lake to the bottom of the lake *Michigan* and,
for aught we know, through all parts of the 3 middle lakes." Some
of the rivers supplying the lakes extended close to the headwaters
of the Mississippi, and Bartram commented on the vast potential
for inland navigation in America.

Bartram and Evans were invited to dine at "the castle" by the
commissary and were joined by the doctor and the clerk. After dinner they "had the satisfaction of swimming in the lake *Ontario.*"
Bartram was told that the Great Lakes are said to "ebb and flood
several times in a quarter of an hour, tho it be perfectly smooth and
scarce any wind." He reported that the extent of the lake had evidently been much greater in times past, apparently having once extended more than a mile beyond its present shoreline. He recalled
that Sir Isaac Newton believed this to be true of all the waters of
the earth, but he suggested that it could have been caused by the
removal of some great obstruction which caused a drop in the St.
Lawrence River or merely by the wearing away of the bed of that
river to greater depth. Bartram decided that he would be content
to leave the decision to "a more able naturalist than myself." He
was familiar with existing maps of the lake and with the supposition that it was 120 miles wide and 200 long, and he noted some
disagreement between the more common maps and that of Bellin
with regard to the direction of the long axis of the lake.

In the evening, while others were resting, Bartram found his
relaxation by looking for plants nearby. After a night in the captain's quarters he was out again early the next morning before the
others were up and around. He collected some seeds, some of which
came from a plant of particular interest in England. This was the
"leonurus" (*Monarda didyma* L.) of Jacques Philippe Cornut
(1600–1651), the French botanist who had published a book on
North American plants in 1635. The plant had once grown in England but had been lost. Collinson successfully raised plants from
Bartram's seeds, which flowered for the first time in England in
1745. The New Yorkers called it "Oswego tea," and Collinson found
it "not unpleasant."[8]

Bartram breakfasted with one of the traders from whom he
and Evans bought some dried beef. They also purchased a gallon of

rum at the castle. They had wanted to buy some biscuit but were disappointed to find that the traders had either disposed of it or packed it for return to Albany. One of the traders, however, went among the others and collected quite a bit for them. After breakfast Bartram "regulated" his journal, "having a convenient private room to do it in." He and Evans again dined at the castle and did not start for Onondago until midafternoon. The return trip was not very pleasant. It was a hot day, and they had heavy packs. To make matters worse, the Indians, glad to be going home, set a fast pace. Bartram was dead tired when they reached the river village about sunset. He had also acquired an indisposition of some sort, which was not much helped by the fact that "The *Indian* Squaws got very drunk and made a sad noise until morning."

When Bartram and Evans arrived at Onondago, they found the Indian delegates still arriving. Meetings began on the afternoon of 30 July and proceeded in a dignified and leisurely manner for four days. There were innumerable speeches, complicated by the fact that the Anticoque Indians could not be understood. An interpreter for them had been brought some 700 miles; he knew some Delaware and some English and could communicate with Weiser, who in turn interpreted for the council. There were formal exchanges of wampum belts and numerous feasts. One of these Bartram found "consisted of 3 great kettles of *Indian* corn soop, or thin homony, with dry'd eels and other fish boiled in it, and one kettle full of young squashes and their flowers boiled in water, and a little meal mixed: this dish was but weak food, last of all was served a great bowl, full of *Indian* dumplings, made of new soft corn, cut or scraped off the ear, then with the addition of some boiled beans, lapped well up in *Indian* corn leaves, this is good hearty provision."

While his two companions were traveling to Oswego, Weiser had remained at Onondago to do as much lobbying as he could with individual chiefs who were present or who arrived before the council meetings began. Bartram mentioned the value of this: "And here I cannot help observing it was scarcely ever known that an *Indian Chief* or *Councellor*, once gained so far as to promise his interest, did break his promise, whatever presents have been offered him from another quarter." Weiser had done his work well and, when they took their leave on 2 August, the Indians bade them farewell with "much affection." Many of the chiefs brought gifts of food for their journey, including bags of parched meal which Bartram thought the best of all provisions for traveling. It was mixed with sugar, and a quarter of a pint with water added provided "a hearty traveling dinner."

Bartram had hoped that they might return by a different route, preferably through Mohawk country to Albany, but Shickellamy could not be persuaded to do so. The chiefs were afraid to permit the whites to undertake it without a guide, so they reluctantly set out by the same trails on which they had come, the Anticoque interpreter deciding to join them for part of the trip. On the whole the return proved to be more pleasant than the journey northward. The weather was cooler, so they were less bothered by insects. Blueberries and gooseberries made a fine addition to their diet. They killed several rattlesnakes, one of which was passed by all five horsemen before it was observed. Bartram found a great cache of fossils but was too burdened to carry any more. He observed many sorts of trees and was impressed by a magnolia (*M. acuminata* L.) 100 feet tall and two feet in diameter. They were all anxious to get home and pushed along as fast as their horses could manage.

Their Indian addition proved to be a problem. One day he set out on his own, ostensibly to hunt. When he overtook the party he had acquired a squaw, who joined them in the cabin where they spent the night. This met with such general indignation on the part of his companions that he sent his "occasional wife" home next day. They met two Indian parties along the way, one a group of half-breeds looking for stray horses with colts to be broken and another of Five Nations Indians returning from fighting the Catawbas in South Carolina with a woman captive. They passed through a former Indian town where they "found plums, peaches, and noble clusters of large grapes growing." As they neared home their horses became increasingly tired and lame. Near Tulpehocken the men walked and led the horses for twenty miles. This provided such opportunity for picking huckleberries that Bartram feared they might become ill. When they finally reached Weiser's home, Bartram's mare stretched out on the grass and did not move for twenty-four hours. Even then she was so tired and lame that Bartram borrowed a horse from Weiser to ride the rest of the way. He finally reached Kingsessing on 19 August.

On such a long journey as this Bartram found that there had

been plenty of time for reflection, even with the unusual distraction of companions:

In this journey into the heart of a country still in the possession of its original inhabitants I could not help sometimes to divert the length of the way by reflecting on their manners, their complection so different from ours, and their Traditions: this led me to conjecture at their origin, or whence they came into *America* and at what time. Perhaps it may be equally hard to disprove or to prove that they were originally placed here by the same creator who made the world, as soon as this part of it became habitable, for it is reasonable to suppose the almighty power provided for the peopling of this, as well as the other side of the globe, by a suitable stock of the human species.

However, if we are to account for their passing from what is called the old world, there are many relations of voyages hither from the North of *Europe* previous to that of *Columbus*, which, though dark and uncertain, are neither evidently fabulous, nor even improbable from either the length or difficulties of the way. That the *Norwegians*, the possessors of *Iceland*, for many ages past had colonies in *Greenland*, is a fact too well attested to admit a doubt, from Greenland the short passage cross *Davis' Streights* brings us into the continent of *America*.[9] If these colonies be put out of the question, it is scarce possible to think that of the numerous fleets with which the *Danes* and *Norwegians* terrified continually the rest of *Europe*, none, tempted by the hopes of gain, or drove by stress of weather, should ever fall in with the coasts of *Newfoundland* or *Gulph of St. Lawrence*. If it be objected that the navigators of those times were too unskilfull to attempt such a discovery does it not furnish us with a reason to account for its being made by chance? If this passage was ever publickly known, which is more probable it was not, might not the knowledge of it be lost as that to *Greenland*, and can we be sure that the *Greenland* of the *Norwegians* was not more to the southward of that country now so called I am not ignorant that these traditions of the *Norwegian* colonies, as well as many others to the same point, particularly that of prince *Madoc*, has been treated as meer fiction; but let us not

forget that *Herodotus's* account of the doubling of the Cape of
Good Hope has been treated so likewise too, tho' the fact be
now established to the degree of moral certainty. . . .

Another manner of peopling this side of the earth, particularly *S. America*, might be by some vessels of the *Egyptians*,
Phoenicians, or *Carthaginians* being blown off the coast of
Guinea to that of *Brazil* or the *Antilles* in their course to or
from the cape of *Good Hope*; in which case, for want of those
Arts and *Sciences* which are not to be found in *America* before its plantation by the whites and which are seldom to be
met with in a ship's crew, they must take to that way of life
our *Indians* now follow. This conjecture is the more probable,
as even in the state of perfection the art of navigation is now
arrived at, this accident is often unavoidable.

In conclusion, Bartram summarized his impressions of the Indians
they had seen of the Five Nations:

. . . they are a subtile, prudent, and judicious people in their
councils, indefatigable, crafty, and revengeful in their wars,
the men lazy and indolent at home, the women continual
slaves, modest, very loving, and obedient to their husbands.
As to the natural disposition of these Nations, they are grave,
solid, and still in their recreations, as well as in their councils. The Delawar's and Susquehanah's, on the contrary, are
very noisy in their recreations, and loud in discourse; but all
when in liquor, whether men or women, take the liberty of
shouting, singing, and dancing at an extravagant rate, till
the operations of the liquor cease; or being wearied they fall
asleep.

The six nations enjoy the character of being the most war-
like people in *N. America*, this they have acquired by the un-
interrupted state of war, they have continued in probably
near 200 years, and which has been attended with such success, that has made them the dread of people above 1000
miles distant.

Bartram thought that these Indians were probably not as
cruel as they had formerly been, perhaps because of their diminishing numbers. The Indians themselves were concerned about this

problem. Instead of killing prisoners, they were now giving them to the relatives of their own people who had been slain and were integrating them into the tribe. Bartram had been very much impressed by the hospitable treatment they had received, and he wrote to Colden: "ye Indians received us very kindly & entertained us with ye best they could afford & why should we expect more."[10] A few years later he made a somewhat similar comment in response to an inquiry by Collinson with regard to intermarriage between whites and Indians: "I don't remember to have known one English man to have married an Indian nymph it would [be] reconed a horrid crime with us but indeed if thay was well dressed & as cleanly as our women thay would make as handsom dutyfull industrious loveing & faithfull wives as many of our own women if we could whiten their skin a little & persuade or compel them not to use strong drink but most of our Indian traders debaucheth them shamefully which is one cause of many that hath eleniated thair respect from us ye young girls & women are generaly very modest unless debauched by Europeans then sometimes thay throw of all restraint."[11]

The return of the travelers was news in Philadelphia. Franklin commented in the *Pennsylvania Gazette*: "We are assured that the misunderstanding between the Colony of Virginia and the Six Nations . . . is now happily accomodated. . . ."[12] Breintnall, who frequently wrote verses to honor his friends, did so on this occasion, imitating the twenty-second ode of Horace:

Whose Life is upright, innocent and harmless
Needs not, O Bartram, arm himself with Weapons;
Useless to him, the Sword, the venomed Shaft, or
            Murdering Musket.

Thus when thou'rt journeying tow'rds wild Onondago
O'er pathless Mountains, Nature's Works exploring,
Or thro' vast Plains where rowls his mighty Waters
            Fam'd Missisipi;

Should the fierce She-Bear, or the famish'd Wildcat,
Or yet more fierce and wild the Savage Indian,
Meet thee, God praising, and his Works admiring,
            Instant they'd fly thee.

Tho' now to piercing Frosts, now scorching Sunbeams,
Now to unwholesome Fogs, tho' thou'rt exposed
Thy Guardian Angel, Innocence, shall keep thee
     Safe from all Danger.[13]

In the spring of 1744 Bartram sent a copy of his journal to
Collinson by Captain Peter Reeves on the *Lydia*. When the French
seized the ship, papers as well as cargo were lost.[14] It was disheartening to Bartram, who thought of the many hours that he had
wasted in the copying. However, when Gronovius wrote him "You
shall very much oblige the learned world with your communications; particular with your Journal to the Five Nations," Bartram
was encouraged to recopy and try his luck again.[15] He was no more
fortunate this time, his manuscript being carried on the *Queen of
Hungary*, which was also taken.[16] A year or two later he decided to
send a copy directly to Holland rather than by way of England,
hoping that it might prove a safer route, but it was not and he gave
up the whole idea. Finally, in June 1750, a gentleman by the name
of R. Poole was in Philadelphia on his way to England. He asked
Bartram to let him carry a copy.[17] Apparently Bartram complied,
and Poole passed the copy on to Collinson. In any event, Collinson
finally received it.[18]

Little did Bartram suspect that the manuscript account of his
travels would prove so popular with Collinson's friends that Peter
would decide to have it printed. Collinson asked his friend Richard
Jackson, a barrister who was deeply interested in husbandry, to
write a preface to the small volume.[19] In it Jackson regretted that
Bartram had not more education, as his style was "not so clear as
we could wish, however, in every piece of his, there are evident
marks of much good sense, penetration, and sincerity, join'd to a
commendable curiosity." Jackson wished that there had been more
detailed descriptions of plants, overlooking the fact that the journal
had been written merely as a running account for Collinson, who
was already familiar with most of the plants Bartram mentioned.
Collinson was reluctant to make any changes since he had not requested Bartram's permission for publication. The manuscript was
sent to J. Whiston and B. White, printers in Fleet Street. Their
interpretation of Bartram's handwriting and spelling resulted in
many mistakes, a rendition Collinson labeled "scandalous."[20] He
wrote to Franklin that Jackson would gladly have read the proof

but that "to save a Little Trouble of sending It" the printers did it themselves. Bartram's first book was published 9 February 1751 and sold for one shilling sixpence. It bore the impressive title of *Observations on the Inhabitants, Climate, Soil, Rivers, Productions, Animals, and other matters worthy of Notice, made by Mr. John Bartram in his Travels from Pensilvania to Onondago, Oswego and the Lake Ontario In Canada.*

Collinson wasted little time in sending copies to various friends, usually with apologies. To Franklin he wrote, "I am Vex'd to see J. Bartrams Journal printed with so many Faults."[21] To the Nuremberg apothecary Jean Ambrose Beurer, he explained that it was printed so incorrectly that he would probably not recognize some plant names.[22] Nevertheless, Gronovius congratulated Bartram: "you have realy obliged the world with some curious observations as you have [made on] most every page. . . . It was to be wished that all Travelers hath been so curious about the nature of the ground, as you have showed."[23]

EIGHT

Of Science and Philosophy

E ARLY IN 1738 a thought had occurred to Bartram that had important long-range conse-
quences although no immediate ones. He considered it for a while
and then wrote to Collinson, asking his reaction. Bartram suggested that a scientific academy or society should be formed at
Philadelphia by a few "ingenious and curious men," there to devote
themselves to a "study of naturall secrets arts & syences." He
thought that they should have a meetinghouse and that they
should communicate their discoveries fully.[1] The reception that the
Royal Society had given his communications to Collinson, the latter's references to the society in his letters, and the *Philosophical
Transactions* had all convinced Bartram that something comparable could and should be established at Philadelphia.

Collinson's reply was more realistic than encouraging. On 10
July 1738 he wrote, "As to the Society that thee hints at, had you a
set of learned, well-qualified members to set out with, it might
draw your neighbors to correspond with you. Your Library Company I take to be an essay towards such a Society. But to draw
learned strangers to you, to teach sciences, requires salaries and
good encouragement; and this will require public, as well as proprietary assistance,—which can't be at present complied with—considering the infancy of your colony."[2] Apparently he misunderstood
Bartram's use of the word "academy."

In spite of Collinson's response, Bartram was not discouraged,
and when he was in Philadelphia he often discussed his idea with
Franklin, who was always eager to stimulate intellectual and scientific pursuits. His printing establishment and newspaper were

now successful enough to allow him to devote time to other things. Franklin had been intrigued by Bartram's far-flung correspondence with men important in world science. He was impressed by the fact that Collinson sometimes presented Bartram's papers before the Royal Society and that some were printed in the *Philosophical Transactions*. Franklin agreed with Bartram that it was high time for the American colonies to have a society of their own, and he had a number of friends who would support such an organization.

Both men being very busy at the time of Bartram's first conception of a scientific society in 1738, actual plans did not materialize until the spring of 1743. At that time Franklin wrote and printed a broadside of their proposal for a learned society, relying heavily on Bartram's ideas and suggestions.[3] It was for an academy quite different from the Royal Society but logical and suitable for North America. Now that "The first Drudgery of Settling new Colonies" was almost over it was time to "cultivate the finer Arts, and improve the stock of Knowledge." The colonies comprised immense variations in weather and soil, and improvements could be made in many fields with the free exchange of ideas and experience by "Virtuosi or ingenious Men" from each colony. If they joined together in an "American Philosophical Society," Philadelphia, being in the most central location, would act as a clearinghouse for their contributions. Distances being too great for members from other areas to meet, the Philadelphia group would meet monthly "to read and consider such Letters, Communications, or Queries as shall be sent from distant Members." They would also report their own experiments and ideas. Those communications which seemed to be of value would then be sent to the absent members quarterly to ascertain their opinions of them. There would be at least seven Philadelphia members, representing botany, geography, mechanics, chemistry, and natural philosophy, in addition to a president, secretary, and treasurer.

Bartram's hand is especially obvious in the suggestion of subjects for study: botanical discoveries, their propagation and possible uses; improvements in the manufacture of cider, wines, and other fruit juices; new medicines and procedures, for both treatment and prevention of diseases; fossils; new mathematical methods; "New Mechanical Inventions for saving Labour; as Mills, Carriages, &c;" methods for pumping water and draining marshes; the latest in maps and charts; studies of soils; "And all philosophical Experiments that let Light into the Nature of Things, tend to increase the Power of Man over Matter, and multiply the Conveniences or Pleasures of Life." Some "intended Members" already corresponded with the Royal Society and the Dublin Society, and such correspondence should be continued by the American Philosophical Society.

To meet the expenses of the organization each member would be assessed a "Piece of Eight" annually. Some of the funds might even be used to finance certain experiments if a vote of the members supported it. At the end of the year a volume of the most important papers would be published and distributed to the membership. Until the first meeting, when regulations would be drawn up and officers elected, Franklin volunteered to act as secretary and promised that, by permission of the Postmaster General, all society correspondence would be postage-free.

The proposal was published on the fourteenth of May. Bartram left for Onondago on 3 July and Franklin spent part of the summer in New England, so nothing was accomplished toward establishing the society. Franklin did mention it to Colden when he saw him, and the doctor was most enthusiastic, interesting New York friends in the idea of the society. When Colden heard nothing more of the organization that fall he wrote to Franklin, who admitted that he had been too busy since he returned home to do anything about it.[4] But the year 1744 saw the first meeting of the American Philosophical Society. Hoping that they could head the membership list with Logan's prestigious name, Bartram and Franklin had shown him the proposal. Bartram was fairly certain that Logan would not be interested, and he was correct. They decided that this "should not hinder our attempt & if he would not go along with us we would Jog along without him."[5] In the absence of Logan, a number of enthusiastic men attended the first meeting. Rules were drawn up and officers elected: a lawyer, Thomas Hopkinson, president; a merchant, William Coleman, treasurer; and Franklin, secretary. Representing the scientific fields were: "Dr. Thomas Bond as Physician; Mr. John Bartram as Botanist; Mr. Thomas Godfrey as Mathematician; Mr. Samuel Rhodes as Mechanician; Mr. Wm. Parsons as Geographer; Dr. Phineas Bond as General Natural Philosopher."[6]

By the end of March three meetings had been held, and there were already members from the Jerseys: Robert Hunter Morris, Archibald Home, and two Trenton men. Interest was being shown in

New England and in the southern colonies of Maryland, Virginia, and Carolina.[7] Bartram sent Colden a copy of the proposal in late March, writing him that "we hope thee will pleas to do us ye honor to be enroled in our number—I hope this undertaking may be of publick benefit to our American Colonies if we act with diligent application in this afair."[8] At the end of April Bartram reported to Colden that seven members had been initiated at the last meeting, of whom one was Colden, who was elected unanimously. Dr. Archibald Spencer, who was then giving "a Course of Experimental Philosophy" at Philadelphia, was present at the May meeting. He found the proposal so estimable that he volunteered to take it with him to the West Indies, hoping to interest people there.[9]

In July Dr. Evan Jones, a neighbor of Colden, sent the doctor a paper on rattlesnake bite, writing that it could be given "for ye approbation of yr Gentlemen in Philada. who have formed yemselves into a Societie for the propagation of useful knowledge please to make my kind regard acceptable to Docr. Thomas Bond also to our Frd James the Botanist & to all ye Gentlemen of yr. Societie."[10] When Colden went to Philadelphia that fall he was disappointed to learn that Franklin had received very few, if any, other papers to be printed in the annual collection. The following summer he suggested that Franklin, as a printer, publish papers sent by friends "by way of Specimen."[11] Franklin accepted Colden's suggestion and planned an *American Philosophical Miscellany*, the first number to be published in January 1746.[12] By that time he was clerk of the Pennsylvania House of Representatives and far too busy to carry out the project. However, in October 1746 he wrote to Colden that he had five or six articles ready for his *Miscellany* and asked Colden to permit him to take some copies from a plate he had of the North American coast. He sent a copy of an article on a wooden cannon for Colden's opinion, another having gone to Governor William Shirley of Massachusetts.[13] Unfortunately the *Miscellany* was never printed, and the contributions have disappeared.

Bartram was reluctant to write to his European correspondents about the society. The Philadelphia members had agreed not to say much about it, hoping to get well organized before they informed their European friends. They should have known better; the international scientific community got the word promptly. As soon as he learned of his election to membership, Colden dashed off a letter to Collinson, informing him of the society. He admitted that

Bartram was the only member known to him at the beginning. He added, "I have not as yet seen any thing from the Philadelphia Society & its probable that the members of the other Colonies will wait for an example from those of Philadelphia before they'l offer anything so that I cannot tell what expectations to give you of that undertaking. We have in America for some time past made great progress in Aping the Luxury of our Mother Country   I am glad that some now indeavour to imitate some of its Excellencies. . . ."[14] It was not long before Bartram learned of Colden's letter and wrote to him: "I find by my correspondents in Europe that they have been informed of our Phylosophycal Society & have great expectation of fine accounts therefrom tho I durst not so much as mention it to my correspondents for fear it should turn out but poorly; but I find the mentioned [it] to Collinson, hee to Catesby, and hee to Gronovius which was to him from Clayton."[15] Gronovius had kept the chain going by writing to Linnaeus in Sweden: "In Philadelphia they have established a Literary Society, and the most worthy members adorn it, such as Clayton, Colden, Mitchell, Bartram, and all who are eager to promote natural history."[16]

Early meetings concentrated on botanical and medical subjects and later, inspired by Dr. Spencer and Franklin, on electricity. In spite of his doubts concerning the chances of success for the society, Collinson had given it his blessings once it was established.

Benjamin Franklin (1706–90)

His earlier reservations unfortunately proved to be well founded. The original enthusiasm of many of the members soon waned, and Franklin was complaining that they were idle and "take no Pains."[17] He, Bartram, and Dr. Thomas Bond did what they could to hold the organization together and recognized that there were extenuating circumstances.

Bartram wrote to Colden in April 1745: "We make at present but a poor progress in our Phylosophick Society: ye tumultous reports of wars Invasions & Reprisals exercises most of our thoughts & discourse & many is under apprehentions of being more sensibly touched with these Calamities altho we cant yet generally agree to put our selves in any posture of defence notwithstanding many is very uneasy in our exposed Circumstance."[18] Bartram did not think the threat of war fully accounted for the problems of the society. He regretted that "most of our members in Philadelphia embraces other amusements that bears A greater sway in their minds—dear friend I sometimes observe that ye major part of our inhabitants may be ranked in three Classes   ye first Class are those whose thought & study is intirely upon geting & laying up large estates & any other attainment that dont turn immediately upon that hinge thay think is not worth thair notice. the second Class are those that are for spending in Luxury all thay can come at & are often ye children of avaritious Parents, ye third class are those that necessity obliges to hard labour & Cares for a moderat & happy maintainance of thair family & these are many times ye most curious tho deprived mostly of time & material to pursue thair natural inclinations."[19] Bartram was convinced that the society could make progress if "we could but exchange ye time that is spent in ye Club, Chess & Coffee House for ye Curious amusements of natural observations."[20]

Dr. Phineas Bond returned to Philadelphia from Leiden in the fall of 1743, bringing with him a letter to Bartram from Gronovius, desiring a correspondence with him and a gift of two books. Soon afterward Bartram received from Gronovius a copy of Part II of the *Flora Virginica*. Bartram was delighted by these overtures and reciprocated with a letter and a specimen of a red-bellied snake.[21] This was the beginning of an exchange between the two men which continued sporadically for a number of years. Gronovius wrote that Bartram would never "believe how our Virtuosos are pleased to see the cells of the wasp nests filled with Spiders, of which they never have heard before. Professors Muschenbroek and Luhots cannot enough admire that mechanica." He thanked Bartram for a shell containing a hermit crab and for various bivalve mollusc shells. The hermit crab gave Gronovius particular satisfaction for it helped him to disprove a contention of Jan Swammerdam, the great seventeenth-century Dutch biologist. The crab occupied a different kind of shell from that of other specimens that Gronovius had and he wrote: "By these two different Lodgings it appeared that Swammerdam is mistaken when he says, that this Crab liveth only in one sort of shel which is created only for his use: and it appears more that he is mistaken by the shell you send to me, which is the Cochlea perlata Bonnaru . . . and a very different shell from that which Catesby painted. . . . So that the Hermit Crab is found in two different species of shell as well in America, as in Europe."[22] In his first letter, Gronovius had assured further shipments from Bartram by writing him that he should "very much oblige the learned world" with his various communications.[23]

Gronovius had great hopes for the American Philosophical Society and lost no time in writing to Bartram about one study he hoped they would promote: "Now dear Sir, as you are now setting up a Philosophical Society at philadelphia I think you have the best occasion to propagate the Naturall History of Fishes, of which the Europeans are very well described by Artédy. But of the American ones we know nothing."[24] To encourage the idea he sent a copy of the *Philosophical Transactions* that contained an article on classifying and preserving fish.[25] Two fish that Bartram had sent to him were spoiled on arrival so Gronovius sent two prescriptions: one for a "varnish which preserves the fishes" and the other a powder "by which any creature, as quadrupeds and birds, are preserved and become very hard." He also sent specimens of fishskins dried and mounted so that they might be "kept as plants in an Herbarium."[26] He had questions about muskrats so Bartram sent him a muskrat skin.[27] Bartram did not send the great number of fish for which Gronovius was hoping, but he did send a variety of zoological specimens, although he did not enjoy collecting animals of any kind. He confessed: "as for the animals and insects it is very few that I touch of choice, and most with uneasiness. Neither can I behold any of them, that have not done me a manifest injury, in thair agonizing, mortal pains, without pity. I also am of opinion that the creatures commonly called brutes, possess higher qualifications, and more exalted ideas, than our traditional mystery mongers are willing to allow them."[28]

In May 1744 Bartram received a letter from Dr. John Mitchell. Mitchell was born in Lancaster County, Virginia, and had been educated at the University of Edinburgh, where he studied medicine. He had returned home in 1732 and was now practicing at Urbanna, Virginia. He was busy studying the colony's flora and fauna, sending reports on his observations to Collinson and the Royal Society. Like Bartram, Mitchell collected mosses for Dillenius and was a friend of John Clayton. Bartram hastened to reply to Mitchell's letter, deploring the fact that they had not been in touch sooner. He discussed at some length his Virginia trip of 1738, which had taken him within a few miles of the doctor's home. Bartram added a summary account of his travels, mentioning the Catskills and his most recent trip to Onondago.[29]

Mitchell was pleased by Bartram's letter and gratified to have been elected a corresponding member of the Philosophical Society. For these reasons and the very poor state of his health, he determined to visit Philadelphia early in the fall. When he called on Bartram he received a warm welcome. The two men tramped through Bartram's gardens and around his farm, examining the diverse plants which Bartram had planted in places best suited to their ecological requirements. Mitchell saw many that were new to him and begged specimens and seeds. Very little persuasion was required to convince him that he should spend the night, for they still had much to discuss.[30]

Mitchell had brought with him two papers which he thought might interest the Philosophical Society. One of these was an account of his experience in treating a disease reaching epidemic proportions in Virginia in the years 1737, 1741, and 1742. He had diagnosed it as yellow fever, after performing a number of autopsies.[31] His second paper, a description of the pines of Virginia, interested Bartram even more. Mitchell's meticulous study recognized only two species of pine in Tidewater Virginia but gave good descriptions of the common variations that he did not consider to be species. He discussed ecological influences, details of reproduction, and uses, both medical and commercial. Bartram borrowed the paper to copy, later returning the original to Mitchell. Lewis Evans then made a copy from Bartram's to send to Colden.[32] Mitchell had written a third paper that he discussed with Bartram. Irked by existing systems of classification, Mitchell had made quite a study of the subject. He was convinced that the only valid basis for determining the genuine relationships between plants, or between animals, should be actual breeding experiments. He had sent this proposal with descriptions of what he believed to be thirty new genera of plants to Collinson in 1741. The latter was making arrangements to have these published.[33]

Bartram was delighted with Mitchell. He took the doctor to Philadelphia to find a place to stay and introduced him to Franklin and other members of the Philosophical Society, and to various friends and acquaintances. Franklin took Mitchell to visit Logan, another kindred spirit. The doctor was so delighted with all of this scientific interest that he remained in Philadelphia for several weeks, revisiting Bartram a number of times. Philadelphians were equally impressed by Mitchell. Franklin borrowed his essay on yellow fever and had it copied. He was eager to publish it, but Mitchell refused permission. Bartram described Mitchell for Colden as "an excelent Phisition & Botanist & hath dipped in ye Mathematicks which inclined A Gentleman in Town well known to us to say to me that our docters was but novices to him, but another person more volatil & more extravagantly expressed his value for him tould me thay had not ye Millioneth part of his knowlege."[34]

The state of Mitchell's health had concerned Bartram, and nothing that he heard after the doctor left did anything to reassure him. He felt that Mitchell would not survive long unless he left Virginia.[35] Mitchell had reached the same conclusion. In 1746 he went to England, where he lived for twenty-two years and continued a sporadic correspondence with Bartram and Franklin.[36] Mitchell was elected a Fellow of the Royal Society and became an intimate friend of Catesby and Collinson. He also made new friends who became important to Bartram.

Among them was Archibald Campbell (1682–1761), third Duke of Argyll. The Duke owned very large estates in Scotland at Inveraray and elsewhere and a house in London. Much of his time, however, was spent at Whitton, his home on Hounslow Heath, near London. He had purchased a tract of land there in 1723 and had developed one of the most elaborate gardens in eighteenth-century England. Early in the century, English gardeners had begun to turn away from formal designs in the French and Italian style toward a more natural landscaping, making use of natural contours or creating the desired effects by grading. The gardens at Whitton covered nearly thirty acres in addition to a nine-acre nursery and kitchen garden. When Mitchell first knew them, they had been developing for more than a quarter of a century. Trees from many parts of the world shaded nearly a mile of carefully tended gravel walks. There were fishponds, a canal, an aviary, sundials, and statuary. A Gothic tower topped a man-made hill. There were large greenhouses, an orangery, a bowling green, and a Chinese summer-house.

In his nursery and greenhouses Argyll raised trees, shrubs, and herbs from all over the world, not only for planting at Whitton but for moving to his estates in Scotland. He was a great and practicing advocate of forestation, not only raising trees but purchasing seedling evergreens in numbers exceeding 100,000 annually. Mitchell, with his interest in botany and his knowledge of North American plants, was immediately welcomed by the "tree-monger," as Argyll was sometimes called. Mitchell was soon spending a great deal of time with the duke and his nephew, John Stewart (1713–92), Lord Bute. Mitchell requested seeds and plants for them from Bartram, which were sent with the usual shipments to Collinson. The first of these orders was sent in 1747 and was shipped on 30 January 1747/48. Many others followed during the next ten years.

Soon after Mitchell's arrival in England, Bute became Lord of the Bed-Chamber. At about the same time, he acquired from Argyll Cane Wood (now Kenwood) on the Hampstead-Highgate road, with fine views of the city of London. He began renovating both the house and an eight-acre garden. Bute was an even more ardent botanist than his uncle and collected exotic plants not only for himself but for the gardens of Frederick Louis, Prince of Wales, at Kew. The gardens at Kew had been originally laid out by the well-known horticulturist Sir Henry Capell, who filled them with rare plants much admired by his friend John Evelyn. The gardens had later been restored by William Kent, the landscape gardener, under the direction of Frederick and Augusta, when Frederick acquired the property in 1730. Both the Prince and his wife were dedicated gardeners. Mitchell's close association with Argyll and Bute introduced him to many of their friends among the nobility who maintained fine gardens. It was not long before Bartram's seeds began to supply not only the Prince of Wales but many others of this group.

Mitchell had not long been gone from Bartram's house that fall of 1744 when Colden appeared on Bartram's doorstep. The doctor spent the night and went with his host to call on James Logan the following day.[37] On his return to Coldengham, he wrote to Bartram, thanking him for "the Civilities" he had received, and added:

I shall have the greatest pleasure if I can be a means of persuading you to make your knowledge more publick & of consequence more usefull & I perswade my self it will not be difficult for me to perswade you to it for the greatest pleasure a good man can have is in being usefull to the community & in what I am about to propose I likewise hope that you'l find a private advantage in it. It is to communicate your knowledge of our American plants to the publick. This I believe may be done with most advantage to yourself by publishing it by Subscription in monthly papers of about one shilling Value & to take Gronovius' Flora Virginica for the foundation of your work & method. It will be necessary for you to have at least six months papers ready before you begin to publish that the work may be continued with sufficient care and without Interruption.[38]

Bartram was impressed by such encouragement but he was cautious:

I am obliged to thee for thy kind advice & offers to assist me in publishing A description of our American plants which I have thought of Many times but am not yet very hasty in entering upon a Performance that requires mature consideration I have had severall years past A specimen of A performance of this kind from ye Medical Society at Boston with an account that Doctor Douglass had described (according to that specimen which was done well according to Turnfort's method) eleven hundred plants growing round and adjacent to Boston—allso ye Ingenious Dr. Mitchel hath discribed curiously many of ye plants in Virginia & hath promised me A book as soon as possible he hath sent it to london to be printed When I am furnished with these materials than I shall be better enabled to proceed warily in so difficult an affair.[39]

Waiting to see these two publications before starting one of his own discouraged Bartram. Dr. William Douglass died in 1752 without publishing his descriptions. Mitchell's Tidewater Virginia plants did not appear as a book but rather as an article in Latin, dealing mainly with principles of classification. It was published in German in a Nuremberg journal but not until 1748.[40]

Although Bartram was well aware of the hazards to which he was exposed on his travels he was less conscious of those at home. On several occasions he received bad cuts on his legs, but in the spring of 1745 he received a more serious injury. He was kicked in the back by a horse. Unable to breathe and in great pain, he writhed on the ground as members of his family tried to assist him. He was sure that he could hear his ribs "slip in & out of ye socket" of his backbone as he tried to breathe. He was carried to his bed as soon as he could bear to be moved and prescribed for himself ten drops of oil of turpentine with a little sugar to overcome faintness and shock and "hinder ye blood from coagulating." Ann was horrified by the dark and ugly swollen bruise on his back and worried about internal injuries. She, too, could hear noises from his ribs as he breathed. She was able to give him some relief by massaging his back with rum and salt, and he continued to take turpentine drops every few hours. Although whichever way he tried to lie in bed was painful, Bartram managed to stay there for two days, admitting it "a great affliction to me who can't rest long without action nor endure confinement." On the third day he was up and walking about his room, supported by a "strengthening plaster" on his back and a "discutient plaster" on his chest, which Ann had prepared. In a few days he was back at his usual routines.[41]

Accidents were not the only health problems that year, for there was an unusual amount of sickness in the Philadelphia area. In July, when Bartram wrote to Colden, he was feeling bad and supporting "my acking head on my hand & ellbo leaning on ye table while I scrible over this paper I hardly know how, my neibouring town ships is sorely distressed with Fluxes & fever in ye City many children dieth & in ye Countrey many lusty young men so that I think it not convenient to leave my family of little helpless children. . . ."[42] The following summer was no better. Bartram wrote to Colden that people "suffered with four different kinds of mortal distempers viz ye small pox which now begins to be very malignant   ye bloody flux grievous lingring feavours commonly Called ye dumb ague & ye sore throat   all these is generaly thorow ye countrey   very few families escapes some or other of them & abundans dies both men women & children as it is ye dryest Summer that ever was known since ye English setled here so it is ye Sickliest so that we are dayly prest by naturall affection or ye ingagements of humanity to condole near relations & friends afflictions instead of amuseing or diverting our selves with curious speculations."[43]

In July 1746 Colden sent two copies of his newly published treatise, *An Explication of the First Causes of Action in Matter*, to Franklin, one to be delivered to Bartram and the other to Evans. The essay was an attempt to explain gravity by means of various "mathematical demonstrations." Colden must have been disappointed by the two recipients, for Evans simply told Franklin that he did not understand it, while Bartram, with more tact, told Franklin "that he could not read it with the necessary attention, till after Harvest, but he apprehended he should find it out of his reach."[44]

Another aspect of science was baffling Bartram, namely electrical phenomena. Like many others he had been fascinated by Dr. Spencer's demonstrations. Electrical experiments were popular in Europe, and Spencer had brought them to Boston in 1743, where Franklin had seen them. The doctor's Course of Experimental Philosophy did not attract many in the New England city but proved very popular in Philadelphia the following April. He was forced to repeat the series several times throughout the summer. A year or so later Collinson sent an early model of the Leiden Jar, an electrical condenser or storage battery invented in that city, to the Library Company. Franklin was instantly fascinated. His house "was continually full for some time, with People who came to see the new Wonders." Finally, to alleviate the problem, he had some glass tubes blown for his friends that they might perform their own experiments.[45]

Among Franklin's audience on at least one occasion when he demonstrated his new toy was his old friend Bartram, who later described the "ball turning many hours about an Electrified Body" and other facets of the experiments for Logan's amusement.[46] Bar-

tram had to share his excitement with Colden as well: "I suppose
thee hath allready heard of ye Electrical experiments which thay
can so efectualy apply to A man as well as to many other objects as
to fill him so full of fire that if another man doth but put his finger
to ye electrified person ye fire will fly out & strike that part which
approacheth nearest I take this to be ye most Surpriseing Phenomena that we have met with & is wholy incomprehensible to thy
friend."[47] Colden was fascinated and promptly requested Franklin
to send him a similar apparatus so that he and some other New
York gentlemen could experiment, too. Franklin obliged and sent
him the beginning of his "Electrical Journal" as well.[48]

The winter of 1747/48 was a trying one for Philadelphians for
reasons other than sickness. Many of the citizens expected an attack by the French in the spring. The city was poorly prepared to
defend itself but was doing what it could to get ready. Bartram
wrote to Collinson that many people were "daily exercising and
learning the martial discipline, in order to oppose them, if they
should attempt to land,—and are making preparations for forts and
batteries, to stop any vessels that come in a hostile manner. Ye
clergy exercises thair talents with all thair force of eloquence to
persuade thair hearers to defend thair country, liberties & families
by ye sword & ye blessings of God, but our Society opposeth them
by pamphlets, persuasion & threats of reading them out of our
meetings for breach of our discipline in taking up ye carnal weapon
which unreasonable proceeding I suppose hath made a hundred
hypocrits to one convert for thay can't bind ye freedom of thought."[49]

NINE

The International Scientific Circle

O NE MORNING in September 1748 three gentlemen from Sweden called on Bartram.[1] One of them, Gustavus Hesselius, a painter of note, had been in America since 1711. The other two had landed three days previously. Peter Kalm (1716–79), a former student of Linnaeus, had accompanied his professor on a tour through Russia and the Ukraine in 1744. Kalm had been elected to membership in the Royal Swedish Academy of Sciences in 1745 and two years later was appointed professor of agriculture at the University of Abo in Swedish Finland. He was already on leave of absence from this post. The Swedish Academy had requested him to seek American plants of economic value which could survive in the Swedish climate. The third member of the party calling on Bartram was Lars Jungstrom, an expert gardener and artist, acting as Kalm's assistant.[2]

On their way to America, Kalm and Jungstrom had been delayed for some months in London, waiting for a ship. They had occupied their time studying English and talking to people with some knowledge of American plants. Having introductions from Linnaeus, they had met Catesby, Collinson, and Mitchell and had spent a great deal of time with them. Few people could have better advised them of what to expect in the New World. When they left London they had been given letters to both Bartram and Franklin by their London friends, and they already had a letter from Linnaeus to Bartram.[3]

Bartram made his guests welcome and read their letters. Kalm very soon found him to be the mine of information which the London botanists had claimed him to be and proceeded to take full advantage of it. It was exciting for Bartram to have a student of Linnaeus as his guest, and his pleasure was magnified by knowing that Kalm had a personal acquaintance with his London friends. He would be delighted to assist Kalm and Jungstrom in any way possible. One of Kalm's first requests was that Bartram send some seeds to Linnaeus. Bartram agreed, but he told Kalm that he had previously sent them to Linnaeus in care of Swedish ministers returning home and had received no acknowledgment of them.

Later in September Kalm was again Bartram's guest. Among many other things, he asked for more information about persimmons and their uses. Bartram told him that they were sometimes served as table sweetmeats and that wine could be made from them. He was amused by Kalm's account of Jungstrom's introduction to them. On their first visit to Bartram, Hesselius had gathered some persimmons for Jungstrom to taste and "the poor credulous fellow had hardly bit into them when he felt the qualities they have before the frost has touched them, for they contracted his mouth so that he could hardly speak."[4] Bartram took Kalm into his garden and provided him with some ripe persimmons, which Kalm thought delicious.

Kalm was interested in Bartram's conviction that the oceans had once covered much more of the land than at present. He gave Kalm a number of reasons for this, principal among which were deposits of what seemed to be seashells that he had found on the Blue Mountains and in various parts of Virginia, Maryland, Jersey, and New York. Another curious point was that many of the petrified shells that Bartram had found on the northern mountains differed from those found along the sea at the same latitude. In fact, they were more like those known to be found in South Carolina. He believed that this supported Dr. Thomas Burnet's theory that the earth was in "a different position towards the sun" before the flood. If this were the case, then areas that were presently cold had formerly been tropical.[5]

Bartram showed Kalm some of the more unusual plants in his herbarium. The professor was interested to find a few with which he was already familiar, since they were found in northern Europe. Among these were the white birch, a gentian, *Potentilla*, *Myrica*, and a specimen of *Linnaea borealis* var. *Americana*, which had been sent to Bartram from the Canadian mountains.[6] Kalm asked his new friend if he agreed with Catesby, who believed that trees and plants decreased proportionately in size as they were brought further north. Bartram had long observed this ecological phenomenon and replied:

If the question were more limited, then my answer would be more worthwhile. There are some trees which grow better in southern countries, and become smaller as you advance to the north. Their seeds or berries are sometimes brought into colder climates by birds and by other accidents. They gradually decrease in growth, till at last they will not grow at all. On the other hand, there are other trees and herbs which the wise Creator destined for the northern countries, and they grow there to an amazing size. But the further they are transplanted to the south the smaller they grow, till at last they degenerate so much as not to be able to grow at all. Other plants love a temperate climate, and if they be carried either south or north, they will not succeed well, but always grow smaller. Thus, for example, Pennsylvania contains some trees which grow exceedingly well, but always decrease in proportion as they are carried further off either to the north or to the south.[7]

As Kalm traveled more widely in North America, he found Bartram's statement to be correct.

Kalm returned frequently to confer with Bartram and was always welcome. On a visit in November, Bartram showed him his collection of pieces of Indian pottery and one unbroken pot. The latter was unglazed but had elaborate ornamentation. Bartram had obtained it from a man who found it in an abandoned Indian village and used it to store a fat or wax with which he waterproofed shoes and boots. Bartram called Kalm's attention to differences in the composition of the clay fragments and told him that they were related to locations of the Indian tribes. The seashore Indians mixed pulverized shells with clay; those inland used mountain crystals. It was obvious that none of the pottery had been long-cured for it was quite soft. Since the Indians had begun purchasing cooking utensils from the Europeans, such pottery was rare. Kalm was interested in some samples of slate that Bartram showed him. He told Kalm that there were large deposits along the Schuylkill. Although a little thicker, it was similar to table slate used in Swe-

den. In America, roofs were made from it which were impervious to
heat and cold as well as extremely durable. The local caves fascinated Kalm. Although Bartram had sent his samples of stalactites
from the caves he had explored to London, he described them for
Kalm at length.[8]

Through the fall and winter Kalm traveled the general area
of the Jerseys, Maryland, Delaware, and Pennsylvania, visiting the
Swedish settlements and collecting odd bits of information and history as he went. In mid-April 1749 he was again at Bartram's
home, and the two men spent some time studying a pair of wasp
nests high in a maple overhanging a brook. They observed the
three combs in each, with the largest at the bottom, making the
nest triangular in shape. Bartram recounted his experiments in
burning different parts of the nests.[9]

The longer Kalm knew Bartram, the more he admired the
man. He wrote to Linnaeus in May that Bartram was "everything,
farmer, joiner, turner, shoe-maker, bricklayer, gardener, minister,
carpenter, and I don't know what else, a brilliant fellow." Kalm
could tell that Bartram "was a mightily exact observer" although a
"lazy writer." From what Bartram and Colden had told Kalm of Canadian plants, he was anxious to investigate them and decided to
travel north that summer.[10] He had kept careful meteorological records ever since he had landed and now was loathe to discontinue
them. Since Jungstrom would accompany him, Kalm asked Bartram to continue his observations. Kalm provided him with his
thermometer and explained what information he would like to
have recorded. He was somewhat disappointed later to find that,
while Bartram had noted the temperatures, he had not recorded
some of the additional observations, but he conceded that Bartram
had many other matters of greater consequence to occupy him.[11]
Kalm and Jungstrom started north on 31 May 1749 and visited
Lake Champlain, Montreal, and other parts of Quebec. In August
Kalm sent Jungstrom back to Philadelphia with the request that
Bartram advise him on the collection of grape and mulberry
seeds.[12] Kalm remained in Canada until mid-September in order to
collect seeds there.

It was not until February 1750 that Kalm was introduced to
James Logan, and the elderly gentleman did not appreciate the de-
lay. He expressed his irritation to Collinson the same night: "I have
Spent most of this day for the first time with thy friend Kalm, ac-

companied with B. Franklin, and I know not what to make of him, nor of his journey to Canada, where, after the whole last winter spent at a Swedish Woman's House near Newcastle, he spent near five Months, and dined many times at the Governors at Quebec, without Seeing, during the 8 months or more that he had been here, any one person I could hear of, but B. Franklin and Jno. Bartram. . . ."[13]

During the summer of 1750 Kalm traveled through Iroquois territory to Oswego on horseback and then by boat for six days of rowing to Fort Niagara. From the fort he traveled to Niagara Falls. His dramatic description of the falls in a letter to Franklin was published by the latter in the *Pennsylvania Gazette* for 20 September. Collinson obtained a copy and had it inserted in the Royal Society journal, and the printer added it to Bartram's *Observations* to help fill out the small book. Kalm returned to Philadelphia in October and again spent some time with Bartram. For the most part, Kalm was given serious answers to his many questions, but Bartram, like Catesby and Mitchell in London, could not resist taking some advantage of his credulous nature. Kalm recorded that "Mr. Bartram told me that when a bear catches a cow he kills her in the following manner: He bites a hole in the hide and blows with all his power into it till the animal swells excessively and dies, for the air expands greatly between the flesh and the hide."[14]

Kalm and Jungstrom sailed for England in February and had a short stay there before going on to Sweden. Kalm took with him from North America a large herbarium—great collections of seeds, plants, and zoological specimens. Many of his plants appeared under his name in Linnaeus' 1753 *Species Plantarum*.[15] Kalm's report of his travels was published in three volumes between 1753 and 1761 and went through numerous translations. It is a somewhat rambling and disjointed account of his experiences. In it he readily recognized his indebtedness to Bartram: "I . . . owe him much, for he possessed that great quality of communicating everything he knew. I shall therefore in this work frequently mention this gentleman."[16] This he did, quoting Bartram's comments on a wide range of subjects: botany, zoology, geology, the silk and wine industries, medicinal uses of plants, and plant geography.

Kalm's North American friends took for granted that they would maintain a correspondence with him when he returned home, and both Franklin and Bartram expressed themselves strongly when he never wrote. The latter wrote to Linnaeus in March 1753: "We are all surprised that we have not one letter from Peter Kalm whom we are ready to tax with ingratitude."[17] When Bartram learned that the 1753 edition of the *Species Plantarum* had been published, he wrote to a friend that he understood it contained all of the North American plants that Kalm had found, adding, "I showed him many, that he said were new Genera, and that Linnaeus must make many alterations, when he was by him more truly informed of their true characters, as I should soon see when they were printed. I long to see these books,—to see if they have done me justice, as Kalm promised me. Dr. Gronovius promised to send them to me, as soon as they came to his hand."[18] If Bartram ever saw a copy of Kalm's *Travels*, he left no comment on it. Kalm did see a copy of Bartram's account of his journey to Onondago and remarked that "the book did Mr. Bartram more harm than good, for, as he is rather backward in writing down what he knows, this publication was found to contain but few new observations. It would not however be doing justice to Mr. Bartram's merit if he were to be judged by this performance. He had not filled it with a thousandth part of the great knowledge which he has acquired in natural philosophy and history, especially in regard to North America."[19]

Bartram's journal was not his only publication in 1751. On 27 June an advertisement appeared in the *Pennsylvania Gazette*: "Speedily will be published, and sold by B. Franklin and D. Hall, at the Post-Office, in Market-Street, MEDICINA BRITTANICA . . . with a preface by Mr. John Bartram, Botanist of Pennsylvania, and his Notes throughout the Work, Shewing the Places where many of the described Plants are to be found in these parts of America, their differences in Name, Appearance and Virtue, from those of the same Kind in Europe; and an Appendix, containing a Description of a Number of Plants, peculiar to America, their Uses, Virtues, &c." Bartram may have been his own publisher; he gave David Hall a bill of exchange for £25 on 22 June.[20]

This was the third edition of Thomas Short's work, first published in London in 1746. The American edition appeared on 5 September and sold for eight shillings.[21] Bartram's preface was a short review of the history of medicine, with emphasis on the part played by plants. His notes on Short's medicinal plants revealed that few of the English ones were available to Americans. Of seven that

Bartram had tried to raise, only three had survived. A few English plants had American counterparts close enough to the English to have value in treatment. Many had similar and misleading names but were unrelated. Bartram's comments were often pungent, as were those about toadflax (*Linaria linaria* [L.] Karst): "This species is called by our People Ransted's Weed, or Dog Piss Weed; a troublesome stinking weed, is no native, but we can never I believe eradicate it."[22]

Bartram's appendix, containing a list of native medicinal plants growing in the northern part of America, is of particular interest. He gave a description of each plant, the method of preparation of the drug, and its use in treatment. Some plants on Bartram's list are still used as drugs today although the specific medical applications may be quite different. A preparation made from the roots of *Collinsonia canadensis* L., or horse balm, was "much commended for Women's After pains." It has many uses today: diuretic, diaphoretic, tonic, and astringent. Bartram gave Dr. Colden's recommendation for *Sanguinaria* (*S. canadensis* L., bloodroot) mixed with "Small Beer" as a cure for jaundice. It is now employed as an expectorant and an emetic. *Apocinum* (*Asclepias tu-*

Peter Kalm (1716–79)

berosa L., chiggerweed) provided a cure for the "Bloody Flux," and Kalm considered it excellent for "the hysteric passion." Today it is used as a diaphoretic, diuretic, and expectorant. *Eupatorium perfoliatum* L., or boneset, was good as a "Vomit in intermitting fevers, and used as a Fomentation for Pain in the Limbs." This herb has a long history as a medicinal plant. Even today, it is used as a diaphoretic in the treatment of systemic colds. There were others. This appendix has been called "an early American pharmacopoeia"[23] and was of assistance to Schoepf in preparing his *Materia Medica Americana.* In late 1752 Bartram sent two copies of the book to Collinson with the request that one of them be forwarded to Linnaeus.[24]

A friend to whom Collinson sent a copy of Bartram's *Observations* was Arthur Dobbs (1689–1763), of Castle Dobbs, near Carrick-fergus, Ireland. He was Engineer-in-Chief and Surveyor-General of Ireland and was a great promoter of forestation. Another interest of Dobbs was the increased settlement of the colonies and the improvement of trade between them and both England and Ireland. In 1745 he had acquired title to lands in Rowan County, North Carolina, and was sending German settlers there.[25] Bartram had sent two boxes of seeds to Dobbs at Collinson's request in 1748. The following year Dobbs wrote directly to Bartram, ordering four five-guinea boxes of seeds for fall shipment.[26] His share would be one-eighth, the remainder being divided among friends. In a separate order for himself, Dobbs wanted some ginseng and rattlesnake root plants and seeds, some indigo or other *"Curious Dying Woods,"* prickly pear, and several other unusual plants. He reported that most of the previous year's acorns were rotten and that some of the seeds were very dry. Some had come up but others had not, and he hoped that they might be the type that required two years for germination. Worst of all, the seeds had become so mixed that it was difficult to identify them. Dobbs' optimism concerning the germination of his seeds after two years proved ill founded. None of them sprouted. Many of those in the three boxes sent in the fall of 1749 failed, and in 1750 the shipment was lost at sea.

Dobbs' letters were not confined to botanical subjects. In 1749 he queried Bartram concerning the growth of the colonies and the number of German settlers who had come. He wanted to know whether the frontier settlements were increasing, their extent, and if they now went beyond Lord Fairfax's grant to the branches of the

Ohio and Allegheny rivers. He told Bartram that such settlements and proper treatment of the Indians should make the English secure from the threat of French encroachments. Bartram replied that 10,000 Germans had arrived and settled in the backwoods. His description of the Jersey cedar swamps convinced Dobbs that they were identical to Irish bogs and that American white cedar would flourish there.[27] On 28 February 1750/51 Dobbs communicated Bartram's account of American trees and of the white cedar to the Dublin Society as well as the Pennsylvanian's offer to correspond with them and send seeds.[28] The secretary was ordered to convey the society's thanks to Dobbs for communicating Bartram's letters. Dobbs was requested to ask his friend to be kind enough to send seeds and plants that would survive the Irish climate.

In the summer of 1749 Bartram and Lewis Evans had become involved in plans for another expedition that would concern the Indians. Since their return from Onondago, Evans had been very busy making a map of Pennsylvania. To support himself while he did so he had a shop in Strawberry Alley, where he sold such diverse items as "fine Crown Soap" and the new stove designed by Franklin.[29] He was also available for surveying and for drawing up deeds. In June 1749 the Proprietor of Pennsylvania, Thomas Penn, was worried about the possible encroachment by the Ohio Company on lands granted to the Proprietary and wanted someone to reconnoitre the boundaries of Pennsylvania secretly. He thought John Bartram and Lewis Evans would be ideal. They could carry out the project under pretense of collecting plants and making observations for further corrections to the latter's map without arousing suspicions. When Evans agreed but Bartram did not, it was suggested that Conrad Weiser help run the line. He was no more enthusiastic than Bartram, saying that the Indians would no longer trust him if he were involved in this. Collinson advised Bartram to remember his family obligations since it was a dangerous expedition, which Bartram had already concluded.[30] Both he and Evans remained safely at home.

Bartram may have wished that he had gone somewhere as the summer of 1750 was a painful one for him, both as a botanist and as a farmer. He wrote to a friend in July:

. . . we have now the driest season that, I believe, ever was known. The ground near us has not been wet plough-deep,

since the beginning of March. Our spring was extremely dry,
windy and cold; and since June, the weather has been very
hot and dry. Our fields have no more grass in them than in
the midst of winter; and the meadowground, that used to
bear two good crops, has no more grass than the middle of
the street, both root and branch being scorched as with fire;
and the ground is as dry as dust, two feet deep. The very
briers are withering, and the fruit upon them appearing
scorched, and drying up. Our springs have failed and the
runs dried up. Yet, notwithstanding this extraordinary
drought, we have rarely been without rain for five days, since
March; and during the winter we were not so long without
snow, though we had but three snows that staid long with us,
all the winter; most of the rest would hardly cover the
ground. Thus in the summer, one week's rain, every day,
would scarcely afford as much moisture as one common
nightly dew.[31]

Sometime in the early fall of 1750 Bartram received a letter
from John Mitchell written in August, thanking him for several
letters and for plants sent to the Duke of Argyll. The doctor had
just returned from a long trip to Scotland with Argyll. The latter
did not need any more plants at the moment, but Lord Bute had
given Mitchell an order for a five-guinea box of seeds for the Prince
of Wales, and there were orders from Lord Strafford and the Earl of
Galloway.[32] These orders inspired Bartram to make a trip beyond
the Blue Mountains, following the river through the Delaware
Water Gap again that fall. He sent a description and drawing of the
gap to Gronovius, both of which impressed the doctor. Sensing a
kindred spirit in Gronovius, Bartram later sent him a vivid account of how such mountainous scenes affected him:

But when we ascend to our mountainous country, then we
view nature in her ragged, torn, and tattered crags, in be-
holding the exalted towers, those dreadful precipices of rocks
washed bare, many undermined by furious torrents and tum-
bled down into the water courses; others hanging over or
standing tottering on the others' shoulders, deep valleys
more of the solid rock the mighty ridges move through, that
vast bodies of water might pass through with their sandy or

muddy contents; vast lakes drained dry, at the bottom of
which is now excellent rich soil and many that it so filled up
by the wash of the adjacent mountains as to become marshes
of large extent many great lakes very much diminished in
depth and extent by wearing the falls below deeper, so as to
drain the water so much off, the adjacent shores is now become rich low land. Your opinion of these great mutations
would much oblige your friend. . . .[33]

Inorganic evolution was a very real and awe-inspiring phenomenon
to Bartram.

As early as 1736 Collinson had encouraged Bartram's interest
in geology and paleontology, sending him fossil specimens and indicating his own interest in them. Geology was still an infant science, not yet taught in the universities.[34] The principal interest in
the subject was in the exploitation of metals. Such possibilities had
not gone unobserved in Pennsylvania. In 1698 Gabriel Thomas had
written a pamphlet to promote the settlement of the Proprietary. In
it he noted various rocks, copper, a mineral spring, and the possi-
bility of coal deposits.[35] By 1737 there were beginnings of a broader
interest in geology. During the winter a group of men met every
Saturday evening in Leiden to discuss scientific matters and eventually involved Bartram. Among them were Linnaeus, Gronovius,
and Isaac Lawson, an English medical student.[36] Together they
studied flowers, insects, fish, and minerals, attempting to place all
of these into categories according to Linnaeus' system of classification. Lawson was particularly fascinated by minerals. Having continued his studies in Germany, he returned to England in 1738. To
further his collection of mineral specimens, he prepared a list of the
sorts of things that he desired, and a copy of this was sent to Bartram by Collinson. As Bartram was already sending fossils to
Catesby, Collinson, and Sloane, he gladly obliged by remitting
some to Lawson.[37]

When Dr. Thomas Bond returned to Philadelphia from London in the early 1740s he sang the praises of his friend Dr. John
Fothergill to Bartram and mentioned the doctor's interest in geology. Bartram sent Fothergill a specimen of cotton stone and some
fossils in 1743. The English physician wrote a lengthy letter of appreciation, and thus another correspondence began which continued until Bartram's death and with his sons afterward.[38] Fother-

gill's scientific interests were broad, but when his correspondence with Bartram began he was concerned with the possibilities of American medicinal plants and mineral springs. He inquired about the latter and asked Bartram to preserve some sassafras flowers in rum as he wanted to distill them. Bartram did not receive the request until after these flowers had been shed in 1744, but he did discourse about mineral springs and their virtues in medicine. He thought that many people tended to misuse them, dosing themselves with the water with little regard to quantity, the nature of the illness, or the age of the patient. When no immediate cure occurred, they abandoned the water for some other treatment.[39]

Fothergill was convinced that he had aroused Bartram's interest in mineral springs and that between them they could make an extensive study. Accordingly, in the summer of 1745 he sent Bartram an essay by Lyncom Spane, which gave instructions for the chemical testing of springs, and a box containing the necessary chemicals. There was syrup of violets which would turn green in an alkaline solution and red in an acid one. A jar of powdered galls was included for the preparation of a tincture or infusion of galls. This would give a deep purple or black color in water if iron was present. Oil of tartar would form a white precipitate if calcium was to be found. A solution of silver in aqua fortis (nitric acid) would form a blackish sediment if there was sulphur in the water. Fothergill not only wanted to have Bartram run all of these tests on the springs' water, but he wanted him to evaporate four gallons of it from each spring and to send him the remaining sediment for further analysis. A special vessel would be needed for this evaporation, and he would send one of block tin for the purpose.[40]

Bartram replied to the letter on 7 December, sending the sassafras flowers but regretting that "I have not yet made much observation on our mineral waters, for want of time to examine them, being hurried in the fall to procure forest seeds for my correspondents; and indeed, if I should make diligent and proper observations on all of our mineral waters, it would take up most of my time, or, I am sure, more than I can spare, beside serving my benefactors in Europe and my plantation at home, and still worse, because most of the trials must be made a great distance from home. . . . I like very well to serve my country, but as I have nine children alive, most of which are not able to help themselves, it is my duty to provide for them." He discussed various mineral springs of which he had heard, one of which was rich in sulphur: "Several men and women, passengers that were going up the river, drank at this spring to quench their thirst, which purged them stoutly, & put them in a nasty trim on board ye sloop." Dr. Shaw, a brewer in Burlington, had told him "that a Spa water broke into his well, which he brewed beer with, which affected the beer so much that it purged those who drank it so much, that they thought he put a trick upon them. So he was forced to throw away fifty pounds worth of beer. . . ."[41] In a letter to Colden, Bartram discussed Fothergill's proposal and the amount of time it would take and added, "But ye main spring of motion still hath not its proper temper but he saith he is not without hopes that he can engage some to assist him to remedy that defect."[42] Perhaps the doctor never was able to "temper the mainspring," as apparently Bartram was unable to find time to carry out his request concerning the mineral springs. Neither does he appear to have sent samples of water and the "earth, salts, &c" around the spring which "turned iron to copper" requested by Dr. Mitchell of both Franklin and Bartram a little later.[43] When Bartram declined the role of chemist, two of his friends took it up. Dr. Phineas Bond and his brother, Dr. Thomas Bond, advertised in the *Pennsylvania Gazette* that they intended inquiring into the nature of medicinal springs, using European methods of testing. They invited reports of gentlemen's experiences with springs.[44]

From time to time Colden and Bartram exchanged bits of geologic news. Colden remarked on New York's mineral springs when Bartram informed him of Fothergill's request.[45] They traded notes on locations and quality of copper mines.[46] When Colden sent a pamphlet on Gowan Knight's discoveries concerning the magnetism of steel, Bartram experimented with a steel bar three and a half inches long and three-quarters of an inch in diameter. With it he was able to hold up a medium-sized key or three ten-penny nails by their points. He balanced four large knitting needles on one end by the key at the other. He later used the magnet to test for iron particles in sand and soil.[47]

Bartram's geologic interest was stimulated far more by Gronovius than by anyone else. The Leiden doctor had drawn up a catalogue of his rock collection and had it printed.[48] It was a copy of this and Linnaeus' *Characters* that he had sent to Bartram by Dr. Bond in the fall of 1743.[49] In June of the following year Gronovius received a huge collection of curiosities from Bartram: shells, rocks, fossils, and bits of old Indian pottery. He hastily wrote to Bartram that his generosity would not be selfishly hoarded. He would make public such things and share them with the learned world by means of a second edition of his *Index*. He would classify the geological specimens in their orders, classes, genera, and species. He would add the following paragraph to his preface:[50] "We must now pass to such stones as have a resemblance of some animal, or of its shell or covering, and which authors commonly call petrifactions, and which they make no doubt in producing them as proofs of the ancient deluge. This excellent man [John Bartram] observed these, variously situated on the ground: some on the surface of the earth, others sunk deep; for what he found in the *southern* parts of Pennsylvania, towards the great Lakes of Canada . . . lay on the surface of the ground; and in a journey which he made of some hundreds of miles, he found them scattered everywhere."[51] Unfortunately, this paragraph was in Latin so Bartram had to wait for Colden's translation. When Bartram replied to the Leiden doctor, he suggested that in the future Gronovius should confine his letters to English since "I can make but A poor hand of latin & we have very few or none that can assist Mee."[52]

Gronovius proposed to draw up a monograph, similar to the *Flora Virginica*, with Bartram supplying North American rocks as Clayton had done plants. With such a prospect, Bartram was determined to send Gronovius all that he could manage. One of Gronovius' queries was in regard to the lodestones that Bartram had sent. Bartram had gone out to the quarry where he purchased two for Gronovius' friends, Professors Peter van Muschenbroek and Johann Lulofs, who had requested them. He discovered that the ten-to twenty-yard-wide lodestone vein, running approximately east and west, continued for sixty to seventy miles. Mixed with it was some asbestos. The earth surrounding it was very black, producing *Lychnis* and *Alsine*, and considered to be an excellent fertilizer.[53] In spite of this, little else grew in the area, which was known as "the Barrens." When he sent the lodestones, Bartram told Gronovius he would be happy to correspond with the professors, "for I am ready to learn of any learned person that will be so kind as to instruct me in any branch of Natural History which is my beloved amusement." Muschenbroek was grateful to Bartram and assured Gronovius that, when he wrote a report of the lodestone, he would give Bartram proper credit.[54]

Bartram's correspondence with Gronovius was interrupted by war for four years. When Gronovius wrote again in March 1750/51 the new edition of his *Index* was in press. Bartram hastened to reply, delighted to resume his overseas correspondence. Writing in January, he informed Gronovius that Collinson had finally received the journal of his trip to Onondago and would be glad to lend it to him. Gronovius had been disappointed by the many delays in receiving the journal; he had hoped to translate it into Latin and include it in the new edition of his *Index*, but it was now too late. He sent a copy of the *Index* to Bartram in June, with a copy of Linnaeus' *Bibliotheca Botanica*, just published in Amsterdam, which would have mentioned Bartram's journal had it arrived in time.[55]

Gronovius had promised Bartram that his book would include "an ecomium and thanks for all the benefits you have bestowed on me," and he was as good as his word. He referred to Bartram as "the most knowledgeable Pennsylvania naturalist, to whose offices I owe much." He included some seventy specimens that Bartram had sent to him, with descriptions and, in many cases, the locations where Bartram had found them.[56] Among them were various quartzes, flint, jasper, marble, mica, talc, serpentine, amianthus, iron pyrites, zinc, iron, copper, lead, silver, and tufa. Bartram continued to send Gronovius specimens from time to time but heard little of or from him. Gronovius was not well, and his son, Laurens Theodore, was gradually taking over his father's scientific interests. The younger Gronovius included some of Bartram's geological contributions in a manuscript entitled "Lithophylacium," which he never published but which survives in the library of the University of Amsterdam.

Many of the fossils Bartram found raised questions in his mind concerning their origins. Among these were belemnites, internal shells of an extinct species of cephalopod mollusc.[57] He queried Collinson about them and was told that they were surely the remains of some marine organism, although many still believed them to be stones. Collinson added that earlier in the century a Frenchman had gone to "the Inquisition for arguing an organic origin" of these objects, but that it was now permissible, even fashionable, to attribute the location of fossils to the deluge.[58] When Bartram replied, he invited Collinson to consider some further speculation. Why might there not be "many species of shell-fish on shoals very remote from the shores, never yet exposed to our sight or knowledge, which may agree with many fossil bodies found very far in land, which carry the strongest marks of their having existed in another element"?[59] Later he wrote to Gronovius along the same lines:

I have had several accounts from curious observers, of many fish which have been catched near the middle of ye Sea, in which there have been shellfish, and sand reptiles, and several such like submarine fish, whose abode is on sandy shoals; which inclines me to query whether there may not be vast chains of mountains, of many hundred miles extent in the sea, as well as at land; and whether the tops of these may not be large sand-banks, which may produce food for many kinds of fish (that never swam near the shore), which resort to these banks for their daily food, whose summits may be nearer the surface than most people expect, and where they may suppose it to be unfathomable; as there are islands already known, many of which are dispersed in most parts of the sea, at unequal distances, where ships take their course in sailing to the East and West Indies; and it's very likely many more are yet undiscovered, by reason of the vast tract of sea where ships have not yet sailed, as may be observed by consulting the Sea Journals.

These islands being the tops of vast mountains, appearing above the surface, so I think it's very likely that hundreds of them may be placed as different in altitude as magnitude, or distance; so, consequently, many of them may be in the reach of common sounding, not yet known, by reason that the navigators never sound but when they expect they are near some coast. But if our cruising vessels (for merchant ships can't lose so much time, unless in a calm), were to sound every day far from shore, perhaps they might find fine banks, where many kinds of fish frequent for food, and might be improved for good fisheries, for the benefit of mankind. *Query*, whether these vast chains of mountains, if there be such, may not be, in part, the cause of the currents in the sea which our navigators complain so much of; and is it not probable, that there may be various kinds of fish in the great vales, between these ridges, which never appeared, nor can live, near the surface of the water?[60]

In a letter to Collinson in 1751, Bartram allowed his far-ranging thoughts free expression. He was convinced that the fossils found on the mountains originated far earlier than the biblical flood. He believed that "Where marle or clay prevailed, the shells entered into the formation of lime stone, marble, or flint; but where sand superabounded, there these shells entered into the composition of gritty rock which hath, by degrees, cemented into the hard compact state that we now find them in unless where the currents of water have worn them away, or where they have been exposed to the air, rain, or frost, which had dissolved their original cement." He continued:

> I cannot agree with Dr. Woodward, that the rocks and mountains were so dissolved at the deluge as he represents; nor with Burnet that there were no rocks before the flood.— Moses expressly says, that *all the hills were covered.*
>
> In most of the northern countries may be found fossil bodies, both animal and vegetable, which are well known entirely to agree with others found in warmer climates. The great variety of fossil shells near Limington in Hampshire is a farther confirmation, as they were altogether like those found in the West and East Indies. This to me seems a demonstration, that our earth's axis was in a different position to the sun before the flood; and if *our country*, as well as *yours*, hath received much alteration by earthquakes, might it not be some very violent shock that altered its poles?—These hints and conjectures I submit to more mature consideration.[61]

Collinson had nothing to add to all of this speculation. He did comment on Bartram's theory concerning marble and limestone: "thy notion of its formation by a mixture of slime, or mud, with what thee calls nitrous or marine salts, enters not into my comprehension. So thou hath it all to thyself."[62] He nevertheless found Bartram's theories sufficiently provocative to have his long letter published in the *Gentleman's Magazine.*

Gronovius had been surprised that belemnites should be found in North America. He did not believe that they were the result of the deluge and suggested that there may well have been several different times when the oceans overflowed the lands. This would account for the various strata. He agreed with Bartram that there were oceanic mountains below the surface of the oceans. Such thoughts inspired Bartram to further speculation about geological history. While he had a "very indiferent opinion" of priests, he still felt that they had often been the only repository of history in the day when it was handed down by word of mouth. Thus, the tales told to Plato of Atlantis may well have had a factual basis:

how do [we] know but that was part of America & Joyned to or near ireland & that to England that to France & is it not probable that Spain joined to Africa at ye straights of gibralter   that asia & Europe Joyned at ye propontis that ye mediteranian was high enough to cover part of ye islands contained therein & might not ye deserts of libia & Arabia be ye sandy bottoms of ye sea 100 or 200 fathom deep   might not waters of ye flood or not long after   cut its way thorow ye straights of gibralter & ye black sea through ye propontise might not britain be separated from france & ireland & ye atlantis which be low loose & sandy be washed away or sunk there is found in several northern countreys plants & shells which appears to be ye production of prety warm climates   I cant at present see how this can be accounted for better then by these two ways that I shall mention   either that thay growed in or near where we find them or that thay was brought from ye southeastward or southwest from ye places of thair original growth by very strong winds & currents; if thair original growth was where we now find them or near it & by winds & mighty current of water such a vast body of soils covered them we may reasonably suppose ye countrey there was once a warmer climate & consequently ye earth run paralel with its equinox   this will perhaps make some start but pray consider we read in ye book of Joshua that ye sun & earth stood still a whole day & I think it would require no greater power to incline ye earth 25 degrees then to stop its or ye suns motion   now dear Peter I have sent a confused heap of broken links[63]

Bartram's belief in the reality of an Atlantis was further bolstered when he was told of a Philadelphia ship captain sent to the Azores who was unable to find certain islands in the latitude and longitude where they had formerly been. He was interested in the cap-

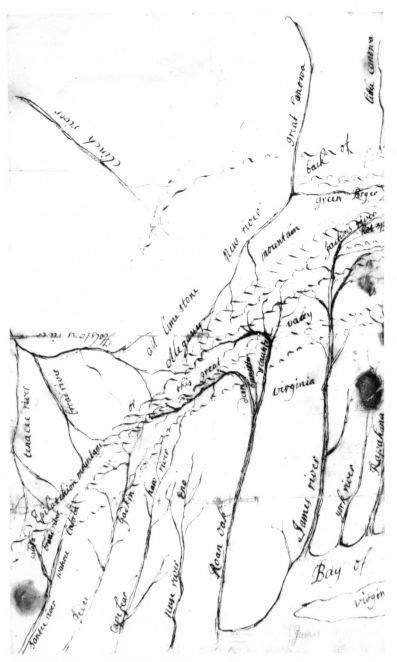

Bartram's drawing of the Chesapeake Bay river system (courtesy American Philosophical Society)

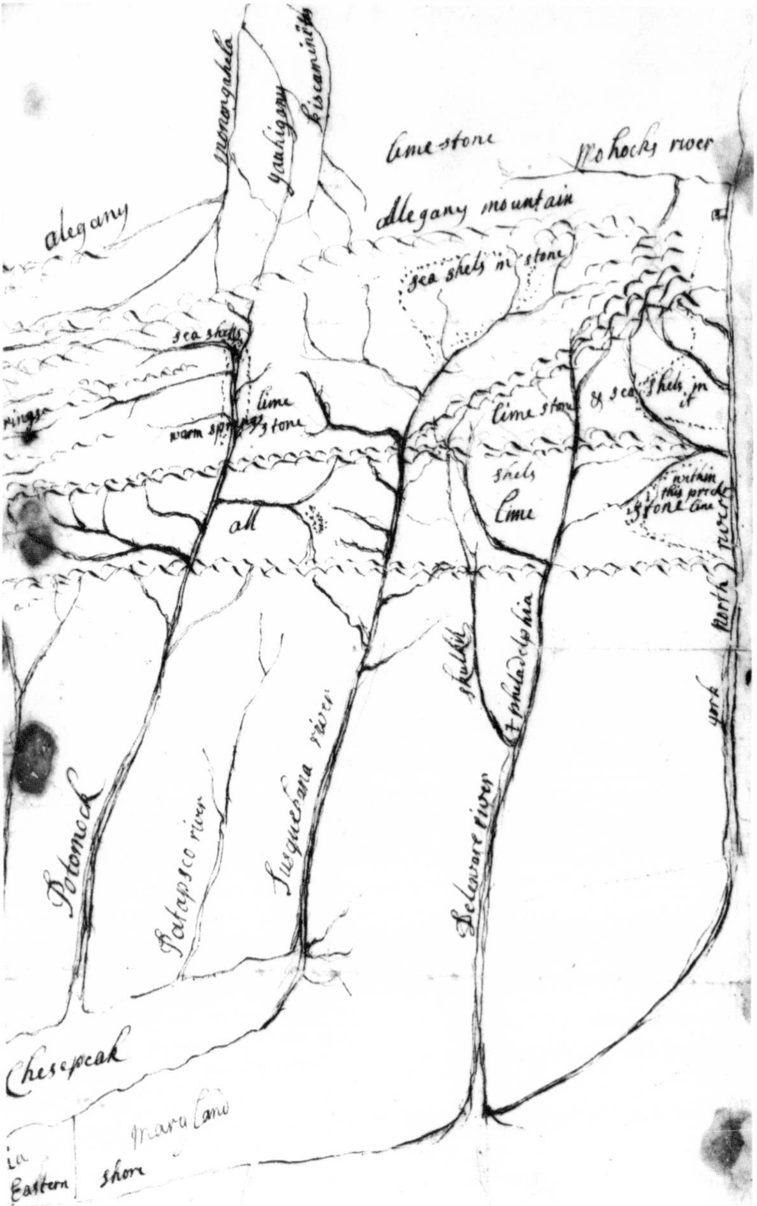

monongahela

Yauhiogany

Kiscaminitas

Lime stone

Mohocks river

alegany

Alegany mountain

sea shels in stone

sea shels

lime stone & sea shels jn

ringo

lime stone

warm springs

shels

Lime

within this prect of stone lime

oh

Potomack

Patapsco river

Susquehana river

shels

Philadelphia

Delaware river

York river

york

Chesepeak

ia Eastern shore

mara land

tain's suggestion that they had sunk beneath the surface of the sea.

Bartram's interest in geology extended beyond the possible existence of historic land bridges and what are today called "sea mounts." He was curious about what might be learned by exploring beneath the surface of the earth and proposed a systematic survey suggestive of "mohole" (a National Science Foundation project for the study of the earth's crust). Specifically, he believed that responsible people in each province should be appointed "to bore the ground to great depths, in all the different soils in the several provinces, with an instrument fit for the purpose, about four inches in diameter. The benefit which I shall propose from these trials, is to search for marls, or rich earths, to manure the surface of the poor ground withal. Secondly, to search for all kinds of medicinal earths, sulphurs, bitumens, coal, peat, salts, vitriols, marcasites, flints, as well as metals. Thirdly to find the various kinds of springs, to know whether they are potable, or medicinal, or mechanical." Careful records of the type and depth of each stratum were to be recorded and mapped. He was convinced that "vast beds of rock salt" could be discovered and that sandy soil covered beds of marl which could be used to enrich it. In any event, he was certain that such a study would result in a "curious subterranean map." This suggestion of "what amounted to provincial geological surveys . . . long anticipated any actual organization of official surveys in this country."[64]

Bartram once drew another type of geological map, a paleontological one, for Franklin, who found it "curious." It covered an area from the Mohawk River in New York to the Wateree River in South Carolina and from the Eastern Shore of Maryland and Virginia west to beyond the Alleghenies, showing the sources of the Great and Little "canowa," the Monongahela, and others. All of the eastern rivers were depicted. The map was roughly drawn and out of proportion but served Bartram's purpose of showing the location of great shell deposits and the limestone region of the Shenandoah Valley.[65]

[The mapping of mountains and valleys beneath the seas, which Bartram first suggested, was not begun in his lifetime. The great explorations of the British ship *Challenger*, sent out to seek "living fossils," did not begin until 1872. The first detailed sea floor maps are only a few years old, and in June 1977 the discovery in the South Atlantic of "two submarine canyons more than twice as deep as the Grand Canyon" was announced by the National Science Foundation. We are indebted to William Maurice Ewing and his associates and students for carrying out in the mid-twentieth century the kinds of studies that Bartram envisioned in the mid-eighteenth century. It is interesting to note that much of their early work was done from a ship named the *Atlantis*.[66]]

TEN

A Companion for His Travels

B ARTRAM had long complained that he could
find no one who would join him on collecting
trips and must make most of them alone: "Our Americans have
very little taste for these amusements. I can't find one that will
bear the fatigue to accompany me on my peregrinations. Therefore,
consequently thee may suppose I am often exposed to solitary and
difficult traveling beyond our inhabitants, and often under dangerous circumstances, in passing over rivers, climbing over mountains
and precipices amongst the rattlesnakes, and often obliged to follow the track or path, of wild beasts for my guide through these
desolate and gloomy thickets."[1] From time to time he made short
local jaunts and took some of his children or farm workers with
him, but it was the long expeditions which were usually lonely. He
was by nature a sociable man and liked the company of congenial
people who stimulated his thinking and on whom he could try ideas
of his own. His love of nature kept him happy in the wilderness,
but he did wish for company with whom to share its wonders. He
was pleased indeed to be able to include his "little botanist," his son
Billy, in his plans for a trip to the Catskills in September 1753.[2]
Billy was then fourteen and had already made short trips with his
father. Of all the Bartram children Billy had most clearly inherited
his father's appreciation of nature and would be the most congenial
on such expeditions.

Leaving on 1 September they traveled ninety miles in two
days and on the third crossed the Jersey section of the Blue Mountains.[3] Bartram pointed out to Billy a variety of mountain oaks—
Spanish, red, and chestnut—as well as many other kinds of trees.

In swampy areas they found an abundance of ripe fox grapes and ate as many as they dared. As they rode down the mountain to the Minisinks, Billy saw a large rattlesnake tightly coiled in a circle the size of a hat. They dismounted and observed the snake for a time. Bartram tried to persuade it to uncoil by prodding it with a stick, but it only coiled more tightly. It did swell with indignation and exhibited a brightening of its colors. They wished that Billy had brought the paint box and paper given to him recently by a "Switzer" and could record the snake in all its beauty. Toward sunset they came to a tavern perched on a stony hill from which they could see the Blue Mountains beyond the lowlands of the river bottom three miles away. They arranged for the care of their horses and then went for a tramp along the river. The Delaware was so low from the drought that they were able to walk three-quarters of the way across by leaping from stone to stone. Bartram showed Billy how these rocks had been worn smooth by the action of the river and regaled him with his theories of the long action of water on the rock and soil of such places.

Bartram roused Billy early next morning, and they were soon on their way. Not long after they started Bartram spied some Scotch lovage (*Ligusticum scothicum* L.), which he had only found once before. They turned toward Goshen so that Bartram could show his son this awesomely desolate area. Along a riverbank they noted alders fifteen to twenty feet tall with leaves that were like silver underneath (*Alnus rugosa* var. *americana* [Regel] Fern?). They finally found a not very prepossessing cottage where they could spend the night. The owner assured them that there were very remarkable plants growing on his land, so they hurried out to collect but found nothing unusual. They were happy to depart next morning after sharing the cottage, "hardly big enough for a hen roost," with five or six other people and innumerable lice. Soon after daylight they were on their way to Coldengham.

The Bartrams arrived just in time for a midday dinner but were sorry to find that Colden had gone to New York. Bartram had brought him "Some Meterological Conjectures" from Franklin.[4] The family made them welcome, and they spent the afternoon plant collecting nearby. After supper they persuaded Colden's daughter, Jane, a very capable botanist, to show them her plant collections. In the morning Colden's son took them to the home of Dr. Evan Jones to see his pines, and after dinner they collected arborvitae seeds from trees along the river. They spent a second night at Coldengham and were urged to stay longer since Bartram had a fever. He felt capable of traveling, however, and declined their hospitality.

At Catskill Bartram hired a guide for four shillings. He was still feeling very unwell when they started up the mountain the next morning. The steep and difficult climb, in addition to his fever, made him painfully thirsty. He kept looking for the cool springs that he remembered from his previous visit, but most of them had dried up. They were halfway up the mountain before they found water. By that time Bartram felt so weak that he let the guide carry his pack and still had all he could do to force himself to the top. They reached the summit about noon and picnicked by North Lake. After an hour's rest in this beautiful place, Bartram felt sufficiently revived to undertake a three-mile walk to see the "Great Falls of the Kaaterskill." They circled the lower end of the lake where the yellow buds of "opulas" (*Viburnum opula* L.) peeped out from beneath low branches of balm of gilead firs, hemlock, and spruce.

As they made their way toward the falls they found a ledge of rock five feet above the ground and large enough to shelter 100 men.[5] They left their packs there and followed the stream down to a series of small falls and finally found the one "great gulph that swallowed all down." They dropped stones down the falls and counted until they could hear them reach bottom, estimating the sheer drop to be one hundred feet. On their way back Billy, leading the way, saw what he took to be a great mushroom and was about to kick it. Fortunately, he discovered his error and warned the others of a rattlesnake. Bartram wrapped his handkerchief around a stick and poked it at the snake, which ignored him. It did sniff at Bartram's hat when presented with it but then withdrew. As it was departing the guide killed it, saying that he never allowed a snake to escape.[6]

They returned to their rocky ledge, where Bartram was very glad to lie down while Billy and the guide made a large fire and prepared beds of moss. Bartram hoped that he might feel better next morning but actually felt worse. Nevertheless, they spent the morning collecting seeds, and since nothing would persuade the guide to climb and Bartram did not trust Billy to do so, he climbed a number of tall firs himself. Seeds of all kinds were surprisingly scarce, but they collected what they could. They also gathered small plants of firs, spruces, pines, striped maples, dwarf cornel, "herb paris" (mayapple), and others. In the afternoon they made their way down the mountain, reaching their lodging at sunset. Bartram was too exhausted to eat and afraid that he might be too ill to travel next day. Much to his surprise, his fever seemed to be gone in the morning.

They headed south, stopping from time to time to rest their horses and investigate for seeds and plants. At one point they climbed a crumbling cliff and found marine fossils. They amused themselves sliding down "ye scaleing declivity often sinking to ye ancles in ye Mouldering scaley spoils of ye perpendicular rock." After having been caught in a deluge of rain, they stopped at the first house they could find and dried out by a fire. Billy had developed a fever and was glad to spend the night. Fortunately, both of them were able to travel next day and continued home without further problems.

Upon his return, Bartram was busy collecting seed locally and preparing his usual shipments for England. Four boxes were sent to "R. H. Prince of Wales," which were probably intended for Princess Augusta, her husband having died in 1751.[7] Bartram's collections and shipments in 1753 were the most impressive that he had ever achieved. In the *Gentleman's Magazine* for 24 February 1754 appeared "A List of Seeds of Forest Trees and flowering Shrubs gather'd in Pensilvania, the Jerseys and New York, by John and William Bartram, and sent over the last year to their Correspondent, being the largest Collection that has ever been imported into this Kingdom." The list contained exactly 100 items. Some months later a comparable list of seeds for sale by N. Powell & Co., Fetterlane, Holborn, was published by the same journal and referred to Bartram. Nathaniel Powell had written to Bartram on 14 August 1753 requesting "a box of seeds, pray let me have as great a variety of new sorts as possible. Consider that I have them to sell again, let me have larger quantities than you send Gentlemen for thare own use." He did not suggest that he was prepared to pay a higher price.[8]

Bartram's five-guinea box now became completely standardized, but the content was impressive. There were seeds from more than 100 different species of trees and shrubs, varying only slightly when some seed became unavailable. The quantities of each are not known but certainly varied with the size of the seed concerned and its rarity.[9] Preparing these boxes for shipment was a chore of no small proportions. Presumably Bartram made the wooden boxes himself or with the assistance of his sons as they became old enough to help. The actual packing was most onerous to Bartram, as he indignantly wrote Collinson who had made a suggestion of carelessness on John's part:

> I have this week received my dear peters letter of May by ye packet which at first sight allmost made my Heart leap for Joy but when I read but for want of care & exactness or perhaps left to some careless person to pack up one of ye Boxes had but 8 sorts of seeds instead of 104 this knocked me down at once   but considering this was not ye 1st or 2d or third time that I have been rashly censored & reproached when I have hazarded life & limb both my own & childrens   using my utmost endeavour to oblige my correspondents I revived again   surely you must think I am a careless fool When I know from long experience that ye least neglect will heap coals of fire upon my head: but ye method I take its impossible to make such a mistake   I make up ye Boxes ready before I begin to pack   then I set one half in my room where I

William Bartram (1739–1823)

pack them & mark those which is for perticular persons then
I divide my seeds in two parts   then measures or numbers
each box its share with its number which is entered in ye
catalogue as thay are put in   I assist in every box & trust no
living creature but my two sons which is very carefull. I
dayly searcheth every box while they are packing & placeth
every list & lid to every box & marks them myself help to
load every one & sees thair shiped but I cant watch them all
along after until thay come to your hands nor keep them
from being rifeled neither on board ye ship nor after thay are
landed:[10]

Collinson was often horrified at the state of Bartram's shipments when they arrived in England. Sometimes the sailors had
neglected to water the plants or seawater had ruined them. Mice
and rats burrowed into the boxes of seeds. Sometimes it was the
contents which caused the trouble. Live insects, sent inadvertently,
damaged plants or seeds. Labels rotted or became detached. A present of a squash for Collinson became overripe, exuding its yellow
stain over other items.[11] There were cases of theft, with the boxes
left partly filled. More destructive were the delays in sailing occa-
sioned by bad weather, causing shipments to be partly or completely ruined.

The number of Bartram's overseas correspondents increased
in 1754. Franklin showed him a letter from Thomas Francis Dalibard (1709–79), a French scientist who had translated Franklin's
electrical experiments. Dalibard wrote that he was sending his
Florae Parisiensis Prodromus (Paris, 1749) to Bartram.[12] The latter
was delighted and immediately sent seeds and specimens to the
Frenchman.[13] In January, George Edwards presented a paper on
the ruffed grouse to the Royal Society.[14] The description he gave of
the bird was that which Bartram had sent to Collinson in 1750.
With the latter's permission, Edwards took an exact copy of Bartram's letter to be included in his *Essays Upon Natural History and
other Miscellaneous Subjects*.[15] He used the two birds that Bartram
sent to Collinson as models for his print of the grouse and as type
specimens for *Tetrao Umbellus*. From this beginning, a correspondence between Edwards and Bartram developed. Bartram supplied
Edwards with information about various birds and other animals,
some of which he included in his *Essays*. He also used items from

Illustration of ruffed grouse which Bartram sent to George Edwards in 1750. It accompanied the article "A Letter to Mr. Peter Collinson, F.R.S. concerning the Pheasant of Pennsylvania and the Otis Minor. By Mr. George Edwards, College of Physicians," *Philosophical Transactions of the Royal Society* 48 (1754):499.

Bartram's Onondago journal and his notes on the bears' custom of seeking snails and slugs under the bark of old trees. Bartram sent Edwards an account of snowbirds and arranged for Billy to send him specimens of the small birds that Edwards wanted.[16] Variations in the migratory habits of birds particularly interested Bartram:

Many birds in their migrations, are observed to go in flocks, as the geese, brants, pigeons, and blackbirds; others flutter and hop about from tree to tree, or upon the ground, feeding backwards and forwards, interspersed so that their progressive movement is not commonly observed. Our blue, or rather ash-coloured, great herons, and the white ones, do not observe a direct progression, but follow the banks of rivers—sometimes flying from one side to the other, sometimes a little backwards, but generally northward, until all places be supplied sufficiently where there is a conveniency of food; for when some arrive at a particular place, and find as many there before them as can readily find food, some of them move forward, and some stay behind. For all these wild creatures, of one species, generally seem of one community; and rather than quarrel, will move still a farther distance, where there is more plenty of food—like Abraham and Lot; but most of our domestic animals are more like their masters: every one contends for his own dung-hill, and is for driving all off that come to encroach upon them.

It is very probable that many kinds of birds, in their migrations, fly out of our sight, so high as to be unobserved,—as for instance, our Hooping Cranes, in their passage from Florida to Hudson's Bay. They fly in flocks of about half a score, so exceedingly high as scarcely to be observed, but by the particular noise of their loud hooping. We then can but just see them, though so particularly directed where to look for them. Altho such a very large bird thair flight is near circular with a progression in lines after this manner ◌◌◌◌◌ one after ye other by which we have an opertunity of observing thair motion by seeing & hearing for several minits time (but there may be millions of smaller birds fly over our heads much lower than these & not one of them seen) next to these of our larger fowl flyeth lower   ye brant then ye geese then pidgeons then blackbirds I mean in thair highest stages of flight in thair migrations.[17]

During the early summer of 1754 Bartram received from Collinson one of the many botanic publications of John Hill (c. 1716–75), probably some of the early parts of *The British Herbal*. Bartram was well pleased with it, although he found it "to be very far from being exact, true, or fully intelligible: on the contrary, he hath not gone half way through with it. There are many great omissions, and errors, I suppose for want of opportunity to examine the subjects himself; and doubtless there are also neglects, by being concerned in other business, which diverted him from taking so much notice of minute particulars, as he might otherwise have done: yet nothwithstanding these deficiencies, there are many curious observations, and certain truths contained in it."[18] Hill was a highly controversial character, and Collinson was one of many who disapproved of him. However, knowing that Bartram had enjoyed Hill's herbal, Collinson sent his friend a copy of the doctor's *History of Plants* in June 1756.[19] Had Bartram seen *A Review of the Works of the Royal Society*, he might have shared Collinson's feelings about Hill. In it Hill berated the society for referring to Bartram as an M.D.: *"John Bartram* is an Inhabitant of Pennsylvania, a Planter of the meaner Sort; so mean, indeed, that he owes the little Knowledge we have of him, to his having been some Years employed, at a very small Price, to travel over his own and some of the neighbouring Colonies, to Collect the Seeds of the *American* Trees, for the Curious here."[20] With his well-known brashness, Hill, a few years later, ordered several pounds of various medicinal plants from Bartram, closing his letter "I always have, and always shall espouse your interest."[21]

Bartram and Billy went to the Catskills again in the late summer of 1754. They ascended the mountain by a different route, several miles from where they had climbed previously. The ground was almost covered with wild lilies-of-the-valley under mountain cherry trees forty feet tall. Bartram's favorite striped maples were abundant, and there were thousands of white birch. The Bartrams again visited Coldengham. As a small token of appreciation of former hospitality, Bartram brought his hostess a gift of some of his best Dutch bulbs, including some fine tulips and snowdrops. Mrs. Colden was not at home, but the family planted the bulbs for her and her son David wrote her of the "gaudy shew" that she would have the following summer.[22]

Dr. Colden was at home, and he and Bartram had many things to discuss. Among these was Franklin's *Observations Concerning the Increase of Mankind*. Colden had written to Franklin some months previously that he was "exceedingly pleased" with it but agreed with "our friend Bartram that the last paragraph is the only one liable to Exception, and I wish it had been rather somewhere in the midle than at the end of that discourse because the reader should be most fully satisfied when you take leave of him." The manuscript had already gone to be printed so it was too late to modify the ending, but it was omitted in later editions. Franklin had deplored the "darkening" of the white population by the importation of negroes and wished that the population of whites was greater.[23]

During the Bartrams' visit, Colden had another visitor who delighted both Colden and Bartram. Dr. Alexander Garden (1730–91), even though a much younger man than either, had much in common with them. Like Colden he was a Scot, and like both men he had an avid interest in natural history in all of its aspects. He had studied both at Marischal College in Aberdeen and at the University of Edinburgh, where he attended Charles Alston's botany classes. He had emigrated to South Carolina in 1752 and was practicing there. Like Mitchell, Garden had come north hoping to recuperate from a general debility. He questioned Bartram closely about many things, especially minerals and fossils, which he was eager to collect. Garden was much impressed by Bartram's "strong natural thoughts on gems, as to their *structure, use, time and properties*" and thought it a shame that he did not know and understand Loefling's *Dissertation on Gems*. Both Colden and Bartram showed the younger man letters that they had received from Linnaeus. Garden gave them glowing accounts of the flora and fauna around Charles Town, and Bartram promised himself and Garden to make an expedition to the Carolinas. He asked Garden to send him seeds of a number of plants that he wanted, and he extracted a promise that Garden would stop for a visit at Philadelphia on his way south, if at all possible.[24] The Bartrams made their way home while Garden spent some time in the mountains collecting rock specimens, to some of which he had been directed by Bartram.

The doctor arrived in Philadelphia in mid-October and called on Bartram one day, accompanied by Dr. Bond and Governor Tinker. Garden was amazed by the "ease, Gaiety & happy Alacrity" with which Bartram received his unannounced guests. He urged them to stay for dinner, but the governor was expecting guests himself and had to leave. Since there had been no time for Garden to really visit, Bartram went to town one day and insisted that he come out to see his garden. As they rode toward Kingsessing, Bartram kept Garden so occupied pointing out rocks, trees, and other plants that he forgot how hungry he was. Equally fascinating to the doctor was Bartram's library, where he first saw Linnaeus' *Critica Botanica* and *Systema Naturae*. Garden said that Bartram did not let him escape for two days, "during which time I breakfasted, Dined & supped Sleep't & was regaled on Botany & Mineralogy, in which he has some excellent Notions & grand thoughts." Garden found the diet nourishing, for he returned with a young Jamaican doctor and spent another night before he departed for Charles Town.[25]

A few months after his return, Garden used his meeting with Colden and Bartram as an excuse to initiate a correspondence with both Gronovius and Linnaeus. To the latter he commented about his new friends: "How happy should I be to pass my life with men so distinguished by genius, acuteness, and liberality, as well as by eminent botanical learning and experience!—men in whom the greatest knowledge and skill are united to the most amiable candour!"[26] This was high praise indeed from the young doctor, who was very caustic on occasion concerning the intellectual interests of most of his South Carolina colleagues. He wrote belatedly to Bartram, thanking him for his hospitality, and sent some of the seeds that Bartram had requested. Bartram, in return, sent Garden a choice collection of Dutch bulbs.[27]

For some time Bartram had been observing with great interest Billy's increased preoccupation with drawing. Even as a small boy he had shown aptitude for this sort of thing. He had made some quite good sketches of birds, and his father had encouraged him to draw plants. Early in 1753 Bartram had sent some of these sketches to Collinson, who declared that Billy's "pretty performances please me much."[28] Perhaps because of Billy's artistic ability or his delicate health, or simply because his father recognized unusual qualities in him, Bartram had him entered in the

"Academy" in 1752.[29] He was the only one of Bartram's children so favored. Franklin had proposed the academy (which was to become the University of Pennsylvania) in 1749. It officially opened 7 January 1751 and was housed in the building constructed for the preaching of the Reverend Whitefield. The curriculum offered was broad: Latin, Greek, German, English, history, geography, chronology, logic and rhetoric, writing, gauging, navigation, astronomy, "drawing in perspective," "other Mathematical Sciences," natural and mechanical philosophy, and still other subjects. Tuition was four pounds per year, and there was an admission fee of twenty shillings.

In the spring of 1755 Bartram sought Collinson's advice: "My son William is just turned of sixteen. It is now time to propose some way for him to get his living by. I don't want him to be what is commonly called a gentleman. I want to put him to some business by which he may, with care and industry, get a temperate, reasonable living. I am afraid that botany and drawing will not afford him one, and hard labour don't agree with him. . . . Pray, my dear Peter, let me have thy opinion about it."[30] Bartram had thought a medical career might be the solution but never could persuade Billy even to read books on the subject. When Garden volunteered to take Billy as his apprentice, Bartram had to write the doctor that Billy "longs to be with thee; but it is more for the sake of Botany than Physic or Surgery."[31] Bartram concluded that busy doctors had little time for drawing so perhaps a mercantile career was the answer.

In the meantime he set Billy to drawing turtles. Since he was still a student, Billy's time was limited to Seventh Day afternoons and First Day mornings. His father forwarded some of his drawings to Collinson, who found one of a marsh hawk admirable and thought that neither Edwards nor Georg Ehret (1708–80), England's most renowned botanical illustrator, could do much better. The drawing of the horned turtle was incomparable.[32] When Billy had completed his series of turtle and tortoise sketches, which were accompanied by his father's remarks, Collinson called the attention of the editor of the *Gentleman's Magazine* to the fact that Catesby's *Natural History of Carolina* did not include a tortoise: "Wherefore I procur'd these accurate drawings to be taken from a living subject, by William Bartram, an ingenious young man, to be engraven for your Magazine; which, if you get well executed, may probably encourage the artist to supply us with other curious and to us, unknown productions of nature to supply the deficiencies of Catesby and his brethren."[33]

Billy continued to draw, and as the years went by his artistic gift was acknowledged by all. There were frequent remarks by Collinson, who predicted that Billy would "be another Ehret, his performances are so elegant."[34] When Collinson showed the young man's drawings to that famous illustrator, Ehret admired particularly a painting of the "Red Centaury."[35] Not only were the drawings and paintings exquisite in appearance, but they were usually accurate so that they were of value not only artistically but scientifically.

In addition to worrying over the problems of his son's career, Bartram was disturbed by the military situation during that summer of 1755. For several years the English and the French had been trying to outmaneuver each other in a contest for North American Indian territory that eventually culminated in the French and Indian War. In June 1754 Franklin had been one of twenty-three delegates, representing six colonies, who met at Albany, New York, for a conference with 150 Iroquois chiefs of the Six Nations. The chiefs were less impressed by English promises than by French fortifications and made no assurances. Franklin was one of several who made proposals for a union of the colonies for their mutual defense, but these were not well received by either the colonists or the English.[36]

Throughout his life, Bartram had very mixed feelings about Indians. As a Quaker he was inherently a peaceful man, avoiding conflicts of any kind. As an honest and accurate observer of the world around him, he could recognize both Indian virtues and inhumane treatment of Indians by Europeans. At the same time he was a realist, and it was more difficult for him to take the detached view of the Indian problem that Collinson and his Quaker friends in London espoused. Although he never commented on the matter in his correspondence, he must have been greatly influenced in his youth by the fact that his father and most of his Carolina neighbors had been slaughtered by Indians with whom they thought they were friendly. He had seen something of Indians in his boyhood days at Darby, when they came frequently to the house.[37] When Bartram began plant collecting, Indians became increasingly a factor that he had to consider. He traveled thousands of miles through thinly settled or unsettled areas, usually alone or accompanied by

one of his young sons. Indian-white relations were always in a
state of flux and subject to abrupt change as they were manipu-
lated by both French and English. Even at times when the Indians
were supposed to be peaceful, a single unarmed man with a good
horse would seem to have been a temptation to those who encountered him far from home.

Accordingly, Bartram's travels were always planned with due
regard for the current state of Indian relations, and at times he had
to forego trips because he knew traveling would be too dangerous.
It is strange that he seems seldom to have met Indians in his travels or to have had trouble with them. He did have his favorite horse
stolen, but not necessarily by Indians, and he did mention an occasional meeting: "Many years past, in our peaceable times, far beyond our mountains, as I was walking in a path with an Indian
guide hired for two dollars, an Indian man met me and pulled off
my hat in great passion, and chawed it all around—I suppose to
show me that they would eat me if I came in that country again."[38]

In the fall of 1754 Bartram planned that his next trip would
be to the mountains of Virginia and Carolina. By March 1755, however, he told Collinson he had been "informed of ye great danger of
travelling near those delightful situations I must forbear at present, but am sadly afraid your ministry will be fooled by ye french
who no doubt will pretend thay will not act in a hostil maner in
order that you may forbid us to drive them back." A month later he
wrote, "Our philadelphia people seem at ease, and disolved in luxury. I think two twenty-gun ships could take the town in two hours
time."[39]

It finally became apparent to the English that military action
was essential to counter French activity in the colonies. General
Edward Braddock was sent to assume the post of commander-in-
chief of British forces, arriving at Alexandria, Virginia, in April
1755. He planned to direct his first campaign toward forcing the
French out of Fort Duquesne, which they had constructed after
driving Captain William Trent from the fort that he had started
there. Again Franklin became involved. The Pennsylvania Assembly asked him to visit Braddock, ostensibly in his capacity as Postmaster General but primarily to do what he could to counteract
Braddock's reputed prejudice against the assembly. The general
and his men were camped at Frederick, Maryland, waiting for men
to return who had been scouring Virginia and Maryland for horses

and wagons needed for the move against Fort Duquesne. Franklin spent several days with Braddock and managed to reassure him of the good intentions of the assembly. While he was there, the men seeking horses and wagons returned with only a small fraction of those needed. Franklin was persuaded to help obtain 150 wagons and 1,500 additional horses in Pennsylvania and did so.[40]

Franklin had "conceiv'd some doubts and some fears for the event of the campaign" as he listened to the general and his officers. Finally, he could not resist telling Braddock that, while he did not doubt of the success of his men if and when they reached and attacked the fort, he was concerned about the problem of getting there: "The only danger I apprehend of obstruction to your march is from ambuscades of Indians, who, by constant practice, are dextrous in laying and executing them; and the slender line, near four miles long, which your army must make, may expose it to be attack'd by surprise in its flanks, and to be cut like a thread into several pieces, which, from their distance, can not come up in time to support each other. He smil'd at my ignorance, and reply'd, 'These savages may, indeed, be a formidable enemy to your raw American militia, but upon the King's regular and disciplin'd troops, sir, it is impossible they should make any impression.'"[41]

Just how tragically mistaken Braddock was has been many times described but never more vividly than by Bartram:

both town & country is now in ye utmost astonishment & moved as ye leaves in ye trees with a wind & ye sea with a storm at ye relations of such a tragical sceen that tho it is confirmed by several letters daly for near a week yet it is so incredible that it seems more like a dream than real fact: but I doubt ye dreadfull consequences will soon convince us that it is too true; General Bradock is overthrown   600 of his men slain & wounded   most of his officers killed & ye artilery taken by 300 Indians. Oh stupid obstinate Briton: that would not be moved By his soldiers falling round him in garments stained with blood nor ye agonies & groans of his valient Captains at his feet rolling in gore nor ye earnest entreaty of those more superficially wounded who begged leave to take 200 or 300 men & rouse ye hidden enemy up from behind ye trees & bushes from whence thay took such sure Aim that thair balls seldom failed of opening canals for ye efusion of

sanguin streams while our mens offenceless bead onely sa-
luted its mother earth or grained ye bark of senseless trees.
general would not break his ranks or turn or turn [sic] out of
his ould beaten path   his foot he kept in a lump   his Captains on horseback all exposed to ye fire of ye secreated
enemy who could not desire a better opertunity to embrace ye
limbs of those who if thay had liberty could have bound them
hand & foot   Oh how are ye french now strengthened by our
spoil & enriched by our treasure   thay have arms to fight us
& cloaths to keep them warm all brought to their dore & a
great road ready cut at ye great toil of ye provinces   this is
now common report.[42]

Along the eastern coast things were still fairly peaceable, and
Bartram decided to visit New England, which he had long intended. Again Billy would accompany his father. Bartram had
some prejudice against New Englanders, wanting "to se what sort
of a clownish sanctified people thay are. several of them have come
to my house   I showed them what civility I was master of."[43] He
had had another unfortunate experience with the Yankees. At the
request of Franklin, he had sent ginseng specimens to two Bostonians, who neither thanked him nor even acknowledged the gift.[44]
Bartram was glad to be leaving home, where he could only survey
the weather's devastations helplessly. It had been another cruel
year. There had been only three rainless days all winter until
April. Then, early in June, a hard frost had killed most of the crops,
even those two feet tall. This was followed by one of the most severe droughts the province had ever known. Now the hayfields lay
brown and powdery underfoot, and even the leaves on the trees
were curling and withering.[45]

One objective of this expedition was to call on Jared Eliot
(1685–1763), a Presbyterian minister of Killingsworth, Connecticut. He was a graduate of Yale and practiced medicine but was also
intensely interested in agriculture.[46] He and Bartram had been corresponding for four years. On Christmas Eve of 1751 Franklin had
written to Eliot, "I send you also enclos'd a Letter from my Friend
John Bartram, whose Journal you have read. He corresponds with
several of the greatest Naturalists in Europe and will be proud of
an Acquaintance with you. I make no Apologies for Introducing
him to you; for tho a plain illiterate Man, you will find he has

Merit. And since for want of Skill in Agriculture I cannot converse with you on that valuable Subject, I am pleas'd that I have procur'd you two Correspondents who can."[47]

Eliot and Bartram exchanged several lengthy epistles on agricultural subjects that were important to them both. Collinson did much to encourage the friendship by forwarding recent agricultural pamphlets from England, which they both read and discussed by letter, particularly those of Richard Jackson who had written the preface to Bartram's journal. When Bartram had requested information on modern English agricultural practices, Collinson had sent him some of Jackson's essays.[48] Bartram was able to give Eliot the benefit of his extensive travels with a description of the soils of many of the provinces. Eliot had asked Franklin how the teeth were placed in a certain type of hay rake, but Franklin was unable to answer his question. Instead he wrote to Eliot on 31 August 1755 that Bartram was "upon one of his rambles in Search of Knowledge, & intends to view both your Sea Coast & back Country," thinking that he might answer the query. Franklin added, "He delivers you this, and I need not recommend him to you, for you are already acquainted with his Merit tho not with his Face & person. You will have a great deal of Pleasure in one another's Conversation; I wish I could be within hearing; but this cannot be."[49] Not satisfied with this, Franklin also gave Bartram a formal note of introduction: "I wrote to you yesterday, and now I write again . . . For I not only send you *manuscript* but *living* Letters. The first may be short, but the latter will be longer and yet more agreable. Mr. Bartrams I believe you will find to be at least 20 folio Pages, large Paper, well filled on the Subjects of Botany, Fossils, Husbandry, and the first Creation. . . . Read them both. 'Twill take you at least a Week. . . ."[50]

Traveling for the Bartrams was simplified since the road from New York to Boston went through the Connecticut coastal towns including Clinton, near which Eliot lived. Bartram found Eliot much as he had imagined: "a good sort of man, and endeavours for the general good of mankind." Having corresponded for so long, Bartram and Eliot felt like old friends immediately. Eliot showed Bartram around his farm and pointed out that some of it was quite useless since there were many acres of salt marsh lying along Long Island Sound. At the time Bartram could think of no solution to the problem but later suggested that, if Eliot plowed the drained marsh several times and planted it with Indian corn, he thought that after a few years meadow grass or wheat could easily be raised. With the exposure of the land to the action of the sun, the rain, and the frost, much of the salt would soon be leached out. Among other subjects they discussed were methods of splitting rock. Bartram said that he had been told that in some countries grinding stones and mill-stones were split by driving wooden pegs around a cylinder. For some reason Eliot thought that his friend had used this method for splitting stones. Later Bartram disabused him of the idea and wrote him lengthy instructions for the method he did use. Eliot spoke of his friend, Thomas Clap, rector of Yale College. Bartram and Billy called on Clap, and on their return home Billy sent some drawings to him in a tube filled with indigo seed. Some of the sketches were intended for Eliot and were so marked, but Dr. Clap never delivered them.[51]

On their way home, the Bartrams traveled inland to explore a bit. Bartram was interested to find that some of the New England plants were similar to plants that had been sent to him from Acadia and Newfoundland.[52] They came upon a drained beaver pond near the Connecticut River in which was growing a handsome dwarf *Crataegus*. It was only two feet tall but drooping with the weight of a fine crop of juicy black berries. In order to extract the seeds they put the berries in a bag, squeezing the juice through,

Jared Eliot (1685–1763)

much as one does in jelly making. Bartram took a rooted plant home, which grew well. To his surprise, it was as covered with berries the following July as it had been the day they found it, 11 September.[53] They crossed the North River (the Hudson) south of the Highlands, for Bartram wanted to show Billy the extraordinary falls on "Second River." The rocky cliffs banking the river are only ten feet apart at this point, where the water plunges down sixty feet vertically. There they found the same species of "herb paris" that they had collected in New England.[54]

ELEVEN

Affairs of Family and
of Conscience

U PON THEIR return home in late December
1754, Bartram and Billy found everyone
alarmed by Indian attacks encouraged by the French. There were
scalpings and murders of families in the Tulpehocken Valley near
Weiser's home. There had been raids near the Delaware Water Gap,
and seventy-eight people were killed in the Jerseys at Minisink.
Almost the whole area around Easton had to be evacuated. A reward of £700 was offered for the heads of the Indian leaders, Singas
and Captain Jacobs, and £350 each for those of the Delaware chiefs.
Franklin and 160 men of the Philadelphia Regiment were sent to
Gnadenhuten and were reported to be building a fort.[1] The great
numbers of pacifist Quakers presented a problem in Pennsylvania's
defense, and the situation worsened daily. Bartram described the
attacks to Collinson:

By what we can understand, by the reports of our back inhabitants, most of the Indians which are so cruel, are such as
were almost daily familiars at their houses, ate, drank,
cursed and swore together—were even intimate playmates;
and now, without any provocation, destroy all before them
with fire, ball, and tomahawk. They commonly, now, shoot ri-
fles, with which they will, at a great distance, from behind a
tree, fence, ditch, or rock, or under the cover of leaves, take
such sure aim as seldom misseth their mark. If they attack a
house that is pretty well manned, they creep behind some
fence, or hedge, or tree, and shoot red-hot slugs, or punk, into
the roof, and fire the house over their heads; and if they run

167

out, they are sure to be shot at, and most or all of them killed. If they come to a house where the most of the family are women and children, they break into it, kill them all, plunder the house, and burn it with the dead in it; or if any escape out, they pursue and kill them. If the cattle are in the stable, they fire it, and burn the cattle: if they are out, they are shot, and the barn burnt.

If our captains pursue them, in the level woods, they skip from tree to tree like monkeys; if in the mountains, like wild goats, they leap from rock to rock, or hide themselves, and attack us in flank and rear, when, but the minute before, we pursued their track, and thought they were all before us. They are like the Angel of Death—give us the mortal stroke, when we think ourselves secure from danger.

O Pennsylvania! thou that was the most flourishing and peaceable province in North America, art now scourged by the most barbarous creatures in the universe.[2]

Meanwhile Bartram continued to be concerned about a career for Billy and sought advice. He wrote to Collinson that because "Botany and drawing are his darling delight," he had considered surveying as a career for Billy. It would give him the opportunity to collect and study plants. Unfortunately, there were already five surveyors for every opening. Collinson suggested that Billy might become a printer: "Never let him reproach thee, and say, 'Father, if thou had put me to some business by which I might get my bread, I should have by my industry lived in life as well as other people.' Let the fault be his, not thine if he does not."[3] This was just what Bartram feared.

The original suggestion of printing as a career for Billy had come from Franklin, who had offered to take him as an apprentice.[4] One evening at the end of May, when Bartram was with his friend, he told Franklin that he appreciated his offer but had some reservations about it. He reasoned with Franklin "about the difficulty of falling into good business; that, as he well knew, he was the only printer that did ever make a good livelihood by it, in this place, though many had set up, both before and since he did, and that was by his extraordinary and superior abilities, and close application; and merchandizing was very precarious; and extreme difficult to make remittances to Europe. He [Franklin] sate and paused awhile, then said that there was a profitable business which he thought was now upon the increase; that there was a very ingenious man in town, who had more business than he could well manage himself, and that was engraving; and which he thought would suit BILLY well."[5] When nothing came of Franklin's suggestion, Bartram returned to his earlier idea of a mercantile job. He apprenticed Billy to Captain James Child, whose son Billy had known at the academy. Child had been master of the *Beulah* in 1748,[6] then had opened a store on Water Street, between Market and Arch streets, in 1750. There he sold a great variety of merchandise: dry goods, pewter, snuff, window glass, frying pans, tin and earthenware, copper kettles, and other items.[7] By September 1757 Bartram could report to Collinson: "My Billy comes on finely with Captain Child, who is very kind to him, and keeps him very close to his business."[8]

Billy's older brother, Moses, had had no doubts about what he wanted to do and had gone to sea at an early age. In 1751 the nineteen-year-old was stranded in London, his ship having been summarily sold from under him. While trying to discover a berth on a westbound ship, he called on Collinson, who was delighted to see the son of his old friend. Moses' good nature and frankness appealed to Collinson, and he listened to his account of his unsuccessful search for a chance to work his passage home. There were few ships going west at this time of year, and those that were were bound for Maryland, Virginia, or the West Indies. Collinson would not hear of Moses going to the West Indies because he would have to "associate with our London common sailors, who are a most profligate crew, and, if possible will never be easy until they make him like themselves." Collinson bought clothing for Moses, as Bartram had asked, and entertained him when he could.[9]

One fine September day, Collinson took Moses out to Ridgeway House.[10] In 1749 Collinson's father-in-law, Michael Russell, had died and left his home at Mill Hill to his daughter, Mary. Collinson had just spent the last two years moving his garden from his country villa on the Surrey side of the Thames at Camberwell, Peckham, to Ridgeway House.[11] Moses studied the garden with great interest for he knew that his father would want a precise and detailed description. He found many things wanting which the Bartrams could supply. It was December before he finally persuaded the last Pennsylvania ship to let him work his passage home. He kept so busy for several weeks before they sailed that he had no time to visit Collinson in the country and could do so only rarely in the evenings in town. Nevertheless Collinson admired his industry, which he was sure would eventually "turn to his advantage."[12] Moses carried home laurel and horse chestnut plants, which Bartram had been unable to grow from seed, and part of the preface to Colden's book, all gifts from Collinson.[13]

Moses continued his life at sea. It involved great uncertainty, for he seldom knew where the next voyage would take him. His parents never knew where he might be until a letter suddenly appeared from some faraway place. Being young and adventurous Moses found this life appealing, but his parents worried over the dangers of a maritime career. Collinson shared their concern about his young friend. He wrote in January 1756: "Poor Moses has been tumbling and tossing about the world."[14] Twice, Moses' ships took him to London where he enjoyed visits with Collinson. By May 1756 Moses was master of the snow *Corsley*, belonging to Captain Child.[15] Still the young man continued to baffle Collinson: "Moses is yett Here, I wish'd he had gone home in some of those ships but he will Try his Fortune in an adventure I don't understand."[16] In

Moses Bartram (1732–1809)

July 1757 the Bartrams frantically tried to locate Moses. Two prominent Quaker merchants, Edward Pennington and Samuel Shoemaker, were building a ship.[17] The two men were considering the appointment of Moses as master of the new vessel and had consulted Captain Child in regard to the young man's ability. The Bartrams had received three letters from Moses that spring but had no idea where he could be reached at the moment and were afraid that he might miss this fine opportunity.[18] Their suspense was not relieved until October when Moses landed in New York after a prosperous voyage to the northern ports of Europe, which had enhanced his reputation. Moses immediately set to work supervising the finishing of the ship of which he had been made master and "to whom ye vesail & Cargo" was consigned.[19]

There were two sons who apparently never gave their parents any serious anxiety, Isaac and James. Isaac was the child of Bartram and his first wife, Mary. Little is known of Isaac's education and training, but like his father he was interested in medicinal plants as well as other aspects of natural history.[20] He had been apprenticed to an apothecary, possibly Thomas Say. The colonial apothecary was somewhat comparable to today's general practitioner except that he filled prescriptions for other doctors as well as for his own patients.[21] Isaac had spent three to five years mixing medicines, studying anatomy, and learning to pull teeth, to bleed patients, and to apply leeches. In 1756, at the age of thirty-two, he went into partnership with Say.[22] Their shop was at the Sign of the Bottle and the Three Bolt Heads in Second Street, where most of the apothecary shops were located. There they mixed "all sorts of chemical preparations" and herb prescriptions in addition to selling patent medicines imported from England. They fitted out medicine chests for ship captains, and their store had some of the versatility of today's drugstore, once advertising "a riding chair, tobacco engine, press and boxes, parchment, wool combs, a large boiler, sundry locks and hinges, sundry sorts of saddlery ware, fringe, worsted reins, &c, &c."[23] Isaac married Sarah Elfreth in 1747, by whom he had nine children.[24]

James, oldest son of Ann and John, married Sarah Bunting, daughter of Samuel and Sarah Fearne Bunting, in 1751.[25] He farmed the land that his father had bought from Andrew Jonason. It lay on the northwest side "of the great road leading to Darby," some of which his father gave him in return for an annual payment of £2 to his mother.²⁶ James did not have the same congeniality with his father as some of his brothers and was never mentioned in Bartram's letters. There had been another marriage in the family. On 17 December 1754 nineteen-year-old Mary married Benjamin Bonsall.²⁷ He was the son of Benjamin and Martha Fisher Bonsall and grandson of Richard Bonsall, who had come to Pennsylvania from Derbyshire the same year as had Mary's great-grandfather. This was a joyous occasion for the Bartrams. Aside from the fact that the two old families were united, Benjamin was "a very worthy rich young man" whose home was within sight of the Bartrams' and could be reached within a half hour's walk.²⁸

In July 1753 Bartram learned of the death of Collinson's wife the previous March. The *Gentleman's Magazine* had paid tribute to her kindly character in an obituary.²⁹ Bartram hastened to write to his "Dear Afflicted Friend:—As I have been once near, in some respects, in the same gloomy, disconsolate circumstance with thine, I believe I am in some measure qualified to sympathize with one of my dearest friends, in his close and tender affliction."³⁰

A month after writing his letter of condolence to Collinson, Bartram wrote to him again: "I am now very intent upon examining the true distinguishing characters of our forest trees, finding it a very difficult task—as I can have no help from either ancient or modern authors, they having taken no particular observation worth notice. I expect, by our worthy friend Benjamin, specimens of the evergreens of New England,—which I intend to compare with ours, and those of York government; so that I may give a particular account of the evergreens natural to our northern parts, which I hope to send thee, this fall or next spring—with a fuller account of our Oaks and Hickories; and for thy present amusement, I here send thee, as a specimen of my method of proceeding, a near perfect description of the characters of our Hop Hornbeam. . . ."³¹ He described not just evergreens and oaks but walnuts, birches, maples, chestnuts, alders, magnolias, gums, dogwoods, ashes, and viburnums.³²

Bartram even considered including shrubs "which will amount to near one hundred & fifty different species; in the describing of which I have the green specimens before me, taken from trees of midling growth neither too young or ould, too luxuriant or declining." He was well aware of the importance of describing a typical tree. Bartram added, "I first give the general character of each genus; then the description of each species with its particular distinguishing character by which it may be certainly known from other species, in what soil or situation so ever it is found growing in."[33] He included some descriptive items not usual at the time, among them the "form of growth" and the type of bark, both of which he found useful in winter identification of deciduous trees, especially oaks.[34] When he had completed the description of the viburnums, he concluded, "I have taken uncommon pains in describing ye Particular form of ye leaves & ramifications of ye nerves which seem most material of any part of ye plant to distinguish ye species from one another. With the different manner of growth of each species to which I have added ye common perticular appearance which is a signature originally implanted in all plants, shrubs, & trees & can no more be described by writing than ye perticular features of a man's face voice or behavior that distinguishes one man from another."[35]

When Collinson reviewed Bartram's dissertation on American oaks and hickories, he had mixed reactions. He found the descriptions excellent, yet he felt that Bartram had introduced too many species of oaks. There were only two species recognized in England. The differences between Bartram's "Lowland White Oak" and his "Mountain White Oak" could surely be attributed to their places of growth. Likewise the soil and situation caused the variation between the swamp and the mountain chestnut oaks. All Bartram had to do to determine whether or not they were distinct species was to plant the acorns in his garden and evaluate the results! Unless he did this, he might well "be arraigned with want of judgment to distinguish things aright."[36] Collinson was clearly a "lumper" and not a "splitter," but it was Bartram who was more nearly correct. There are at least twenty-seven species of oaks recognized today in the area with which Bartram was concerned.

In July 1754 Bartram replied to Collinson, "I am glad of your remarks on my deficiencies, which I hope you will favourably excuse, and consider that my descriptions were done, and specimens placed, in the greatest hurry; most of them by candlelight, or First days, being hurried in travelling, and gathering, drying and sorting seeds, or labour about my farm."[37] By November he had again heard from Collinson, and his usual calm disposition was beginning to show signs of irritation: "I received thy kind letter of July the 30th. Good grammar and good spelling, may please those who

are more taken with a fine superficial flourish than real truth; but
my chief aim was to inform my readers of the true, real, distinguishing characters of each genus, and where, and how, each species differed from one another, of the same genus: and if you find
that my descriptions are not agreeable with the specimens, pray let
me know where the disagreement is, and send my descriptions
back again that I may correct them,—or if they prove deficient,
that I may add farther observations; for I have no copy, and you
have the original. So, by all means, send my descriptions back
again by the first opportunity; for I have forgot what I wrote."[38]

In December, Bartram shipped a quire of oak specimens on
the *Myrtilla* in care of Captain Budden. He included Billy's sketches
of most of the oak species and all of the birch. He requested Collinson to compare these drawings with those of Catesby. Collinson
would then see that Catesby had not distinguished between "summer & winter acrons [*sic*]," the latter referring to acorns of the
black, red, and Spanish oaks, which require two years to mature.
Additionally Catesby had not delineated with care the manner in
which the leaves grew or the way the nerves projected, although
his leaf outlines were correct.[39] There was a matter of omission on
Collinson's part which irritated Bartram: "thee often year after
year desired me to send thee specimens of our evergreens & that
you knowed but little of that tribe (little to your Credit) in compli-
ance I collected with much pains at great distances most if not all
of ye evergreen trees & shrubs natural to our three or 4 governments in thair perfectest state & sent them carefully above A year
past & yet never since received one line mentioning whether thee
hath received them or not.& all ye reason I have to hope that thee
hath received them is that thee writes no more to ask about them
only those two or three I sent after from terra Labradore." Bartram
had some answer to his question when he read volume twenty-five
of the *Gentleman's Magazine* the following year. In it appeared two
short and superficial articles on pines by Collinson.[40]

Collinson gave the forest tree descriptions to Philip Miller to
examine, and he advised Bartram to contract his descriptions.
Miller believed that leaves and acorns were sufficient factors for
identification. Bartram disagreed. He felt that the type of bark and
form of growth of the tree were very important. From the latter
characteristic he was often able to identify different species of oak
from a distance of one-half mile to one mile, adding "I am sure he

must be very sharp-sighted that can know them, at half that distance, by their leaves, acorns, and cups all together."[41] As soon as Miller had completed his examination of Bartram's descriptions, Collinson sent them, along with Billy's drawings, to Gronovius. Months passed, and there was no word from Leiden. Finally, Gronovius returned Billy's drawings in February 1756, saying that he had found it impossible to find anyone to engrave them. Georg Ehret then agreed to undertake the engraving but gave no indication when he might be able to do so.[42] Apparently Collinson permitted the whole undertaking to die quietly.

The same volume of the *Gentleman's Magazine* that carried Collinson's articles on evergreens also carried an involuntary contribution by Bartram. In October 1754 Charles Alston created something of a stir in botanic circles by an article published in the same magazine. He had reported some experiments that he had performed which had led him to question the existence of different sexes in plants. A number of competent botanists had pretty well settled the matter, or so it was thought. Bartram and John Clayton did not receive their copies of the magazine until some months after their European friends, but in letters to Collinson both were quick to question the validity of Alston's experimental evidence. Collinson was so impressed that he had their comments published in the *Gentleman's Magazine*. Bartram had written:

In the Magazine I read Dr. Alston's observations on the mercury, spinage and hemp, the female produceing good seed at a great distance from the male, which seems curious, and may be true to appearance; yet I can't believe but that the female must be influenced by the male, tho' at a very great distance, as providence acts uniformly in all its operations: But yet it is not impossible, in case of accidents, but that some provision may be made in the female to act in both capacities, especially in what we call annual plants, that are male and female in distinct, separate plants; that if the female grow at too great a distance from the male to attract his farina, there may be produc'd some latent farina to impregnate the female part, altho' before invisible and inactive, and would have remain'd so unless called and rouzed up to assist in the greatest end of nature.

Many genuses of plants are male and female in distinct

trees; of which I have observed many of the fem. trees to have the same anthera, but not to discharge the farina, unless at great distance from the male tree; but this is not always the case; for the roots of *English* briony that I raised bore abundance of fine red berries, but all imperfect being nothing but skin, and watery juice.

I found a fine stalk of *Indian* corn, at a great distance; I cut off the male tassel as soon as it appeared, and there was produced a large ear, but no good grains upon it.

If we plant cucumbers, squashes or melons near the bitter gourd, the fruits of the first will be bitter as gall.—These experiments show how necessary the male farina is to the fructification of all seeds, and how liable plants are to be bastardized by bad neighbors of their own kindred.

This will give a hint how careful a curious gardener ought to be. The way to preserve a good species of any plant is to keep it separate from others of the same kind, that is not of so good a quality.[43]

Two years later, in November 1756, Bartram wrote to Philip Miller that he was sending "some of my observations on forrest trees tho its likely others have done it allready but I have not yet seen any such observations on ye female parts which is distinct on different branches of ye same tree from ye male parts   ye first I took notice of was ye black spruice fir black larix & ye bald cypress of Carolina   all which hath for severall years produced ye female cones to appearance as large & plump as ye most fruitfull with ye appearance of ye seed between each squama but no kernel in them . . . my scotch pine of 3 years old produced last spring several little cones (a specimen of which I sent thee last summer) which fell of ye later end of summer   I suppose for want of being empregnated in ye spring."[44]

In 1757 Franklin was in England as agent of the Pennsylvania Assembly, and Bartram missed him greatly. The loss of his friend's company was admittedly mixed with a certain amount of envy as he wrote to Franklin:

While thee art diverting thyself with the generous conversation of our worthy friends in Europe, and adding daily new acquisitions to thy former extensive stock of knowledge, by their free communications of their experimental improvements, thy poor, yet honest friend BARTRAM, is daily in mourning for the calamities of our provinces. Vast sums spent, and nothing done to the advantage of the King or country. How should I leap for joy, to see or hear that the British officers would prove by their *actions*, the zeal and duty to their prince and nation, they so much pretend in *words.* . . . Pray, my dear friend, bestow a few lines upon thy old friend. . . . They have a magical power of dispelling melancholy fumes, and cheering up my spirits, they are so like thy facetious discourse, in thy southern chamber, when we used to be together.[45]

Reports reached Philadelphia of Indian forays within sight of forts. In November Bartram wrote to Collinson that Fort William Henry "is lost & some few of ye men that ought to have defended it   our poor back inhabitants is weekly murdered. carried into captivity or drove away; ye finest army fleet & artilery that ever came into north America (which was sufficient to have shaken all of Canada & destroyed ye whole french fleet) merely sported themselves at halifax in erecting & taking a sham battery until ye french fleet got safe into lewis burge."[46]

It was in June 1757 that Collinson wrote, perhaps in jest: *"What didst mean, to send me so large a box of seeds? It made much trouble, and time, to part it."* John indignantly fired back, "I reflected upon myself what pains I had taken to collect those seeds, in several hundred miles' travel, drying, packing, boxing and shipping, and all to put my friend to trouble! Indeed, my good friend, if thee was not a widower, I should be inclined to tell thee that old age advanced as fast upon thee as upon myself."[47] Bartram's annoyance, if real, was but temporary, and he managed to collect some seeds of orchis in East Jersey for Collinson's son, Michael.[48]

This same year there was an affair which caused Bartram grave concern. Few incidents in his life show more clearly the independence of his mind, the courage of his conviction, and his refusal to pretend to believe what he did not find rationally convincing than does his difficulty with Darby Meeting in 1757–58. It will be remembered that his father was declared "out of unity" with the meeting when John was a small boy. This did not have any connection with Bartram's problem. He had been an active member of the meeting for fifty years since that incident.

The reason for Bartram's breach with the meeting, unlike that of his father, is very clear and a matter of record.[49] The overseers entered a complaint against him, charging his disbelief in the divinity of Jesus Christ and requested that he "attend meeting" and explain. When he failed to appear, a committee of four men was appointed and directed to "treat with" him. They were able to persuade him to appear at meeting and state his views, which he did. After some discourse, the matter was deferred to another meeting. The next meeting concluded that the charge appeared to be well founded but nonetheless directed that the committee, with two additional members, continue to attempt to show Bartram the error of his ways. When asked for a report the committee reluctantly admitted that not only were they unable to convince Bartram of the divinity of Christ but, on the contrary, he seemed more determined than ever to believe that Christ was a mortal man. Cases of such heresy were rare at this time, and it took considerable courage for Bartram to make such a stand and to maintain it against what appears to have been the virtually unanimous opposition of his fellow members. If he received support, it was not recorded.

Bartram's case was considered at meeting after meeting for well over a year. From the fifth month of 1757 until the seventh month of 1758 some aspect of the matter was debated. Bartram was given every opportunity not only to state his views but to change them, which he steadfastly refused to do. When a "Testification" against him was finally drawn up and deliberated upon, he declined to appear. When he was officially declared no longer a member of the Christian Society in 1758, Bartram continued to attend meeting with his family and friends for the rest of his days.

Let no one conclude from this incident that Bartram was either irreligious or contentious. Nothing could be farther from the case. On a great many occasions throughout his life he gave written testimony to his firm belief in the existence and goodness of God. A careful study leaves no doubt that this was the constant guiding influence of his life and that few have come closer to practicing what they preach. He was a very firm believer in the Golden Rule and practiced it.

There is possibly a connection between Bartram's refusal to

accept the divinity of Christ and his interest in the teachings of Confucius. For several weeks in the late winter of 1737/38, Franklin had printed excerpts from P. Intorcetta's and F. Couplet's translation, *The Morals of Confucius*, in the *Pennsylvania Gazette*.[50] Bartram was so interested that he evidently borrowed the volume from Franklin, finding that it emphasized a concept of God which Bartram repeatedly had expressed elsewhere. In a summary of his reading, he said that Confucius "had the Justest Notion of the deity & of the spiritual worship due him Alone . . . for his Notion of God was, that he was the Supream truth & reason or the fountain from whence truth & reason derived & communicated to man." No mention of Confucius appears elsewhere in Bartram's writings, and there is no way of determining whether reading about Confucius inspired his heresy or merely confirmed views already held.[51]

That his children might be left in no doubt as to his sincere and ardent belief in the Almighty as well as his general philosophy, Bartram committed his thoughts to paper in a lengthy essay of advice for his children in 1758.[52] It began with emphasis on thankfulness to and worship of the "Living God" and his personal interpretation of the Golden Rule. He discussed charity, humility, industry, and moderation in some detail and recommended that everyone take a few moments of "a still quietude in an Evening it Refresheth the Soul & prepares the Mind to receive Divine instructions." He continued with advice on married life, which was astonishingly modern for an eighteenth-century man: "Reason together on the advantage or disadvantage of any important transaction. . . . A prudent wife's advice is often beneficiall and many times Husbands that have rejected it have plunged themselves and family into grievous inconveniences. . . ." He stressed the dangers of living up to one's income and not saving for emergencies. He pointed out that children were greatly influenced in their behavior by that of their parents: "the little Dears Cunning Creatures very soon observe the Conduct of their Parents." Nothing was more important than the proper training of children and he was "apt to think the vitious and exorbitant of the Present age is greatly owing to the neglect of early inculcating of truth and virtue in their tender age of Childhood."

Bartram concluded his dissertation with the problems facing the elderly. These were three: "Drunkeness, Covetiousness and Pevish and fretfull humour." He desired that his friends and children, if they observed such weaknesses on his part, inform him immediately that they might not become habitual. He added that a pious and godly man "altho he appears in a shrivel skin and his Eyes are dim with age yet is he Serounded with Rays of Light their pious minds are waiting to hear the midnight Call with their Lamps trimmed Ready to meet their God whom they have loved hoping he will receive them into the glorious Mansions. . . ."

During some comparatively leisurely hours of an early winter day in 1758, Bartram made a sketch on some of Billy's drawing paper.[53] He had heard so much about Peter's garden from Moses and Kalm that he thought it might amuse his friend to see a rough plan of his. At the top of the page he drew the back of the two-story house with its two chimneys and his study at the left. A path from the study door led toward the river, with a new fenced flower garden to the left and the old one in front of the house on the right. Beyond this, on the same level, lay the upper kitchen garden, separated from the flower garden by another path and behind it a tiny shed, which must have been intended to represent what is presently called the "Seed House," a considerably larger building than the sketch would suggest.

Steps, joined by a picket fence, led down from both paths to the terrace below, sloping gently southeastward to the Schuylkill. To the left lay a fence and inside were three long avenues of trees under which were paths to the river. A tiny figure with staff walking under them could be a self-portrait. All the land on the right, down to the river, was another huge enclosed vegetable garden. Halfway down it was a small pond or "springhead," whose water was piped underground to a springhouse or milk house. With the river four hundred yards wide at this point, it made a pleasant prospect from the house. Bartram sent the sketch to Collinson in January 1759, with the hint that his "new Flower Garden" was designed for English plants. Bartram's drawing was welcomed by Collinson: "We are all much Entertained with thy Draught of thy House & Garden, the situation is delightful; and that for our plants, is well chosen. I shall endeavour to furnish it."[54]

This drawing, however, failed to show the full extent of Bartram's garden. A great many of the trees and other plants he had collected were planted outside of the two acres of the gardens that he had depicted. He was keenly aware of the importance of ecological influences and knew that a plant would not thrive if its new

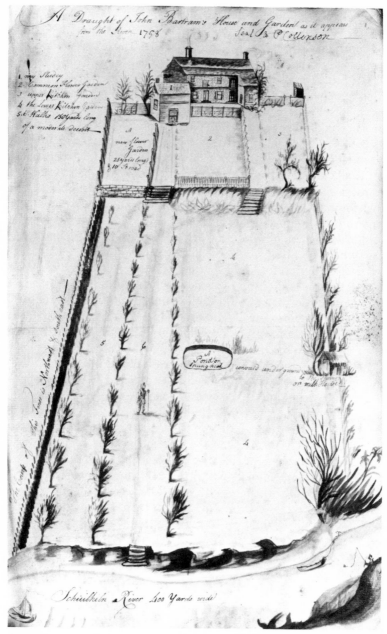

Bartram's drawing of his house and garden which he sent to Peter
Collinson in 1758 (original in the Earl of Derby's library, Knowsley,
England; reproduced with permission)

surroundings differed too radically from those to which it was adapted. He always tried to find a situation as nearly comparable as possible to that in which the plant had been found. In fact, he called his 200- to 300-acre plantation his "garden," which was aptly described by a friend: "His garden is a perfect portraiture of himself, here you meet wt. a row of rare plants almost covered over wt. weeds, here with a Beautiful Shrub, even Luxuriant Amongst Briars, and in another corner an Elegant & Lofty tree lost in a common thicket—on our way from town to his house he carried me to several rocks & Dens where he shewed me some of his rare plants, which he had brought from the Mountains, etc. In a word he disdains to have a garden less than Pennsylvania & Every Den is an Arbour, Every run of water, a canal, & every small level spot a Parterre, where he nurses up some of his Idol Flowers & cultivates his darling productions. . . ."[55] Bartram's letters seldom give a clue to the numbers of plants in his garden or its extent. He wrote a friend that to prepare a list of all of his plants would take far more time than he could spare, but he did draw up a list of 169 North American trees and shrubs as they occurred to him, the majority of which were growing on his land.[56]

One February day in 1759, Bartram found a letter at the post office for which he had to pay two shillings and ten pence postage. He promptly replied to the writer, Philip Miller, that he would gladly have paid three times that amount.[57] Although Miller had been one of his earliest patrons, they had not begun direct correspondence until 1755. During the previous twenty years they had communicated through Collinson. Miller was one of the most knowledgeable of English botanists. His nurseryman father had not only trained him thoroughly in the nursery but had provided him with a sound education, including foreign languages.[58] He had made it possible for his son to travel extensively both in England and on the continent, studying both ornamental and practical gardens. When he later became the gardener for the Chelsea Physic Garden of the Society of Apothecaries, he had enhanced its reputation throughout the world. Many of Bartram's plants had flourished in that garden.

Miller had begun his popular *Gardener's Dictionary* in 1731, and there had been numerous revisions. He had, in most cases, given Bartram full credit for his discoveries and introduction of plants to England. Bartram had long admired the *Dictionary*, which had been sent to him by Lord Petre and by Dillenius, and he was delighted when Miller initiated the correspondence. His only regret was the loss of so many years "wherein we might have reciprocally communicated our observations to each other: and although thee had incomparably the advantage over me, yet, notwithstanding, I love to peep into the abstruse operations of nature."[59] His correspondence with Miller came to fill a place left empty by the deaths of Dillenius (1747) and Catesby (1749) and the ill health of Gronovius, which terminated their correspondence in 1754.

Miller sent Bartram his *Figures of Plants*, later editions of the *Dictionary*, and his *Catalogue of Trees and Shrubs*, all of which were appreciated and enjoyed.[60] He gave Bartram advice concerning the descriptions of trees that he was writing. Bartram sent seeds and plants to Miller and discussed botanic problems with him. In one of his letters Miller protested that Linnaeus had caused confusion by joining together unrelated genera: "The Apple and Pear are undoubtedly of different genera. They will not take upon each other, either by budding or grafting, and it is well known, from experience, that all trees of the same genus will grow upon each other."[61] Bartram was somewhat startled by this curious statement and hastened to assure Miller that he had successfully grafted pears on apple stocks and had seen trees bearing both pears and apples.[62]

A botanic problem of major proportions interested Bartram in the spring of 1759. He sent Collinson "a brief account of thos plants that are most troublesome in our pastures and fields in Pennsylvania; most of which were brought from Europe."[63] Bartram discussed ten plants introduced from England that "have escaped out of our gardens and taken possession of our fields and meadows, very much to our detriment." Few could question that the plants he mentioned were a nuisance, although they might be surprised to realize that they are not native: dandelion, dock, crow garlick, ox-eye daisy, toadflax, mullein, scotch thistle, bouncing bet, and dog fennel. Having discussed the habits of these immigrants and the problems caused by them, Bartram turned to native weed pests: blackberries, raspberries, dewberries, asters, ragweed, chickweed, henbit, sheep sorrel, and pigweed. Lambs' quarter could be a nuisance but "is very tender when boiled." Collinson found this very interesting. He recalled that John Josselyn (c. 1608–75) had called attention to introduced plants in his *New-England's Rarities Discovered* in

1672. Collinson thought it curious that American climate and soil could make a pest of a plant like toadflax (*Linaria*), which was not a pest in England. He enjoyed it in his garden. He admitted that the daisy could be a pest, but he raised it anyway.[64]

Early in 1759 Bartram felt optimistic about the prospect of a long collecting trip in the fall. The French and Indian War showed some signs of diminishing. Fort Duquesne had fallen, and Crown Point seemed likely to follow. Furthermore, he wanted to go south this time, and there seemed to be less trouble in that area. Ever since Garden's visit, Bartram had been eager to visit Charles Town but had not been able to do so. His half-brother, William, had lived in North Carolina for many years and would welcome a visit. Bartram began to plan a trip that would take him south through the Shenandoah Valley and along the mountains to South Carolina. He would return along the coast and visit his brother at the Cape Fear River. One of his sons would accompany him.

It was early in October that Bartram and his son, probably Johnny, started out. In Bartram's favorite Shenandoah Valley they took time to study the manner in which the land was enriched in limestone regions.[65] The streams left incrustations on shrubs, rocks, and the ground whenever they overflowed their banks. Winter frost broke these up and they were absorbed into the ground. An eight-foot bank at a millrace clearly demonstrated such a buildup. Often it practically formed a dam, which caused overflows to fertilize the surrounding fields.

They reached Staunton on 17 October, where they were told that many of the valley settlers just thirty miles south had been murdered by Indians. One of the Bartram horses was proving a poor traveler, and it seemed wise to turn back. They decided to go directly east over the Blue Ridge through Wood's Gap. Ginseng grew along the stream they followed down the mountain. From there, they were pleased to find a good road of red clay and, along Ivy Run, some splendid aconite almost six feet tall, which grew beautifully in Bartram's garden later. That night, spent at the Tirrels', was enlivened by negroes playing banjos. Crossing the Rivanna on a fine bridge thirty-eight feet wide, they found the "spotted asarabaca" or wild ginger. They reached William West's ordinary at the head of Bull Run on the twenty-fourth. The inn had just been opened in 1754 and was doing a fine business since one of the two roads to the valley from Alexandria passed by it.[66] The next night was spent at genial Molata Tom's. He and his white wife made them welcome, showing the Bartrams their fine plantation well farmed by Tom's negroes. A few days later the Bartrams reached home after a frustrating trip.

Bartram found Isaac and Moses busy planning a joint enterprise. Moses had been in Jamaica the past spring and then had been involved in some new misfortune. Collinson wrote in the fall, "I am concerned for poor Moses. Now he has eat his brown bread, his white will come next. I wish he would write a little Journal in his own way and style, from his first going to sea to this present time. *Short hints will do.* I question if it is to be paralleled. We don't know what human nature will bear until it is tried."[67] Whatever catastrophe befell Moses as captain of his new ship must have been the final straw. At this point, Isaac had several years of experience as an apothecary and was ready to strike out on his own. He and Moses formed a partnership in the drug business which lasted for twelve years. Moses had finally found his white bread.

On 28 February 1760 the *Pennsylvania Gazette* carried an advertisement for "Isaac and Moses Bertram, at the sign of the Bottle and Three Bolt Heads," which shop they had taken over from Thomas Say. They carried the usual assortment of drugs, crucibles, galley pots, pewter syringes, mortars and pestles, scales, and boxes or chests of medicines suitable for ships' captains to use at sea or for home use when doctors were too distant for consultation. In the years to come Bartram used his London credit to facilitate purchase of medicines for his sons. Many supplies were bought locally, and "highest prices" were paid for buckhorns, rattlesnakes, oil of mint, snakeroot, and "well faded Roses." From time to time unusual items were offered for sale such as "7 or 8 barrels of best Carolina pork," possibly sent by their uncle. Even that first year Isaac and Moses were ambitious and appealed to the wholesale trade as well as to the retail: "where Shop and Storekeepers may be supplied, with large Allowance to sell again."[68]

TWELVE

To the Carolinas at Last

B ARTRAM had failed to complete his attempted
trip to the Carolinas in 1759, but he had not
lost his determination to get there. Everything that he had heard
about the plants of the region excited him. Since the Cherokee Indians in western Virginia and Carolina were still very much a
threat in the spring of 1760, Bartram determined to confine his
travels to the Atlantic coastal area. He decided to go south by ship
and obtain a horse there to ride home. He had never traveled by
ship but knew that it would save him a great deal of time and effort. He sailed from Philadelphia in the cold and wintry weather of
early March. The sea was rough, and Bartram was devoutly thankful when the ship finally anchored at the mouth of the Ashley
River near Charles Town on 13 March.[1]

The balmy spring weather soon revived him. As he made his
way to Garden's home, he saw spring flowers in great profusion
everywhere. He was welcomed warmly by the doctor, his wife,
Elizabeth, and their two-year-old son, Alex, even though he had arrived at a very inopportune time. There was a great deal of sickness in the city, including smallpox, and all doctors were extremely
busy. Garden would not be free to make the field trips with Bartram that both had hoped for.[2] Bartram had no problem in occupying himself during his eighteen-day visit. He followed Garden's directions for places he should explore. As had long been his custom,
he rose early every morning and departed for the fields and woods.
When he returned, he was loaded with plants to be heeled in until
he packed them for shipment to Philadelphia. Garden promised to
have some of these packed and forwarded in the fall.[3] When the

doctor could manage it, he introduced Bartram to friends with gardening interests. The city had many fine gardens, and Bartram visited a number of them. He saw plants that he coveted, and he made numerous friends. Among them was Thomas Lamboll (1694–1774), a longtime correspondent of Peter Collinson. He and his wife lived in a house at the corner of King and Lamboll streets, where there were large gardens for both flowers and vegetables. Among the many plants that interested Bartram was a white broom from Portugal, sent by Collinson twenty years earlier.[4]

A garden of particular interest to Bartram was that of Martha Logan (1704–81), to whom Bartram referred as an "elderly widow lady" although she was five years his junior.[5] She had, for some years, supported her family with her nursery garden at Trott's Point, which supplied many of the other gardens of the city. Her garden calendar, printed in the local almanac for the years 1751–60, was the first published in America.[6] Bartram had only a brief visit with Mrs. Logan, since it was the height of her spring business, but they both enjoyed it. They agreed to correspond and exchange plants and seeds and did so for a number of years. She promised to send him seeds of horse sugar (*Symplocos tinctoria* [L.] L'Her.) but instead sent two good plants and a silk bag filled with various seeds. Bartram promptly returned the bag with seeds for her. The bag made a great number of trips between Philadelphia and Charles Town.[7]

When Collinson had Bartram's report of his visit to Charles Town, he was amused by Bartram's prowess with the ladies: "I plainly see thou knowest how to fascinate the longing widow, by so close a correspondence. When the women enter into these amusements, I ever found them the best assistants. Now I shall not wonder if thy garden abounds with the rarities of Carolina."[8] Not to be outdone, Bartram replied: "Now I hope to be stocked with Padus [chokecherry], as I have received a lovely parcel this spring from Mrs. Logan, my fascinated widow. I saw the lovely tree growing in Governor Glenn's garden. She also sent me a young tree from there, but the rats demolished it. I have also fascinated two men's wives, although one I never saw; that is, Mrs. Lamboll, who hath sent me two noble cargoes; one last fall, the other this spring. The other hath sent me, I think, a great curiosity. She calls it a Golden Lilly. I thought when I planted it, to be the Atamasco, but the bud seems different." The second lady was Sarah Hopton.[9]

Garden was seldom able to spend more than a half hour with his guest after dinner and supper, but both enjoyed this time. At last Garden had a botanist with an enthusiasm equal to his own with whom to discuss the Carolina plants. Charles Town gardeners had little interest in botany as a science. Garden had thoroughly enjoyed his northern visit with the Coldens and Bartram, but they were unfamiliar with the Carolina flora. He was very helpful to Bartram, and the latter was able to find some plants unknown to Garden. Not long before Bartram started home, the doctor spent two hours roaming the woods with him and was amused by Bar-

Travels in the Carolinas (adapted from map compiled by S. Lewis, Philadelphia, 1807)

tram's excitement when they found something new: "he seems almost ravished of his senses and lost in astonishment." It was certainly a genuine enthusiasm for Bartram for he had fallen in love with the place: "Oh Carolina Carolina a ravishing place for a curious Botanist."[10]

Bartram took ship for Cape Fear, North Carolina, on 1 April and, to his surprise, enjoyed the short ocean voyage. At Brunswick, across the river from Wilmington, he was able to go ashore briefly and saw some shrubs which he did not know and later tried to obtain.[11] There he met for the first time his Irish correspondent, Governor Arthur Dobbs, who had been interested in the region long before he was able to obtain the governorship. Both Dobbs and his deputy secretary of state, William Powell, had a considerable interest in plants, and the latter promised to send Bartram several things that he wanted. Dobbs gave Bartram an order for plants and seeds for fall delivery and later sent him a request for seeds for his kitchen garden. There were not many ships going from Brunswick to Philadelphia, so they had some difficulty in carrying out their plant exchange.[12] At either Brunswick or Wilmington, Bartram made another friend, Dr. Samuel Green (1707–71). He was employed by the provincial government from time to time, attending soldiers and prisoners. He had a large family and, when Bartram urged him to visit him in Philadelphia, said that he had not been further from home than Fort Fisher on the coast since he came there twenty-one years earlier. He was well acquainted with Bartram's half-brother and offered to forward mail or parcels to him. As so often happened with Bartram, he made a friend on brief acquaintance who became a correspondent and sent him plants.[13]

Colonel William Bartram lived up the Cape Fear River in what is now Bladen County.[14] His home, Ashwood, was built on a high bluff above the river. He had prospered in Carolina and owned some 3,900 acres of land, a mill, an ironworks, and several lots in Wilmington and Campbelltown (or did at the time of his death). He was, for many years, a member of the North Carolina Assembly and active in the affairs of the province. His family consisted of his wife, Elizabeth Locke, a son, William, two daughters, Mary (Polly) and Sarah, and a stepdaughter. The colonel, like his brother, was a farmer. With the help of about ten slaves he raised cattle, hogs, sheep, and horses and the crops with which to feed them.[15]

The family reunion was a happy one, and John was able to do

some plant collecting as William showed him his farming operations. Bartram spotted a number of plants that he wanted, including a dwarf palm, a rose mallow, and a deciduous bay. He went with
William to visit Richard Singletary, a friend who lived eight or ten
miles up the Cape Fear River. Here, too, Bartram saw plants that
he wanted, this time some water tupelos. He exacted promises from
William to send him the plants when a ship was going to Philadelphia. He was not returning home by water but was going to borrow
a horse from his brother and ride home.[16]

   Among many things that the brothers had in common was a
concern about the future prospects of a son named William. John
was still worried because his Billy (Will) knew that he wanted to
be a botanist but not how he could support himself. William's "Bill"
(so-called by his father) knew that he wanted to study medicine.
William suggested that John's Billy might consider opening a store
in the Ashwood neighborhood, and John urged that William's Bill
should come to Philadelphia, where he could attend the Academy.
There he could make up any deficiencies in his education before
entering upon medical study with some doctor.[17] Each uncle promised to act in loco parentis if the other decided to send his son. It
was agreed that John would sell William's horse unless an opportunity arose to send it back.[18]

   The third major objective of Bartram's trip was to see John
Clayton at Gloucester Court House. This time he found Clayton at
home, and a joyous meeting it was. No other men in America had
made so extensive a study of plants as had these two, and both had
achieved considerable reputations both at home and abroad as
botanists of ability. Bartram had "corresponded freely" with Clayton at least as early as 1744, and he had long used his *Flora Virginica* and admired it.[19] They had much to discuss and did so at such a
rapid pace that Clayton later complained bitterly of all that he had
forgotten to show Bartram. Clayton was very much interested in
the journeys Bartram had made and one which he planned to make
to Pittsburgh.[20]

   Clayton asked Bartram about a plant that Catesby had called
Meadia, which had an interesting history. Some twenty years earlier a friend of Bartram had told him of a plant he had seen in some
remote place that resembled a cyclamen which he saw in Bartram's
garden. Later the friend was startled to find that Bartram had
found the plant, and it too was growing in his garden.[21] Bartram

had found it in the Valley of Virginia when he crossed the Shenandoah River and had gathered seed, some of which he sent to Collinson. The latter was successful in raising it, and after two years it flowered, in September 1744.[22] Since it was a new genus, Catesby named it in honor of his friend Dr. Richard Mead and included a description of the plant in his *Appendix*. Collinson sent a specimen of it to Linnaeus in 1746, saying that Bartram had collected it beyond the first mountains in Virginia and suggesting that it be named for him. Linnaeus had, by that time, named a different plant for Bartram. When he published his *Species Plantarum* in 1753, he offended some of his English friends by naming this plant *Dodecatheon*. Clayton was curious to know where Bartram had found the plant. Clayton had never been able to discover it, even though he had included it in his new version of the *Flora*. Bartram promised to send his friend a root of the plant and was later reminded of his promise.[23]

Clayton hoped to have his manuscript published shortly in London. He called it the "Flora Virginiana" to distinguish it from the earlier Gronovian edition and told Bartram the curious story of his decision to publish independently of Gronovius. After the latter had published the second part of the *Flora Virginica* in 1743, the two men had continued to collaborate toward a third part, until Gronovius began to think about a new edition. After many years had passed and nothing had happened, Clayton finally had prepared one himself. In 1758 he had sent it to Collinson to publish, and Collinson, Ellis, and others had pronounced it a great improvement. They had decided to have it illustrated by Georg Ehret, and this had delayed its publication. Collinson planned to have it "translated into English & to print the Lattin on one side of the page and the English on the other side—for you must know that very few of the Common People & also of the Gentry who have had a University Education—understand Botanic Lattin for no Dictionary gives the Synonims, & Technical Terms—so it is very Difficult for an English Man to understand Description of plants unless he makes it his whole study."[24]

Clayton and Bartram spent a long time in the garden examining all of Clayton's treasures from forty years of collecting. Clayton was especially proud of a fine English laurel that he had grown from seed. The great majority of his plants were well established in Bartram's own garden, but there were many things on which to compare notes. Clayton promised to send Bartram seed of a plant with a beautiful blue flower which had aroused curiosity in both England and Sweden. Clayton had named the new genus *Amsonia* in honor of his friend Dr. John Amson of Williamsburg.[25] He would send seed of another curiosity, a red-flowered turtlehead (*Chelone glabra* L.).[26]

Clayton would have liked nothing better than to keep Bartram for a long visit. He was particularly concerned to see him leave with a very bad cough and some fever. But Bartram had been away from home a long time and felt that he could not linger. Since he did not know when, if ever, he might ride to Virginia again, Bartram suggested a number of places where he and Clayton might meet and do some collecting together, but Clayton had grave doubts that he would be able to do so. He was relieved to learn that Bartram arrived home safely. Parting with him had made Clayton "very melancholy for some time."[27]

Bartram sent his brother quite a collection of plants which he had found lacking in William's garden: buckthorn, angelica, white raspberry, lily-of-the-valley, iris, columbine, cowslips, saffron, althaea, and violets.[28] He packed his plant specimens for Collinson and entrusted them to his neighbor Andrew Lamb, who was sailing to England.[29] He planted the many plants and seeds that he had brought back for his own garden and the many which he had packed for shipment to himself. A ship had arrived in May with five boxes "well stuft with curious plants & shrubs all which came as good as if taken up ye day before."[30] Bartram was delighted by the many additions to his garden. The plants seemed to thrive, and by September he could report to his cousin, Humphry Marshall, that his garden "now makes a glorious appearance with ye Virginia & Carolina flowers." He was so busy that he failed to send Collinson his journal of his trip until the following year, when he sent it in care of his friend Dr. William Chancellor.[31]

Some seeds were shipped to Bartram in December 1760, which had come a long way. They were sent by John Ellis (c. 1710–76) from London to "all our Govern'rs & Chief Botanists in N. America." Ellis, one of England's foremost naturalists, was forwarding tea seeds which had come from Ningpo, China. They had been imbedded in balls of wax which, he hoped, would preserve them from deterioration in shipment. Ellis was very much interested in finding a satisfactory material for this purpose. Unfortunately, the seeds that he planted in London failed to germinate, and all those that he shipped to America were lost when the ship was seized by the French.[32]

In the fall or early winter Bartram and his twelve-year-old son, Benjamin, went to collect holly berries, which had been requested by the nursery gardener James Gordon. The getting of them "had like to broke" Bartram's bones. He was holding on to the top of a tree when it and the branch on which he was standing broke simultaneously, and he fell to the ground. Benjamin tried to help his father up but was not strong enough. Bartram was in great pain and chilled by a cold wind. There were no houses near from which Benjamin could seek help. Finally, Bartram recovered sufficiently to crawl into his saddle with Benjamin's help and rode the twenty miles home. An injured arm was still bothering him some months later.[33]

The autumn and winter of 1760–61 were well occupied with a project that Bartram had been considering for some time. He wanted a building in which to put "some pretty flowering winter shrubs, and plants for winter's diversion; not to be crowded with orange trees, or those natural to the Torrid Zone, but such as will do, being protected from frost."[34] He did not approve of keeping a greenhouse too hot for plants that were to be put outside later, thinking that too much heat tended to make them tender and sickly. The stone was collected in September. As soon as the harvest was over and his seed shipments had gone, he was able to turn to stonemasonry. Before spring, his greenhouse with two flues in the back was completed. As a final touch, he chiseled into the lintel over the door a quotation from Pope: "Slave to no sect, who takes no private road, But looks through Nature up to Nature's God." Some of Bartram's hints to his friends with regard to furnishing his greenhouse were successful. Gordon sent him a white Persian cyclamen and paduas from Portugal. Collinson sent a blue cyclamen and seeds of geraniums which "have a charming variety, and make a pretty show in a greenhouse."[35] Bartram found the building useful in many ways for the care and propagation of the native plants he had collected. Some of his Carolina plants found the Philadelphia weather a little too cold for their liking and fared better inside. Some seeds sprouted better there and got off to an earlier start than they could outside. There were occasional surprises, such as an East Indian sumac that Bartram grew from seed brought to him by Dr. William Shippen, Jr. It grew like Jack's beanstalk and soon had to be removed to take its chances outside. Still later, Collinson sent an Italian strawberry plant and a pineapple. Bartram felt sure that he had the only plants of these species in North America. This may or may not have been the case, but they were certainly the only ones in Philadelphia and were great curiosities to show to his friends.[36]

Among those who admired Bartram's greenhouse was a new friend, Sir John St. Clair, who had a fine one of his own and gave Bartram many plants. St. Clair, born in Scotland, had made a career of the army. After serving in many places, he had been sent to America to serve as Braddock's quartermaster general. His estate near Trenton, which he called Belleville, had a fine view of the Delaware and was described as being "the most beautiful and neat Place within many Miles."[37] In January 1761 Bartram sent some *Mimosa* seeds to St. Clair and mentioned various plants that he had available. St. Clair thanked him and said that he would send his gardener, Mr. Marshall, to collect them. He urged Bartram to pay him a visit: "I can promise you a hearty Welcome & to show you the best Garden in America which I have neither spared labor or expence to finish. You may easily believe that I have not been able to stock it wt great variety, but what trees I have are good, and this season will show if my flowers answer my Expectations."[38]

St. Clair had really ambitious plans for his gardens and greenhouses. He had ordered all sorts of West Indian plants from Charles Willing at Barbados and bulbs from the Harlem florists, whom he thought far superior to those at Leiden. A friend had sent him curious plants from the Cape of Good Hope. Among the plants which St. Clair hoped Bartram could help him obtain were pomegranates and nectarines. He also wanted to try to propagate the "Red China Orange wt the Nectarine flavour," which he had formerly done successfully.[39] He pressed Bartram to visit him. There were many things about which he wanted advice, including the composition of compost and the proper treatment for scabs on gooseberries. He promised to provide a bed in his library above the greenhouse "where a Gardiner ought to be lodged, and a very hearty wellcome." St. Clair indicated his high regard for the Bartram family by sending Ann a cow of the fine Rhode Island breed, which he had obtained with difficulty and wanted to establish in the area. The cow would calve at Christmastime, and, should the calf be a heifer, St. Clair promised to send a bull calf.[40]

Bartram's trip to Carolina had not only been a thoroughly satisfactory one in itself, but it continued to yield plants for his garden. In the spring of 1761 William Powell sent a box of plants that Bartram had requested. It contained pines, purple-berried bays, hollies, and others. Dobbs personally sent "Paradise berries" (the chinaberry tree, *Melia azedarach* L.), myrtle berries, and date seeds, which his son had sent from Gibraltar.[41] William Bartram wrote from Wilmington, where he was serving as a member of the assembly, again urging that Billy come to Carolina in the fall. After the colonel returned to Ashwood, he sent a box of plants. On rather short notice, he learned that his stepdaughter's husband, Anthony Gully, had been given command of a ship leaving for Philadelphia, so he wrote a hasty note to John. He suggested that this would be a good time for Billy to come south and felt sure that he could prevent him from being drafted to fight the Cherokees. He recommended that among the goods which Billy should bring to sell should be rum, molasses, powder, and lead.[42]

Billy was just completing his apprenticeship with Captain Child and liked the idea of starting a mercantile career in Carolina. Quickly he acquired a stock of goods so that he might go south with Captain Gully.[43] Just before he left, Billy received a handsome present from George Edwards in appreciation of his help with American birds. Edwards sent two volumes of his *Gleanings of Natural History*, finely bound with gilded edges, containing 100 beautifully colored prints described in both French and English. Billy was delighted to find that they included all of the birds that he had sent to Edwards and assured his father that he would write to thank him as soon as he got to Carolina. Not surprisingly he forgot to do so, and Bartram was embarrassed months later when Edwards inquired whether the books had ever been received.[44]

Not long after his arrival in Carolina, Billy sent his father some plants which, unfortunately, were washed overboard from Captain Gully's ship. Bartram wrote in June to thank his son for sending them and for three letters as well. He could not resist adding: "My dear child I have no new advice to give thee but to remind thee of my former general instructions; fear God & walk before him; practice all virtues & eschew all vice take care of being be-

guiled by vain recreations   thay are like ye hornets   hath a sting
in thair tail but keep close to industry temperance & frugality;
thee hath left a good character behind in town   pray don't forget
it   now is ye time to gain it there & establish it in both provinces
by making good remittances to thy creditors here; be Complaisand
& obligeing to all so far as consistent with thy credit & no honest
man will desire more; thy master & mistris gives thee an extraordinary good word & laments thair loss as one of thair family."[45]

If Billy must be away from home, Bartram was glad to have
him where William could keep an eye on him and advise him. He
urged Billy to consult his uncle about merchandising matters and,
when the opportunity occurred, to call upon the governor and other
people of importance, "letting them know that thee art come to
thair countrey in ye way of trade" and offering his services in obtaining goods for them from Philadelphia or London. Bartram was
happy to have Billy in an area where there were so many plants
that he coveted. Those that his brother had sent were doing well,
and Bartram was curious about one of these, a grapevine which
looked "just like our little odius grape." He hoped that Billy would
ascertain what manner of fruit it produced in order that he might
know "what honor to bestow upon it." Bartram mentioned a number of plants that William had not sent and which he wanted. By
way of news from home, he told Billy that he was "all in a flame to
go to Pittsburgh if Providence permits." He planned to go in late
August or early September.[46]

On 6 July 1761 Bartram answered an interesting letter from
England, written the previous September. It had come from Peter
Templeman, secretary of "the Society established at London for the
encouragement of Arts, Manufactures, and Commerce" (the Royal
Society of Arts), of which Garden had been the first American
member. The society had been organized in 1754 and had enjoyed
rapid growth. Templeman wrote that they believed that "the surest
method of improving science is by a generous intercourse of the
learned in different countries, and a free communication of knowledge." The specific inquiry on which they hoped that Bartram could
enlighten them was whether there were species of plants that
flourished in America in winter which cattle could eat, other than
those included by John Ray in his *Synopsis*. The members of the
society reasoned that "the common Parent of all has not left the
preservation of such animals solely to the care and industry of

man." It was hoped that Bartram would favor them with "an account of them, with the nature of the soil they grow in, and the
culture they required."[47]

Bartram replied with a rather long letter. It was his opinion
that Providence had originally placed cows in regions with warm
climates where grasses and other plants grow the year around. If
man transported them elsewhere, it was his responsibility to provide for them during cold weather. There was very little food for
cattle to find in winter in America. Unless food was provided, they
were barely able to survive until spring and then in a very weakened condition. He pointed out that cattle had the peculiarity of
lacking upper foreteeth and were not well adapted to browsing as
horses, sheep, and goats might do. He gave the buffalo as an example, it being the same genus as cattle. In the summer they came
north as far as Pennsylvania to feed on the grass of the rich valleys, retiring south when the first frosts came. He discussed a number of plants that cattle would eat but that were not abundant
enough to support them. In closing his letter, Bartram wrote that
he expected to go to Pittsburgh in September and would like to go
down the Ohio and up to Lake Erie but doubted that the Indians
would permit it. He hoped to find many new plants and fossils to
add to his collection, which lacked few specimens of vegetables
from Nova Scotia to North Carolina and from the Atlantic to Lake
Ontario. He admitted that "ye Botanick fire set me in such a flame
as is not to be quenched until death or I explore most of ye South
western vegitative treasures in No. America or perish in ye attempt."[48]

When Colonel Bartram learned from Billy that his brother expected to be away from home for some time in the fall, he decided
to send his son to Philadelphia in August. He wanted John to be
there to advise Bill and to help him get settled and started at
school. He had written to Isaac and Moses, asking them to let Bill
stay with them if he would be living in Philadelphia. If his decision
was to live out of town, he hoped that John would let him live at
his home. He promised to reimburse his brother for any expense he
might incur on his nephew's behalf.[49]

John and Ann were disappointed that Bill brought no letter
from their son, as they wanted to know how his sales were pro-
gressing. Bill informed them that his cousin was keeping "but little
Company" but that of the best, which was reassuring. He told them

that his father and Billy were talking of a trip to Georgia in the fall. This excited Bartram, who hastily wrote to his son, urging him to collect all manner of seeds. A six-inch bag would do, and he need not bother to separate them. Ann added a postscript to her husband's letter: "I joyn with thy father in the good counsel he gives thee wishing thee health and prosperity in all thy undertaking desiring to hear from thee at all opertunitys and if i have anny in thy father's absence I shall write to thee, from thy loving mother."[50] Bartram and his brother had temporarily exchanged sons. Each of them worried about the conduct of his absent son and enjoyed the visit of his nephew. Captain Gully, whose vessel traveled regularly between Carolina and Philadelphia, kept the brothers in touch as they had not been for many years.

The menace of the Indians gave Bartram definite qualms as he prepared for his trip to Fort Pitt. He wrote to Collinson that he intended to go "if the barbarous Indians don't hinder mee (and if I die a martyr to Botany, God's will be done; His will be done in all things). They domineer, threaten and steal most of the best horses they can." In spite of such misgivings, he left Kingsessing as planned in early September. He was glad to take advantage of the recently completed Forbes Road through Carlisle, Shippensburg, Fort Loudon, Bedford, Fort Ligonier, and finally to Fort Pitt, a ride of close to 300 miles. As he rode west he observed the underground riches displayed from time to time along the road in quarries and strip mines: coal, slate, limestone, marl, and whetstone.[51]

Bartram was welcomed by Lieutenant-Colonel Henry Bouquet (1719–65), commander of Fort Pitt, and the other officers. Bouquet was a Swiss who had joined the British army in 1755. He had spent a year in South Carolina before joining General Forbes in the campaign against Fort Duquesne and its conversion to Fort Pitt in 1758. He was in a ticklish situation, trying to maintain peace with the Indians and enforce the Easton treaty with the Ohio Indian tribes, who had been promised by Pennsylvania that there would be no English settlements beyond the Alleghenies. The Ohio Company was eager to settle Germans and Swiss in the Ohio Valley and disapproved of the Pennsylvania treaty. In spite of these problems, Bouquet was able to spend quite a bit of time with Bartram. He had a genuine interest in botany and did everything he could to help. They both enjoyed talking of their stay in South Carolina. Bouquet gave Bartram nuts from Illinois that he said were hickory nuts. Some of these Bartram eventually sent to Collinson, although he doubted that they would sprout, being a year old.[52]

On 16 September Bartram was taken across the Monongahela by James Kenny, a Quaker friend from Kennett Square, and Kenny's friend, Captain Gordon, to see some plants which had interested them.[53] One of these was a very pretty vine with fruit like a cucumber. It had heart-shaped leaves which were aromatic. Kenny had seen only the one plant in the area. Bartram thought that it might be an *Aristolochia*; if not, it must be a new genus.[54] Bartram spotted a fine violet in bloom and collected it to take home. The following day Bartram and Kenny went out by themselves to explore south of Monongahela Mountain and to see the French lime kiln, the sawmill, and a coal mine.

When Bartram and his friends decided that he should explore the banks of the Ohio River, Bouquet not only encouraged the idea but outdid himself in outfitting the expedition. He provided a batteau with four men to row it and sent Captain Bryen to take charge of them. Kenny and Hugh McSwain, an Indian interpreter, completed the party. They were provided with a tent, food, and even a plentiful supply of liquor. Bartram was not used to collecting in such style. According to Kenny's compass, they traveled roughly northwest from Fort Pitt to Beaver Creek, stopping at islands in the river to rest the men and to give Bartram an opportunity to collect. At one of these, a long island just below Shirtee's Island (Neville Island?), they found dwarf plums and an imposing *Coreopsis* with stalks five to six feet tall.

The party continued down the Ohio to Log's Town, a 100-acre clearing where there had once been a town. Bartram and Kenny explored the nearby woods while the men rested from their rowing and relaxed near the boat. Another eight to ten miles of rowing brought the party to the home of Colonel William Johnson (later Sir William Johnson), known by the Indians as "Gray Eyes," who had been placed in charge of the northern Indian department in 1756. He was not at home, having gone to Detroit, but some women and children were there. His establishment was imposing: a shingled house, cowbarns, and stables, all built by order of General Amherst. Not long after Bartram's party pitched their tent nearby and made a fire to cook dinner, they were joined by two Indians who had returned from hunting. One of them, William Turnum, spoke English and proved to be quite entertaining. He shared their food and drink, and, sitting around the fire later, he gave them Indian names for the various planets and pointed out the North Star, the Great Bear, and other constellations.

The white men had been told of an "oyl Spring" somewhere in the area and were anxious to find it. They inquired of the Indians, but they did not know it. On the following day the party went still further downriver looking for the spring but without success. When they turned back upstream against the current, rowing really became work and they used a sail to help out. Part of the time, Bartram, Bryen, and Kenny walked on shore. About twilight they came upon the remains of a small Indian town about a mile from Colonel Johnson's home. There had been at one time about twenty well-built small houses with stone chimneys, but most of them had been destroyed. This had been a town of the Shawnees, who had been encouraged by the French to settle there and to harass the English. Bartram's group pitched camp there for the night. While they were doing so, McSwain walked on to Johnson's home and came back with some freshly made butter. Next day they returned to Log's Town, where Bartram searched, without success, for horse chestnut trees. He had seen Indian children with necklaces made of the nuts but could not learn where they came from. He did find some plants for his collection: a dragonhead, a jacea, and several ferns.

Bartram spent another day resting at the fort. When he started home he rode up the Monongahela River to Redstone Creek and Fort Burd, where he picked up Braddock's road to Fort Cumberland on the Potomac.[55] Somewhere along the way he found an "evergreen hypericum," some unusual ferns, a "pretty hesperis," and a wild iris quite different from the Virginia species. He stopped at Colonel Thomas Cresap's trading post, where all travelers, Indian and white, were made welcome. The Indians gave recognition to Cresap's hospitality by calling him "Big Spoon." From there, Bartram made his way to the warm springs in Virginia (Berkeley Springs), with stops to see such things as "allum rocks" and a cave.

When Bartram reached home at the end of September, he had traveled more than eight hundred miles, not including some ten days spent on the rivers.[56] He had collected a number of herbaceous plants and plant specimens, yet he felt disappointed since he had not found a single shrub or tree that he did not already have growing on his own land.[57] He had nevertheless enjoyed the trip and had made new friends and improved old friendships. Both Kenny and Bouquet had promised to send him seeds. His bread-and-butter letter to the latter produced Bouquet's promise to visit Bartram the following year and to procure seeds from a sergeant at Fort Burd. Seeds sent by Kenny were enclosed. Bouquet tried to arrange a visit to Bartram by a Lieutenant Brehm, who had traveled to some remote western areas for General Amherst, but Brehm left for New York before Bartram was able to locate him.[58]

Bartram's journal of the Fort Pitt trip was roughly completed the following spring, and Collinson finally received a finished copy of it in October 1762 from the hands of Bartram's friend, a Mr. Taylor, who had agreed to deliver it. As always, Collinson derived great pleasure from the journal, but he admitted to some disappointment at the lack of wild beasts encountered. He had fully expected that a "panther had sprung out of a thicket, or a bear wakened from his den, or a beaver-dam broke up," but the only animals which Bartram seemed to notice were snakes.[59]

THIRTEEN

To Carolina Again

B ARTRAM was a little apprehensive as he prepared his seed boxes for shipment in the fall of
1761. Collinson had aroused his ire by suggesting that his London
customers all wanted new things and were tiring of the old ones.
Bartram inquired: "Do they think I can make new ones? I have
sent them seeds of almost every tree and shrub from Nova Scotia to
Carolina; very few are wanting: and from the sea across the continent to the lakes. It's very likely ignorant people may give strange
names to tickle your ears withal; but, as I have travelled through
most of these provinces, and have specimens sent by the best
hands, I know well what grows there. . . ."[1]

His seed business had increased immensely over the last
fifteen years and had become a brisk commercial enterprise. The
trees and shrubs that he had moved to his plantation as seed
sources greatly facilitated the procuring of large quantities. Stan-
dardization of the five-guinea box made packing simpler and
speedier. The largest number of boxes shipped in one year of which
a record has been found was twenty-nine in 1752.[2] Bartram still
spent time in the field collecting the more unusual items, but the
organization that he had developed made his nursery business far
more rewarding than it had been. Collinson's statement of account
to Bartram for the period 1760–62 showed receipts from customers
of £590.[3] While it seems most unlikely that he was entirely recom-
pensed for the expense and labor of his trips and his nurseries, the
arrangement made such delightful distractions from farming possible.

For Collinson there was only the satisfaction derived from

seeing the results in the gardens of his friends and a dividend of which he may or may not have been conscious—that his ability to procure such curiosities may have opened some doors to him which might otherwise have remained closed. As business increased, Collinson found that he was having to spend more and more time on it, often more than he would like. It involved a plethora of correspondence and "attendance at the Customs house to procure delivery of the seeds and then dispersing the boxes to their proper owners."[4] Even more difficult was collecting money from the customers, particularly the wealthy and noble. Collinson complained that "it is very hard getting money of great people, though I give them my labour and pains into the bargain. They are glad of the cargo, but are apt to forget all the rest. They give good words, but that will not always do."[5] Then the money had to be transmitted to Bartram or kept in his account. After all this, some of the customers, after receiving their boxes, would say "'Pray sir, how and in what manner must I sow them, pray be so good as to give me some directions for my gardener is a very ignorant fellow.'"[6]

The list of Bartram's individual patrons included many of England's, Ireland's, and Scotland's most influential and wealthy men, able to afford elaborate and extensive gardens. They ranged from peers to merchants. Of these, 124 have been documented, among them Frederick, Prince of Wales; the dukes of Argyll, Bedford, Cumberland, Manchester, Marlborough, Norfolk, Northumberland, and Richmond; the earls of Bute, Essex, Findlater, Galloway, Hyndford, Ilchester, Macclesfield, Marchmont, and Telmey. In addition there were at least thirty-three friends and correspondents with whom Bartram exchanged plants and seeds.[7]

The most demanding of Bartram's customers were the seedsmen and nurserymen. In the early years of his collecting all of his customers were individuals. In 1746 he had begun supplying James Gordon, nurseryman of Fenchurch Street, London. The following year John Williamson & Company, gardeners at Kensington, were added. Williamson soon became his largest customer and ordered as many as eight seed boxes per year over a period of sixteen years. It was not long before many other nurserymen were sending orders. There were at least nineteen based in England, many well known and popular with the English gentry. There was Christopher Gray at Fulham, for whom Catesby worked at one time. There were Henry and John DePonthieu, close neighbors of Collinson.

Nathaniel Powell of The Kings Head, Fetter Lane (Powell & Edie after 1760) was probably Bartram's second best customer. John Webb of The Acorn, Bridge Street, was another faithful one. Several of the nurserymen exported stock to Germany: "Balk," "Bert," and John Bush (Busch), in Middlesex, an especially good patron. In Scotland, Bartram supplied William Borthwick at Edinburgh, and in France, Bouchard at Paris. There may have been others. While the list of Bartram's individual customers is fairly easily determined, the extent and number of people who bought from the nurserymen can scarcely be gauged. Bartram was supplying gardens not only in the British Isles but on the continent as well.[8]

Collinson could not complain that he had received nothing new from Bartram in his 1762 box. There were "seven hard and stony seeds, something shaped like an acorn." He thought that John was "a great wag" and had only sent them to puzzle him. He had a great collection of seeds but none like these. He and James Gordon studied them and argued about them. Collinson hoped that they were seeds of the bonduc tree (Kentucky coffee tree, *Gymnocladus dioica* [L.] K. Koch), which he had long wanted. He laughed at Gordon, who thought that they must be some species of hickory. Gordon had the last laugh, for they were nuts which had been sent to Bouquet from Illinois as hickory nuts.[9]

Upon his return from Pittsburgh, Bartram had more opportunity to get acquainted with his nephew. Bill was busy with his studies but managed to visit now and then. Not long after this he became an apprentice of his cousins, Isaac and Moses, with one of whom he was apparently living. Probably he was able to attend the anatomy lectures started that fall by Dr. William Shippen, Jr. The family all found Bill attractive and insisted that he spend Christmas with them. Neither Bill nor his cousin Billy was a satisfactory correspondent. Bartram was continually annoyed because he could get no information from Billy about his business venture, and Colonel William complained that Bill never wrote to his mother. News of Billy was apt to reach Bartram from some friend in Carolina.

Bartram continued to write to his son and, in a letter just after Christmas, discussed several interesting North Carolina plants which his nephew had told him about: "Thee disappointed my expectation much, in not sending me any seeds by Captain Sharpless; and I know your seeds were, some or other, ripening from the day thee set thy foot on Carolina shore, until Sharpless's departure, and such as were within a mile or two of thy common walks, or most of them within sight. And yet I have not received one single seed from my son, who glories so much in the knowledge of plants, and whom I have been at so much charge to instruct therein." His complaint was successful for Dr. Green forwarded a box of plants and seeds from Billy and wrote that the young man had called on him several times.[10] In June 1762 Billy returned to Philadelphia to attend to business affairs, and his uncle found parting with him was more painful than with his own son. He took comfort from the fact that Billy would be returning.[11]

In 1762 Bartram and Collinson began a political debate that continued in their correspondence for several years. As far as colonial affairs were concerned, Bartram shared the views of Frederick the Great, who is reputed to have said of William Pitt, "At last England has brought forth a man."[12] Bartram was distressed when Pitt was forced out of office in January 1762 and wrote to Collinson on the subject. The latter did not admire Pitt and expressed his views strongly: "I don't find any cause to lament his abdication. We go on full as well without him. So prithee, my dear John, revive and don't sink, and be lost in doleful dumps under so terrible an event, which portends no harm that I can see; for we have a brave King, and good men at the helm. Never fear; we shall keep Canada, and have a good peace; and Pitt is as well pleased with his mercenary pension of £3000 per annum, and a title in reversion; and has cleverly slipped his neck out of the collar, when it most became him to keep in, to serve his country, but he preferred serving himself before it." Bartram replied that he would be happy to have an honorable peace but feared that, if Louisiana were not ceded to the English, there would be continuing trouble with the Indians. The French would not only encourage them but would also encroach, and eventually this would lead to war.[13]

Franklin returned in the fall of 1762. With him he brought a magazine, two books, and a letter to Bartram from Collinson. One of the books was a second edition of the *Flora Virginica*, completed by Gronovius' son, Laurens, and sent by him to Bartram. When writing to Collinson, Bartram did not comment directly on the fact that Clayton's manuscript of a new flora had never been published, but he made an oblique reference to it: "My thanks to Gronovius for his new edition of *Flora Virginica*. It's pity the plants beyond the south Mountain, and the draft of that fine country had not been in it."[14] What fate had befallen Clayton's manuscript, which had caused so much enthusiasm in London, remained a mystery. There was some compensation for Bartram to see his name among the "authors cited" and that J. F. Gronovius had written that Collinson had made available to him "the Pennsylvania plants dried by the industry of the most diligent John Bartram."[15]

There was an item of particular interest to Bartram in Collinson's letter. The governor of Virginia had sent Collinson some enormous teeth, the largest of which weighed three and three-quarters pounds and was eighteen inches in circumference. They had been found at a salt lick near the Ohio River by an Indian trader named Greenwood, who had knocked them out of the jaws of the skeletons of six gigantic creatures standing there. Collinson hoped that Bartram would seek out the fossils if his travels took him within one hundred miles of them.[16]

Bartram was already on the trail of the mysterious skeletons before he received Collinson's letter. Colonel Bouquet had informed him that he had received in early July "a very great curiosity, from about six hundred miles down the Ohio;—an elephant's tooth, weighing six pounds and three quarters, and a large piece of one of the tusks; which puts it beyond doubt, that those animals have formerly existed on this continent."[17] Bartram had promptly written to a Quaker friend, James Wright (of Delaware County, Pennsylvania?), and asked him to learn what he could about the skeletons. Wright questioned two of the "more sensible" Shawnees about them. The skeletons were in a large savannah (Big Bone Lick, Kentucky) three miles from the eastern side of the Ohio River and four days' journey from the lower Shawanese town. There were five more-or-less complete skeletons lying with their heads together, and they were incredibly large. The shoulder blades were as long as a tall man, the thigh bones were large enough in diameter to permit a small boy to crawl inside, and the tusks were ten to twelve feet long. The Shawnees told of ancestral men who had been big enough to kill these beasts and carry them home on their shoulders as modern Indians would a deer. They believed that God had killed the animals by means of lightning to protect the present smaller race of Indians.[18]

Thus, Bartram was well prepared to inform Collinson about the skeletons when he received his inquiry. He did not believe that the beasts could have been rhinoceroses, which Collinson or others had suggested. Their presence would be quite as difficult to explain as that of elephants, and the bones were too large to have been either. He thought that the bones belonged to an unknown beast. If he had an opportunity to go there, he would want to study enough bones to make a complete skeleton, for he was critical of the very superficial reports that had been made by "uncurious" persons. He was amused by Collinson's description, which pictured the skeletons standing facing each other "which is impossible. The ligaments would rot, and the bones fall out of joint, and tumble confusedly to the ground. But its a great pity, and shame to the learned curiosos, that have great estates, that they don't send some person that will take pains to measure every bone exactly, before they are broken and carried away, which they soon will be, by ignorant, careless people for gain."[19]

Bartram had written to his brother William in December 1761, "I have a great mind to drink, next fall, out of the springs at the head of Cape Fear River and Pedee, if God Almighty please to afford me an opportunity."[20] He had been tremendously excited by the botanic possibilities of the Carolinas and Virginia, and his longing to return was kept alive by his Carolina correspondents. In the spring he was very pleased to have his seeds from the Pittsburgh trip coming up as thick as hair along with "many from North and South Carolina," but he still planned another Carolina trip.[21] Some of his determination came from a new neighbor who had lived on the New River in southwestern Virginia until driven out by the Indians. He told Bartram of a huge chestnut tree on his old land whose nuts were unfit to eat and which sounded like a nut that Bartram had been given from near the Greenbrier River. The man spoke of other interesting plants that he had never seen anywhere but there. He said the river was more than five hundred feet wide at that point. Other bits of information provided by his neighbor continued to whet Bartram's curiosity. There were catfish a foot long and, on the bank of the river, a mine of such bright silver mixed with lead that the river reflected the glitter. When Bartram expressed an interest in visiting Holston's River, the man gave him a list of the houses on the road and the distances between them.[22]

By August, Bartram's plans were set. Billy would be returning to Carolina with him. They would go down the Shenandoah Valley to the New River, then cross the mountains to the Moravian settlements on the Carolina side along the Yadkin River and then on to the Wateree, all provided that the mischievous Indians did not interfere. John Bush, the London nurseryman, was eager for seeds and plants of the umbrella tree, and Bartram had hopes that he and Billy could find it somewhere along the Yadkin.[23] At the last minute Moses decided to join the expedition. He and Isaac were planning an expansion of their newly established business venture by seeking wholesale drug outlets in the other colonies. Their Uncle William had written the year before that he might be of service to them in this endeavor. They had also written to Dr. Garden of their plans in January, and he had replied that he would be delighted to assist them in any way he could.[24]

Bartram and his sons did not go to the New River on the way south as first planned. Instead they followed the "Great Road" from Philadelphia through eastern Virginia to the Yadkin River, a distance of 435 miles. Bartram amused himself as he went by testing sand along the road for iron content with his steel magnet. For the greater part of the journey they were passing through red clay soil, and the sand that he tested had been washed out of the clay by floods. He found that it would adhere to his magnet just like some sand that Jared Eliot had sent to him. When he reached the twenty-fourth parallel in North Carolina, the soil became very sandy and particles as large as radish seeds stuck to his magnet.[25] At the Yadkin, Moses and Billy turned east toward the coast and Ashwood, while their father continued south. He asked Moses to look out for available land in the neighborhood of his uncle's plantation. Bartram was thinking about acquiring some for his youngest son, Benjamin, now only fourteen but showing an interest in farming.[26]

At the time of parting with his sons, Bartram had planned a visit with a Mr. Mendenhall, a relative of Ann. By chance, however, he met Mendenhall sixty miles from home and so changed his plans, going more directly toward the Congaree River. He had been advised to stay at the home of Samuel Wyly, an Irish Quaker, who had settled near present-day Camden, South Carolina, where he had a store. Wyly was most knowledgeable about the area. He was a close friend of the chief of the Catawbas and had surveyed 144,000 acres for the tribe. He insisted that his guest borrow a horse for a day or two while Bartram's recovered from the long trip. This was a great help and enabled Bartram to continue almost to the Savannah River. He had hoped to find plants in this area that would differ from those of the coastal plain, and he was not disappointed. One plant in particular delighted him: "A glorious evergreen, about four or five feet high, and much branched in very small twigs growing upright. The leaves are much like the Newfoundland Spruce, rather smaller and grow round the twigs close, like it. The seed is very small, in little capsules, as big as mustard" (*Ceratiola ericoides* Michx.?).[27]

After two days at Wyly's, Bartram headed north toward the "Moravian Town" (now Old Salem, North Carolina). He had not progressed far when his botanical instinct led him nearly a mile off his road to find a sweet shrub or Carolina allspice (*Calycanthus*). It had neither flowers nor seeds at this time of year, but Bartram later wrote a description of its location to Wyly, whom he had drafted into sending him seeds. Bartram was delighted when Wyly sent him the plant or one like it which grew vigorously at Kingsessing.[28] Bartram found many other smaller plants as he went, most of which he could take with him. Among these were an *Amsonia*, then very popular in English gardens, and the pyramid of eden, which Alexander Garden called "the glory of the Blue Mountains" (*Swertia carolinensis* [Walt.] O. Ktze.).[29]

From Salem, Bartram rode some thirty miles along a bad road to the settlements in the valley, where he stopped to ask advice about crossing the mountains into southwestern Virginia. He was fortunate in learning of four hunters who were about to set out in that direction, and he was able to join their party. They spent the first night on a small tributary of the New River, not far from the head of the Dan River, and started climbing the mountains the next day. The mountainous terrain impressed Bartram: "The South or Alleghany Mountains, are really very high on Carolina side, and steep, full as high, if not higher, than our Blue Mountains; and still grow much higher against Georgia. There is much middling good land, and fine savannas, and plentiful streams, on these mountains; but it's so cold and wet, and the snow frequently two feet deep in winter (some say in October and November, but I believe not commonly then), that it must be uncomfortable living...." While the hunters stalked deer with which they kept the party's larder well supplied, Bartram was able to collect a few plants, among them the wild lily-of-the-valley.

They reached Colonel Chiswell's lead mine about noon the

third day, and Bartram parted company with the hunters. He spent
the afternoon in the neighborhood and along the New River, collecting numbers of interesting plants. Among them were the
American yew, broad-leaved *Silphium*, the Allegheny barberry, and
a "rudbeckia" witb peach-colored petals.[30] Here he found three different horse chestnuts, but he was unable to find the silver mine
that his neighbor had mentioned as being in the area. He did meet
a man on the road who was sporting silver buttons.[31] There were
other things that Bartram collected, namely some tall tales. One of
his many landlords told him of a spring near the headwaters of the
James River which ebbed and flowed like the seas, running for six
hours and stopping for six. When it ran, it had sufficient force to
turn a mill and did so. Bartram thought this would be a real curiosity if it were true and might have been more skeptical had he not
been told by his grandmother of a spring at the Peak in Derbyshire
that ebbed and flowed. The same gentleman had told Bartram of a
warm spring that emptied into either the Greenbrier River or the
James, he was not sure which. The landlord and many others had
experienced its "excellent virtues" after sitting in it a short time
and breaking out "all in A sweat."[32]

When Bartram left the lead mine, he was again fortunate in
obtaining a guide, for the overseer rode with him, crossing the
river in a boat. As they went in the direction of Holston's River,
Bartram was amused to find that the distances between houses,
which his neighbor had listed, were "surprisingly exact." From Fort
Chiswell (near present-day Wytheville), they proceeded to "the
Ferry," thirty miles away. It was dark when they reached the inn,
and the following day they again traveled until dark, going supper-
less and sleeping on the ground beside the eastern branch of New
River. Bartram's guide left around noon the next day when they
had reached the branches of the Staunton River,[33] and he proceeded
alone. He crossed the South Mountain along a wagon road which
was so steep in one place that the wagoners cut small trees and tied
them behind the wagons to act as a drag going down. So much wood
accumulated at the bottom that big fires were made to get rid of it.
As Bartram went north, he noticed that the rich bottomlands belonged to the wealthy, while the poor farmers had to be satisfied
with the less fertile land on the hills. Gradually wheat and oats
were replacing tobacco, and there were some fine orchards of
peaches and apples, from which brandy was distilled.[34]

It was the end of October when Bartram reached home.[35] Although the trip had been the longest he had ever taken, he thought it had been his most satisfying one. Providence had kept him safe from danger or accident and had directed him to many unusual plants. He was confident that Collinson and his friends would be impressed by the collection.[36] Collinson wrote: "Think, my dear John, with what amazement and delight I, with Doctor Solander, surveyed the quire of specimens. He thinks near half are new genera. This will enrich the fountain of knowledge. The Doctor is very busy examining them. I hope soon to send thee a list of them. . . . But what surprises us most is the Tipitiwichet Sensative."[37]

This "sensative" plant was the subject of a great deal of correspondence before Collinson was finally satisfied about it. In January 1760 Governor Dobbs had sent Collinson a description of it which intrigued him: "But the great wonder of the vegetable kingdom is a very curious unknown species of sensitive; it is a dwarf plant, the leaves are like a narrow segment of a sphere, consisting of two parts, like the cap of a spring purse, the concave part outwards, each of which falls back with indented edges (like an iron spring fox trap); upon any thing touching the leaves, or falling between them, they instantly close like a spring trap, and confine any insect or anything that falls between them; it bears a white flower: to this surprising plant I have given the name of Fly Trap Sensitive."[38]

When Bartram visited Dobbs that spring, it would have been highly surprising if his host had failed to mention it. Certainly someone did, for, in answer to Bartram's request, Billy and his uncle sent some good roots of the plant to Bartram in May 1761; however, they were washed overboard. Bartram thought it would be better to send them between September and April and gave directions for their packing and shipment. The following summer the impatient Collinson wanted Billy to make sketches of the plant and wished that it was safely growing in Bartram's garden: "I then could form some idea of this waggish plant—as waggishly described."[39]

Bartram was already doing his best. A great variety of Carolina plants were doing well in his garden, but there were several that he still wanted, including some sensitive plants, one of which he had from the Congaree. About a month later he had planted some more of the seed from there, but only two seedlings survived.

This was the true *Dionaea muscipula* Ellis, which Bartram found "differs much from ye sensitive bryer [*Leptoglottis?*] which only closeth its leaves at ye touch & ye humble plant [*Mimosa pudica* L.?] both which is very prickley but this is quite smooth slender stalked & both closeth its leaves & gently prostrates my little tipitiwitchet sensative stimulates laughter in all ye beholders." A French visitor from Montreal had been particularly amused. In October 1762 Collinson reminded Bartram that he was impatient to see this plant and again inquired if Billy might paint it. By December he was really tantalized: "Whilst the Frenchman was ready to burst with laughter, I am ready to burst with desire for root, seed or specimen of the waggish *Tipitiwitchet* Sensitive."[40]

When Bartram sent his Carolina collection to Collinson in the fall of 1762, the ship was seized by the Spanish. In January he sent both leaves and the flower of his tipitiwitchet to Collinson in the care of a friend, Thomas Fisher. To Bartram's delight that spring, he found that one of the plants that he had raised from seed was still alive and vigorous. Collinson, too, had reason for rejoicing, for the Carolina specimens which the Spanish had seized had finally been sent on to him and included the sensitive plant. He was ecstatic: "It is quite a new species, a new genus. It was impossible to comprehend from any description, which made me so very impatient to see it. I wish we had good seed; I doubt not but Gordon

"Tipitiwichet sensative"
(*Dionaea muscipula* Ellis)

would raise it." Although he had never received Bartram's letter with the leaves, he sent a specimen of the plant to Linnaeus, telling Bartram, "Only to him would I spare such a jewel. . . . Linnaeus will be in raptures at the sight of it."[41]

Seeds of the sensitive plant arrived from Bartram in December 1763, and Collinson immediately sent them to Gordon. Although Bartram had said that they were good and fresh, they did not sprout.[42] In June, Collinson informed Bartram that there was now little hope of obtaining seeds from Dobbs: "I hear my Friend Dobbs at 73 has gott a Colts Tooth in his Head & has married a young lady of 22 It is now in vain to write to him for seeds or plants of Tipitiwichet now He has gott one of his Own to play with."[43] In 1765, when Bartram visited the area in North Carolina from which Dobbs' plants had come, he noted that this was the extreme range.[44] He made no further mention of it, but many other people then took over the intriguing subject, including John Ellis, who formally described the plant.

Collinson was enjoying a very special gratification in the spring and summer of 1763. The young Lord Petre, son of his old friend, had given him an order for a ten-guinea box of seeds from Bartram, as his father had so often done. Collinson wrote to Bartram of his great pleasure: "It may be truly said the spirit of Elijah rests on Elisha." He had other reasons to be pleased, for many Bartram plants were blooming in his garden: *Calycanthus*, a red-flowered *Acacia*, a laurel-leaved *Magnolia*, and *Rhododendron*, "glorious beyond expression."[45]

In April 1763 Collinson had been unable to resist needling Bartram about the fact that a treaty had been signed without the services of Pitt and that "all Louisiana is yielded to us by an honourable peace. . . . Now, my dear John, does not the ardour of curiosity burn in thy mind to explore the wonders of Louisiana?"[46] Bartram was indeed burning with curiosity to see Louisiana and had already become very much involved in the matter. Soon after his return from Carolina in the fall of 1762, he had received an invitation from Colonel Bouquet to join an expedition to take possession of the land ceded to England by France. Bouquet was to establish the English presence in the newly acquired territory. His party would go by boat from Pittsburgh, and carpenters had already been sent there to build the necessary boats. He hoped to leave by April.

Bouquet assured Bartram that he considered his going to be important, that he would have no duties other than to study the natural
history of the new territory, and that he would be given every assistance in so doing.[47] As an added bonus Bartram would be able to
make a personal examination and measurement of the mammoth
skeletons near the Ohio River. Although Collinson had failed to get
the word, other Bartram friends had heard. Linnaeus learned of
the proposed expedition from Garden, who alerted him to expect
the wonders which Bartram was sure to bring back.[48]

While Bartram was enjoying the prospect of the Bouquet journey, another was proposed to him. James Logan's son, William
(1718–76), suggested that Bartram join him on a trip down the
Ohio to the lower Shawnee Indian town to seek the release of prisoners being held there.[49] Bartram's prospects of joining either or
both of these expeditions dimmed considerably when he developed
a stubborn and painful ulcer on his leg which failed to respond to
his doctor's treatments. Not only Bartram but also Bouquet and the
doctor were upset, the latter two saying that it would be a grave
loss to the nation if he were unable to go with Bouquet. Finally
Bartram gave up his doctor's prescriptions and applied some of his
own. These proved more successful, and he began to think that he
would be able to travel. In the meantime Indians, incensed by the
French treaty with England, attacked the western outposts, and
Bouquet's plans were abruptly changed. He was ordered to lead a
force to relieve Fort Pitt.[50] A bloody battle was fought at Bushy
Run in which the Indians were defeated, but plans for Bouquet's
Mississippi and Louisiana expedition were abandoned.[51]

Bartram made two short trips to Little Egg Harbor and Great
Egg Harbor rivers with John, Jr., in the fall of 1763. With Billy
away, Johnny had now become what Collinson referred to as Bartram's "sheet anchor." Bartram found Johnny a great help not only
on trips but in the care of the nursery as well: "My John is a worthy, sober, industrious son, and delights in plants but I doubt Will
will be ruined in Carolina. Everything goes wrong with him
there."[52] It was well that his father could have such confidence in
Johnny, for Bartram was evolving a scheme which might keep him
away from home for six months to a year. Only if he was assured
that his business could be carried on as usual could he contemplate
such an absence. The *Pennsylvania Gazette* had reported an En-

glish proposal to investigate the natural productions of Canada and Louisiana—their minerals, soils, vegetables, and favorable locations for factories. Bartram considered himself perhaps the best qualified person in England or America for such an assignment. He felt, however, that such an investigation would not be possible until the Indians were thoroughly subdued or "All the discoverers would be exposed to the greatest savage cruelty. . . ."[53]

As the months went by, Bartram's enthusiasm for the proposed exploration grew rather than diminished. He wrote to Peter, "The variety of plants and flowers in our southwestern continent, is beyond expression. Is it not, dear Peter, the very palace garden of old Madam *Flora*? OH! if I could but spend six months on the Ohio, Mississippi, and Florida, in health, I believe I could find more curiosities than the English, French and Spaniards have done in six score years." Collinson pounced on Bartram's mention of Florida to tease him again, since its acquisition could not be ascribed to his idol, William Pitt. Bartram replied with asperity that, could he afford it, he would be content just to explore Florida, Georgia, Alabama, and the Mississippi River, no matter whose it was![54] In June, at last, Collinson acknowledged that he understood Bartram's early subtle hints and later open suggestions: "I wish we had some wealthy, public-spirited people who would encourage a search of those fine countries,—our new acquisitions. No one so well accomplished for that work as thyself; but court politics so engross the attention of the great men, they have no room to think of anything else. It is by no means advisable to undertake it at thy own expence."[55] However, Peter did nothing to use his influence among his noble friends to secure an appointment for John.

Bartram was frustrated that he could not get support for his exploration. Insult was added to injury when friends came to him with the news that William Young, Jr. (1742–85) had been appointed Queen's Botanist at £300 a year. They pointed out that Young had received more preferment "by a few miles traveling to pick up a few common plants," many of which had long been in English gardens, than Bartram had in thirty years of dangerous and distant exploration.[56] The twenty-two-year-old Young was the son of a German neighbor and as a lad had spent many hours in Bartram's garden. In 1761 he had gone to Charles Town, probably with a letter of introduction to Garden from Bartram. The doctor became his patron and wrote to John Ellis in his behalf, saying that Young wanted an introduction to Gray, Gordon, and other nurserymen as well as gentlemen desiring plants. Young would spend his whole time filling specific orders. Ellis was definitely interested since he had been unable to persuade Garden to send seeds or plants in quantity.[57]

In the summer of 1764 Young had the impudence to send a package of plants directly to Queen Charlotte: "He had placed the pacquet unobserved in the bag which is usually kept open at the Coffee-house by ships shortly to clear. Arrived at London the skipper was in a quandary whether to deliver the pacquet, of which he knew nothing, what it contained or who had sent it; but after consultation with his friends despatched it as directed. The Queen, supposing this to be an extraordinarily hopeful lad, had the youthful Young brought to London and placed under the care of the celebrated Dr. Hill. Three hundred pounds sterling was appropriated annually for his use, and after a time Young came back to America, with the title, a large peruque and a small stipend, and fulfilled none of the hopes he had aroused."[58]

Collinson having failed him, Bartram decided to try his own solution. Impressed by Young's success, he packed a small box with his rarest treasures, some of which had never before been sent to England, and addressed it to young King George III. He was curious to see whether their rarity would be recognized.[59] Some of his friends suggested that he send the box in the care of the Proprietor, but Franklin persuaded him to send it to Collinson and "not to pass by his old Friend." Bartram agreed, but with reservations, writing to Collinson that, if he was unable to deliver the box, Franklin had suggested that the queen's physician, Dr. John Pringle, would do so.[60] Not content with sending plants to the English king, Bartram determined to go Young one better; he packed a collection of plants, "ye fruite of near thirty years Travel thro New England, New York East & West Jersey Pensilvania Maryland Virginia North & South Carolina, from ye Sea Coast to that great Lake Ontario & for many hundred miles to ye north of ye great Alegany mountains back of all ye above mentioned Provinces. . . ." These plants he despatched to Queen Louisa of Sweden, with a letter referring to her "surprising Progress in all kind of natural Knowledge. . . ."[61]

Bartram dispensed with hints when next he wrote to Collinson. He spelled out his desires distinctly and specifically: "My good old friend, I am well assured that thee is well acquainted with many of the nobility, some of whom, no doubt, are men of curiosity. Could not they be prevailed upon to enable me to travel a year or two through our King's new acquisitions, to make a thorough natural and vegetable search, either by public authority, or private subscription? And I must insist upon two articles: first, that I have one to accompany me; second, to have an allowance sufficient to make full discovery, and not be hurried for time to make remarks, and carriage to transport what I discover. But I can't expect to be able to perform such a task many years hence. I must yield to the infirmities of age, or death."[62]

Franklin was as upset over the Young affair as were Bartram's other friends, telling Collinson, "I wish some Notice may be taken of John's Merit. It seems odd that a German Lad of his Neighbourhood, who had only got some Smatterings of Botany from him, should be so distinguish'd on that Account, as to be sent for by the Queen, and our old Friend who had done so much, quite forgotten. He might be made happy as well as more useful, by a moderate Pension that would enable him to travel thro' all the New Acquisitions, with Orders to the Governors, and Commanding Officers at the several Outposts, to forward and protect him in his Journeys."[63] Collinson decided to enlist the aid of Lord Northumberland, an ardent gardener who had given much assistance to Lord Bute in the development of the Royal Botanic Gardens at Kew. Northumberland was no stranger to Bartram's abilities, as he had been one of his regular customers since 1747. Collinson expressed the hope that Lord Northumberland would remember to inspect Bartram's box of specimens when next he went to court. The king had expressed his approval of them to Collinson at the last levee. Now that Lord Bute was so busy with affairs of state, he had no time to consider sending Bartram to Florida, but Collinson hoped that Northumberland might forward the idea. Bartram could send seeds and plants to the king from various southern ports. He would be an ideal collector, for he was capable of making observations on the soil as well as the vegetation. Moreover, he was eager to go and a moderate man. He would be satisfied with a small stipend, sufficient to cover the costs of himself and one or two servants.[64]

While Bartram waited to see whether his and Franklin's appeals to Collinson would be successful, his assistance was sought from another quarter. Both Franklin and another old friend, Dr. John Bard (1716–99) of New York, approached Bartram on behalf of Dr. John Hope, professor of botany at the University of Edinburgh. Hope had written directly to Bartram in November 1763 complimenting him on the great reputation that he had achieved and suggesting an exchange of seeds between them. He had mentioned that young Samuel Bard, Dr. Bard's son, was making excellent progress in botany at Edinburgh.[65] Bartram would ordinarily have responded promptly to this sort of offer of a correspondence. If he did in this case, the letter went astray. Not having received a reply, Hope appealed to Franklin, and Samuel Bard wrote to his father. Hope needed help for two programs with which he was associated. He needed plants for a new botanic garden which was being established at Edinburgh. The Royal Botanic Garden and the King's Garden at Holyrood-house had proven inadequate, and a new garden had been laid out near Haddington Place. Second, Dr. Hope was an officer of the new "Society of Gentlemen," concerned with an attempt to reforest Scotland. Young Sam Bard informed his father that a number of Edinburgh gentlemen "have formed themselves into an association for the importation of American seeds and plants, and would be much obliged to you to recommend a proper person as a correspondent, I know of no one who would answer so well as Mr. Bartram."[66] The society had raised subscriptions from a number of men of prominence and was prepared to pay for seeds of foreign trees capable of thriving in Scotland.

Properly flattered by all of these commendations, Bartram sent Hope in October a gift of 100 plant specimens, some of which were rare, and a box of seeds containing 150 species. He also sent in late November a box of forest trees containing about 100 species, at the request of Franklin. He agreed to supply the society's demands, provided that their "generosity is equal to them; for the charges of collecting rare vegetables are in proportion to the distance from home, and hazards and dangers in collecting them."[67] Dr. Hope had received the seeds and plants when he wrote on 7 March 1765 to thank Bartram. For the future he wanted only seeds for the society, since its members lived at widely scattered locations in Scotland and the distribution of plants was too complicated. They were primarily interested in useful trees but had a secondary interest in ornamental shrubs. Since they were particularly interested in woods, he hoped that Bartram would send a sample of the wood of each tree for which he sent seeds "and you have an easy way of executing this, by making the tops, bottoms, sides and divisions of the boxes of different wood, numbering each with references to the catalogue: the whole constituted in the same rough way packing boxes are usually made, beginning with all the woods of one genus, as the Pines, and then the Oaks, &c."[68]

Bartram's comments on Hope's idea of an "easy way" of packing seeds have not survived, but the enterprise got off to a bad start. When he shipped a £15 box of seeds of the 1765 crop, he sent them via Ireland rather than London, as Hope thought he had requested. They were reshipped from Ireland to Chester, where they were seized by the customs agents. When they were eventually released by customs, they were sent by land to London and then on to Edinburgh. They arrived there in time for the 1767 planting season rather than the 1766, which did nothing to improve their germination or the tempers of the members of the society. Collinson forwarded another box to Hope from Bartram in April 1767 and agreed to settle the first £15 charge for half of that sum, but this was the last shipment made to them by Bartram.[69]

On 8 November 1764 a great crowd of well-wishers accompanied Franklin to the ship in which he was to sail for England. Franklin, carrying Pennsylvania's protest against the proposed Stamp Act, later headed the delegation of colonial agents in England. Bartram, "being no party man" and being extremely busy, took no part in the "bon voyage."[70] He had not heard from Collinson since a letter dated 30 June, so when he wrote to Franklin before Christmas, he told him that he was very worried about their friend. He was reassured to hear from Franklin that "Our Friend Peter is not dead, as you apprehended; but, Thanks to Heaven, as well as I ever knew him, hearty, brisk, and active as a Youth." When Franklin showed Collinson Bartram's letter, he said that he had already written. Not only Collinson but others assured Franklin that Bartram's box of plants for the king had been very well received.[71]

With Benjamin overseas again, Bartram often stopped by the Franklins' house to see how the family fared. One late fall day he came by to invite them to celebrate his "Dauters marag."[72] Ann, the Bartrams' youngest girl, was to marry George Bartram in the

Old Swedes Church on 6 December 1764. The bridegroom had emigrated from Scotland with his brother, Alexander, and his mother and sister. He and his brother had gone into the dry goods business with James Dundas.[73] It was thought that the two Bartram families were related since there was great similarity in their coats-of-arms.[74]

FOURTEEN

"His Majesty's Botanist for North America"

O N A pleasant day in the late spring of 1765, there came a knock upon the Bartrams' door. When Mrs. Bartram opened it she saw a youngish man on the step who identified himself as St. John de Crèvecoeur. He had been born in France in 1734 but had emigrated to Canada, where he became a lieutenant under Montcalm. About five years prior to his visit to the Bartrams, he had been employed as a surveyor at Albany. Well educated and unassuming, he was a highly attractive person.[1] To Mrs. Bartram's query as to whom he wanted, Crèvecoeur replied: "I should be glad to see Mr. Bartram."

"If thee wilt step in and take a chair, I will send for him," she cordially invited him.

"No," he said, "I had rather have the pleasure of walking through his farm; I shall easily find him out, with your directions."

Following Ann's instructions, he wandered down to the river and soon came to a newly made dike, on which he strolled for quite a distance. He finally came to a group of ten or so men working and inquired, "Can you tell me where Mr. Bartram is?"

A tall, thin, elderly man in wide trousers covered by a leather apron, answered him, "My name is Bartram, dost thee want me?"

"Sir," Crèvecoeur replied, "I am come on purpose to converse with you, if you can be spared from your labour."

"Very easily," Bartram answered, "I direct and advise more than I work."

They walked to the house where Bartram found his visitor a comfortable chair while he went to wash and change his clothes. Upon his return, Crèvecoeur told him, "The fame of your knowledge in American botany, and your well known hospitality have induced me to pay you a visit, which I hope you will not think troublesome. I should be glad to spend a few hours in your garden."

"The greatest advantage," Bartram replied, "which I receive from what thee callest my botanical fame, is the pleasure which it often procureth me in receiving the visits of friends and foreigners. But our jaunt into the garden must be postponed for the present, as the bell is ringing for dinner."

Bartram led his guest into the hall where a table as long as a Welsh dairy table was laden with food. At the lower end were seated the negroes and next to them the hired men, while the family and Crèvecoeur were near the head, where Mr. and Mrs. Bartram presided. Heads were bowed for silent grace in the Quaker fashion.

"After the luxuries of our cities, this plain fare must appear to thee a severe fast," Bartram remarked to his guest.

"By no means, Mr. Bartram," Crèvecoeur responded, "this honest country dinner convinces me that you receive me as a friend and an ould acquaintance."

"I am glad of it," his host answered, "for thee art heartily wel-

St. John de Crèvecoeur
(1735–1813)

come. I never knew how to use ceremonies; they are insufficient proofs of sincerity; our Society, besides, are utterly strangers to what the world calleth polite expressions. We treat others as we treat ourselves."

While they ate, Crèvecoeur questioned the older man. "Pray, Mr. Bartram, what banks are those which you are making; to what purpose is so much expense and so much labour bestowed?"

"Friend St. John," Bartram answered, "no branch of industry was ever more profitable to any country, as well as the proprietors. The Schuylkill, in its many windings, once covered a great extent of ground, though its waters were but shallow even in our highest tides; and though some parts were always dry, yet the whole of this great tract presented to the eye nothing but a putrid swampy soil, useless, either for the plough or for the scythe. The proprietors of these grounds are now incorporated; we yearly pay to the treasurer of the company a certain sum, which makes an aggregate superior to the casualties that generally happen, either by inundations or the muskquash [muskrat]. It is owing to this happy contrivance that so many thousand acres of meadow have been rescued from the Schuylkill, which now both enricheth and embellisheth so much of the neighbourhood of our city."

Crèvecoeur commented, "It is really an admirable contrivance, which greatly rebounds to the honour of the parties concerned, and shows a spirit of discernment and perseverance which is highly praiseworthy; if the Virginians would imitate your example, the state of their husbandry would greatly improve."

While the two men had been talking, the others had quietly returned to work as soon as they had finished dinner. Hearing the faint sound of music, Crèvecoeur turned questioningly to Bartram, who smiled gently and let him seek out the cause. As the Frenchman climbed the staircase, he discovered an Aeolian harp through which the wind was playing—a complete novelty to him. After some Madeira, the two retired to the garden and greenhouse. So absorbed were they that, before they knew it, sunset was near. Relying on the Quaker's attachment to frankness and lack of ceremony, Crèvecoeur told him how very much he had enjoyed his visit but that it had been much too short. In fact, he openly said he should like to spend several days with him.

Bartram warmly remarked, "Thee art as welcome as if I was thy father; thee art no stranger; thy desire of knowledge, thy being a foreigner, besides, entitleth thee to consider my house as thine own, as long as thee pleaseth; use thy time with the most perfect freedom; I, too, shall do so myself."

Before dark, they walked over to the banks and examined the new meadows which had been made. Crèvecoeur admired the great number of horses and cattle grazing on the land which had so recently been marshy or under water. He marveled at the fine cows as they made their way to the barn, "deep-bellied, short-legged, having udders ready to burst." Bartram took great pride in his soil conservation and improvement and needed no urging to display it. He proudly showed Crèvecoeur the orchard growing on what had once been sterile, sandy ground. He related his particular methods of liquid fertilization, crop succession, and composting and the surprising results achieved. He explained how he irrigated his fields, saying that he was not unique in employing water to increase yields.

For the next several days, Crèvecoeur wandered about the farm and gardens with Bartram. In the evenings, they discussed aspects of botany and Bartram's burgeoning nursery business and correspondence. He was interested to learn that Bartram had sent plants to Antoine de Jussieu but surprised that Dalibard was the only Frenchman with whom he had corresponded. He suggested that Bartram write to Jussieu's brother, Bernard, who was in charge of the king's garden. In his turn, the widely traveled Crèvecoeur regaled Bartram with accounts of Pompeii and other European wonders.[2]

One aspect of the household puzzled the Frenchman, and one evening he asked his host, "By what means, Mr. Bartram, do you rule your slaves so well, that they seem to do their work with all the cheerfulness of white men?"

Leaning back in his chair, Bartram replied at length: "Though our erroneous prejudices and opinions once induced us to look upon them as fit only for slavery, though ancient custom had very unfortunately taught us to keep them in bondage, yet of late, in consequence of the remonstrances of several Friends, and of the good books they have published on that subject, our Society treats them very differently. With us they are now free. I give those whom thee didst see at my table, eighteen pounds a year, with victuals and clothes, and all other privileges which white men enjoy. Our Society treats them, now, as the companions of our labours; and by this management, as well as by means of the education we have given them, they are in general become a new set of beings. Those whom I admit to my table, I have found to be good, trusty, moral men; when they do not what we think they should do, we dismiss them, which is all the punishment we inflict. Other societies of Christians keep them as slaves, without teaching them any kind of religious principles: what motive beside fear can they have to behave well?

"In the first settlement of this province, we employed them as slaves, I acknowledge; but when we found that good example, gentle admonition, and religious principles could lead them to subordination and sobriety, we relinquished a method so contrary to the profession of Christianity. We gave them freedom, and yet few have quitted their ancient masters. The women breed in our families; and we become attached to one another. I taught mine to read and write; they love God, and fear his judgments. The oldest person among them transacts my business in Philadelphia, with a punctuality, from which he has never deviated.[3] They constantly attend our meetings, they participate in health and sickness, infancy and old age, in the advantages our society affords. Such are the means we have made use of, to relieve them from that bondage and ignorance in which they were kept before. Thee perhaps hast been surprised to see them at my table, but by elevating them to the rank of freemen, they necessarily acquire that emulation without which we ourselves should fall into debasement and profligate ways."

"Mr. Bartram, this is the most philosophical treatment of negroes that I have heard of; happy would it be for America would other denominations of Christians imbibe the same principles, and follow the same admirable rules," Crèvecoeur commented.

On Sunday two wagons took all the members of the household to the meetinghouse in Chester. Bartram and Crèvecoeur rode on horseback. The latter was surprised by the simplicity of the meetinghouse, its white walls gleaming, its benches comfortable, but no pulpit, no font, not even an organ or an altar. He quickly put his hat back on, which he had automatically removed. Even with 200 or so in the congregation, it was peacefully silent for half an hour. Then a lady arose, announced that the Spirit moved her, and discoursed with great dignity for forty-five minutes. After another fifteen minutes of silence, everyone arose and left the meetinghouse. Then Crèvecoeur was made so welcome by the Friends that he spent two months as guest of the various farmers in the community.

Bartram lost no time in writing to Bernard de Jussieu (1699–1777), telling him that he had planned to send him plant specimens in 1755 but the war had intervened. He sent him examples of spring plants, promising to forward a complete collection in the fall similar to those he dispatched each year to Sweden, Denmark, Scotland, Germany, and so forth. In a postscript, he added that his "Friend St. John," who admired Jussieu as much as he did, had promised to forward his letter to Paris and to inform Jussieu of the best method of directing any letter to Bartram via London.[4]

In February 1765 Collinson was optimistic about Bartram's chances of receiving some recognition from the king. Both the Earl of Northumberland and Lord Bute had agreed that the exploration of Florida was a necessity and that Bartram was the obvious person to do it.[5] Franklin, encouraged by Collinson, ended a letter to Bartram, "In the pleasing Expectation of a happy Meeting with you after your Return, hearing your curious and judicious Observations, and enjoying your agreeable and instructive Conversation. . . ."[6] Weeks went by, however, without further word.

There was a brief distraction for Bartram in mid-May, a visit of Lord Adam Gordon (c. 1726–1801), accompanied by the governor, Colonel Bouquet (now General), and a number of other prominent people. Gordon returned for a second visit later in the week, and Bartram returned his calls at General Bouquet's house. Gordon was a colonel in the Sixty-sixth Regiment of Foot and the son of the second Duke of Gordon. He had spent several winter months at Charles Town and had come to know Alexander Garden well. Gordon represented Aberdeenshire, the doctor's home territory, in Parliament, and the two men shared an interest in botany as well. Gordon was so impressed by Bartram that he invited him to go to Quebec with him at his expense and promised to pay the cost of Bartram's return to Philadelphia.[7]

Bartram was tormented by invitations he could not accept. Lord Gordon wanted him to go to Quebec. General Bouquet wanted him to go with him to Florida, where he would furnish him with a servant to wait on him and "an escort through dangerous passes." He would very much like to do either but felt that he must decline both until he heard from Collinson.[8] Tantalizing advertisements in the *Gazette* announced the sailing of the *Florida Packet*, and there were announcements of land grants and invitations from Governor Grant to prospective Florida settlers.[9] Actually a letter from Collinson was on its way. He had written on 9 April: " . . . my repeated solicitations have not been in vain; for this day I received certain intelligence from our gracious King, that he had appointed thee his botanist, with a salary of £50 a year."

This was not a very munificent sum, being just one-sixth that paid to Young by the queen. Bartram's duties were carefully outlined by Collinson: he was to make observations on the soil and the country and to collect specimens of ores, plants, and fossils and send them to such shipping points as Pensacola, St. Augustine, and Charles Town. Collinson advised him to provide himself with large paper for specimens, leather covers for the paper, and leather saddlebags in which to carry them. As a personal request he urged that Bartram acquire a supply of small boxes for insects, land snails, and river shells. Collinson suggested that he go by sea to Charles Town and procure horses there.[10] Collinson had been disappointed in his attempts to get official letters of recommendation to all of the governors, but John Ellis, who was agent for West Florida, had written to the governors of both East and West Florida.

Bartram had very mixed reactions, as well he might. The honor of the title of King's Botanist was impressive and flattering, but the stipend was ridiculous. Collinson recognized that Bartram would not think the remuneration was enough and that he would have to "use it or refuse it" as he thought best.[11] Bartram expressed himself strongly, but Collinson wrote in November that there had been a change in the ministry and that Bartram's friends were now out: "So pray, make no more remonstrances on that head, for I am tired with a repetition of them in every letter. . . . I allow all thou says The premium is not equal to the risk; but in these precarious, unsettled times, there is no hope for an alteration."[12]

Bartram's friends were pleased to see him honored. Thomas Lamboll wrote, thanking him for a letter of condolence on the death of his son and congratulating Bartram on his appointment. Lamboll wished him "a Continuance of health, and enjoyment of the Royal Favour and Bounty."[13] This seemed to be the general sentiment, but Garden, while pleased for Bartram's sake, had some reservations. He expressed them to his friend John Ellis: "Is it really so? Surely John is a worthy man; but yet to give the title of King's Botanist to a man who can scarcely spell, much less make out the characters of any one genus of plants, appears hyperbolical. Pray how is this matter? Is he not rather appointed or sent, and paid, for searching out the plants of East and West Florida, and for that service only to have a reward and his expenses?"[14]

Garden's question was a pertinent one. Although Collinson had clearly written to Bartram that the king "had appointed thee his botanist," he wrote again in May saying that he had some doubts about the matter. In September he explained his doubts: "A horse is a necessary article for a King's botanist. But dost thou know who thou art to thank for that title? Between ourselves, *an old friend*, who knew thou deserved it; but under what character the King is pleased to rank thee, I do not know. Only this I know, he allows thee £50 per annum."[15]

While Bartram was understandably not happy about the small amount of money to be allowed by the king, he could not resist the temptation provided by both the title and the excuse for doing what he wanted to do anyway. He would have liked to take quite a bit of time in planning and preparing for a long absence from home, but General Bouquet was eager to have him take passage on the same ship with him as far as Charles Town, leaving about the first of July. Bartram wrote to Billy, asking if he would like to go to Florida. Collinson had proposed that Bartram might take him so that he could make sketches in the field, completing them at his leisure. In order that his son might settle his affairs with expedition, Bartram suggested that he sell his stock at public auction and turn over his accounts to an attorney, who would be better able to collect his debts than Billy. His son should write to his creditors immediately and explain the situation. Bartram would have to make other arrangements if Billy was not going.[16]

On the morning of 1 July 1765 Bartram gathered together his luggage, said good-bye to his family, and went to Philadelphia. Three days later the *Pennsylvania Gazette* noted: "On Monday last, Mr. JOHN BARTRAM, His Majesty's Botanist for North-America, embarked for South-Carolina, in the schooner East Florida, Captain Beckop; from whence he is to go to East and West Florida, in order to discover the curious and most valuable vegetable and mineral Productions of these Countries." The ship weighed anchor at four o'clock in the afternoon and set sail with a brisk breeze.[17] They proceeded down the Delaware River and by morning passed two men-of-war anchored near Wilmington. At noon they stopped for an hour at Reedy Island, where another passenger boarded. It was a leisurely progress; within the hour the ship paused, this time at Bombay Hook, where livestock were loaded.

The favorable breeze held throughout the night, and by Wednesday morning they had passed Cape Henlopen and were out in the rough Atlantic. Bartram immediately became "extream sick and head very dizzy" and continued ill until he reached Charles Town. He had decided to spend some time in the Carolinas before starting south. There were a number of preparations to be made, and he wanted to find cooler weather when he arrived in Florida. James Island, off Charles Town, was reached six days out of Philadelphia, but the ship's captain hove to all night, not wanting to chance "overshooting the bar." By ten o'clock next morning the ship anchored off Johnston's Fort, and Bartram lost no time in landing and making his way across town to Garden's home.

Only a few hours were required for Bartram to recover his bounce. In the late afternoon he and Garden called at the home of Colonel Henry Laurens (1724–92), a wealthy merchant of Huguenot extraction and Garden's close friend. Laurens' handsome gambrel-roofed house on East Bay, built five years previously, stood in the midst of a four-acre lot, but it was his ambitious garden that was causing something of a sensation in Charles Town. Laurens had brought over John Watson, an English gardener, especially to design and lay out his brick-walled garden, which was 450 by 600 feet.[18] Bartram had seen the garden before, but he found many improvements.

Having seen so little of his guest in 1760, Garden was determined to enjoy his visit this time and took some days off from his busy practice. In the morning he and Bartram called upon Thomas Lamboll and Dr. William Keith. After dinner they saddled up and rode out to see a newly appointed member of the Governor's Council of East Florida, Major John Moultrie, Jr. (1728?–98), who Garden thought might be of assistance to Bartram.[19] Moultrie had received a medical degree from the University of Edinburgh. While there he had had Carolina seeds and plants sent for the botanic garden, so he was interested to hear that there was a new one and that Bartram was to supply North American seeds for it. Perhaps what interested Bartram most was Moultrie's method of reclaiming salt marshes for rice fields. Constructing banks of earth around a future field, he gradually washed out the saline content by means of rainwater, which was regularly emptied out by means of sluices and the process repeated until the land was sweet.

The night was spent at Thorogood, the plantation of John Deas on Goose Creek, twenty miles from town. Below the lawns at the front of the house lay flat lands composed of stiff clay. These had been originally planted in rice but, not being enriched by manure, had become exhausted. To return them to their former fertility, steep banks had been made, resulting in a series of ponds so deep that they were stocked with fish of all sorts which multiplied rapidly: pike, gar, trout, mullet, bream, mudfish, carp, silver roach, and perch. Numerous herons and gannets haunted the ponds. Bartram was interested in the fine kitchen gardens at the back of the house where there grew grapevines and apple trees whose nine- to ten-foot branches were so laden with fruit that many almost touched the ground.

Deas and his guests were up early in the morning to ride to one of his quarters, where he wanted to show Bartram a new idea that he had introduced into farming: the planting of corn rows ten feet apart with indigo planted between. The indigo was interesting in that the lowest pods were already hardening while the upper branches were still in flower. It was about ready to be harvested, and Deas said that he hoped to cut it twice more before frost. Riding on, they passed through a field worn out from rice where Bartram dismounted to gather specimens of a fine spotted lily, whose petals turned back. Not far away they found a curious formation of limestone in which were impressions of seashells, some tinted by iron deposits. These were near the borders of Daniel Blake's plantation, Newington, whose fine brick house they reached just before dark and where they spent the night. Blake showed them his ten-foot cork oak tree, a native of southern Europe and northern Africa. After a hearty breakfast, they returned to Thorogood, leaving there at three o'clock for Charles Town, "haveing been exceeding diverted with Complaisant agreeable company & observed numerous species of curious plants & found one new genus. . . ."

On 10 July Garden returned to work and left his guest to his own devices. Bartram had his journal to update as well as letters to write. The next day he joined the Lambolls for a visit to their country seat on James Island. On this plantation, which had been acquired by Lamboll's father in 1696, there was a two-story house approached by an avenue of trees. The land was mainly sandy, sometimes covered with oyster shells, but some of it was of a rich black color where it had not been worn out by the planting of the Indians or white men. Bartram was surprised by the variety of trees growing in such sandy soil: hop hornbeam, magnolia, dogwood, linden, myrtle, pitch pine, beech, several species of evergreen oaks, pignut, and many others. Lamboll told him that there were many trespassers. Some came to hunt, and others brazenly dug earth from his banks and took it away.

Another day was spent wandering about Charles Town. Bartram liked the great brick marketplace, with its welcome shade and numerous stalls. The growth of Carolina fruit astonished him. One of Colonel Laurens' grapevines was seven and a half inches in circumference with 216 bunches of grapes, and there was a nectarine seven inches around. When Bartram wrote up his journal at night, he summarized all sorts of miscellaneous information that he had collected during the day, including Charles Town's population, rainfall, and temperature. He was meticulous in recording soil information. The ecological aspects interested him. He was told that the amount of tar produced from pines was dependent upon the amount of clay bottom. Firing the bay swamps when very dry killed all vegetation and resulted in a savannah covered with coarse grass. The rich-looking black soil, where grew the tall pines, was misleading. When cleared and planted, it produced only one or two crops before the topsoil washed away, leaving sterile sand. This, deep down, generally had a clay base, as did the great deposits of seashells, some of which were fine as sand. In either case, wherever a hole was dug, it began oozing water at ten to fifteen feet, sometimes even at six.

William Hopton invited Bartram to accompany him on a visit to his plantation, which he called Starve Gut Hall. On 14 July they crossed the Cooper River and rode ten miles northeast to the Hopton plantation on the southern bank of the Wando River. The principal crop raised was rice. An avenue of live oaks led to a rather small brick house where they spent the night. Bartram explored the salt marsh swamps with Hopton, observing many of the dwarf palmettoes.

Although Garden was busy, he managed to accompany Bartram on some of his rambles. He had been concerned that what he

thought to be Bartram's lack of understanding of generic characters might handicap him in his Florida explorations, so he spent as
much time as he could demonstrating taxonomic principles. He was
surprised to find that Bartram had a better grasp of them than he
had realized, although he thought him prone to confuse varieties
with species. He was again amazed by Bartram's tireless energy
and his knowledge of soils and timber but decided that perhaps his
greatest asset as a botanist was his lack of credulity.[20] They were
able to spend many of their evenings together in wide-ranging conversation, which both enjoyed. Bartram did not want to overstay
his welcome. He decided that he would ride north to Ashwood for a
visit with his brother and wait a bit for cooler weather before he
started south. Billy would return with him to Charles Town a few
weeks later.

His riding at Charles Town had been on borrowed horses, but
now he bought one of his own. He found one that he thought would
have the stamina it would need for his traveling and paid £40 for it
in the Carolina currency, the equivalent of £6 sterling. Collinson
thought £40 would make a large hole in Bartram's annual salary
and was pretty steep for a horse in a country "where they breed
wild and are had for the catching."[21] Bartram left Charles Town on
16 July for the ride of 170 or 180 miles to Ashwood. The weather
was hot for both horse and rider, so he made frequent stops to rest
and make observations of plants, soils, rocks, and other items of
interest. He felt under no time pressure and traveled at a leisurely
pace. This was probably just as well, for there were numerous fer-
ries: the Santee, the Black River, the Pee Dee, and the Waccamaw.
He was fortunate in finding hospitable hosts who provided food and
lodging. One, Herman Rust, even rode with him for some miles and
provided good company. Bartram took six days to reach Ashwood
and arrived there in a downpour of rain, which was welcome to his
brother if not to him. North Carolina had been in the midst of a
prolonged drought with serious injury to crops.

The rains continued intermittently next day while Bartram
relaxed and enjoyed the company of his son, his brother, and other
members of the latter's family. He still managed to sneak in a little
plant collecting between showers. Next day he was ready to go
again and rode up the Cape Fear River to Richard Singletary's
home. Along the way he tested a gravel bank for iron, observed "a
lovely species of onobrichis" (*Psoralea canescens* Michx.?), known

locally as "buckroot," and, most interesting of all, saw petrified tree trunks along the river. One of these was eight feet long and two feet in diameter. He was very much impressed by the fine variety of the living trees on the rich neck of land along the river, especially the large hickories. He took note of a white-berried *Cornus* (*Svida femina* [Mill.] Small), "a fine new genus."

On the following day they made a visit to a small lake on the northeast side of the river. The lake was roughly circular and about a mile and a half wide. The principal reason for their visit was to show Bartram the lotus flowers or "Colocasias," as he called them (*Nelumbo lutea* [Willd.] Pers.), growing in water eight to ten feet deep. These had very large circular leaves, sixteen inches or more in diameter, and cream-colored flowers nine inches in diameter. The vast number of them in the lake made a truly glorious sight. Bartram also found plants of what he thought to be another species of "Colocasia" washed in on the shore. These had finished blooming but had fruit and seed.

After several days in which wet weather largely confined him to the house, Bartram was able to resume his exploration of the environs of Ashwood, usually accompanied by Billy. He gave particular attention to geology, studying the strata to be seen on exposed banks along roads, streams, and lakes. On one of these days he rode fourteen miles to Lake Waccamaw, a large lake for this area, being approximately eight miles long and five wide. The banks along the shore of the lake were twelve feet high in places and provided an excellent cross section of soil strata for study. He noted an upper stratum of sandy loam beneath which was some four feet of clay or marl, some of which was brown and some red. Below this layer was a deposit of loose oyster shell, under which was limestone filled with shells of various kinds. He made fairly detailed notes of his observations for his journal, including commentary on the character of the country, the weather, trees and other plants, and soil, taking particular note of the unusual, such as the petrified trees.

On 6 August Bartram and Billy headed south. Colonel William, reluctant to part with them, rode along for a while before turning back. They were fortunate in finding places to stay each night, although some of them were a bit unusual. One of their hosts, "skinking more" (Schenckingh More), was a "new light baptist," many of whose brethren lodged with him and joined him in extensive prayers both night and morning. At Brunswick the Bartrams paid their respects to Governor William Tryon, who had been appointed when their friend, Arthur Dobbs, died the previous March. They traveled even more slowly than Bartram had on his way north and did not reach Charles Town until 15 August. Here they were welcomed by the Lambolls and provided with a large, attractive upstairs room with a balcony and fine views of the bay and of James Island across the Ashley River.

Bartram had once more served as rainmaker, so he spent most of the sixteenth mounting plant specimens and writing his journal. He and Billy lingered in Charles Town for two weeks, preparing for their long trip, taking care of specimens, and visiting new and old friends. Billy did some drawing, and they rode out of town for collecting. The weather was very unsettled, which prompted Bartram to discussions of the subject with his friends. From one of them he obtained an account of the hurricanes of 1700, 1713, 1716, 1722, 1728, and 1730. Among the people they met was Colonel John Stuart, superintendent of Indian Affairs for the Southern Department, to whom they were introduced by Garden. Stuart had been at Pensacola when Bartram was in Charles Town in July and would leave soon for a congress at St. Augustine. He was cordial and invited them to dinner a few days later. He promised to do everything he could to promote their friendly reception by both Indians and whites in the area that they hoped to explore.

Letters from Philadelphia brought Bartram and Billy up to date on the family there. These had been sent by Ann under cover of a letter to Garden written only ten days earlier.[22] Billy and his father accompanied the Garden family to Sunday service at St. Michael's and dined with them afterward. They called on Henry Laurens again and were pleased to learn that he planned a visit to St. Augustine during the coming winter and might see them there. They checked with Captain Beckop about a chest that he had taken to St. Augustine for Bartram in July and learned that it had been left with John Willson, a merchant there, who would care for it until they arrived. Finally they prepared and packed a box of plant specimens for the king and one for Collinson.

Bartram had been amused to learn at Ashwood that Colonel William, inspired by his brother's example, had shipped a heavy box of mineral specimens to George III. Collinson was *not* amused when they arrived, and he wrote indignantly to Bartram on 19 September: "Thy brother's making so free with the King is ridiculous, and giving me a great deal of trouble at the custom-house, and himself to the expense of 6s. 6d., which I have charged to thy account, as else I must dispose of the ores to pay it. You don't know the difficulty, trouble and attendance to get things to the King. Though I undertook it for thee, I shall not for anybody else."[23]

FIFTEEN

On to Florida

O N THE last day of August 1765 the *South Carolina Gazette* informed its readers that "Mr. Bartram, his Majesty's botanist for North America, who arrived here some time ago from Philadelphia, has since been to North-Carolina and returned here, and on Thursday last he set out, accompanied by his son (who is an excellent draughtsman) for Georgia, and East and West Florida, intending also to go as far back of those countries as the Indian nations may permit him."

If Bartram had been much of a believer in omens, he might well have returned to Charles Town on Friday.[1] In their travels he and Billy had very rarely, if ever, met with a lack of hospitality when they sought lodging for the night. Their first night on this trip was a distinct exception. Somehow they missed a turning of the road that they were to follow. The approach of darkness found them very weary in the Willtown community of the lower Edisto River. Twice they were refused shelter. When they reached a third house, again they found no welcome. They were so insistent that they could go no further that the owner finally agreed to permit them to use the poorest of his outbuildings, an old corn crib scarcely fit for a pig sty. The debris was more or less removed and an ancient mattress placed on the floor. Mr. Willson, their host, provided them with some hominy, horn spoons, and a candle in an old bottle, leaving them to share the place with the rats, bugs, and mosquitoes. This particular community had little use for strangers and was prejudiced against Quakers.

The second day was a complete contrast to the first. The Bartrams stopped early at the large farm of a Mr. Dupont near Jacksonburgh. He not only made them welcome but rode about the farm with them, pointing out plants that his family had used medicinally to treat themselves and their neighbors. The Bartrams spent a night with him and were loaned horses next day to ride with their host to inspect a canal that he was having dug to irrigate 200 acres of rice land. The canal would be between a quarter and a half mile long and eight to twelve feet deep. It was being dug by 130 negro men and women slaves, using hoes and throwing out the dirt with their hands. Bartram wondered why no spades were used to save both time and labor.

From Jacksonburgh the Bartrams made their way to Savannah, which they reached on 4 September. Bartram believed the South Carolina roads to be the best in North America. The road they followed was a few miles from the coast. Crossing the salt marshes with causeways, interspersed with bridges where necessary, the road ran straight, mile after mile. Tall oaks, pines, tupelos, and sweet gum provided shade, for it was against the law to cut trees bordering a road. In the distance could be glimpsed gentlemen's estates, often with large ponds that had formerly been used for growing rice but now produced fish. To offset the pleasure of the good road, insects continually harassed the travelers. Bartram did not lose sight of the fact that he was being employed to make observations as well as collections, and his journal recorded much information concerning the country through which they rode. The absence of certain plants as well as the presence of others was noted. Changes in the terrain, the nature of the soil, and the crops being raised were all made a matter of record. From Purisburgh, the Bartrams traveled ten miles down the Savannah River in a batteau and were delighted to see alligators diving as the boat approached.

Bartram had brought with him a letter of introduction to James Habersham (1712–75) of Savannah from their mutual friend Charles Magnus Wrangel (d. 1786), pastor of the Old Swedes Church, where young Ann Bartram had been married recently. Bartram had a profound admiration for Wrangel, whom he thought "the most indefatigable and zealous minister that ever crossed the seas, of any sect whatever."[2] Habersham was a member of the governor's council and urged that the Bartrams pay their respects to Governor James Wright and then return to spend the night. Bartram needed little urging to do either. He and Billy were graciously received by the governor, who promised any assistance which he might be able to render. Bartram did not plan to linger at Savannah but to leave the coast and go inland to Augusta. He wanted to be at St. Augustine by 1 October, but he would not know until he reached Augusta whether he could go directly from there through the lands of the Creek Nation or whether he must return by way of Savannah. He did take time to dash off a hasty letter to his wife to let her know that they were still well, signing it, "dear love, in the meantime, I remain thy affectionate husband, John Bartram, In great haste."[3]

On the morning of 5 September it was 87°F when the Bartrams rode northwest toward Augusta, following a road along the Savannah River. Bartram was surprised to see a great deal of *Collinsonia* (*C. tuberosa,* Michx.) growing along the road, never having seen it in the coastal areas of the Carolinas. He took note of a variety of other plants, including witch hazel and Indian pinkroot (*Spigelia marylandica* L.), and commented on the very large number of sturgeon leaping from the river. Toward afternoon the land became more hilly, and by dusk they reached Ebenezer, a village of about twenty houses, near which they saw orchards of peach and mulberry trees. They learned that a number of the residents were raising silkworms successfully, although the project suffered from a scarcity of labor. The second night was spent at "Revels," perhaps near Blue Springs, and the third at a "dirty tavern," after what Bartram described as the longest and most tiring day's ride that he had ever made. They had ridden over forty miles by his estimate and the temperature had reached 90°F or more.

The eighth was another hard day for horses and riders. The weather continued very hot, and the country became increasingly hilly. Fortunately, they traveled in the shade of large tulip poplars, beech, and cypress trees, crossing many fine streams. Their most interesting discovery of the day was an outcropping of flint rock with pieces in all manner of shapes and sizes lying on the surface of the ground. Bartram suspected that it might be one of the Indians' "factories." He inquired of a fellow traveler whether arrowheads and other Indian artifacts were often found in the area and was assured that they were very common. The Bartrams spent the night with a farmer named Read, who was so hospitable that they decided to remain another day and night to rest their horses. Mr. Read took them to see a bluff on the opposite side of the river, which was about 200 yards wide at this point. He produced a home-

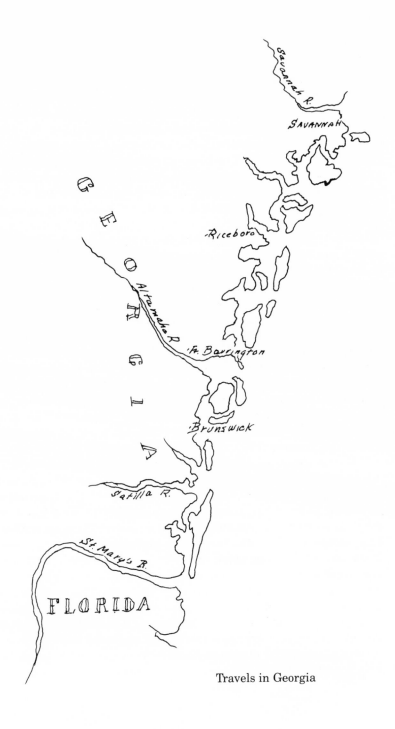

Travels in Georgia

made boat which Bartram thought was more raft than boat. The bluff did prove interesting, rising nearly 200 feet from the water's edge and revealing a series of strata. Bartram was particularly interested in the exposed fossil shells of oysters, eighteen inches long. He learned that the deposit of giant shells extended for several miles and that the settlers burned them to make lime. In typical Bartram fashion he observed the presence of worm holes in the shells, as he commonly had seen in modern shells along the seacoasts.[4] The bluff was attractive botanically, having many familiar Pennsylvania plants including maidenhair fern, Solomon's seal, bellwort, and mitrewort. He was told that ginseng grew there, but he did not see it.

When they took leave of Mr. Read, they came down to lower ground and crossed the river on a ferry to the Carolina side. Another eight miles of riding brought them to the home of George Galphin, an Indian trader who had been recommended to them by friends in Charles Town. Galphin, a native of Ireland, had received a large grant in this area in 1734 and had established a trading post. Bartram realized how successful Galphin had been when he learned that he used 400 packhorses in carrying on his business. His friendly relations with the Indians had led to his appointment by the governor as an assistant in Indian affairs. The Bartrams spent three nights with Galphin, who was delighted to have a guest with geological interests. He insisted that they must go to see bluffs along the river, where the Spanish had tried, unsuccessfully, to establish a silver mine.

It was quite an expedition. Galphin provided two batteaus, five or six men, and provisions for a noonday meal. They traveled some twelve miles down the river to a bluff not far from the one previously seen. A magnificent stream of cold water poured from a spring at its base. While some of its characteristics were similar to those of the earlier one, there were differences. Here the oyster shells, ground to a fine sand, had become a conglomerate that Bartram likened to the "bermudous rocks used for building. . . ." He found that he could cut it easily with his knife. The bluff was only about 200 yards long at the river's edge and receded at each end some distance from the river, leaving rich bottomland. The local settlers, by digging five to six feet into the ground, could expose the layer of giant oyster shells that apparently extended at least thirty miles to another bluff, where it was exposed.

The "Silver Bluff" was a mile below Galphin's house. Since the silver deposit lay under the Savannah River, the Spaniards had attempted to divert its course. Before the project had been abandoned, either because of Indian threats or the excessive cost, they had dug to a depth of thirty feet, twenty of which was composed of mould and sand. Below this were masses of fuller's earth in a sand stratum. Beneath was "very black sulphurous earth," similar to that which Bartram had seen at Cape Fear. In this, at the water's edge, were large trees driven down by floods, among which were pyrites and some petrified wood. The day was so interesting to the entire party that darkness was approaching before they reached their starting point on the river, and they had to tie up the batteaus and travel on foot. Bartram spent much of the next day observing Galphin's farming operations and writing in his journal.

On 12 September, Bartram and Billy rode on to Augusta, crossing the river to the town. Directly opposite the ferry was a 100-foot bluff which had as fascinating a display of colors as Bartram had ever seen. Near the water were patches of red, yellow, and purple, some tinged with white. Bartram noted:

thence A ten foot strata began of a whiteish glittering slipery micatious substance mixed toward ye uper part with coarse sand, then A deep strata white coars sand which gradualy came to yellow, mixed with red. in many places large masses of very red clay or marl higher up great masses of feruginous compositions of coarse sand then stratas of gravel alternately toward ye top mixed with Geodes & severall thin strata of dark congelations so[me]thing approaching to ye appearance of ye blood stone: here is in this part of ye countrey a prodigious deep strata of very tenatious clay or marl being originally formed at ye bottom of ye then present sea. which in process of time was by ye surging waves & ye great accumulation of sand & different soiles brought down from ye mountains in furious floods covered over to very uncertain depts . . . where ye strata is very different as to color quantity & quality as thay was deposited by ye flood in various curls, eddies & furious direct currents. . . .[5]

Bartram was interested in indications that the river had made a number of changes in its channel. An old channel was now a sand bed fifteen feet above the present river. An old fort lay below thirty feet of water. This change had occurred in just three decades. He was impressed by the tenacity of the cypresses growing along the banks, their great, spreading roots making a formidable defense against the floodwaters. As the Bartrams watched the stream, they saw sturgeon attempting to leap the falls, and an occasional alligator was seen. The river was about 300 yards wide, flowing very rapidly over many projecting rocks with considerable noise. In spite of Augusta's beautiful location, the town did not appear prosperous. The Bartrams returned to Galphin's next day and stayed with him for five more. The cool weather continued, with morning temperatures in the low sixties. In a jacket and coat, working in his bedroom, Bartram sometimes still felt chilled. He was busy stitching his specimens while Billy worked on a drawing of a snake.

With the thermometer at 56°F, the Bartrams set off for Savannah on the morning of the eighteenth. They had been advised not to go directly to St. Augustine but by way of Savannah. It was not much further, and the traveling would be less hazardous. Galphin and some of his men accompanied them, as they were to visit one of his cowpens twenty-five miles away. Bartram considered these one of the great curiosities of the country. A cowpen usually consisted of a rough cabin near a spring, where a white overseer and four or five negroes lived. They provided care of sorts for a large number of cattle and horses which ranged over an area of six to ten miles' radius from the cabin, summer and winter. A general watch was kept on livestock, and some animals were brought to corrals near the cabin when care was needed. Here, at last, Bartram found the wild horses to which Collinson had referred, and he found that the Georgia cowboys were adept at catching and breaking them.

This particular cowpen was located near an unusually fine spring which formed a large creek. Since Bartram found both flints and pottery, he realized that this must once have been the site of an Indian settlement. Most interesting of all were several bushes of "evergreen caseena" (*Ilex vomitoria* L.), a coastal plant. The Creeks planted it near all of their settlements and used the dried leaves as tea. Bartram was surprised that it would survive that far from the coast. He thought it was a mistake for whites not to use it more, for he had found it more efficacious than tea imported from the East Indies.

The Bartrams left Galphin and his men on 20 September, reaching Ebenezer the next day. Bartram was interested to learn more of the silk industry there, which occupied most of the inhabitants. The labor of three boys and three girls was required to make 400 pounds of cocoons. The price had once been three shillings two pence per pound, but now they only received a little over two shillings. The importance placed on this infant industry became apparent at Savannah. The silk house was the same size as the council house. Only the Church of England church was larger. The ride back to Savannah was in heavy rain, which had begun during the night and continued steadily all day. Water was "belly deep" on the causeways. Bridges had washed out at several places where they had to persuade their horses to swim. The Bartrams and all of their belongings were thoroughly soaked. They arrived at Savannah in a sorry state, reflecting that it was fortunate that they had left their specimens behind to be sent down by Mr. Galphin.

The next morning, the twenty-third, Bartram went seeking advice about the best way to reach St. Augustine. He was somewhat disconcerted when told that the rains had made it nearly impossible. He and Billy dined with Governor Wright the following day and found him more encouraging. The governor wrote a letter to Fort Barrington's commander, instructing him to provide a guide from there to St. Augustine. The Bartrams spent a week in Savannah, waiting for the waters to go down and resting their horses. Bartram found it a pleasant, relaxed town. It stretched over a half mile on the top of a great bank of sand about fifty feet high. The clearing of vegetation for the houses permitted brisk winds to stir up minor sandstorms, a continual irritation to the inhabitants and a scourge to their gardens.

The houses were similar to those of Charles Town, with their great piazzas which screened the houses from some of the sun's heat and acted as breezeways. Bartram found that much of the visiting was done on these porches. It was a viciously hot day which could not be spent pleasantly on them. He was struck by the fact that at Charles Town and Savannah most of the more prosperous people lived in town but were supported by their plantations, operated by slave labor. By contrast, if a Philadelphia man owned a country estate, it was for recreation. He was supported by his business in the city. As a result the southern cities lacked the noise and bustle of their northern counterparts. Bartram's observations were not all of a social nature. He lowered one of his thermometers into the water of a thirty-foot well and was a bit surprised to find that the temperature was 80°F, only five degrees cooler than that of a shady room.

On 25 September, a fine cool day, Bartram and Billy rode twelve miles to Bethesda to see the orphanage established by George Whitefield. Bartram made note of every detail, for he knew that not only Collinson but Franklin would expect a complete description. Whitefield had told Franklin that many of the Georgia settlers were ill equipped for pioneering and were lazy as well. As a result many died leaving helpless children, for whom he had established the orphanage. Bartram observed corroboration of this among the Scottish Highlanders who had settled in the vicinity of Savannah. They were indeed poor settlers, for they were lazy, careless, and made few improvements. Franklin, unsuccessful in persuading Whitefield to build the orphanage in Pennsylvania, had felt a certain reluctance to contribute to his fund raising. He gave a fine tribute to Whitefield's powers of persuasion in his account: "I silently resolved he should get nothing from me. I had in my pocket a handful of copper money, three or four silver dollars, and five pistoles in gold. As he proceeded I began to soften, and concluded to give the coppers. Another stroke of his oratory made me asham'd of that, and determin'd me to give the silver; and he finish'd so admirably, that I empty'd my pocket wholly into the collector's dish, gold and all."[6] Bartram could now report on how well the money had been spent.

Almost from the beginning the orphanage had provided for between seventy and a hundred children, so it was fortunate that the main building was large and well planned. It was approximately sixty feet long by forty wide, painted inside and out. The basement kitchen was walled with brick, extending four feet above ground level. The first floor was circled by a ten-foot porch and had nine large windows on each side. A hall extended through the house with staircases of "sweet red bay much like mahogany" at either end. On one side of the hall were the library and parlor with a chapel between them. On the other side was another parlor and a huge airy dining room. The second floor was similar, with large bedrooms opening off the hall. There was a big, well-finished attic with "dormant" windows providing additional sleeping quarters. The acre and a half of level ground surrounding the main building

was completely enclosed by a fence. On one side there was a saltwa-
ter creek that was dry at low tide. On another there was a two-acre
kitchen garden. On still another side the schoolhouse stood next to
the stables and other outhouses. As the Bartrams rode back to Savannah, they stopped at a plantation with the finest orchards they
had seen in the area: oranges, nectarines, peaches, figs, and pomegranates. They ate their fill of the last as they rode homeward.

The box of plant specimens forwarded by Mr. Galphin arrived
on the twenty-seventh, and the day was spent in sorting and numbering. There was still some to be done next day as well, letters to
be written to Collinson and others and the journal brought up to
date. Packing occupied another day, and it was not until the thir-
tieth that the Bartrams actually left for St. Augustine, having
spent the night at Beverley, Habersham's country seat. Their way
led through much low and swampy ground with a fine stand of
pine. Bartram measured one tree as eighty-one feet from the
ground to the first limb and another fifty-four feet to the top. He
saw another that was thirty inches in diameter, ninety feet to the
first limb, and another twenty-eight to the top. They had timed
their trip well, for it was clear and cool. The roads were surprisingly good, even though many rice fields had been flooded by the
recent heavy rains.

After a night spent at Mr. West's, near Riceboro, Georgia, they
came to the road which some had thought they might find impass-
able. Many of the bay swamps through which they rode were so
difficult that they doubted that their horses could make it, but they
managed to cover about twenty miles. This area had abundant deer
and turkey. It became very dry in dry seasons, and traveling was
then comparatively easy. In a wet season a large part became
flooded, resulting in a huge swamp. The Bartrams managed to find
a spot a few feet above water level on which to eat their lunch of
bread and pomegranates. They had hoped to reach Fort Barrington
before dark but missed a turning and had to spend the night about
four miles below the fort. Although the day had been difficult, they
had found some "very curious shrubs." One of these is today known
as the fever tree (*Pinckneya pubens* Michx.).

The second shrub or small tree has never been found anywhere else in the wild, yet it was not specifically mentioned by Bartram in his journal. Only through Billy's later writing do we know
this: "This very curious tree was first taken notice of about ten or

twelve years ago, at this place, when I attended my father (John Bartram) on a botanical excursion; but, it being then late in the autumn, we could form no opinion to what class or tribe it belonged."[7] The tree has disappeared even in this area, having last been seen there by John Lyons in 1803. Ironically, it grows today in many gardens here and abroad, bearing the name of Bartram's beloved Franklin, *Franklinia alatamaha* Marsh. Had the trees been blooming, Bartram could not have failed to describe them, exhausted though he must have been from struggling through twenty miles of bog and swamp.[8] Bartram never saw the small tree's beautiful flowers, for Billy did not bring back the seeds of it to their garden at Kingsessing until January 1777.[9]

When they arrived at Fort Barrington the next morning, they were delighted with the situation. The twenty-foot-square wooden fort, with a gun on each wall, was built on a bank twenty feet above the 300-yard-wide Altamaha River. On the northern side a lovely lagoon extended for half a mile, and on all sides the view encompassed miles of lowlands and cypress swamps. The fort was only thirteen miles on a direct line from the coast, but it was thirty miles by the winding river. The incoming tide raised the river level two feet there and for ten miles above the fort, yet Bartram found it fresh, not brackish. In the spring floods large areas were underwater. A similar situation now existed, for the unusual rains of the

Franklinia alatamaha,
Marsh.

past few days had been the worst remembered in forty years and had destroyed most of the rice crops. As the Bartrams had ridden along, they had seen the rice straw broken off and floating downstream. Profitable as rice was in a good season, Bartram questioned the healthiness of the inhabitants living by the stagnant water necessary for the flooding of rice fields. In addition to floods local farmers had another problem—sudden cold snaps. Bartram could hardly believe this in the apparently balmy climate, whose heat he would have thought to have been a far more serious threat. However, the fort commander confirmed the fact, telling Bartram that the tops of his orange trees were killed annually and that he had even crossed a shallow pond on ice without breaking through.

Bartram and Billy spent the next two days exploring and listing the interesting variety of trees. The most exciting were groves of tall trees growing in the water along the river's edge. Their leaves had fallen, but they were liberally decorated with a great crop of scarlet fruit the size of olives. Bartram thought it must be a very rare tupelo or gum. When he questioned people, they said they called them limes and often used them for punch.[10] Bartram and Billy resumed their journey on the fifth, along the old post road to St. Augustine. Away from the coast the road was on higher ground and avoided most of the numerous creeks and swamps. After a night spent under a pine they continued to ride along the pine barrens, now carpeted with palmettoes and dwarf oaks. "A very odd Catalpa with pods round as an acron [sic] & short" (*Pinckneya?*) provided relief from the monotony. Again the Bartrams "lodged in ye woods under A pine amongst ye palmettoes & near A pond & musketoes."

They were on the road by sunrise on 7 October. Three hours later they reached the Great Satilla, now in flood, fifty miles from Barrington. They had passed two cowpens, one at Warsaw and one at Carney's, where again they saw the unusual "catalpa." Some of the land here was suitable for rice, but most of the country from the Altamaha to the Satilla was of poor, white, sandy soil over a "whiteish clay mixt with sand." Under this was a clay stratum. All it managed to support were pines and a coarse grass. The banks of the Satilla were a welcome contrast, composed of rich black earth. The river there was about 450 feet wide and fifteen feet deep at low water. The Bartrams swam their "horses over at 2 shilling Apiece."[11] The next few days took them through similar pine barrens but they were improving in quality. The pines were taller and the grass thicker. When they reached Cabbage Swamp, they were delighted by the groves of cabbage trees, *Sabal palmetto* (Walt.) Todd., which Bartram called "tree palms," being thirty feet tall. The nearer they came to St. Augustine, the poorer the land became. The trees were stunted and the grass miserable. They reached the city before sunset on 11 October. There Bartram was shocked to learn of Bouquet's death. The general had arrived on 23 August and had died of fever ten days later. It saddened Bartram's arrival, for he had looked forward to many visits with his friend.[12]

The following day, Bartram and several Carolina gentlemen dined with the Florida governor, James Grant (1720–1806). A career military man, Grant had fought in Flanders, Ireland, and North America. He had just succeeded Major Ogilvie as governor. His house, with belvedere and portico, had piazzas on two sides, overlooking the great parade ground with a church at one end and the guardhouse at the other. After dinner, the Bartrams explored some of St. Augustine and found it fascinating. Since they stayed there from 11 October until 19 December, with the exception of one week, they came to know it well. By Philadelphia's standards, the streets were extremely narrow, a bare fifteen feet wide. Even the main avenue was but twenty-two feet wide, and the six or eight lanes intersecting were only twelve feet wide.

There was no regularity about the location of the houses. The principal Spanish citizens had been military, but there had been a few priests, merchants, and men from the civil government. They had built fine houses in the Spanish style of architecture, which was well suited to the climate. They were constructed of hewn stone, usually with flat roofs, ornamented with battlements that contained clay pipes for gutters and downspouts. There were no chimneys, and there was no glass in the windows. The roofed balconies were supported by double beams, with the houses built around inner courtyards in whose centers stood wells. Along these inner walls were walks covered by an extension of the main roof, supported by pillars forming a colonnade amply supplied with benches. At one end a staircase led to the upper chambers. The houses of the wealthy had windows projecting on the street, but they were crossbarred in elaborate designs and shuttered. All of this caused the rooms to be cool but very dark. Where English officers had preempted homes, they had immediately removed such impediments to light and substituted glass windows as well as adding chimneys.

Bartram noticed that the soldiers and the poorer people in general had constructed their houses by building forms and pouring mortar mixed of sand and lime shell, into which they pounded osyter shells before the mortar hardened. The forms were then raised and the process repeated until the walls reached the desired height. These walls easily supported a second story and a thatched palmetto roof. Additions were made as they could be afforded, and there were often cracks between the original walls and the additions. Sometimes there was a smoke hole in the roof. These houses had the same latticed windows as the more expensive homes, so convenient for watching the street without being seen. They were particularly valued by the young girls of both rich and poor families, who were practically sequestered from all but their family from the age of twelve. Even at mass they were heavily veiled.

Spanish kitchens were quite different from any that Bartram had seen. The three-foot fireplace was raised two feet from the floor and extended the full width of the room. It was open to a slanted roof, which protected it from rain but permitted the escape of smoke. Several pots were permanently fixed in the fireplace and were used for making soups. Bartram thought the whole scheme inefficient and reminiscent of Indian cabins. He gathered that the Spanish diet differed considerably from that of the English. They ate little meat but enjoyed fish and oysters, highly spiced with herbs, especially garlic. Some salted beef or pork stewed with pumpkins, herbs, and red pepper was eaten. Few cows were kept, and butter and cheese, when available, were imported, as was English flour.

One of the two old churches had been converted for use by the Church of England, but the other was falling apart. Not far from town was a Dutch church which the soldiers had been tearing down for firewood. In fact, this was a general practice of the English military, who had almost wrecked the town, pulling down houses and cutting down fruit and shade trees. Bartram felt ashamed of his English origins. He thought that the finest of the churches, architecturally, was one that had been built for the Indians and was known as the "Milk Church." It was situated in a small Indian village on St. Mark's River, not far from the town. The fluted columns on the gable end had Doric bases and capitals, and there was much stone carving. He thought it strange that the Spanish had devoted so much more work and expense to this Indian church than to either of their own in the town.

The most impressive structure in St. Augustine was the main fort, the Castillo de San Marcos, near the bay. On Sunday following their arrival, Bartram and Billy attended church services and then strolled down to see the fort. They found it remarkably well built, costing the king of Spain "many millions." Bartram concluded that the fort had never been completed, for there were some very large hewn stones bearing the Spanish arms and other carved ornamentation still lying nearby. The Bartrams walked two miles northwest to old Fort Mosa, on the edge of the swamps, looking for plants. There were two small forts at the southern end of town, each with six guns. One was near the sound and the other about 1,200 feet away, close to a tidal creek. The latter had round sentry boxes with covers and mouldings projecting from each corner. There was still another battery on the same creek, nearer to town, at the far end of the governor's garden.

There were letters for Bartram to write to his family, to Collinson, the Lambolls, Garden, and others. Everyone wanted to hear about the newly acquired lands. Many of his letters were necessarily short, and they exasperated his correspondents. Collinson wanted more details of St. Augustine. A letter from Garden, enclosing one from Ann Bartram, urged Bartram to "Tell me what you are discovering; for I know your imagination and genius can't be still. How many wonders of creation do you daily see? Why won't you let me know a few?" He added that he had forwarded Bartram's letter to one of his sons as requested.[13] When Garden wrote again, a note of envy as well as of annoyance crept into his letter; he complained that the only letter he had received was not only short but had no botanical news: "Think that I am here, confined to the sandy streets of Charleston, where the ox, where the ass, and where men as stupid as either, fill up the vacant space, while you range the green fields of Florida, where the bountiful hand of Nature has spread every beautiful and fair plant and flower, that can give food to animals, or pleasure to the spectator."[14]

Throughout their travels, Bartram had methodically kept a meteorological journal. His recording of Charles Town's temperature had interested Isaac, who found that Philadelphia's temperatures were far higher that summer.[15] Now Bartram sent the data on the weather on to Collinson, as well as some of his journal, his specimens, and a number of Billy's drawings.[16] By Wednesday morning he had finished much of his writing but, to his great annoyance, he felt quite ill, shaking with chills and fever. He continued sick for several weeks, better at times, exhausted at others, and always miserably feverish on alternate days. He was evidently suffering from malaria, acquired from sleeping unprotected from the mosquitoes along the swamps. When he felt up to it, he wrote or prepared and stitched his specimens onto sheets of paper. On the twenty-first he managed to ride twenty miles but was in bed again the next day. While his father was sick, Billy twice visited Anastasia Island, and sometimes David Yeats, a doctor attached to the military hospital, kept him company on rides out of town gathering specimens. A strong northeast wind blew for days, preventing ships from entering or leaving the harbor. Those at anchor were safe behind the shelter of Anastasia Island, which lay like a protective barrier, lengthwise to the town. There were no wharves, but the Spaniards had made a massive stone mole, five to six feet thick and half a mile long. When Bartram again felt up to an expedition, he and Billy rowed over to the island, where they spent the night. In a leisurely fashion they explored the sandhills, Billy finding some curious plants and Bartram gathering seeds. By 1 November Bartram was feeling much better. His customary fever did not appear, but he was cautious for the next ten days, walking and riding some and dining with the governor. In spite of this the fever returned Sunday night after church service. It was very disheartening, since he was afraid he might miss the imminent meeting of the governor and Colonel Stuart with the Indians at Picolata.

The governor and his party left for the meeting on Wednesday, 13 November. Bartram and Billy, "with severall Gentlemen whose curiosity led them to be present there at a Congres with the Creek Indians," planned to leave at seven the next morning. At the last

Governor's house, St. Augustine, Florida (drawn from plate in Francis Harper's annotated edition of John Bartram's "Diary of a Journey")

minute one of the horses was missing, so they postponed their departure until Friday, which gave Bartram another day of rest. Friday was a perfect day, and they left an hour after sunrise. The countryside through which they rode was not inspiring, mainly open, with little grass and many palmettoes. Occasionally there were a few scraggly pines, shrubby evergreen oaks, andromeda and such. At least the swamps offered some variation, and Bartram spotted some small orchids and pickerel weed. At Picolata, about eighteen miles west of St. Augustine, the Spaniards had built a fort to guard the St. Johns River and to keep open communications down St. Mark's Creek. It was set back from the river about 100 feet and was not very large, but there were four swivel guns on the walls. Knowing of Bartram's illness, one gentleman had a tent ready for him and Billy, but they accepted the offer of a room in the fort instead, since it would be warmer. The walls of this fort were two feet thick. To enter it they had to climb a ladder. There were windows on three sides with another ladder leading to a room over it. The magazine and storeroom were on the ground floor, and the kitchen was just outside but within the stockade.

Having observed the meeting with the chiefs of the Six Nations at Onondago, Bartram was curious to compare it with this meeting of southern Indians. When he and his party arrived, a pavilion for the meeting had already been erected. It was roughly twelve by thirty-six feet, with a roof of pine branches that had also been used in forming the back wall and half of the side walls. The governor and John Stuart would sit at a table at the back, facing the open end of the pavilion. Down each side was a long blanket-covered bench for the Indians. Bartram was a little weary after the early morning ride but accepted an invitation to dinner with the governor and "chief gentlemen" on board a schooner anchored off the fort. He ate heartily but felt no ill effects that night.

When the congress began the next day, all four guns at the fort were fired. A soldier stood at attention on either side of the pavilion entrance while the main body of soldiers was drawn up a short distance away. Facing the pavilion, perhaps 500 feet away, fifty or more Indian chiefs had assembled. They advanced in columns of six; on one side two carried twenty finely dressed buckskins, and on the other two carried eagle-feathered pipes. They were accompanied by an interpreter. They advanced with deliberation, breaking into dances now and then, singing, shouting, and then pausing. When they were within twenty feet of the pavilion, they stopped, and the two chiefs with the pipes approached the governor and superintendent, stroking them with the eagle feathers. The remaining chiefs then approached by twos and fours, shook hands with Grant and Stuart, and took their seats on the sides. Finally the skins were presented by the two chiefs who had carried them. The peace pipe was passed around, and Stuart addressed the chiefs. He told them of a similar congress held with the western chiefs the previous spring. He expressed the hope that this meeting might also result in mutual satisfaction. The governor then made an address, followed by one of the chiefs, acting as spokesman for the group. At last they got down to discussion of the English proposals, which requested more land than had previous treaties.

The meetings continued on the sixteenth but without much ceremonial. It had been expected that the Indians would be insistent upon provisions of previous treaties, granting lands only as far as the tide reached up the rivers. To the surprise of the English, the Indians conceded from twenty-five miles above Fort Barrington across to St. Marys, about sixty miles north of Picolata, a far larger area than Grant had anticipated. While the meetings were in session on the seventeenth, Bartram and Billy took the opportunity for some exploring and "rowed" a canoe six miles up the St. Johns River, here as broad as a bay. The following day was appropriately beautiful for the signing of the treaty. The chiefs placed their mark upon the two deeds, one to be kept by them and the other deposited at St. Augustine. A peace pipe was smoked, and silver medals, ranging from dollar to palm size, were presented to the chiefs, according to their importance. These were strung on two-yard-long silk ribbons, which the governor hung around the neck of each chief as the drums beat and the guns from the fort answered. A similar congress was to be held in the spring to determine the Georgia boundaries. During the next two days additional gifts were given to the chiefs: hoes, guns, linen, blankets, and kettles.

On the last day of the congress Bartram and Billy again took a canoe to look for plants. Along the river there were interesting coves and luxuriant swamps in which grew elms, maples, the ash with "shorter seeds," loblolly bay, dahoon holly, buttonbush, and spider lilies. Curiously, there were few cypresses, and these were quite small. As they returned, walking through a swamp close by the fort, Bartram urgently called to Billy, who stopped immediately. There, in front of him, was coiled a huge rattlesnake. One more step and he would have tramped down upon it. Billy was so startled that he became angry. Cutting a sapling, he killed the snake. Then, he felt remorseful and resolved never again to kill one, a promise that he broke on at least one occasion.[17]

The six-foot-snake was too big to be carried easily, so Billy tied a vine around its head and dragged it into the fort. He was soon surrounded by an admiring throng of English and Indians, astonished by the size of the snake. It was not long before the fort's commander heard the commotion and sent an officer to ask if he might serve the snake for dinner, provided that it had not bitten itself. Later, the Bartrams were invited to dine with the governor, who also had a taste for rattlesnake meat. Billy's trophy appeared in several dishes, and he made himself taste it but could not bear to swallow it.

When everyone was preparing to leave Picolata the following morning, the Bartrams' horses were found to be missing. Bartram was able to hire one, but Billy had to walk the twenty or more miles to St. Augustine in the rain. Someone returned their horses three days later, at a cost of two dollars. For the next several weeks, the Bartrams lingered at St. Augustine until Bartram should feel strong enough to undertake a strenuous trip. Governor Grant was eager for him to explore the headwaters of the St. Johns River and was prepared to bear all expenses of the trip, including a boat, a guide, and a cook.[18] Bartram and Billy were equally eager to go, but it was no undertaking for anyone in a poor state of health so Bartram had to rest a bit. In the meantime he and Billy made local explorations around St. Augustine to such places as Woodcutter's Creek. A sharp frost the first week of December killed the pumpkin vines and the leaves of the Carolina peas as well as the tops of the cotton plants but did not harm the tomatoes. The governor told Bartram that it was more severe than the freeze of the previous Christmas. Bartram noted on 30 November, with the same brevity used for recording the weather, that the "man of war came with stamps." Although the Stamp Act, which had become operative 1 November, had been the subject of violent discussion all over the colonies for months, Bartram made no remarks upon it. Perhaps this was because the journal would be sent to England, where colonial feelings would not be welcome. He learned later that Colden, then lieutenant-governor of New York, had been pulled from his carriage, which was destroyed by a mob angered by the Stamp Act, and had been burned in effigy.[19]

SIXTEEN

The River St. John

THE GROUND was a glittering white with frost when Bartram, Billy, and Dr. Yeats left St. Augustine on 19 December on the first leg of their search for the source of the St. Johns River.[1] They spent that night at Greenwood's, twelve miles south of Cow Ford, present-day Jacksonville. Here there was a beautiful woodland of ancient oaks, magnolias, and sweet gums nearly 100 feet tall. On a bluff eight to ten feet above the river was a grove of what Bartram called "guilandina."[2] Next day, the party reached the home of Robert Davis, whose son Governor Grant had "ordered" to act as a guide for the party. Young Davis was reputed to be an excellent hunter and could keep the party supplied with meat. Provisions would be carried in a batteau, and one of Davis' negroes would row the boat and cook. They would travel in style this time. On the morning of the twenty-first, they embarked but soon returned. The southern wind was so strong that they could make no progress against it and had to impose on Mr. Davis' hospitality for another day and night. He walked with them about his land, where the Bartrams saw red bays two feet in diameter and 100 feet tall. There were purple-berried bays, Hercules'-club, and many orange trees.

The party set out again on the twenty-second and appeared to be more fortunate, but when after several miles they again found the wind too strong, they landed and walked along the shore. Here they found many tall evergreen shrubs eight to ten feet high, known by the settlers as wild limes, which produced an edible nut about the size of an acorn. Bartram found the nuts so delectable that he thought they could easily compete with almonds.[3] The shores of sand and black mould along the St. Johns at this point shoaled gradually into swamps and then pineland. Between the latter two were great masses of palmettoes. The party camped by the river and were not surprised to see a large alligator. After a night at Picolata they proceeded upriver, where they found hunting profitable. Davis brought in a deer and the negro a turkey.

While the hunters were thus occupied, the Bartrams investigated the woods with a man who was looking for honey. The first tree that he cut had only a yellow wasp colony, but then they came to a hollow tree in which was a swarm of bees and honey. Bartram was told that both Indians and whites often gathered as much as ten gallons from one tree in addition to the wax. The Indians garnished venison with honey. They also used it to sweeten sour oranges. One end of the fruit was cut off, then honey was poured over the pulp and the mixture scooped out. Christmas Day dawned cool and hazy. Being Quakers, the Bartrams did not celebrate in any way but continued their travels. They came to a great abandoned plantation where there were many orange trees. Beyond it, there was a seventeen-foot bluff extending about a half mile, with small swamps on either side. On top of it they found the remains of a Spanish fort, about thirty-six by forty-two feet. Open to the river it had five-foot walls on the other three sides.

Just inland from the fort was the town of Charlotia, or Rolle's town, where they were welcomed by a Mr. Banks, whom the Bartrams found "a sober, careful, and agreeable man." Rolle's town had a particular interest for Bartram. It had been founded by one of his diverse acquaintances, Lord Denys Rolle, former member of Parliament for Barnstaple. Bartram had met him in Philadelphia in 1760 and had given him a letter to Lamboll at Charles Town.[4] Rolle was then on his way south to look for land on which to found a colony to rehabilitate unfortunates. He had found it and returned to England. Four years later, he had brought over a number of indentured settlers, some of whom he was accused of kidnapping. He again called on Lamboll at Charles Town, where some of his settlers deserted. Rolle had planned to settle at St. Mark's, but when he arrived with his 100 families, he failed to land there and came to St. Johns instead. He explored upriver and was so impressed that he planted his colony there with the idea that it would be convenient to the capital, St. Augustine. He claimed 20,000 acres on the east side of the river. His project suffered various mis-

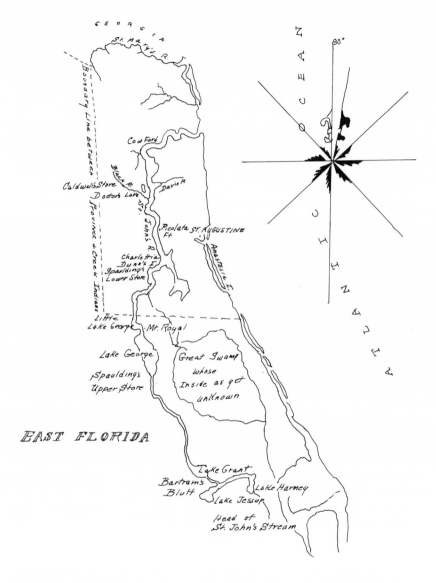

Travels in East Florida (adapted from William De Brahm's *Map of the General Survey of East Florida . . . 1766–1770*, pl. 7, in Harper, William Bartram's *Travels*)

fortunes, including fevers and the departure of many settlers tempted by the capital's promises. Rolle had again returned to England to round up more colonizers, leaving Banks in charge of the town while he was absent.[5]

Charlotia was a half mile in length, although it contained but ten houses of round logs. Precisely laid out, one street was 100 feet broad and the other, at right angles, was sixty feet. The surrounding land was far from inspiring to a farmer such as Bartram, producing mostly scrub oak and pines. To him it hardly appeared the paradise described in the January issue of the *Scots Magazine*, which remarked upon the prosperity of Rolle's settlement in a "healthy, elevated spot" producing large "rice, corne, pulse, and cotton" crops as well as melons, cucumbers, and other garden truck.[6]

The next day they explored land for which another of Bartram's friends, Lord Adam Gordon, had petitioned. This was Dunn's Island (now Murphy's Island), a 1,500-acre tract with an abundance of turkeys and alligators. Bartram thought the middle section would be fine for corn. They spent that night at Spalding's Lower Store, six miles southwest of Palatka. James Spalding, a Scot, had arrived in Charles Town in 1760, and when Florida became a British possession, he established trading posts there.[7] The morning of the twenty-seventh was beautiful, and after five miles in the batteau the Bartrams took to the shore, crossing streams and swamps. The jungle atmosphere was intriguing: "monstrous grape-vines, 8 inches in diameter, running up the oaks 6 foot in diameter" and "the constant evergreen shade rotting to soil." As they descended a hill they came upon a spring (Funk's Spring?) issuing from its foot with such force that it appeared a fountain and was strong enough "to turn a mill." They eagerly drank of the beautifully clear water but found it had "a very offensive taste, and smelt like bilge-water, or the washings of a gun barrel." They came to another spring, equally vile, later in the day (Nashua Spring). There was still a third sulphur spring at the head of a cove almost a quarter of a mile from the river (Welaka), whose volume was so great as to form a creek 120 feet across. It was full of gar, catfish, mullet, and other fish as well as alligators.

As they entered Little Lake George the following morning they were greeted by the sight of a huge shell mound, which Bartram christened Mt. Hope. The mound, fifty yards long, thirty yards wide, and twenty feet high, was composed of snail and mussel shells. Since these mounds disintegrated, the Indians found them extremely fertile in comparison with the other land. Evidence of their usage for agricultural purposes was found by Bartram at such sites: bits and pieces of pottery and sometimes "vestiges of the corn hills." They killed one of the many alligators to examine it, finding that both of its jaws "open by a joint nearly alike to both." Six miles upriver they came to Mount-Royal, where there had been a plantation of some sort, for fifty acres had been cleared and there were many orange trees growing in the woods. From here there was a glorious view of Lake George. As Bartram and his party camped that night they went to sleep listening to the roars of a bear on a nearby island.

Doggedly they made their way upriver, surveying its meanderings, testing its depths, observing the soil and the possibilities of its cultivation. Every now and then they investigated the small tributaries, landing and proceeding on foot when they became too shallow. Bartram noted the trees, shrubs, and plants, recording daily temperatures as well as information for mapping the river. Where it entered Lake George, they found "prodigious quantities of pistia" (*P. stratiotes* L.) being driven downriver by the current. Some of it lodged along the shore and islands, where it "entangled with a large species of water-numularia, persicaria, water grass, and saxifrage, all which send down very long fibrous roots deep into the water by which they are nourished, growing all matted together in such a manner as to stop up the mouth of a large creek, so that a boat can hardly be pushed through them, though in 4 foot water." Storms broke off quantities of the plants, which floated downriver and again took root. There they gathered mud and bits of flotsam, eventually becoming islands that in turn attracted more plants to their shores. Very little in the way of ecological influences escaped Bartram's notice.

On New Year's eve they reached "Spalding's Upper Store." As they continued south, the river became less broad, and there were many streams leading to it. With the ubiquitous flatland curtained by trees, they sometimes resorted to climbing one to gather some general idea of the terrain. One day the temperature dropped to 26°F, and the ground was frozen an inch thick on the banks. They heard later that this freeze killed the citron, lime, and banana trees in St. Augustine. Another day they explored a creek, ending up at Blue Springs. Near here was a mound which Bartram called

Mount Joy. They visited other springs at Lake Monroe, and as they went further upriver they sometimes found great beds of reeds. As the river flooded, these caught trash and gradually built up into banks. On these "the alligators love to bask in the sun-shine, every 20, 50, or 100 yards distance."

The Bartrams first heard the howling of wolves in Florida on 9 January. The next morning they found a "great nest of a wood-rat, built of long pieces of dry sticks, near 4 foot high and 5 in diameter, all laid confusedly together; on stirring the sticks to observe their structure, a large rat ran out, and up a very high saplin with a young one hanging to its tail."[8] Now there were more branches than ever leading into the river, islands everywhere, and small ponds. It became very difficult to determine the main river. Only the strong current gave a clue. They reached the lakes, Ruth and Loughman, on the twelfth. Here they found that the reeds and water plants completely blocked passage. They realized that this was the end of their outward journey and turned homeward the next day. Having mainly followed the eastern banks of the river coming up, they returned by way of the western.

On the fifteenth they camped at Lake Jessup, where Davis killed a 400-pound bear whose forepaws were five inches broad and whose fat was four inches thick, yielding about sixteen gallons of fine oil almost as sweet as that of the olives. Neither Bartram had ever eaten bear meat, and they were delighted to find it "mild and sweet." The skin was sixty-five inches by fifty-eight when stretched. The expedition was well provided for at this point, for they already had a buck and three turkeys. They took a day to barbecue the bear meat, having no salt with which to preserve it. In addition to meat and oranges, their diet was supplemented by the tender white top bud of the tree-palm or cabbage tree. This was about twelve inches long and four in diameter. Boiled with a little bear oil added, Bartram found it very satisfying and much milder than cabbage—so mild, in fact, that he found he could eat twice as much as he ate of that vegetable. The hunters often ate it raw, sometimes subsisting on it for several days. Bartram was so pleased with the bluff where they felled the cabbage palms that he christened it Bartram's Bluff.

The nights of 19 and 20 January were spent at Spalding's Upper Store; the wind was blowing too hard to sail on the lake, and Davis was anxious to dry his skins some more. The store's manager decided to go hunting for wild geese, which often landed on the

many shallow ponds in the vicinity to feed on the grass. The Bartrams went with him, for they had not seen a single goose in all of
their travels although there were "multitudes of ducks" along the
river. Bartram remarked to their host that he had not discovered
any good clay up the St. Johns River and was told that there was
some excellent white clay on the western side of the river where
the manager's house stood. With a hoe Bartram cut out a piece.
When he examined it, he found that the part above water was composed of ground-up seashells but that below water it had become
almost claylike in substance, the more so the deeper it lay. This
raised a question in his mind as to whether other types of clay
might have been formed from shells.

Because of bad weather their progress was slow. By 23 January, they reached Silver Glen Spring, which Bartram named "William's Spring." Thousands of orange trees grew so thickly on the
shell bluff above that it was difficult to pass between them. Nearby
was another bluff on which the Indians had planted crops. These
were the only areas which they farmed, since they would not
bother with the nuisance of raising rice, the only crop that could be
grown in the swamps and marshes. The next day the Bartrams visited a spring where Billy spotted "a lovely sweet tree, with leaves
like the sweet bay, which smelled like sassafras. . . . some of them
grew near 20 foot high, a charming bright evergreen aromatic."
Bartram gathered some specimens of the "very strange kind of seed
pod" produced by the tree (*Illicium floridanum* Ellis), but he was
too late for seed.[9]

Mount-Royal, Dunn's Island, and Charlotia were revisited.
Landing at the first, Bartram studied the Indian tumulus carefully.
It was 300 yards in diameter and almost twenty feet high. He knew
it was very ancient from the size of the live oaks upon it. The
height astounded him when he considered that the only means of
transporting the necessary sand that the Indians had were their
baskets or bowls. Although there was a slight indentation near the
mound, he did not think it deep enough to have supplied the sand.
He found an explanation looking north, where there was a great
avenue sixty yards wide with foot-high banks sixteen feet broad,
taken from where the surface of the road had been leveled. At the
end of this, three-quarters of a mile away in a savannah, there was
an oblong pond 250 by 300 feet. The banks of this were four feet
high, sloping down to the water, which was shallow and covered

with grass. Since the pond was of such a regular shape, Bartram was convinced that it was artificial and that the sand had been the source for the tumulus, which he thought might have been "their burying-place or sepulchre."

They reached Picolata at noon on 1 February and proceeded to Caldwell's Store, where they paused to explore Black Creek and Doctor's Lake, arriving at Mr. Davis' home on the sixth. The Bartrams stayed there for several days, making short trips. They rowed down below the "Cattle-ford," an area new to them, where "high oak-banks" alternated with marshes and pines. Small ponds and sand hills could be seen in the distance. At Forbes' bluff they saw rushes which were much prized for chair bottoms and mats. One morning they enjoyed "a mess of tenniers, a species of eddo" for breakfast, which Bartram found excellent when boiled with meat.[10] After breakfast they resumed their travels, continuing to the mouth of the river near today's Pilot Town. They walked down the beach to an inlet and visited a plantation on St. George's Island. It belonged to a most successful planter, a Mr. Hazard, with whom they spent two nights. They returned to the Davis' home on the twelfth. After spending the night, they rented horses, parted company with their guide, and returned to St. Augustine after an absence of eight weeks.

Bartram reported to Governor Grant, who gave him a room where he could prepare a map of the St. Johns River and complete his journal of their expedition. For the next month he was occupied with this, but he and Billy made short trips around the area, looking for more plants. Billy had become enchanted with Florida and determined to remain there. He had an excellent opportunity for doing so when Gerard De Brahm (c.1717–90), the cartographer, who was making a survey of the area, offered him a job as his draughtsman. Billy declined the offer, having decided to become a planter although strongly advised against it by his father and others.[11] Billy had never shown any aptitude for farming in Pennsylvania, and to create a plantation, even in this semitropical region, would require experience and stamina that he had never previously demonstrated. His father had already helped him try several enterprises at which he had failed dismally. Bartram was not optimistic about this one but permitted Billy to persuade him to finance the venture. They looked for an available piece of land for which Billy could claim a patent from the governor by bringing in the minimum number of slaves, which his father would purchase at Charles Town. They finally found a place that Billy liked, on the river near the mouth of Six-mile Creek.[12]

By the middle of March 1766 Bartram had completed his map and report for the governor and reserved passage on a ship for Carolina. His chest went on board the fifteenth, and he embarked two days later. The ship passed over the bar the following day but was soon becalmed and had to anchor for another twenty-four hours. On the twenty-second Bartram was dining with Garden at Charles Town. He spent nearly three weeks there as guest of the Lambolls. It was a busy twenty days. He completed part of his journal for Collinson. He prepared three quires of plant specimens and seeds for the king. He packed Billy's drawings for shipment and made many purchases for him. These required that he draw several bills on Collinson, one of which exceeded £150. He had already drawn on him at St. Augustine for the expense of their maintenance and for supplies for Billy.[13]

Most of the money Bartram was spending went for the purchase of slaves for Billy. Their Charles Town friends who had seen and admired Billy's drawings were horrified to hear of his adamant determination to relinquish his painting for the life of a Florida planter. They prophesied dire catastrophies. The negroes would surely either murder him or run off and leave him in the wilderness. None of this helped to reassure Bartram, who already had many reservations about what he had agreed to do. But since he had been foolish enough to promise Billy, he must keep his word. He therefore sought the help of friends in finding the right slaves. When he asked Lamboll for advice, he was told that Billy should have nothing to do with slaves, for they were the "greatest curse that ever came to America." When pressed by Bartram, Lamboll admitted that it was impossible to raise rice without their help. Since rice would have to be one of Billy's principal crops, his father had little choice. He spent almost two weeks in his selection. Colonel Laurens, who was reckoned the most expert in selecting slaves, helped Bartram with his choices. Dr. Garden checked their health. Everyone to whom Bartram talked agreed that the negroes recently imported were superior to those born in this country who had been exposed to "mischievous practices." In fact, he found that people thought most of them were "either murderers, runaways or robers or theeves."[14]

By April, six young negroes had been delivered on board the *East Florida* in Captain Peter Bachop's charge. There was Jack and his wife Siby, from New Guinea. Two other men, Jacob and Sam, were small, being five feet and four feet seven and a half inches, respectively. The other woman was Flora, of a paler complexion than most Coromantees, the most popular of the slaves. She came highly recommended by her master and mistress, who declared that she had never been exposed to the usual vices since she had never been allowed to go out at night. She was well trained as a laundress and seemingly so responsible that Bartram thought she might be left in charge in Billy's absence. She had a small boy about four years old, and Bartram thought she might make a fine wife for Jacob. Both women were pregnant. Dr. Garden warned Bartram that Billy must be alert concerning the slaves' health and their clothing, for they never bothered to take care of themselves. When in a sweat from pounding rice, they were apt to run outside into the cold air and develop pleurisy. They were equally likely to fell trees on one another. Bartram did not send Billy the bill of sale for the slaves, for he wanted to wait until he returned home and could adjust his will in fairness to his other children.[15]

Outfitting Billy as a plantation owner from scratch was a tiring undertaking. It was only due to Bartram's usual efficiency that he was able to accomplish it in such a short time. Tools had to be selected: a heavy Pennsylvania axe, a broad axe, an adz for making watering troughs, bowls and trays, a shovel, a saw, a Jack plane, a whetstone, hooks and lines, a dozen sickles, lead with which to make bullets, millstones, and a grindstone. There were household goods to be bought as well: smoothing irons, twenty yards of burlap, some coarse sacking to fill with moss for mattresses, and pots. Mrs. Lamboll sent Billy a pot of sugar and one of ground nuts as well as a bed cloth to be filled with duck and turkey feathers. She also included a kettle, several bushels of peas, taniers, and garden seed. Bartram knew that she would be very pleased if Billy sent her one of his drawings.[16]

Before Bartram had left St. Augustine, he had ordered all sorts of garden seeds to be sent to Billy: squash, pumpkins, melons, beans, peas, and others. He had left money with a Mr. Cummins, with which Billy could buy two cows and a mare and a colt. Now he sent white and red yams and ordered a barrel containing five bushels of seed rice. He suggested that Billy set fire to the twenty-acre marsh to clear it for the rice. If it was too wet, it could be hoed into ridges, for he had been told that water covering the young plant would kill it. Under the tall pines, where the grass grew so luxuriantly, would be a fine spot for a corn crop after the trees were cut. Through Colonel Laurens, Bartram ordered two barrels of corn for £14−4−6, one barrel of rice to eat, at £15, and a barrel of pork, at £11. The colonel added a cask of salt as a gift. Such provisions were expensive, having risen in price just since Bartram had reached Charles Town. He suggested that Billy plant as many peas (blackeyed?) as he could, for everyone recommended them as food for the negroes. He thought it would be wise to plant a great many of the wild limes in fence rows. Friends told him that they were considered to be the coming crop of East Florida, since the market for oil and tallow was never satisfied. Even the remains of the kernels, after the oil had been expressed, would make a very rich hog food.[17]

Bartram developed a wretched cough that kept him awake at night. Tired from all of his activities for Billy and half sick, he was annoyed when a ship came from Florida on 9 April but there was no letter from his son. Bartram had talked to Francis Kinloch, who was sailing back with Captain Bachop. Kinloch was bringing sixteen negroes and provisions and would be settling at Dunn's Creek above Rolle's town. He thought that he might persuade the governor to allow the captain to come up the St. Johns River to land both his and Billy's supplies right at the door. In a letter Bartram enclosed two guineas for Billy's further encouragement.[18]

With his usual pessimism when embarking on a sea voyage, Bartram boarded the *Charlestown Packet*, Captain Thomas Eastwick, the following day. He was not only seasick but had a recurrence of malaria. He landed in Philadelphia on the twenty-fourth where he found his family all well. When he sent Collinson some more Florida seeds, he wrote, "I have left my son Billy in Florida. Nothing will do with him now, but he will be a planter upon St. John's River. . . . This frolic of his, and our maintenance, hath drove me to great straits; so that I was forced to draw upon thee, at Augustine, and twice at Charleston. . . ."[19]

Bartram's feelings toward Billy were not improved by the first letter that he received from him. It had been written on 6 June but only mentioned one of the two letters that his father had sent, nor was there any mention of the two guineas, the grindstone, millstones, tools, and other things that had been sent. When Bartram replied, he remarked bitterly, "I suppose thy usual ingratitude would not suffer the to mention; thay cost me dear & so much that I am still in debt for them." Bad weather had caused Billy to lose his first chance for a crop and had left him depressed. In spite of his irritation Bartram sent more provisions and cloth from Philadelphia in July. He wrote that he would send either an order or money to Mr. Cummins as soon as Billy let him know how much he already owed Cummins but added that he would "not answer any extravagant draught   I am not against finding thee real necessaries this year but thee must expect to suffer ye first year as all do in new settlements."[20]

Billy was more wretched than his father realized. His nearest neighbor lived six or more miles away. Few boats passed by on the river. Some form of fever had weakened his never robust health. The heavy manual labor of cutting trees, clearing away the brush, grubbing out bushes and, all that went with preparing land for planting was almost more than he could manage. Only two of his slaves were handy with axes, and one of them was so insolent that Billy was afraid of him. Provisions were low, and the heat and humidity were extremely oppressive. Whatever shelter he had been able to construct was scarcely adequate for him and his slaves and not proof against rain. He was very soon completely disillusioned with the enterprise that he had been so determined to undertake.

As early as late spring he had begun to talk to a friend about abandoning it. The friend persuaded him to wait at least until after the promised visit of Henry Laurens. Sometime around the middle of June, Laurens arrived and was shocked to find Billy shaking with fever and living under appalling conditions. Billy showed him peas, corn, beans, and yams which he had planted and which had just come up. These looked flourishing at the time, but when Laurens stopped by about 6 July they did not seem to have grown at all. He had advised Billy to continue his swamp clearing and found that he had cleared part of another acre. He suggested that he plant rice immediately, even though it was late in the season. He thought that good rice crops could be produced here but had grave doubts that Billy could do it. He was not even sure that the young man would be capable of making shingles from the cypress, which were always profitable. Laurens promised Billy that he would write to his father about his problems.

Laurens did write when he got back to Charles Town on 9 August. He wrote at length, painting a very dark picture of Billy's dire state, with apologies for what might seem to be impertinence from a casual acquaintance: "Possibly, sir, your son, though a worthy, ingenious man, may not have resolution, or not that sort of resolution, that is necessary to encounter the difficulties incident to and unavoidable in his present state of life. You and I, probably, could surmount all those hardships without much chagrin. I very believe that I could. But, at the same time, I protest that I should think it less grievous to disinherit my own son, and turn him into the wide world, if he was of a tender and delicate frame of body and intellect, as yours seems to be, than to restrict him, in my favour, just in the state that your son is reduced to."

Laurens wrote that he was taking the liberty of sending Billy some provisions and would charge them to Bartram. He said that he would have preferred to send them as a gift but was afraid that he might offend.[21] He shipped a keg of biscuit, half a cheese, brown and loaf sugar, coffee, and tea. In addition to these basic needs, he sent some spirits to add a bit of cheer, four gallons of rum and a dozen bottles each of wine and beer—a rather surprising quantity, especially the rum. He wrote to Billy, enclosing a letter from his father. He told Billy that his father thought that he should dispose of his property and return home. He urged that Billy take his advice.[22]

Portions of Bartram's southern journal had been forwarded to Collinson as he finished them. Collinson received his Georgia account with a short description of St. Augustine and some "thermometrical" observations in May 1766, but it was not until December that Bartram found a safe conveyance for his "true and general Journal" by the hands of Captain Falconer, who did not expect to sail until early spring.[23] In the meantime Governor Grant had sent the report that Bartram had prepared for him to the English Board of Trade, and it was already in print by October 1766. It was added to a second edition of William Stork's *Account of East Florida*, which had been published six months previously. Stork was a physician sent to Florida by the government for the express purpose of writing a promotional description of the newly acquired colony with the hope of encouraging settlers. This it had done, resulting in 120 applications for land grants to the Board of Trade before October. The second edition bore the title *An Account of East-Florida with a Journal kept by John Bartram of Philadelphia, Botanist to*

His Majesty for the Floridas; upon a Journey from St. Augustine up the River St. John's. It was published by W. Nicoll and G. Woodfall and cost four shillings. Stork introduced Bartram's journal as follows: "Mr. John Bartram, a native of Pensylvania, the Author of this Journal, is well known, and well respected in the learned world, as an able Naturalist; his knowledge in Botany has recommended him to the esteem and patronage of the Great, and has procured him the honour of being Botanist to his Majesty for both Floridas. The usefulness of his Journal, in making known to the world the nature of the country to which it relates, is the best proof of the usefulness of his appointment." Stork, or someone else, added notes on various plants mentioned, emphasizing their usefulness.

Bartram's account ends with a section entitled "Remarks on the River St. John's," which does not appear in his original version. The implication is that he was the author, but it sounds far more like a promotional blurb. There are descriptions of "extensive savannahs" with fine grass on which "great numbers of cattle can be raised." Many cypress swamps would make ideal rice fields. Pinelands, cultivated and fertilized, would produce corn, cotton, and potatoes. Where the palmettoes flourished both indigo and corn could be raised. The actual depth of the "rich mud" in the swamps along the St. Johns was unknown, but undoubtedly these lands, when drained, would yield "great crops of corn and indigo and without much or any draining a fine increase of rice." Shingles, pales, and boards could be produced from the cypress and shipping timbers from the live oaks as well as masts from the longleaf pine. Supplies of seafood, both shellfish and freshwater fish, were in abundance.

The publication was duly announced in the October issues of *The Scots Magazine* and in *The Gentleman's Magazine*. The latter added tartly that the journal "can afford entertainment only to a botanist, and to a botanist not much." In spite of this, in April they published a long extract of Bartram's Georgia travels taken from the original manuscript sent to Collinson.[24] Peter's pride had been deeply hurt when others received Bartram's account before he did. He did not write until February and then was still bitter:

> . . . Inquiries I Drew up in peruseing thy Journal which I could not Borrow before the 4th of January for few will Buy so Dear a Book but as my Friend John did not think Mee

worthy of the Original I found no Obligation to Purchase a
Coppy

If thou hast Intended to Lett Stok puff off his Book with
thy Journal to publish the Same as Kings Botanist to the
World which by the way is a Title thou assumes without the
Kings Leave or License which is makeing very free with Majesty it is possible for this undue Liberty thy annuity may be
withdrawn but I hope not because thou Well Deserves It and
as thy Eyes are bad & the Coppy of the Journal to send to
Mee might have been Ill convenient to thee yett if thou
hadst an inclination to oblige a Friend that has Served thee
& Family for so many years I should expect to have heard
thee saye I know my Friend Peter would like to Peruse the
Journal but my Eyes are bad & I Cant undertake it Come
Moses Do thou Do It to oblige an Old Friend I know Moses
would have readily undertaken It but if this was to great a
Favour the Least thou couldest have done was to Engage
Stok to Send & Complement Mee with a Book but not the
least Notice is taken of Mee Doth not this show a Gratefull
Friendly Mind Such kind usage I never expected from John
Bartram. . . . Docr Stork is very Superficial in many things &
Some Improbabilities but I have not Time to point them out

I read one Davis was killed by the Cherokee Indians I
hope it was not that Davis that went with thee[25]

Bartram, who almost certainly knew nothing about his report
to Governor Grant having been published, did not appreciate being
falsely accused of ingratitude by Collinson. He labored to complete
a copy of his actual journal, some of which he had already sent, and
fired it off to Collinson at the first safe opportunity with some caustic comments. These have not survived but can be inferred from
Collinson's reply of 31 July: "My dear John hath at last gratified
my longing wishes with the sight and perusal of his laborious, entertaining Journal, full of fine discoveries, useful reflections and
pertinent observations. I can take a squib from John Bartram,
without the least resentment. Friends may be allowed to rally one
another, when it is not done in anger, or sharp resentment, which
I never intended, however my words may be taken. If I can be
thought too quick, my dear John, thou wast too slow, and so we will

let the matter go."[26] Collinson compensated for his behavior by preparing three indexes to the journal, one botanical, the second geological, and the third general.[27]

Dr. Mitchell was most interested to see the original manuscript. He had probably seen Bartram's report sent to the Board of Trade as well. He was shocked at the changes that had been made in Bartram's work before publication in order to insure that Florida's weaknesses were omitted and her virtues extolled, whether they were based on fact or not. He took pains to call attention to this in his own book, *The Present State of Great Britain and North America*, published in 1767. In a footnote to Bartram's statement concerning the sandy soil of the pine barrens in the published report, Mitchell wrote: "See *Bartram's* journal, *manuscript*; which passage we do not find in the edition that has been published; although it is the most material of the whole, as it contains a general description of the country, and the author's opinion of it, after he had viewed it; but as this is not in the favor of the country, it was not deemed fit to print."[28] Mitchell highly disapproved of the acquisition of East Florida and Canada rather than an expansion to the west, and Bartram's low appraisal of Florida's value bolstered his opinion.

In 1769 Nicoll, in conjunction with Thomas Jefferys, geographer to the king, brought out another edition of Stork's and Bartram's work. Jefferys added a very poor map of the upper portion of East Florida. Another addition was a list of plants by John Ellis, giving their binomials with the page references in the second edition of Linnaeus' *Species Plantarum*. These were plants that he thought might be raised successfully in Florida, including various madders, pistachios, cottons, camphor and caper trees, bamboo, olives, and many others. He even suggested Angora goats. A final edition was published in 1774.

Whatever reaction Bartram had to the liberties taken with his manuscript, it is to be hoped that he read Bernard Romans' remarks on the subject. At the request of the Board of Trade, the cartographer published *A Concise Natural History of East and West Florida* in 1775. In discussing the St. Johns River, he remarked:

the journal of Mr. *Bartram* as published by Dr. *Stork*, may give a tolerable idea of the banks of this river, and consequently of the west part of this peninsula; but this journal, though a very loose performance, and principally defective where we might expect it most compleat, viz. in the botanical articles, yet such as it is, the Doctor who wanted to extoll this province beyond reason, has not thought fit to give it to us in its native dress, but mutilated and unfairly modelled it to answer his own purpose, which has given another author* a handle for depreciating this country still more below its value than the Doctor has endeavoured to raise it above; however, all such prejudiced writers being below contempt, let us leave them   *Present State of Great Britain and North America.[29]

SEVENTEEN

New Honors for a Scientist

B ARTRAM had been away from his home and
family for nearly ten months, far longer than
any previous absence. He was gratified to find how well the family
had conducted his affairs in his absence, particularly by Johnny's
management of the seed and plant business and care of the garden.
Johnny had made all of the usual fall shipments and had a letter
from Collinson saying that all had arrived safely and well packed.
Collinson was especially appreciative of a box containing a loblolly
bay to replace two that thieves had stolen from his garden.[1]

Seeds and specimens from North Carolina, Georgia, and
Florida, which Bartram had shipped in the fall, had been received
and delivered by Collinson to the king's representative.[2] Shortly
after he returned home Bartram shipped another box, and still another was sent in December. During 1765–66 he sent a total of 259
plant specimens for the king's herbarium.[3] He was a trifle disillusioned to learn that the freight costs for all his shipments were
charged against the meager honorarium that he had received. He
considered sending some of his Florida treasures to the queen, but
Collinson advised against it. Bartram was reminded of her whenever he saw her protégé, William Young, in Philadelphia. One
could hardly fail to see him, as Bartram admitted: "He cuts the
greatest figure in town, struts along the streets, whistling, with his
sword and gold lace &c." Young even visited Bartram several times
at Kingsessing, and although he was very respectful and admiring
Bartram viewed him with suspicion.[4] The fact that Young was receiving a £300 pension still rankled.

Even though Ann and his sons had taken excellent care of his
gardens and farm while he was gone, there were still many things

to occupy Bartram on his return. Among these were several matters involving land. He and Ann had sold the farm inherited from his Uncle Isaac to Robert Pennell some years earlier and had bought lots in Philadelphia. This was the land on which Bartram had built the three stone houses mentioned earlier. In July 1754 Thomas Penn had written to his agent, the Reverend Richard Peters, that Bartram should have lot number 60 as well and that it should be included in his patent. Seemingly nothing was done about this until 13 May 1767, when the Board of Property ordered a survey made, and the patent was formally issued by Richard and Thomas Penn on 26 January 1768.[5] Bartram had probably instigated some action concerning the title to the land, for he wanted to dispose of some of it. The money he had spent on Billy's behalf had made him conscious of the necessity to provide fairly for his other children. He and Ann now disposed of part of the Philadelphia tract, including a house, to Isaac for the sum of five shillings, acknowledging in the deed "the natural love and affection which he the said John Bartram hath and doth bear towards his son, and for his better advancement in the world, and for divers good causes."[6]

Billy seldom wrote. The fall months went by with no word. It was mid-December when news of Billy reached them from Thomas Lamboll. De Brahm had arrived in Charles Town from St. Augustine. He reported that Billy had abandoned his plantation and had worked with him for some time. The two men had been running lines for a colony on the Mosquito River being established by Dr. Andrew Turnbull. It would be colonized by emigrants from Greece and Minorca and would be called New-Smyrna. De Brahm said that not long after this Billy had boarded a ship at St. Augustine which had later been shipwrecked. Nothing more had been heard of the young man.[7] Bartram suffered not only the great sorrow of the loss of a son but a feeling of guilt as well. He blamed himself for having permitted Billy to persuade him to do what his own better judgment told him was unwise. He had long been afraid that Billy might come to a tragic end, and now this premonition appeared to be realized. Bartram was aware that he had always tried to shield Billy from the hard realities of life more than he had his other children. He now asked himself whether this had been a mistake. He and Billy had spent so much time together on their trips that they had shared a special relationship. Until more definite word could be received, he and Ann refused to give up hope.

In March 1767 Bartram was confined to the house by two serious attacks of vertigo. He was recovering from the second of these
when a letter from Lamboll arrived on 2 April with the news that
Billy was alive and at St. Augustine.[8] Billy did not return to Philadelphia until some months later. He then told his parents that, in
his desperation, he had written to Collinson, hoping that he might
know of some opening in London for which his pencil and brush
might qualify him, but he had received no reply. Bartram now
understood some of Collinson's remarks that had puzzled him. Referring to Billy, Peter had written on 10 April, "I have often
thought what a pity it is that his ingenuity could not be of service
to him. I have, for years past, been looking out for him, but no
opening has offered. The difficulties to introduce an entire stranger,
are insurmountable; for whilst he is attempting to make himself
known, he may be starving, which has been the case of some ingenious people in his way (that I have known) that have been foreigners. If my advice may have any weight with him, it is, to get him a
good, notable wife,—a farmer's daughter, and return to his estate,
and set his shoulders heartily to work to improve it. . . . "[9] Collinson finally wrote to Billy on 28 July, having just received Bartram's
manuscript journal and Billy's accompanying drawings, about
which he wrote: "It's with concern and regret, that I see so much
skill lavished away on such vile paper, that deserves the finest vel-
lum. But I suppose necessity has no law,—no other was to be had.
Poorly set off as they are, they have been much admired by the best
judges." Collinson was sympathetic to Billy's disappointments and
constantly alert to any opportunity for him but with no success. He
added that "to come over on speculation and uncertainty will never
do."[10] Billy found work as a laborer, a dismal prospect for an artistic
twenty-nine-year-old. Collinson bemoaned such "servile drudgery,"
intimating that surely his father, with his many friends in business, could find something better for his son.[11]

In spite of aching muscles and roughened hands, Billy spent
as many hours as he could at his drawing board. When Bartram
packed up the king's specimens and some for Collinson, the shipment included a letter and a box from Moses, a box of insects from
Johnny, and sketches of red *Hibiscus*, scarlet sage, *Colocasia*, and
other plants from Billy, as well as "Curious Dissertations on the
Productions of Florida."[12] The water lily painting was especially appreciated by Collinson: "I and my son opened my ingenious friend

WILLIAM's inimitable picture of the *Colocasia*. So great was the deception, it being candle-light, that we disputed for some time whether it was an engraving, or a drawing. It is really a noble piece of pencil-work; and the skill of the artist is shown in following nature in her progressive operations: I will not say more in commendation, because I shall say too little where so much is due. I wish the King had any taste in flowers or plants; but as he has none, there are no hopes of encouragement from him, for his talent is architecture. But I shall show it, with thy other curious performances, to Lord BUTE, who is the only great man that encourages ingenious men in painting botanic rarities."[13] Collinson requested Bartram to pay Billy a guinea sterling in colonial currency as some recompense for the time and paper used, adding, "What pleasure it must give thee to have such ingenious sons. WILLIAM and MOSES in his way; and JOHNNY in his way for plants and insects. . . ." The *Gentleman's Magazine* had published Moses' "Observations on the American Locust."[14]

In July 1767 Margaret Cavendish Bentinck, the Duchess of Portland, dined with Collinson. Her great hobby was the collection and study of shells and other marine curiosities. Collinson seized the opportunity of displaying Billy's drawings, which she greatly admired. She ordered sketches of the *Faba Egyptica* and of shells from land, river, and sea, "from the very least to the greatest," for which she would pay Billy twenty guineas. If these were satisfactory, there should be subsequent orders. Collinson specified that the artist should not crowd too many on a page and that no shading should be done since it obscured the shapes. Notes as to color and a short description should be appended.[15] A few days later Dr. Fothergill breakfasted with Collinson, was shown the drawings, and likewise ordered sketches of "Land, River and Sea Shells" of all sizes. As the doctor was in no great hurry, Billy could send several as he completed them. Fothergill was also interested in turtles and terrapins, wanting sketches of both the upper and under shells. A short natural history of each should be included.[16] Collinson had provided the opportunity that Billy had long wanted, to establish an artistic career if he would work at it.

Collinson, now seventy-four, reveled in his Ridgeway House garden. It had reached a maturity and beauty that satisfied even so ambitious a gardener as Peter. Several years earlier he had written to Bartram, "I forgot in my last to tell thee my deciduous Mountain

Magnolia I raised from seed about twenty years agone, flowered for the first time with me; and I presume is the first of that species that ever flowered in England, and the largest and tallest. The flowers come early; soon after the leaves are formed. The great Laurel Magnolia and Umbrella, both fine trees in my garden, showed their flower-buds the first of June. My Red flowering Acacia is now in full flower, and makes a glorious show, as well as the White. But above all, is the great Mountain Laurel, or *Rhododen-dron*, in all its glory. What a ravishing sight must the mountains appear when clad with this rich embroidery!"[17] Collinson gardened year-round. He could step from his parlor into his forty-two-foot greenhouse, which made "a pretty walk to smell the sweets of so many odoriferous plants winter without and summer within."[18] William Bennett, a gardener of some note himself, considered Collinson's collection of North American plants the finest of any individual in England, perhaps in Europe as well.[19] Such choice plants drew artists such as George Ehret and William King of Totteridge, seeking rare botanical models.[20] They were also tempting to thieves, who twice robbed Collinson's garden of some of his choice plants, including a number sent by Bartram. Plant robbery became so commonplace in the great English gardens that a bill was passed by Parliament declaring it a transportation offense to steal curious plants.[21]

To Collinson, his garden was something very personal—a bridge to his friends, many of whom he never saw, and a communion with them through their gifts. Where a visitor might only see a fine spruce and a handsome larch, he saw them as Colden's representatives. Lord Northumberland was there in the person of the "curious Firr from Mount Ida." The Duke of Richmond lived on in his cedars of Lebanon, which would "Endure when you & I & He is forgot." Fringe trees, *Stuartia*, and *Halesia*, were deputies for John Clayton. Innumerable plants reminded Collinson of Bartram.[22] The former could take great satisfaction not only from his own garden but from others as well. In 1763 he wrote, "I often stand with wonder and amazement when I view the inconceivable variety of flowers, shrubs, and trees, now in our gardens, and what there were forty years ago; in that time what quantities from all North America have annually been collected by my means and procuring. . . ."[23] The great majority of these had come from Bartram.

In early August 1768 Collinson was at the home of young

Lord Petre. He always relished these visits to Thorndon Park, where he could view the results of many of his importations and suggestions. This time he became ill and returned to London, where he died a week later. It was many weeks before Bartram heard of his friend's death. He was hurt that the news did not reach him from Collinson's son, Fothergill, Franklin, or any of his English correspondents. Even though Bartram and Collinson had never met, theirs had been a very close association for thirty-five years. They had shared so much both in the botanical world and in their own personal interests. A deep and abiding intimacy and affection had developed. Traveling and plant collecting lost much of their fascination for Bartram now that his discoveries could no longer be shared with Collinson. There was no other friend left abroad of their generation. Catesby, Dillenius, Gronovious, and Mitchell, all were gone.

In one of Collinson's last letters, he had reported that the king desired arum roots, which Bartram had procured. He wondered now what to do with them. He wondered, too, whether his pension would still be paid and even whether he would ever see the money that Collinson had held for him in his account. Bartram kept thinking that Franklin would soon be home and that he could ask his advice. He was sure that Franklin must be on his way or he would surely have written about Peter. In November, however, he wrote to his "dear ould Friend" asking him if he would see to the delivery of the king's box, which he had already shipped. He would have written to Collinson's son instead had he known his given name. When Franklin received the letter some months later, he immediately wrote to Michael Collinson, asking him if he would deliver Bartram's box. If he was unable to do so, Franklin asked Michael to let him know to whom to deliver it. Michael directed that the box be sent to Lord Bute and was much offended that Bartram had not written to him. Franklin informed Bartram of what he had done.[24]

A few days before Bartram received Franklin's letter, two other letters arrived from England that had been delayed six months in transit. The reason for Michael's annoyance was explained. On 22 September he had written a sympathetic and affectionate letter to Bartram, giving a detailed account of his father's last days.[25] Dr. Fothergill had written on 29 October, referring to the great loss they had both undergone in Collinson's death. He only wished that he could take over some of Collinson's services to Bartram, but unfortunately a doctor's busy life precluded that. He was indebted to Bartram for the fine box of flourishing plants that he had sent.[26]

Fothergill's garden was in the country, so he only saw it once a week. In 1762 he had bought a thirty-acre estate, Rooke Hall, at Upton, which he later enlarged. With ample funds, he gradually developed a very beautiful and famous garden, with which Sir Joseph Banks said no other in Europe could compare for rarities. A glass door from a sitting room in the house opened into a 260-foot greenhouse, which eventually contained 3,400 species of tropical plants.[27] Fothergill wrote Bartram that there was a ready market in London for North American seeds to be shipped to Germany. He suggested that two-year-old plants might have a better market in England than seeds, which often failed to germinate. Bartram was interested in this idea, immediately making plans to enlarge his nursery garden. Fothergill ordered a collection of Turk's-cap lilies and some *Colocasia* roots in a tub of mud. He confirmed his order for Billy's drawings and notes, saying that twenty guineas' payment had been mentioned when he talked to Collinson but that he would not restrict him to this.[28] He felt that it was important that accurate drawings be made of all species of animals and vegetables, for a certain species might die out or become so rare as not to be found.[29]

Although Fothergill could not himself handle the business end in England for Bartram, he persuaded his nephew, James Freeman, to undertake it. Michael Collinson, knowing how much of his father's time had been required, had refused to do it. He was even unwilling to take Bartram's annual pension from the king when Sir William Bretton approached him. He requested Bretton to keep it until Bartram informed him to whom he wished it paid. Michael did write to Bartram that he would be delighted to assist him or any of his family in so far as his intimate acquaintance with the Earls of Bute and Northumberland and other members of the nobility would permit, as Bartram wryly wrote to Fothergill.[30] Michael had been completely ignorant of his father's financial affairs and at a loss as to the amount due to Bartram. Settlement was further delayed until Michael returned from a six months' tour of Europe, having leased Mill Hill for two years. It was not until early

1770 that the ledger with Bartram's account was found. Michael was astonished to learn that the estate owed Bartram such a large sum. He wrote that in his last years his father's business had "totally declined" and that he had even "solicited a small pension" but had been refused.[31]

Freeman, a mercer, was presently living in Collinson's London house. Since he knew little of plants, Bartram had to advise him as to prices, with Fothergill assisting him as well. Bartram was pleased with the new arrangement and directed that his pension be paid to Freeman. There had been many things that Bartram could do to oblige Collinson, but he knew of no way in which to oblige Freeman, so he paid him full commissions for his trouble.[32] Although Fothergill was not able to undertake Bartram's business affairs, he did a great deal to provide Bartram with an affectionate and concerned correspondent abroad, helping to fill the great void left by Collinson's death.

In packing up some *Colocasia* roots for Fothergill and the king, Bartram noticed several bullfrogs, which frequented their broad leaves, floating on the water's surface. A pair, male and female he thought, had just come into his springhouse to winter, so he caught them for the king, writing Fothergill:

> thay may be heard near or quite half A mile roaring like A bull & when half A dosen is roaring at A minits distance of time between each at A perticular noise made by one   all is hushed in A minute until perhaps Half or a quarter of an hour. then thay roar again until ye common signal for cessation is given. we suppose it is onely ye males that roars which is very diverting to some. an Irish girl tould me that soon after she came into ye country she was sent to A neibours house back in ye woods where she lost her way in A swamp   in ye night when ye Bull Frogs set A roaring she thought she was surrounded with bears or beasts of preay she then down on her knees in prayer to God to deliver her from those ravenous beasts . . . our Gentry catcheth numbers of them, Cuts of thair hind quarters of which thay make fricasees & esteems them A more delitious morsell then any chicken   if thay should increas in ye pond in St. James park thay would surprise & divert all ye adjacent inhabitants of

London but I think at present it would be beter to turn them
into ye pond at kew garden as being more private until thay
have increased thair number

Bartram suggested that Fothergill empty the whole barrel, frogs
and roots, in a pond at Kew, removing some roots for his own use.[33]
As soon as the shipment arrived Fothergill delivered the *Colocasia*
to Kew and planted some at Rooke Hall. Although he informed the
king of the frogs' arrival and sent a transcription of Bartram's remarks about them, he was given no directions as to their disposal.
Realizing that the king was involved at the moment in more important affairs, he put the frogs in a small goldfish pond at Upton.[34]

To demonstrate his affection for Bartram, Fothergill ordered a
bound copy of the translation of the Bible by the Quaker Anthony
Purver, to be picked up at Thomas Fisher's store in Philadelphia.
When Bartram went to get it, there were no bound Bibles, but Mr.
Fisher offered to get one. Bartram was, however, well contented
with an unbound one and found that the shoemaker had "mollified
many harsh Calvinistical expressions," which pleased him.[35] Not
long afterward Fothergill sent Bartram a copy of John Ellis' pamphlet on the preservation of seeds, one of which Bartram had already received from the author himself. The doctor suggested that
Bartram correspond with William Aiton, the head gardener at
Kew. Bartram wrote but received no reply.[36]

It was a joy to Bartram to hear regularly from Franklin, who
advised him to desist from his lengthy and dangerous travels. Instead Bartram should employ his "leisure hours in a work that is
much wanted, and which no one besides is so capable of performing
. . . the writing of a Natural History of our Country." Bartram protested that there was little interest in such travel journals as he
could write, that the public preferred accounts of man-made objects, modern or relics, such as temples, pyramids, castles, bridges,
and pictures. Franklin disagreed with him, saying that there were
a great number who would be most interested in the type of work
that Bartram would give them if he would but compile his observations, theories, and advice. Franklin admitted that he was one of
this category: "I confess that if I could find in any Italian Travels a
Receipt for making Parmesan Cheese, it would give me more Satisfaction than a Transcript of any Inscription from any old Stone
whatever."[37]

With his failing eyesight Bartram felt reluctant to undertake any lengthy piece of new writing, but he wrote to Franklin that he had sent Collinson the journal of his southern travels in 1765–66. Of course the part dealing with the St. Johns River had been published with Stork's volume and an excerpt on Georgia in the *Gentleman's Magazine*, but much of it had never seen print. He was certain that Michael would willingly lend it to Franklin "if thee should think it worth printing it I have nothing against it with proper correction which I know thee is very capable of doing." Either Michael could never find the manuscript or Franklin was too involved, for it was never published.[38]

Franklin was concerned for his friend, who seemed at a loss with Collinson gone. He continued to find excuses to write to him often and sent him seeds of "naked oats," Swiss barley, green peas, and some Chinese caravances, or chick-peas. With the last he included Father Navarette's recipe for a cheese made from them. For his part Bartram checked on the Franklin family. In November he reported that he had seen Mrs. Franklin, Sally Bache, and Franklin's "fine grandson," as well as his sister, Janet Mecom. They were all to visit Kingsessing the following day.[39]

The late summer of 1769 brought an extremely welcome communication to Bartram—a shining accolade for his years of devotion to natural history:

The Royal Academy of Sciences of Stockholm wished to show in the only way it can how much it regards the merits of the celebrated man JOHN BARTRAM, Royal Botanist in North America of the British Domain, and for that reason it has received this MR. BARTRAM into its fellowship and among the members of the Academy April 26, 1769. Therefore I salute him as a fellow with these presents in the name of the Royal Academy of Stockholm. In evidence of the matter I affix the Large Seal of the Academy,

PETER WARGENTIN
Permanent Secretary[40]

Bartram had been elected to a foreign society "known for the greatest delicacy in choosing members of distinction and note."[41] Both John Clayton and Collinson were members. If Bartram had ever felt any disappointment that the Royal Society of London, to which he had made so many contributions, had never so honored him, this Swedish compliment more than made up for it.

In September 1768 Bartram's dear friend, the Lutheran minister Charles Wrangel, had sailed for home, where he was appointed court chaplain and later bishop. The following July he wrote to Bartram that it had disturbed him, while in America, that his native country had not given Bartram proper recognition "and therefore it gives me great satisfaction, when I now assure you, that you are well known here, from the throne to every one that regards learning; and the Society of Science in Stockholm . . . has manifested their great regard for you by choosing you a member, unanimously, at the proposal of Professor Bergius." Wrangel had been present at the 26 April meeting of the academy and had presented the society with some of Billy's drawings and a few things from Bartram that had been intended for Linnaeus. Wrangel explained that Linnaeus was so accustomed to receiving presents from all over "that he hardly thinks of it," so Wrangel had taken this liberty.[42]

Linnaeus had been among those instrumental in founding the academy and had been elected its first president in 1739. As he was still president, it was to him that Bartram wrote, thanking the academy for the honor that they had done him. As evidence of his appreciation, Bartram sent them his own theories on two natural phenomena that had been the subject of much discussion among the learned. He hastily added that his dissertation was in the form of queries rather than explanations. His discussion included evaporation of the earth's water, the moon's influence on tides, and a detailed analysis of North American plant distribution according to latitude. He attributed the lower temperatures here in comparison to those of Europe of the same latitude to the lack of mountainous protection from arctic blasts. He concluded with his conviction that the sea once covered much of eastern North America and his reasons for believing so.[43]

In North America there was now a revival of interest in some sort of scientific academy. The Reverend Ezra Stiles of Newport, Rhode Island, amused himself for several years, drawing up proposals for an "American Academy of Sciences" or an "American Anti-European Academy of Sciences," so detailed that he even determined upon officers and council as well as members. Harvard professor John Winthrop should be president. The council would include Franklin, Bartram, and Benjamin Gale. Since he thought that Colden was contemptuous of colonial scholarship, Stiles refused to consider him. Nothing came of his plan at the time, but Stiles used it after the Revolution, when he was one of those instrumental in establishing the Connecticut Society of Arts and Sciences.[44]

There was a renewal of scientific interest in Philadelphia. The original proposals of the American Philosophical Society were reprinted in the 26 January 1768 issue of the *Pennsylvania Gazette*, with the following explanation:

Several Gentlemen of this City and Province, in Conjunction with some others, of the neighbouring Colonies, did in the year 1743, form themselves into a Society for promoting Useful Knowledge in America, which Society hath subsisted ever since, but with frequent and long Interruptions of their Meetings, on Account of the occasional Absence, and many Avocations of some of their principal Members. Nevertheless, many valuable Papers having been Communicated to them, and regularly entered in a Book, the surviving Members, after divers Consultations and Meetings during the last Year determined to enlarge their Design, by an Election of new Members, which they have done, to the Number of near fifty respectable names.

Although seven of the original members still survived, only three took part: Dr. Thomas Bond, Dr. Phineas Bond, and Samuel Rhoads. Franklin was in England and the others, like Bartram, had reached an age when they were inclined to leave new undertakings to younger men. The reactivation of the Philosophical Society had undoubtedly been inspired by that of the "American Society for promoting and propagating usefull knowledge, held in Philadelphia." Founded in 1750, it had been revived in 1766. Both Isaac and Moses Bartram were members, and their father was elected a member on 19 February 1768.[45]

While all of his brothers and sisters seemed to be leading normal and peaceful lives, trouble continued to haunt Billy. After a period of manual labor he returned to merchandizing in Philadelphia. He was again unsuccessful and by the summer of 1770 had accumulated numerous debts. One angry creditor so terrified Billy that he departed next day without a farewell to any of his family. It was not until months later that a letter came from him. Meanwhile George Bartram, Billy's brother-in-law, had paid off the man who had threatened Billy. Bartram and George then persuaded Billy's creditors to settle his debts for £100, which George advanced on his father-in-law's account.[46] Billy had fled to Ashwood, where he was sure of a welcome and where he hoped to collect money owed to him.[47] It was an unfortunate time for a visit. Only a few weeks after Billy arrived his uncle died, on 24 October, and his cousin Bill shortly thereafter. Bill had spent six years in Philadelphia, prolonging his medical training by working in his cousins' apothecary shop. Young Dr. Bartram had apparently returned to North Carolina in August 1767, for at that time he borrowed £45 from Isaac and Moses and purchased £34 worth of medicines on credit.[48]

Matters other than Billy's problems occupied the Bartrams that spring of 1771. They had two sons courting and two daughters being courted. Johnny married Eliza Howell on 9 May. She was Bartram's great-niece, James' granddaughter. Benjamin was interested in the daughter of the wealthy John Knowles. Elizabeth, Billy's twin, was being courted by William Wright of Lancaster County. The other daughter, Mary, at twenty-five, was the widow of Benjamin Bonsall. She had two children, Ann and James. Bartram thought her suitor unlikely to succeed.[49] Not long after his granddaughter's marriage, James Bartram died. His death had been expected for weeks. To his granddaughter, Eliza Howell Bartram, he left £100 and his house and lots in Wilmington. To his nephew and namesake, John's son James, he left £15.[50]

Bartram, now seventy-two, turned over his nursery and plantation business to Johnny, reserving only a part of the garden for his own use. He and Ann also gave the house to the bride and groom and made their home with them. Determined to settle his affairs, Bartram rewrote his will. His eyesight was failing badly, and he was unable to recognize his children a few feet away.[51] Franklin sent Bartram a whole series of spectacles numbered one to thirteen so that he might have the time necessary to select the proper ones. Franklin suggested that his friend could keep all those with higher numbers and give the others to friends.[52]

In the early fall there were letters from Freeman and Michael Collinson, both of whom became regular correspondents. Freeman's letters were largely about business, but Bartram relished young

Collinson's discussion of his travels and all manner of other subjects. Bartram's enthusiasm for conservation and concern about the threatened extinction of many species had found Michael sympathetic. The latter was especially upset over the thousands of pelts imported to England annually. Like Bartram, he had long given up killing any creature and admired Bartram's protection of even the rattlesnakes.[53] Michael had returned to Ridgeway House to live and well remembered Moses' visits. His particular interest was orchids, but, like his father, he studied plants wherever he was. He acknowledged Bartram's draft of £200 against him for the amount that his father had owed him. The small remaining balance of £22:2:3 Michael paid to Freeman in 1773.[54]

In midsummer 1772 a letter arrived from Billy which did little to reassure his parents. During his year in Carolina he had spent much of his time reviewing his past and planning his future. He concluded that any mercantile career involved him too much with people and trivialities, leaving him no hours of quiet for his real interests—drawing and studying nature. He was now determined "to retreat within myself to the only business I was born for, and which I am only good for (If I am intitled to use that phrase for any thing)."[55] In his letter to his parents Billy wrote that he was planning to go to Florida again. This time Bartram could no longer restrain himself and wrote to his son in no uncertain terms that he thought the idea ridiculous. He had no intention of making any financial contribution to it. He thought that Billy should come home, where family and friends could help him to find a way to support himself.[56]

Billy had also written to Fothergill, enclosing some drawings with his letter and asking his assistance with a botanical trip to Florida. Here he found a sympathetic ear and a generous proposal. The doctor was not willing to support Billy but thought that his talent should be encouraged. Moreover, Fothergill was most interested in collecting American plants hardy enough to withstand English winters.[57] He instructed Billy, if still in Charles Town, to consult their mutual friend Dr. Lionel Chalmers (1715–77), to whom he also wrote. Fothergill would allow Billy ten guineas for his equipment and fifty guineas per annum. In return Fothergill would expect Billy to collect not only seeds but plants for him. Expenses for freight the doctor would meet himself; he would also pay additional monies for any drawings, commensurate with their accuracy

"The old chimney-corner," from Howard Pyle, "Bartram and his garden"

and quality. These could be of birds, insects, and snakes as well as
of plants, but all should be drawn from life.[58] Billy returned briefly
to Philadelphia to prepare for his new enterprise. There was much
news to be exchanged and many calls to be made. His parents reveled in their son's visit, relieved to have a solution to his problems.
Billy sailed on 20 March 1773 on the Charles Town packet.[59]

Not long after Billy left, a letter from Dr. John Hope, forwarded by Franklin, arrived for Bartram. Two years before, the society that Bartram had supplied in Edinburgh through Dr. Hope,
and on whose order he had taken a loss, had found sufficient funds
to make it up. In order to show Bartram their respect and to honor
him, they had a medal struck rather than sending cash. It was of
gold, weighing 487 grams. On one side was a laurel wreath surrounding the word "Merenti." The other side was inscribed "To
John Bartram from a Society of Gentlemen at Edinburgh 1772."[60]
This was a very satisfying memento. Bartram placed it near Sir
Hans' silver cup under the affectionate gaze of his old friends' pictures: Linnaeus, Franklin, Edwards, and Collinson, whose portrait
Franklin had sent. These hung in his "new stove and lodging
room," built in 1770, where he could commune with his friends. He
was still lacking Fothergill's likeness. He did not consider himself
"a picture Enthusiast" but loved "to looke at ye representation of
men of inoceincy integrety ingenuity & Humanity."[61]

Franklin continued to send seeds for him to test. Among these
was rhubarb seed from plants growing just outside the Great Wall
of China, where the climate was similar to that of Pennsylvania.
Bartram was interested in certain Lucerne seed, but Franklin was
unable to learn anything about it. He sent all those who wanted
American seeds to Freeman but felt that the young man should advertise when they were available.[62] John Ellis gave Franklin seeds
of Upland Rice from Cochin China and some of the Chinese Tallow
Tree for Bartram.[63] Franklin had discovered a new turnip called the
"cabbage turnip" and sent seeds of that and of "Scotch cabbage" as
well as a new pea. The most severe weather could not discourage
this turnip, which made it ideal for spring cattle fodder.[64] Bartram
enjoyed experimenting with all of these strange seeds and was delighted to find that both the rhubarb and some turnips germinated
and flourished.

True to his usual form, Billy seldom bothered to write to his
family. News of him came secondhand, through Charles Town

friends. Dr. Chalmers had written to Bartram shortly after Billy had arrived there: "Your Son has all the Requisites & Application to Researches of this Sort, that his Father had before him—And indeed it Surprises me, that You Should not have encouraged this Genius of his as a Naturalist Sooner; for, tho' you endeavour'd to curb it by putting him to a Mercht &c, yet Nature prevailed So far as to disqualify him from Pursuits of this Sort—On the whole John Bartram has a Son, who I hope will perpetuate both his Father's & his own Name, for the Advancement of Natural Philosophy, as well as Science in general."[65] Being human Bartram could not help but consider such criticism unjust, but being a father he hoped that Chalmers and Fothergill were correct. He trusted that Billy would live up to their expectations. In October 1773 Lamboll wrote to Bartram that Billy had gone to the Cherokee nation.[66] Seven months passed before Chalmers wrote that Billy was safe. He wrote again two months later that he had heard nothing for three months. At least Billy was in no financial difficulties; he had only drawn twelve guineas in addition to the original ten, although forty were about due.[67]

Fothergill was not too happy with Billy's accomplishments. He wrote to Bartram in September 1774 that he had heard that Billy was on his way to East Florida. Fothergill had received about a hundred dried specimens from Billy but had no seeds or plants from him and only a few drawings: "I am sensible of the difficulty he is at in travelling through those inhospitable countries; but I think he should have sent me some few things as he went along. I have paid the bills he drew upon me; but must be greatly out of pocket, if he does not take some opportunity of doing what I expressly directed, which was, to send me seeds or roots of such plants, as either by their beauty, fragrance, or other properties, might claim attention. However, I shall hope he will find means of fulfilling my orders, better than he has done hitherto."

Fothergill closed his letter saying, "Do not imagine that all the people in this Country are against America. We sympathize with you much."[68] The Boston Tea Party had resulted in a ban on the port and the Coercive Acts, but the townspeople refused to let the merchants pay for the tea. The other colonies supported the city by sending in necessary food and livestock. An intercolonial congress had been proposed the previous year, and now the universal discontent underlined its need. The first Continental Congress met in Philadelphia on 5 September 1774. Fothergill's nephew was likewise concerned over the worsening situation, writing Bartram, "I sincerely sympathize with the children of an ungrateful mother. . . ." He thought that the colonies would have to make some concessions first before there would be a true conciliation. He hoped that Thomas Penn, who had just arrived in England, might be bringing some such offers from the Continental Congress.[69] One of Bartram's correspondents was not as broad-minded. As a merchant trading with the colonies, Michael Collinson felt bitter and had written the previous year: "As to the conduct of the Bostonians, it ought, I think, to excite the indignation of every honest mind. In all their late resolves and meetings, we hear of no proposal whatever to pay the East India Company, for the goods they robbed and plundered them of. . . ."[70] This appears to be the last letter that Michael wrote to Bartram. Communication between the colonies and England was interrupted shortly after Freeman's letter of September 1775, and it was the last one that Bartram received from him and the end of export of plants and seeds. When the Revolution interrupted English sales of North American seeds to France, Franklin was in Paris, in May 1777. He found that there were many French customers there who had formerly sent their orders through London. He offered to forward their instructions to the Bartrams and to dispose of the filled orders when they came.[71]

With all the complications of the war, Bartram was relieved that he no longer had to cope with the problems of the nursery business but only to give advice. Sometimes there were small personal matters to attend to, such as a loan of £200 to Susannah Morris, endorsed by Dr. Benjamin Rush, of which £112 was repaid 15 April 1777 by his brother Jacob Rush.[72] On the whole, however, Bartram could relax and garden in a leisurely fashion. He and Ann had time for each other, their children, and grandchildren. The only anxiety they had was a nagging worry about Billy, which had been a habit of many years. It was difficult ever to become reconciled to their son's custom of seldom writing, particularly since his travels were taking him into the Indian lands where a white was often unwelcome. Billy had been gone twenty-three months in April 1775 when the Bartrams received a long letter.[73] Their son had returned to Charles Town and was staying at the home of Lamboll's daughter, Mary Thomas. After his visit to the Cherokees and Creeks his planned trip to East Florida had been delayed by his illness and unsettled conditions, but he had eventually revisited the area. He complained that he had heard nothing from his father or mother. Billy had decided to spend another year traveling. His parents heard nothing further from him for almost two years until he appeared at their door in January 1777. He had been to Lake Pontchartrain and beyond until he finally reached the Mississippi in October 1775. A severe eye problem had prevented him from further exploration. He had returned to Savannah the previous January.[74]

Both children and adults were eager to hear of Billy's adventures, but his most enthusiastic listener was his father. Bartram could now understand how Collinson must have felt, reliving the excitement of the traveler without the dangers, discomforts, and ill health. Billy described the three-guinea sailboat in whch he had left St. Augustine. With a good breeze he had left Spalding's Lower Store about the middle of May, passing Mount Hope, which his father had named. Bartram was interested to learn that the orange grove there had been replaced by indigo. Billy said that he had again found the wild lime, which his father had first called a Tallo Nut because of its hard oiliness. The description which Bartram most enjoyed was that of the new small tree, much like the *Gordonia*, which he and Billy had found near Fort Barrington on the Altamaha River. This time Billy had seen it in all of its magnificence, for it was in full bloom yet simultaneously bearing ripe fruit, some of which he brought home. He told his father "that the flowers are very large, expand themselves perfectly, are of a snow white colour, and ornamented with a crown or tassel of gold coloured refulgent stamina in their centre. . . ." Billy had been eager to find another colony but was unsuccessful, although he searched all the way to the Mississippi. He and Bartram decided to name it for their old friend Benjamin.[75]

In his new leisure Bartram found many hours in which to philosophize: to contemplate the universe, man's place in nature, and his own life. Summarizing his thoughts he put them in the form of advice for his children, "to encourage them to the practice of piety & Virtue," as he had twenty years previously.[76] Throughout the several pages of his collected wisdom runs the recurrent theme of God's majesty and man's need to worship, to praise, and to depend on the Almighty. God was omnipresent in Bartram's world—an abiding force clearly apparent in the wonders of nature and in man's proper relation to his fellowman. Of all virtues he believed moderation was the finest: "Moderation or ye Golden Mean is a Lovely practiced human qualification & balance Against all extremes. A Virtue that Controls all passions; A sweet Calmness & Tranquility of mind, proper to Receive by Contemplation & Divine Influence; & will lead us from pride extravagance & high mindedness ye Common attendants of Prosperity, and much aleviate ye gloomy anctious affections of adversity." To the virtue of moderation he added gratitude, patience, and prudence. The last he defined as "a disposition of Mind to regard distant good equal with present pleasure." He spelled out each with very practical examples, and, in turning to the liar and the adulterer, he plainly showed that there was little profit for either. In all of his philosophy his love, gentleness, and kindliness are apparent.

In conclusion he added a postscript of comfort for his children, being under no illusion concerning his health. He told them that for several years he had had no wish for a long life but was "Resigned to the divine Will & Waiting for his Call." His persistent fear of storms was finally gone, for he now considered death by lightning one of the "Easiest deaths." There were no prolonged and painful infirmities involved, and "ye Grosse incumbering Mortal Body is instantly separated by a Blasting Stream of Light." There was no death by lightning for Bartram, but he did avoid a lengthy illness. He remained active to almost his last hours and died following a very brief illness on 22 September 1777.[77] Thus ended a life which had followed well the precept that he had frequently advocated to his children: "Do Justice, love Mercy, and Walk Humbly before God."

Bartram was buried in the Darby Friends Burial Ground, established in the year that his grandparents came to Pennsylvania. In accordance with Quaker custom, no stone was placed to mark his grave.[78] The will that he had drawn in 1772, naming Isaac, Moses, and Johnny as executors, had remained unchanged.[79] James Bartram and Thomas Say were appointed to make an inventory of the estate, which was substantial. His library was valued at £1,000. The bulk of the estate was in land and buildings, a fortunate circumstance since paper money had already been badly inflated by the Revolution. Bartram's land was left largely to his sons. A lot on the northside of Market Street was to be divided equally between Isaac and Moses. To his eldest, Bartram also left

£200 and his treasured silver cup from Sir Hans Sloane, and to Moses £150. James received the remainder of the land that his father had purchased from Andrew Jonason, some of which had previously been given to him. Benjamin inherited all of his father's land and buildings at Darby and an acre of Jersey cedar swamp bought by Bartram from William Harrison. The remainder of this purchase went to James and Johnny. To the latter went the home place at Kingsessing, with the proviso that his mother should retain the rooms which she and Bartram had been occupying since Johnny's marriage and that he should pay her "yearly ten pounds, and is to find her sufficient firewood cut and hauled to the dore of her kitchen and keep her a cow and horse winter and summer on good grass or hay and allso a sufficient spot in his garden to sow or plant on, and full liberty to pass and repass to the well. . . ." Bartram's daughters, Ann Bartram and Mary Bonsall, received his house and lot on Callow Hill, adjacent to one owned by Moses. The twins, Elizabeth and Billy, received cash, the former £100 and the latter £200. Elizabeth had probably received an adequate dowry, and Billy had received much of his patrimony for his Florida venture. Each of the grandchildren received £5.

EIGHTEEN

"Like Newton, in Simple Facts he saw Great Principles"

IT IS customary, and with good reason, to think of Bartram as a botanist. Much of his life was devoted to the study of plants, and he made important contributions to the world's knowledge of those in North America. Yet he was almost constantly concerned with other aspects of science: conservation, ecology, entomology, ethnology, geology, materia medica, meteorology, ornithology, paleontology, zoology, and related fields. Scientific areas were not sharply delineated in his day, and he clearly considered all of nature to be his study. He had a keen perception of the importance of the balance of nature.[1]

Both his contemporaries and modern writers have overemphasized his lack of formal education. There were advantages as well as disadvantages in this. He was less bound by the hypotheses and theories of others and more free to seek his own explanations of the natural phenomena that he constantly observed. It is doubtful, however, that he would have permitted further education to restrict his thinking. His most striking characteristics as a scientist were intense curiosity and complete independence of thought. He had a gift for accurate observation, even of small details. His analytical mind demanded rational explanations, whether in the realm of botany, theology, psychology, or paleontology. These characteristics attracted him to a remarkable array of more highly educated men both at home and abroad. These also enabled Bartram to make some contribution to a surprising range of scientific disciplines.

In evaluating Bartram's contributions to scientific knowledge, it may be well to keep in mind that many better known scientists of his day, even in such erudite circles as the Fellows of the Royal Society of London, debated what now seem to us to have been rather foolish questions. One, which aroused quite heated controversy in England and on the Continent, was whether or not swallows hibernate under water. Even the great Linnaeus was counted among the affirmative in this lengthy debate. Bartram was seldom to be found in support of absurdities, and this was no exception. His usual skepticism was well expressed in his reply to Collinson, who had written him concerning the "great Water Turtle of New England:" "But as for their barking, I believe thy relator *barked*, instead of the turtle."[2]

It has been mentioned that Bartram collected a great diversity of zoological specimens for Catesby, Collinson, Gronovius, Sloane, and other European friends. As a zoologist Bartram was by no means solely a collector or merely an observer of morphological characteristics. He was a keen student of animal behavior and recorded many observations on the subject, some of which were published. He acquired, for example, a surprisingly good grasp of the life cycles of a number of insects for one who was extremely busy with many other matters. This is well illustrated by his accounts of the mayflies and dragonflies of Pennsylvania, which he sent to Collinson.[3] He described the emergence of the adults, the casting of the skin, the impregnation of the females, the depositing of their eggs, the death of the adults, and the development of the larval stages from the eggs.

A number of Bartram's communications to Collinson were read to the members of the Royal Society, where they were well received and were published in their *Philosophical Transactions*. It may be surprising to some to realize that *all* of these published accounts (see the bibliography for the complete list) were concerned with zoological rather than botanical matters. A number of them dealt with insects, entomology having always been a special interest of Bartram. His observations continue to be cited by students of the subject. As recently as 1957 Howard E. Evans noted that "the first recorded observations on an American Bembix published in 1763 by John Bartram, undoubtedly pertain to *spinolae*, although the species were not described until over 80 years later. Bartram called it the 'Yellowish Wasp.' He described briefly the opening and closing of the nest during provisioning, the manner of carrying the fly, and other details. He was well aware that this wasp practises progressive provisioning in contrast to other wasps familiar to him."[4]

Other aspects of animal behavior on which Bartram made specific commentary include such diverse topics as the noises made by frogs and the way the sounds are made; the hibernation of bears; the migration of birds; the courting rituals of the ruffed grouse; the nest construction of hornets and wasps; the "charming" of their prey by snakes, if any; and the "natural history" of moles. European zoologists took note of his observations and made use of them. George Edwards copied his account of the ruffed grouse. Thomas Pennant cited his comments concerning the black bear, the black rat, the fisher, the ruffed grouse, and the passenger pigeon. It would seem fair to say that Bartram contributed as much as any man of his day to European understanding of American animals.

Fossil animals interested Bartram almost as much as the living ones. Whether this interest was spontaneous or whether it was stimulated by Collinson's request for specimens is not known, but quite early in their correspondence Bartram's strong interest in fossils became apparent. He collected them for Lawson, Catesby, Gronovius, Sloane, and others, as well as for Collinson. The fact that he found what were clearly marine fossils in the mountainous regions of New York and Pennsylvania, long distances from the sea, stimulated his thinking about the past history of the earth and its evolution. There was no doubt in his mind that these regions of the earth had once been under the oceans. He not only realized that many organisms had become extinct but predicted that many more, such as the beaver, buffalo, and rattlesnake, would become so. He shared the general excitement caused by the discovery of the mammoth skeletons in what later became Kentucky, and his ideas about them were more logical than those of some of his European friends. He urged that they be carefully studied and measured before they became irretrievably lost.

Although his understanding of geology seems to have been almost entirely self-acquired, he acquired a surprisingly good grasp of it. Throughout his travels he made and recorded observations of soil strata wherever he had an opportunity to observe them. His description of these in the Lake Waccamaw area of North Carolina is considered to have been probably the first of what is known as the Duplin formation.[5] His suggestion that limestone and marble are of organic and marine origin seemed to startle Collinson, who

replied that Bartram had the idea all to himself.[6] Bartram supplied
Gronovious with large numbers of geological specimens which the
latter valued and published. Studies of fossils and of geological for-
mations led Bartram to speculation concerning not only the history
of the earth but the lack of knowledge of some aspects of its current
state. He had no difficulty in accepting the idea that land bridges
and ocean levels of the past had changed, or even that the angle of
the earth's axis toward the sun had shifted. He believed that mountains existed under the sea, affecting ocean currents, and he urged
that vessels make soundings to locate and map them. He advocated
the systematic boring of the earth as a means of locating and mapping the world's geological resources. As a geologist his ideas were
distinctly advanced for his time.

There can be little doubt that, had Bartram been given the
opportunity in his youth, he would have chosen to study medicine.
He said that this had been one of his earliest interests, and it certainly was a major one throughout his adult career. A great many
of his friends and correspondents were physicians who clearly
found him congenial. They had, of course, the common ground of
an interest in medicinal plants, with which eighteenth-century
physicians were necessarily much involved. Bartram's interests
went beyond this, including medical practice and medical problems
generally. Bartram had some familiarity with the history of medicine and carried on a very limited medical practice among his
poorer neighbors. He was on at least a few occasions consulted by
more affluent patients, including James Hamilton, lieutenant-governor of Pennsylvania.[7] Bartram's correspondence includes a number of medical discussions, particularly that with Colden. His most
notable contribution to the medical science of his day was his introduction and appendix to Short's *Medicina Britannica*. Neither was
very extensive, but they earned him a place in the history of pharmacognosy and materia medica. Many of the plants that he included in his appendix are still used medicinally and are included
in standard texts of pharmacognosy.

The scientific contribution of Bartram that has had the greatest impact on scientific thought, and that continues to do so, is perhaps the least widely known and appreciated. This was his concept
of an American Philosophical Society. That the original idea was
his, and that he and Franklin jointly developed and promoted it,

seems clearly established. The far-ranging influence of this society on world science needs no discussion here.

The many years which Bartram devoted to seeking out new plants, transplanting them to his garden, and trying to persuade them to live and thrive there naturally led him to a keen interest in and study of many aspects of botany other than merely identification and classification, or taxonomy. He became increasingly concerned with the distribution of plants, or plant geography, and the interrelationship between plants and their environment, or plant ecology, which determined where they would or would not thrive. Closely allied to these two aspects of botany is a third, plant physiology, which, while primarily concerned with processes that occur within the plant, nonetheless also involves many external influences such as soils, rainfall, temperature, and light. All of these were of the utmost interest and concern to Bartram and were repeatedly discussed in his letters. The science of genetics did not exist in Bartram's day. The fundamental discoveries that established it were not made until nearly a century after his death. Questions concerning plant reproduction and inheritance, which genetics would eventually answer, were of concern to Bartram, and he had some conception of the factors involved from his experiments in plant hybridization. His early studies of floral anatomy and his later detailed descriptions of trees both serve to demonstrate his extensive studies of plant morphology. He was clearly aware of evolutionary changes in the inorganic world but does not appear to have related it to the organic, in spite of his very considerable interest in extinct species.

No aspect of botany had more appeal for Bartram than that which we presently call ecology. He seldom wrote to anyone about plants without some mention of their ecological relationships, and he had a good grasp of such ecological concepts as plant succession. As early in his botanical career as 1738 he wrote to Collinson concerning the succession of plants on lands which the Indians had once cultivated. He recognized that plants are subject to a variety of influences, all important in their total growth and development. He commented that we can "observe in plants how absolutely necessary earth & warmth is to raise ye plant from seed yet ye air & sun is necessary to make it produce flowers & good seed."[8]

Bartram was well aware that distinctions between species

might involve physiological processes as well as morphological details and that these might determine the distribution of species. Thus, he pointed out to Collinson in March 1755 that "Our black walnuts rarely grow beyond ye 41 or 42 degree Northward but ye white or butternut grows much farther north."[9] In April of the same year he wrote, "Thou art very much mistaken in the striped Maple being a seminal variety, or an accidental one either. It is a very particular, distinct species, both in its manner and place of growth. It hath the most constant appearance of any species I know; and place of growth being particular to the northern ridges of our Blue Mountain, from the North River to Susquehanna. I never observed one to grow on the three southern ridges or between them and the sea."[10]

Physiological processes of plants interested Bartram, and his understanding of them is surprising. He was aware, for example, that transpiration plays a part in the rise of water in stems and that pressures can be built up by imbibition in plant tissues. He was quite familiar with the various aspects of the water cycle in nature and discussed it in some detail in a letter to Alexander Garden.[11] He wrote of the evaporation of water from the seas and other large bodies of water, its condensation when moist air encounters high mountains or colder temperatures, and its falling to earth as rain or snow. Then the plants "by the transpiration of the vapour by their leaves & things cause the roots to attract moisture to supply that expense but there is another method by which nature acts very powerfully in the Conveyance of fluids which altho it is by organized Vacuum yet not by direct tubes but by the proper arrangement of vesicles as in sponges. . . ."

Many of Bartram's letters contain discussions of the character of soils and the influence of soils on plant growth, another concern of modern plant physiology and ecology. He was impressed by the importance of organic matter in the soil and was aware that too frequent plowing can deplete it. He made extensive use of composts in both farming and gardening operations. He was conscious of the necessity of turning plant crops under to mellow clay soil and keep it from baking. In his farming operations he practiced both the rotation of crops and the planting of legumes.

There can be no question about the fact that Bartram was extremely well informed about most aspects of botany that were understood by other botanists of his day and that, being a farmer as well as a botanist, he put his knowledge into practice in both farming and gardening. He was equally at home in discussion of either theoretical or practical botany, having no hesitation in expressing his views to any of his more educated friends and correspondents. His opinions were well received and respected by them both at home and abroad. Those who have tended to picture Bartram as merely a plant collector have had little understanding of the man. He was a well-rounded and well-informed botanist. Although he was very competent in a number of other fields of science and had a broad and philosophic point of view toward natural history in general, there was never any doubt as to his first love: "O, Botany! delightfulest of all sciences! There is no end to thy gratifications." [12]

Although Bartram frequently wrote in haste and in a rather rough and ready fashion, he was quite capable of using a surprising vocabulary. At times he became quite eloquent in expressing his love of plants, displaying that gift of language inherited by his son and more often associated with William. This was particularly stimulated by Bartram's young friend, Alexander Garden, to whom he wrote in 1762: [13]

My dear worthy friend, I am much affected every time that I often read thy pious reflections on the wonderful works of the Omnipotent and Omniscient Creator. The more we search and accurately examine his works in nature, the more wisdom we discover, whether we observe the mineral, vegetable or animal kingdom. But, as I am chiefly employed with the vegetable, I shall enlarge more upon it.

What charming colours appear in the various tribes, in the regular succession of the vernal and autumnal flowers—these so nobly bold—those so delicately languid! What a glow is enkindled in some, what a gloss shines in others! With what a masterly skill is every one of the varying tints disposed! Here, they seem to be thrown on with an easy dash of security and freedom: there, they are adjusted by the nicest touches. The verdure of the empalement, or the shadings of the petals, impart new liveliness to the whole, whether they are blended or arranged. Some are intersected with elegant stripes, or studded radiant spots; others affect to be genteelly powdered, or neatly fringed; others are plain in their aspect,

and please with their naked simplicity. Some are arrayed in
purple; some charm with the virgin's white; others are
dashed with crimson; while others are robed in scarlet. Some
glitter like silver lace; others shine as if embroidered with
gold. Some rise with curious cups, or pendulous bells; some
are disposed in spreading umbels; others crowd in spiked
clusters; some are dispersed on spreading branches of lofty
trees, on dangling catkins; others sit contented on the humble shrub; some seated on high on the twining vine and
wafted to and fro; others garnish the prostrate, creeping
plant. All these have their particular excellencies; some for
the beauty of their flowers; others their sweet scent; many
the elegance of foliage, or the goodness of their fruit; some
the nourishment that their roots afford us; others please the
fancy with their regular growth; some are admired for their
odd appearance, and many that offend the taste, smell, and
sight, too, are of virtue in physic.

But when we nearly examine the various motions of plants
and flowers, in their evening contraction and morning expansion, they seem to be operated upon by something superior to
only heat and cold, or shade and sunshine;—such as the surprising tribes of the Sensitive Plants, and the petals of many
flowers shutting close up in rainy weather, or in the evening,
until the female part is fully impregnated: and if we won't allow them real feelings, or what we call sense, it must be
some action next degree inferior to it, for which we want a
proper epithet, or the immediate finger of God, to whom be
all glory and praise.

What botanist has better depicted the infinite variation and fascination of plants?

POSTSCRIPT

Bartram left behind him a goodly number of descendants who have
continued to reflect credit upon his name.[14] His garden, too, lives
on, and has been a source of great interest and pleasure to many. It
has had periods of both care and neglect in the two centuries that
have passed since his death. The battle of Brandywine had occurred
a few days before he died, and his home and garden seemed threat-

ened by the fighting in the vicinity and the British occupation of
Philadelphia. Some British officers were quartered there, but the
property is said to have been given protection by Sir William
Howe.[15] The garden, however, was neglected at this time, as attested by a description of it written two years after Bartram's
death. The secretary of the French legation, M. de Barbé-Marbois,
visited the garden on 16 October 1779: "We found a house, detached
and solitary, surrounded by fine orchards, and decorated on the garden front by a column of rustic design. We thought it worthy to be
the dwelling of the American Linnaeus. But the garden! . . . It was
in a state of neglect which caused us actual pain . . . in a word an
air of abandonment which I should call criminal if I had the honor
to be a botanist. We entered a little drawing-room while we waited
for the master of the garden. We saw his portrait there. The painter
has represented him leaning on a box of pineapples, holding in his
hand a book with blank pages. If I had not feared to violate the
laws of hospitality, I should have written on the pages this verse of
Racine: 'And I, unknown son of so glorious a father.'"[16] Possibly the
Frenchman thought better of Billy after his *Travels* were published
in 1790.

By 1784 Billy and Johnny had restored some order to the garden and resumed the plant and seed business. They printed a catalogue, listing trees and shrubs available in or near their garden. A
year later their relative Humphry Marshall published a much
more ambitious work, *Arbustum Americanum*, which included a
great many of the shrubs and trees in the Bartram garden.[17]
Among many items of interest in this was the *Franklinia*, about
which Marshall wrote that it had been first found by Bartram and
the seeds brought back by Billy from his second Florida trip. Plants
raised from these had flowered in the fourth year.

Johnny and Billy soon found that the garden continued to be
a mecca for important visitors as it had been during their father's
lifetime. George Washington, James Madison, Thomas Jefferson,
Alexander Hamilton, Manasseh Cutler, and many others came
from time to time.[18] In 1786 Jefferson sent Johnny from Paris an
English translation of Linnaeus' *Systema vegetabilium* and a large
order for plants and seeds for a French friend. Again in 1802 Jefferson gave Johnny an order from the Agricultural Society of Paris,
who had requested the president to obtain seeds for them.[19] André
Michaux was a frequent visitor during the years 1788–94. He had

been brought to this country by Bartram's old friend, Crèvecoeur, in order to establish a garden at New Haven.[20] The weaver from Scotland, Alexander Wilson, settled nearby and became a protégé of Billy, who encouraged his ornithological studies.[21]

Botanists and their students frequented the garden: Benjamin Smith Barton, G. H. E. Muhlenberg, Thomas Nuttall, Frederick T. Pursh, and others. By 1807 Johnny was able to write in his catalogue of the "Kingsess Botanic Gardens": "Thus these extensive gardens became the Seminary of American Vegetables, from whence they were distributed to Europe, and other regions of the civilized world. They may with propriety and truth be called the *Botanical Academy of Philadelphia*, since, being near Philadelphia, the Professors of Botany, Chemistry, and Materia Medica, attended by their youthful train of pupils, annually assemble here during the Floral season."[22]

When Johnny died in 1812, the plantation and garden were the inheritance of his daughter Ann and her husband, Robert Carr. Her grandfather would have approved, for she was both a botanist by inclination and an artist skilled in sketching and painting from nature. She had been trained by her Uncle William. The Carrs continued to maintain the garden for some years.[23] In 1831 they employed an English gardener, William Wynne, as foreman. In writing of Philadelphia gardens for the London *Gardener's Magazine*, Wynne stated that there were at that time more than 2,000 varieties of native plants in the six acres of the main Bartram garden. The finest feature of the garden he thought to be the mature and superb collection of shrubs and trees, then producing a great quantity of seeds for the annual shipments to "London, Paris, Petersburgh, Calcutta, and several other parts of Europe, Asia and Africa."[24]

It was the Carrs who turned over all of the Bartram correspondence to Dr. William Darlington to edit, since he was already doing that of Humphry Marshall. For Darlington's great patience and hard work, historians of science and many others have long been grateful. They could have wished that he had made fewer or no omissions from the letters that he edited.[25] The Carrs had no children; when they felt too old to maintain the property, they permitted it to be taken over by Andrew M. Eastwick, who held a mortgage on it. For a time Eastwick hired Thomas Meehan to superintend the garden. This was an extremely fortunate occurrence for the garden and for posterity. Meehan only worked there for two years, but his interest in and affection for the place continued.[26] When he later published his *The American Handbook of Ornamental Trees*, he dedicated it "To the Memory of John Bartram the Patriarch of American Arboriculture" and included 129 trees from the garden, some of which had been planted long after Bartram's time.[27]

With Eastwick's death, the garden was neglected and vandalized. Even worse depredation than that caused by plant thieves was the dire effect of débris from the oil refineries along the river and the devastating fumes of the factories.[28] Harvard professor C. S. Sargent interested enough subscribers to agree to buy the garden around 1880. The executors at first agreed to the price and then reneged. Starting in 1882 Meehan, who had become a well-known nurseryman, fought to have the city take over the garden as a park. Through his magazine, *Meehan's Monthly*, he waged a campaign, and as a city councillor his efforts were finally successful. In 1891 the city took it over, and Meehan earned the soubriquet of "The Father of City Parks."[29]

Four more years passed before some restoration work started, and this was minimal. In 1923 responsibility for the garden was given to the Fairmount Park Commission, and a list of the eighty-two surviving plants was made. While efforts were made to replace some of those known to have been planted by Bartram, it was now impossible to grow all of them due to recent adverse conditions of the soil and air of an industrial area. Other plants were no longer available since nurseries had developed improved varieties. However, an ambitious planting program to restore Bartram's garden was started. Across the railroad from the house, a garden was established for the teaching of schoolchildren and others, but it is not limited to plants of the eighteenth century. A retaining wall along the river had succeeded in redraining the marsh by the oil works in 1908. A similar one was built for the same purpose in the 1930s.[30]

Meehan and the city of Philadelphia were not the only ones to work toward the preservation and restoration of Bartram's garden. Bartram's descendants had begun to hold family reunions, which eventually led to the formation of the John Bartram Association. In 1923 they permitted interested outsiders to join their ranks. It was this organization which repaired and furnished Bartram's house and barn. The members issued an informative booklet written by Elizabeth O. Abbot in 1904 and reissued it in 1907 and 1915. Photographs of garden and house were made by them to sell as postcards. It was they who persuaded the Park Commission to undertake the replanting. They helped in the support of the magnificent research done on John Bartram and his son William by the late Dr. Francis Harper.[31] Much of the credit is due to two women: Mrs. Bayard Henry, president of the association for twenty-five years, and Mrs. Edward Cheston. Emily Read Cheston is the author of a new pamphlet published in 1938 and a second edition in 1953. Mr. Joseph B. Townsend, Jr., an active member of the society, says that Mrs. Cheston is known to them as "Mrs. Bartram" because of her great knowledge of "Bartramia."[32] The association is affiliated with the Garden Club Federation of Pennsylvania, and they superintend the house and garden, which are open to the public. The entrance is on Elmwood Avenue and can be reached by public transportation.

In 1789 Johann Hedwig (1730–99) revived the generic name *Bartramia* for the species of mosses which today honor Bartram's name. The large number of new plant genera laboriously discovered and distributed by Bartram were described and made known to the world by others and hence are not associated with his name. The specimens collected by him, and the information sent with them, provided the basis for the official descriptions. Some of these are still preserved in herbaria, notably the Dillenian and Sherardian herbaria at Oxford, the Sloane Herbarium at the British Museum (Natural History), and the Muséum National d'Histoire Naturelle. A few Bartram specimens, once in the possession of Lord Petre, are today in the Sutro Library, San Francisco.

Appendixes

Appendix 1. WILL OF RICHARD BARTRAM OF CLIFTON, parish of ASH-
BOURNE, fellmonger. (Lichfield Joint Record Office, Lichfield Consis-
tory Court)

23rd September 1660.

To my loving wief Mary Bartram £10 in the hands of William
Fearne of Markeley also one Bond dated 2nd April 1659 wherein
William Cooper of Snelson standeth bound to me, also my three
cowes and also one greate brasse kettle.

The rest of my estate after the payment of legacies, funeral
expenses, etc. to my wiefe and son John Bartram.

I give to John Bartram of Marchington Woodlands 10s. and to
his daughter Joane Bartram 20s.

To Richard Fearne of Briss . . . 10s.

To Elizabeth Hunt, widow, of Ashbourne any monies due from
her to me.

Exor. :—My wiefe Mary and son John Bartram

Signed:—Richard Bartram

Witnesses:—Henry Elliot, William Cooper, Richard Hill
Inventory dated 14th May 1661 appraised by Richard Hill, Thomas
Titterton, Robert Fearne. Amount £30.9s.4d.
Proved by the exors named 10th May 1661

Appendix 2. Extract from Franklin's *Poor Richard's Almanac* for 1741

Many Persons being at a Loss to know the Plant which is the true INDIAN PHYSICK, *I thought it not amiss to give the Publick a distinct and plain Account of it.*

The Root hath the Appearance of the true *Ipecacuana,* Branching from the Centre every Way near the Top of the Ground, or about two or three Inches deep, from which riseth one Stalk, finely chaneled with redish Lines; from the Sides of which grow alternately, about the Distance of two Inches, from near the Bottom to the Top, three distinct Leaves, two Inches long, and near an Inch broad, finely toothed round the Edges, and pointed at the Ends, but joined near the Stalk; out of the Bosom of which ariseth Branches of every Side the Stalk, which are in large Plants again divided into several Branches, and three Leaves joined together accompany the Beginning of every Branch, both which diminish the nearer they are to the Top; where there is commonly, set upon Foot-Stalks half an Inch long, three white Flowers, consisting of five Leaves to each Flower: the Plant groweth from two Foot to four Foot high, in hilly Ground; in these Northern Provinces the whole Plant is bitter in Taste. This is the true INDIAN PHYSICK mentioned in that valuable little Book entituled, *Every Man his own Doctor,* written by a learned Gentleman in Virginia, whom I had a Letter of Recommendation unto from London: I enquired of him, particularly, concerning the Ipecacuana mentioned in his Book, and he shewed me a large Quantity of it, which was gathered for his own Practice: He told me, that less than *Sixty Grains* was not a full Dose for a Man. This I mention because many in Pensilvania and Maryland use a Species of the Spurges, which yieldeth Milk when broken, and is a violent Medicine, instead of this which the Gentleman designed.

JOHN BERTRAM [*sic*]

Appendix 3. *Philosophical Transactions* of the Royal Society of London 43 (1744):157–59: VI. *Extract of a Letter from Dr.* John Bartram, *to Mr.* Peter Collinson, *F. R. S. containing some Observations concerning the* Salt-Marsh Muscle, *the* Oyster-Banks, *and the* Fresh-Water Muscle, *of* Pensylvania.

Read Nov. 8   I have observed something of an extraordinary Na-
1744.   ture in our *Salt-Marsh Muscle*: By its fibrous Roots,
which strike deep into the Soil, it seems to be of a vegetable Nature; for, it is highly probable, the Animal draws some part of its
Nourishment through them: They are fixed by these two thirds of
their Length in the Sand with their broad Ends uppermost, which
open at every Return of the Tide, to be replenished by the Salt-
Water: When it is retreated, they are found lodged in the Grass,
Sedge, Creeks, and Banks, singly and together in Plenty.

I herewith send you a Specimen, which will give you a better
Idea of this wonderful Creature.

There you may plainly observe the Ligaments draw their Origin from the principal Parts of the Animal, and unite near the Ex-
tremity of the Shell, which they pass through on that Side of the
Muscle that opens to let in the Water; then they divide again into
many capillary Roots or Fibres, which penetrate and extend themselves into the Mud or Soil of the Marsh; which, by long Observation, seem to me for two Uses; first, as I have above observed, to
convey Part of their Nourishment; which seems probable by their
being dispersed through the Body of the Muscle (This is better seen
when alive; but now they are dry, one of the Specimens plainly
shew it). . . .

The other Use of these fibrous Roots (for so I must call them),
by their striking deep into the Mud or Sand, is to secure the Creature from being carried away by the Rapidity of the Tide: So that,
in this Circumstance, thay are somewhat analogous to Plants,
whose Roots both nourish them, and secure them from the Injuries
of Wind and Flood.

OUR *Oysters* are of an oblong Figure; they grow at the Sides
and Bottoms of Creeks, Rivers, and Bays, near the Sea; but mostly
in such a Situation where they are near or quite dry at low Water:
They have the Power of Opening and Shutting, like the Muscle, to
take in and retain the Salt-Water, which is their principal Nourishment; Tho' they stick in the Mud, they are not so secured as the
Salt-Marsh Muscle before-mention'd; and tho' these Oysters grow
in great Clusters or Heaps, commonly called Oyster-Banks, yet
every one that is alive hath free Communication with the Air and
Water, and Liberty to open and shut. If the Oyster's Way of growing
may be compared to that of a Plant, I think there is great Similtude
between it and the *Opuntia*, or *Indian* Fig; a Leaf produces and

supports a Leaf, and so on: Thus the young Oyster grows on the Sides of the old one, which, by degrees, is so deep immerged in the Mud, that it dieth; but yet it serves to support the young one upright, until it comes to Maturity to produce others; and then that, by degrees, subsides, so that, by this Method, Banks of dead and living Oysters are extended of an inconceivable Length and Breadth through all our Coasts.

OUR common *Fresh-Water Muscles* differ from our Salt-Marsh Muscle, in that they are not fixed to any Place or Thing, but have a Method of trailing along on the sandy Bottoms of Creeks and Rivers: They have the Power not only of opening and shutting their Shells at Pleasure, but have, moreover, the Power of creeping (*a*) along as it were like a Snail, by turning upon the upper Edge that opens, and so work themselves along the soft yielding Sand in little Furrows about half an Inch deep. I have traced them for several Yards, by these little Chanels, when the Tide is down, and left the Sands bare.

If these few Observations prove acceptable, it will be a Pleasure to

Your Friend,
John Bartram.

Appendix 4. List of seeds contained in Bartram's five-guinea box, as given in Fox, *Fothergill*, pp. 163–65, original in the British Museum (Natural History).

Weymouth or White Pine or
    Mast Pine
Hemlock Spruce Fir
Tulip Tree
White Ash
Striped Bark Mapple
Silver Leaved Mapple
Sugar Mapple
Dwarf Mountain Mapple
Chinquapin
Sweet Chesnutt

Swamp Pine
2 & 3 Leaved Pine
Small Magnolia
Red Flowering Mapple
Judas Tree
Shagged Bark Hickory
Balsamick Hickory
Small Turgid [Twigged] Sweet
    Hickory
Common Rough Hickory
Red Cedar Berries

Poplar Leaved Birch
Sarssefrass
Beech Mast
Dog Wood
Black Mulberry
Red Cedar
Lime Tree
Mountain Chesnut Leaved Oak
White Oak
Swamp White Oak
Champain Oak
Spanish Oak
Black Champian Oak
Barren Black Oak
Scrubby White Oak
Bastard Champian Red Oak
Dwarf Scarlet Oak
Scarlet Leaved Oak
Willow Leaved Oak
Tusselo [Tuppelo] or Nissa or
    Bla: Gum
Black Spruce Firr
Great Mountain Magnolia
Red Bud Andromeda
Broad Leaved Andromeda
White Spirea
Prinos or Red Winter Berry
Hydrangea
Black Larch
Silver Leaved Alder
Common Pensilvania Alder
Padus or Cluster Cherry
Broad Leaved Euonymus
Blue Berried Cornus
Toxicodendron Triphyllon
Toxicodendron or Poison Ash
Johnsonia
Ptelea arbor Trifolia.
Broad Leaved Swamp
    Viburnum

Ceonothus or Red Root
Great Mountain Kalmia or
    Rhododendron
Olive Leaved Kalmia
Thyme Leaved Kalmia
Candleberry Myrtle or Mirica
Evergreen Privet or Prinos
Pensilvania Elder
Great round leaved Viburnum
Red Berried Viburnum
Mountain Viburnum
Arbor Vitae
Sweet Black Birch
Benjamin or all Spice of
    Pensilvania
Clethra or Sweet Spirea
Stones of the Papaya Tree
Lotus or Celtis with Yellow
    Fruit
Jersey Tree an Epigea
Fringe Tree
Beach or Sea Sumach with
    lentiscus Leaves
Horn Beam
Spiked Andromeda
Ash Leaved Mapple
Cephalanthus or Button Wood
Large Beach Cherry
Hamamelis or Gold Fringe Tree
Sweet Gum or Liquid Amber
    Tree
Red Sumach
Swamp Spanish Oak
Black Walnut
White Walnut
Honey Locust or 3-Thorn'd
    Acacia
Platanus Occidentalis
Euonymus Scandens
Narrow Leaved Thorn

Blackberried Crataegus

Redberried Crataegus

Dwarf Birch

Aralia Spinosa or Angelica Tree

Broad Leaved Thorn

Highland Roses

Swamp Roses

Lesser Kalmia

Spiny Viburnum

Tough Viburnum

Red Spirea

Appendix 5. From Bartram's "Description of Native Trees" BP 1:32:1, 1:41:1–14

Our spring red maple

ye male flower buds hath comonly 10 scales & 4 or 6 lateral buds in a cluster each bud produces 4 or 5 flowers & each flower 4 5 or 6 stamina ye centeral buds in each ramification produce ye leaves & shoots for ye enlargement of ye tree ye female flower groweth in ye same manner but differs in this thay have each two stigmas & ye apices rarely bursts except as I suppose there be no male tree near enough to empregnate them thay flower in ye beginning of march if ye weather is warm or later if cold & makes a glorious appearance very early in ye spring long before any of ye leaf buds opens or any other we have & is ripe about ye 10th of may when ye keys is on some trees of a fine purple in others yelowish green but ye fin a little purplish ye colors is very unconstant ye trees grows with us in moist swampy ground with a clay or gravelly bottom by runs or rivulets generaly with a tall slender bole & smooth bark but where thay grow single thay branch very regular & upright some grows 5 foot diameter ye young branches is generaly redish ye leaves is divided into 3 lobes & serrated on thair edges wheather this is originaly a native of ye ridge of our mountains I will not say but it grows very plentifuly on them & I think no other kind comonly I observed near a spring head in ye desert in Jersey a fine recedental variety of this kind as I am apt to believe for I could not find any esential diference ye leaves was much less & more round & not so much divided ye comon appearance & growth of leaf & tree different.

perticular characters of are ye leaves are divided into 3 lobes ye blosoms are very red in clusters early in spring ye tree is of a single upright growth thay grow generaly prety regular are indented & ye flowers are male & female distinct on diferent trees &

come out ye latter end of february or beginning of march according
to ye coolness of ye season & perfects thair seed ye latter end of
April   some trees produceth keys very red while others is much
paler when ripe   ye bark of ye tree while young is smooth & whit-
ish but when ould it hath many perpendicular cracks & of a darker
color   ye wood is very strong & tough & turns very smooth if ye
grain be curled   it is highly esteemed for cabinets & all Joyners
ware   & for cart wheels

Appendix 6. Lists of Bartram's Customers

There is a list of customers supplied by Bartram in the British
Museum (Natural History). It was made by Collinson and appears
in his manuscript entitled "Introduction of American Seeds into
Great Britain." Some of the information on nursery gardeners came
from John Harvey's interesting monograph on *Early Horticultural
Catalogues*. An asterisk preceding a name indicates those on Collinson's list for whom there is no supplementary documentation; a
plus sign signifies that the customer appeared on his list and is also
mentioned in letters; others appear in correspondence only.

Nursery Gardeners	First year in which Bartram filled their orders
1. Balk, who sent seeds and plants to Germany	1760
*2. Bert, who also sent nursery stock to Germany	1755
3. William Borthwick, merchant and seedsman, Edinburgh	1763
4. Bouchard, Paris	1755
+5. John Bush (Busch), Hackney, Middlesex, nur-seryman, with German customers. Seldom did Bush order fewer than two boxes and often he or-dered three. In 1764 he complained that the boxes were not up to par and his German clients were unwilling to pay the full price.	1760
6. Cross, "Seedsman."	1760
7. Fern	1760
8. Robert Frazier, "Gardener."	1751
+9. James Gordon, *The Thistle & Crown*, 25 Fen-	1746

church Street with nurseries at Mile End & Bow, Middlesex. One of Bartram's best customers, seldom ordering fewer than two boxes and sometimes ordering three. They developed a personal relationship due to Collinson's close association with Gordon.

+10. Christopher Gray, Fulham, Middlesex, King's Road. Like Borthwick and Gordon he once wrote directly to Bartram but this was unusual. Most orders went through Collinson's hands.   1750

+11. Thomas Greening, "Gardener" at Kensington and St. James Palace (possibly his son, H. T. Greening).   1753

12. Edward Gross, seedsman in Fleet Street.   1763

*13. Parson Hanbury, Church Lane, nurseryman although "bred a clergyman." At his request, Collinson ordered boxes from Bartram for several years.   1759

14. Thomas Kirkham, *The Woolpack & Crown*.   1754

*15. Mr. Manner "for Germany."   1759

16. Pike or Pine.   1761

17. DePonthieus, Henry and John, close neighbors of Collinson, who corresponded with Bartram, sending him seeds of Alpine plants. Excellent customers.   1761

+18. Nathaniel Powell, *The Kings Head*, Fetter Lane. Powell & Edie after 1760. He probably was Bartram's second-best customer over the longest period of years, at least through 1763. The *Gentleman's Magazine* for January 1755 (p. 82) gives a list of Powell's North American seeds for sale, possibly all from Bartram.   1750

19. John Swinhoe, Brompton Park, Kensington. He bought the nursery from London & Wise, which had been started in 1685, and eventually sold it to John Jeffreys in 1756. For the three years in which he was in business, he sent many orders to Bartram.   1753

20. John Webb, *The Acorn*, Bridge Street, another faithful customer.   1760

+ 21. John Williamson & Company, gardener at Ken-   1747
sington, who took over from Robert Furber, The
Pineapple, Picadilly. Williamson was Bartram's
best customer. He sometimes ordered as many as
two ten-guinea boxes and two five-guinea ones at
the same time. In 1751 he ordered eight boxes,
probably the largest order Bartram ever had
from a single customer. Williamson's orders covered a period of at least sixteen years, and he
seemed to have registered no complaints.

Individual Customers   First Mention

1. J. Allen, mentioned in John Watts' Letterbook   1763
(1682–1771), Historical Society of Pennsylvania
library.
+ 2. Archibald Campbell, 3d Duke of Argyll, whose   1747
orders came through Dr. Mitchell over a period of
ten years.
3. Peter Bayard, of Bohemia, Cecil County, Mary-   1741
land.
+ 4. Julian Beckford, alderman, London.   1753
+ 5. John Russell, Duke of Bedford, orders at least 1742
through 1747.
6. Benez.   1763
+ 7. Mr. Bercley (possibly David, a linen merchant   1751
and Collinson's close friend).
8. Beverly, Esq.   1752
*9. William Blackburn.   1743
10. J. Blackburne, Orford, near Warrington, corre-   1765
spondent of William Logan, to whom he wrote 24
September 1765, "of yee Seeds from Mr. Bertram
the swamp Pine, water Tupelo & Stewartia are
come up, the Pine is the Sort I wanted & ye others I believe what he called them, but ye quantity of seeds was so small I have only one plant of
each sort" (American Philosophical Society library). Collinson wrote that Blackburne spared
"no expense in building a variety of stoves for all
species of exotics; has much the largest Toda

Panna or Sago Palm in England, and has a very great collection of all kinds of plants" (Dillwyn, *Hortus*, p. 47).

*11.	Peter Burrel, Esq.	1751
+12.	John Stuart, 3d Earl of Bute, first prime minister under George III (through Dr. Mitchell).	1747
*13.	Lord Cadogan.	1756
14.	Alexander Catcott, "divine and geologist," corresponded with Bartram.	1741
*15.	Lady Mary Churchill.	1756
+16.	Lord Clifford.	1758
+17.	Bishop of Clogher.	1752
*18.	Sir General Colebrooke.	1762
19.	Alexander Colhoun, surgeon attached to British troops in New York; ordered ginseng and seneca root.	1739
20.	Collinson's friend in Prague.	1760
21.	Anne Conolly of Castletown.	1754
*22.	J. Conyers, Esq.	1751
+23.	William Augustus, Duke of Cumberland, George III's brother, whose last order was in 1765.	1751
24.	Thomas François Dalibard asked Franklin to engage Bartram to collect seeds or cuttings of all Pennsylvania trees and shrubs and forward them to M. de Buffon (Labaree, *Franklin*, 10:63).	1754
*25.	Sir James Dashwood.	1757
*26.	Sir Willoughby de Brink.	1762
27.	Gov. William Denny of Pennsylvania ordered ten boxes sent "home."	1757
*28.	Lord Derford.	1750
29.	Lord Deskford (same as above?), James Ogilvy, Earl of Findlater, Earl of Seafield, "styled" Lord Deskford, sent orders over a period of ten years.	1747
+30.	Arthur Dobbs gave many orders of his own and for friends in Ireland over a period of fourteen years.	1747
31.	Dublin Society.	1751
32.	Edinburgh, Society of Gentlemen.	1764
*33.	Elliot, Esq.	1751
+34.	John Ellis	1766

*35. Sir Harry Englefield.   1756
*36. Earl of Essex.   1756
 37. Lord Farnham   1759
*38. Sir Matthew Fetherstonhaugh.   1762
+39. Robert Fenwick, Liverpool. Bartram wrote to   1744
     Collinson, "I am not surprised at fenwick's knav-
     ing being [thee] tells me he is a lawyer" (10 De-
     cember 1745, BP 1:31).
 40. George Fernat.   1758
 41. Lord Fitzmaurice.   1753
*42. Thomas Fitzsimmons, Esq.   n.d.
 43. Andrew Fletcher, Esq., Mitchell's friend, Member 1767
     of Parliament and secretary to the Duke of Ar-
     gyll.
+44. Benjamin Franklin. He ordered a box for a friend 1757
     while in England and a box sent to Paris in 1777
     (MJB, p. 406).
*45. Fraser, Esq.   1752
 46. Frederick, King of Prussia, who ordered a guinea's 1751
     worth of white mulberry seed to grow feed for his
     silkworms (PC to JB, 24 April 1751, BP 2:86).
+47. Frederick, Prince of Wales. Dr. Mitchell was in- 1750
     strumental in the ordering of the first box, as his
     friend, Lord Bute, gave the order. Four boxes
     were ordered in 1752.
 48. William Gallagher.   1760
 49. Alexander Stuart, Earl of Galloway, through   1750
     Mitchell.
 50. Colonel Ganzel.   1767
 51. King George III. Bartram sent him a box of   1764
     specimens in 1764 and, as King's Botanist from
     1765, he sent him specimens yearly.
*52. Sir Archibald Grant.   1759
 53. Mr. Gynonder.   1749
 54. Richard Hall, Esquire. Over a period of ten years 1747
     ordered several boxes.
+55. Charles Hamilton, Esq., Dublin.   1747
 56. B. Hammet, London, through Thomas Ord (Ord   1763
     to JB, 10 October, BP 4:93).
*57. Capel Hanbury of Mark Lane.   1751

*58. Earl Harcourt.	1757
*59. Lord Helsborough.	1755
*60. Sir Henry Hemlocke.	1756
61. William Hird of Woodhouse near Bradford in Yorkshire.	1738
+ 62. Dr. John Hope, Edinburgh.	1763
+ 63. John Hope, 2d Earl of Hopetoun.	1748
*64. Colonel Howard.	1754
65. John Carmichael, 3d Earl of Hyndford. Dr. Mitchell acquired at least two different orders for ten-guinea boxes from him for Bartram (Mitchell to JB, 30 March 1751, BP 4:8).	1750
*66. Earl of Ilchester.	1756
*67. J. Jackson ordered two boxes and another two the following year, possibly more.	1751
68. Captain Thomas Jones, of the Royal Artillery, New York, ordered a large box of garden seeds to send to a "Person of Distinction" in England, who should be in a position to recommend Bartram to others (Jones to JB, 2 July 1769, BP 4:55).	1769
69. John Kell, a relative of Collinson.	1757
*70. Lord Kenmont.	1759
*71. Mr. Kennedy (possibly Lewis Kennedy of Kennedy & Lee, the nurserymen).	1756
+ 72. James Fitzgerald, Lord Kildare, of Ireland, over a period of thirteen years, ordered seven boxes.	1756
*73. Duke of Kingston.	1758
*74. Lord Lamhan, Ireland.	1760
75. John Lane, London.	1766
76. Edwin Lascelles, Esq., ordering through Thomas Ord, desired six five-pound boxes (BP 4:93).	1763
+ 77. Lord Leicester, over a period of eight years.	1749
78. John Lewin, London, insects and plants (Lewin to JB, 23 October 1769, BP 4:70).	1769
+ 79. Henry Fiennes Clinton, 9th Earl of Lincoln.	1747
*80. Sir William Louther.	1756
*81. McWard, Esq.	1751
*82. Earl of Macclesfield.	1757
*83. Duke of Manchester.	1761

+ 84. Hugh Hume, 3d Earl of Marchmont, was very in-   1749
     terested in husbandry, forestry, and gardening.

+ 85. Charles Spencer, 3d Duke of Marlborough.   1749

  86. Mears.   1753

+ 87. Philip Miller who, with Lord Petre, was among   1735
     the first to encourage Bartram.

  88. Maj. Al Moneypenny, New York (BP 4:88).   1760

*89. Sir John Mordant.   1757

  90. Lord [John?] Murray.   1767

*91. General Napier.   1757

+ 92. 10th Duke of Norfolk, cousin of Lord Petre, who   1740
     made elaborate plans for the reforestation of the
     duke's park at Worksop Manor and undoubtedly
     suggested Bartram's services to him.

+ 93. Hugh Percy, 1st Duke of Northumberland, the   1747
     former Sir Hugh Smithson, contributed many
     plants to Kew and ordered some of them from
     Bartram. One of his illegitimate sons was the
     James Smithson who endowed our Smithsonian
     Institution.

+ 94. Robert Nugent, Earl Nugent.   1750

+ 95. Charles O'Hara, Esquire, Ireland.   1759

+ 96. Mrs. [James?] Parsons.   1752

+ 97. Thomas Penn, eleventh child of William Penn by   1743
     his second wife. Born in Bristol, he spent only
     nine years in Pennsylvania (1732–41). With the
     death of John Penn in 1746, he inherited three-
     quarters' interest in the Proprietary.

  98. Peters, possibly of Bristol.   1763

+ 99. James Robert, 8th Baron, Lord Petre, the first of 1734
     Bartram's wealthy English patrons.

+ 100. Lord Petre, son of the above, the 9th baron.   1763

*101. Pitts, Esq.   1751

*102. Lady Plymouth.   1761

 103. C. Polk, of Polhill.   ?

+ 104. William Pole, Esquire, Ireland.   1750

 105. Ralf.   1763

+ 106. Charles Lennox, 2d Duke of Richmond. After   1736
     Lord Petre, he and the Duke of Norfolk were
     Bartram's best supporters. Seldom did a year

pass that he did not order a five-guinea box (once a ten-guinea one) until his death.

107. Charles Lennox, 3d Duke of Richmond, also a good customer.	1757
*108. Earl of Rockfort.	1757
109. John St. Clair.	1761
*110. William Petty, Lord Shelburne, 1st Marquis of Lansdowne, Ireland. He was a friend of Arthur Young and attempted to introduce English agriculture into Ireland.	1754
111. William Shirley, governor of Massachusetts, ordered two boxes from Bartram "for one of the Royal Family" (Shirley to JB, 5 May 175?, BP 4:102).	175?
112. Humphrey Sibthorpe, professor of botany at Oxford.	1762
113. William Wentworth, Lord Strafford. Again, it was Dr. Mitchell who found this customer for Bartram.	1750
114. The Right Honorable Lord Viscount Sudley, Ireland.	1760
*115. Talbert, Esq.	1751
116. Tazer, Esq.	1752
*117. Earl of Telney.	1756
118. Governor Thersley.	1751
*119. Sir James Throgmorton.	1753
+120. Ward, Esquire.	1763
*121. James West, Esquire.	1749
*122. Viscount Weymouth.	1762
*123. Sir Charles Hanbury Williams.	1754
124. Wood.	1753

In addition to his customers, there were at least thirty-three friends and correspondents with whom Bartram exchanged plants.

Appendix 7. List of Some of Bartram's Geological Specimens. (Written on the back of John Bush's letter, 8 June 1764, BP 3:52)

1   Piece of Carolina quartz
2   Carolina petrified pine
    with its bark
3   Sea limestone Antigo
4   Black slatish stone from
    Carolina
5   iron oar from Carolina
6   petrifactions from our back
    mountains
7   common Cotton stone
8   Marchasite from Carolina
9   Alum native & its oar
10 black spotted stone from
    Jamaica
11 fine bole from lead mine in
    New run
12 petrified snail from Cresops
    hall
13 flint from Virginia
14 great shells petrified from
    no river
15 thin plate limestone fort
    cumberland
16 cubical Marchasites
17 petrified impressions in
    Sandstone
18 petrifactions
19 petrified Cockel shells from
    Jersey
20 good touch stone Jamaica
21 smooth white Compo stone
    Jamaica
22 thin plate of Spar in bed of
    gravel
23 parts of Indian pots
24 cours ruby from banks of
    Delaware
25 from our sea coast
26 Curious kind of flint field
27 gray sandstone Conestoga

28 seems to be petrified chip
29 glittering geode from
    Jersey
30 iron oar from Carolina
31 earth from pequea lead
32 petrified impressions from
    ye Ohio
33 from a cole mine at ye Ohio
34 pet wood from spar at ye
    End of Carolina
35 red clay from my Sand pit
36 striped stone from Crum
    Creek
37 ground muscle
38 crystal from skulkill gulph
39 choice plated iron oar from
    Jersey
40 petrified wood hicory from
    Carolina
41 coper oar from Jersey
42 star stone from under
    ground Carolina
43 coper color scaly earth ye
    back countrey
44 coal from pitsburgh
45 from ye Gret Valey in
    search of copper
46 asbestos I dug out of a
    lodestone quarry
47 lead oar containing silver
    susquehana
48 from ye same mine
49 white earth detached
    masses in gravel
50 clay stone from Stanton
51 my son split it out of a rock
52 a belemnite
53 Iron sand from new
    england

Appendix 8. Extract from Bartram's Letter to Linnaeus in the Fall of 1769. (Original in the Linnean Society of London)

[Latitude]

43 the farthest I have travailed northward was to Lake Ontario about 43 degrees No. latitude between which & Latitude 42 I observed these folowing trees & shrubs Sasafras, Liriodendron evergreens all growing little further northward; white, red, spanish & chestnut Oak; black beried tupelo, grapes, alder ash, dirka, Elder, Cephalanthus, prinos, viburnums, lotus, two leaved pine, three leaved pine, plum tree, Gale Espleni folio, Hamamelis, red flowered Maple, Hickories several sorts, birch, beech, willow, hornbeam, azalea, spirea, these continueth all ye way to floridas; silver leaved maple, Larix, Balm of Gilead fir, black & red spruice of newfoundland, silver leaved spruice, white pine, arbor vita, yew, dwarf birch, paper birch, red birch, red currants, gooseberries, dwarf Zoxilam, long walnut, yew dwarf Calmia, red bud, cornus, Colored viburnum with heart shaped leaves, Hidrangia, holly, rhus lentils, mountain magnolia, mountain chestnut Oak, pinast with narrow leaves, Rhododendron, Azalea, Benzoin;

42 here begins several of ye southward trees as Liquid amber, candle berrie mirtle, Robinia, cluster cherry, large & dwarf spirea opuli folio, viburnum with red & large black fruite, silver leaved alder, chestnut & dwarf oak, & large chestnut, poplar leaved birch, swamp magnolia, white ceder, crategas, vitis idea; many kind poplar, small viburnum black Diorvila

41 here ends several of our northern plants & Trees as ye white striped maple Larix, red & black spruice of new foundland sweet gale white pine white long walnut & ye black begins ink berries, evergreen prinos, poplar leaved birch, poison sumach or toxicodendron anona diospiros clethra ash leaved maple willow leaved oak swamp spanish & swamp white oak various kinds of andromedas fring tree itea chinkapins thime leaved Kalmia olive leaved Kalmia Siliquastrum great hors chestnut with yelowish flowers Uva ursy sanecio aborescens here ends to ye southward dwarf yew Rhododendron red currants gooseberries silver leaved alder Larix firs & spruice hidrangia striped bark maple balm of gilead fir pinaster vi-

burnum with heart shaped leaves, dwarf birch & dwarf cluster cherry & wild cherry

39 these following continueth most of them all way to florida anona bald cypres,

38 narrow leaved shrub hypericum, beech plums   here ends ye white long walnut broad leaved shrub Hypericum, Ptelia Gleditsia & here ye mountain magnolia ends

37 sorrel tree, yapon evergreen oak   periclimenum; here ends ye arbor vita Carolina

36 canes, dwarf berbery   Burrea or sweet wood & ye shrub yelow root

35 here ye silver leaved maple ends unless on ye north side of A mountain by chance umbrela tree   kidney bean tree; stewartia lobloly bay, sweet red bay purple berried bay, halesia, several sorts of evergreen oaks, philadelphus   horse sugar or yelow leafe pavia   small palmeto   dionea or flytrap   this grows near ye sea coast near which it extends about 60 miles & near 50 miles up ye countrey   I have been several times round where it grows   it prospers there in A moistish ground in an open suny savanah chiefly on ye So. side of Cape fear river but there is no general plant   here & there a patch at 5 10 or 15 miles distance & will bear ye cold that freeseth water an inch thick in one nights time & will bear ye heat of 88 degrees farenheits thermometer

34 long leaved pine   great magnolia   dwarf bay with ye scent of Sasafras

33 small narrow leaved bay   great palmeto   Adams needle or palmeto royal so called & A thorny little tree with box leaves falsly called wild olive

32 great red water tupelo with red acid fruite   short poded Gleditsia & catalpa with short pods no longer then acrons & A dwarf running oak with smooth shineing leaves about A foot high & A curious kind of andromeda three foot high

31 ye bonduck & ye several curious evergreen shrubs A fine variety

30 is a little patch of ye star Annis shrub grows ten foot high a sweet evergreen

I have here given A prety near account where I observed ye natural growth generaly of ye several genus of trees & shrubs of North

America where I have travailed from North to South & where I first observed ye southern trees to grow naturaly toward ye north toward ye sea coast but as our great mountains generaly runs N E & S W our Northern trees will grow on ye top of Northern expositions of them 2 or 3 degrees farther South then on ye plains & many times some odd seeds will be brought down ye rivers by floods from ye mountains yerely & be deposited on thair overflowed banks where thay may vegitate where thay make A feble growth & those seeds that is carried by ye birds from ye South, altho thay grow & flower northward yet ye cold nips them before ye seed is perfected

Appendix 9. Transcription of letter of disownment to John Bartram from the Darby Monthly Meeting.

Whereas by the prevailence of a report Concerning John Bartram (who had his birth and education amongst Friends and made profession with us from his youth, up to this time) viz that he disbelieved in the divinity of our Lord and Saviour Jesus Christ as being perfectly God as well as man, it became the tender Concern of Friends to enquire of him whether he had given occation for such a report by believing and uttering as above, the which he did not deny but rather appear'd to vindicate, and Notwithstanding our earnest Labour of Love from time to time Cannot be prevailed with to decline such a belief and by publick testimony Clear our Society from the great reproach of being unsound in the Christian faith Wherefore fully believing in the Miraculous Conception birth, Miracles death, glorious Resurrection and Assention of our blessed lord and Saviour, Jesus Christ as recorded in holy writ; we can do no less for the Clearing of truth than give forth this testimony against such [marked out] dark notions and hereby declare the said John Bartram to be no member of our Christian Society Untill by Unfeigned repentance he renounces his Corrupt [marked out] opinions and witness forgiveness for the same the which we sincerely desire he may
Given Forth by Our Monthly Meeting held at Darby the 1 day of the 2m 1758 and on behalf and by Order of the same

signed by Abram Bonsall

Whereas by the prevailence of a report Concerning
John Battram, (who had his birth and education
amongst Friends and made profession, with us from
his youth up to this time) viz that he disbelieved in
the divinity of our Lord, and, Saviour Jesus Christ
as being perfectly God, as well as man, it became the
tender Concern of friends to enquire of him, whether
he had given occation, for such a report by believing
and uttering as above, the which, he did not deny
but rather appear'd to vindicate, and Notwithstanding
our earnest Labour of Love from time to time cannot
be prevailed with to decline such a belief and by
publick testimony Clear our Society from the great
reproach of being unsound, in the Christian faith
Wherefore fully believing in the Miraculous
Conception, birth Miracles death, Glorious Resurrection,
and Ascention, of our blessed, Lord, and, Saviour Jesus
Christ as recorded in, holy writ: we can do no less for
the Clearing of truth, than give forth, this testimony
against such dark notions and
hereby declare the said, John Batram, to be no member
of our Christian, Society Untill by Unfeigned, repentance
he renounces his Corrupt opinions and witness forgiveness
for the same the which we sincerely desire he may

Given Forth, by Our Monthly Meeting
held, at Darby the 1 day of the 2m 1758
and on behalf and by Order of the same
Signed ———— By, Abrah: Bonsall the

Letter of disownment to John Bartram from the Darby Monthly Meeting
(courtesy West Chester Historical Society)

Notes

THE following abbreviations are used in the notes:

BP, Bartram Papers, The Historical Society of Pennsylvania.
JB, John Bartram.
PC, Peter Collinson.
KT, Peter Kalm, *Travels in North America* (from 1770 London ed.). New York, 1937.
LPCC, *Letters and Papers of Cadwallader Colden*. New York, 1910.
MJB, William Darlington, *Memorials of John Bartram and Humphry Marshall* (facsimile of 1849 ed.). New York and London, 1967.

NOTES TO CHAPTER 1

1. John Bartram (hereinafter cited as JB) to Archibald Bartram, 1761, quoted in William Darlington, ed., *Memorials of John Bartram and Humphry Marshall* (hereinafter cited as MJB), p. 416; will of Richard Bartram, 23 September 1660, Lichfield Joint Record Office (see appendix 1). A fellmonger removed hair or wool from hides to prepare leather.
2. Edward Watkins, "Friends in Derbyshire 1647–1808," p. 4 (manuscript in the Friends' Reference Library, London).
3. Personal communication from Miss Helen Forde, London, England.
4. Joseph Besse, *A Collection of the Sufferings of the People Called Quakers*, 1:140.
5. Minutes of Derbyshire Monthly Meeting. West Chester Historical Society.
6. Besse, *Sufferings*, 1:142. Compton and Clifton were across the river from Ashbourne.
7. James Bowden, *The History of the Society of Friends in America*, 2:10, 12.
8. JB to Archibald Bartram, 1761, MJB, p. 416.
9. Morgan Bunting, "The Names of the Early Settlers of Darby

Township, Chester County, Pennsylvania," *Pennsylvania Magazine of History and Biography* 24 (1900):182–86.

10. Minshall Painter, "Notes from Darby Meeting," manuscript, Chester County Historical Society.

11. *Records of the Courts of Chester County*, 1681–97, 1:59.

12. *Proceedings Centennial Anniversary Friends' Meeting House, Darby, Pa., 1805–1905*, pp. 7–11.

13. *Records of the Courts of Chester County*, 1:64–313 passim.

14. George Smith, *History of Delaware County, Pennsylvania*, p. 524.

15. Painter, "Notes."

16. Joseph Jackson, *Encyclopedia of Philadelphia*, 3:810.

17. Painter, "Notes."

18. *Records of the Courts of Chester County*, p. 407. This record reads "John Hood Attorney for John Bartram past a Deed to John Bartram the yonger for one hundred and ten Acres of land lying in Darby the Deed bearing Date the nineth of the first month 1696/7." Since John, the younger, died in 1692 and since the Holmes map showing the original purchasers of land from 1681 shows "William Bartram 100 A. March 9, 1696–7," it seems evident that William was the person intended (Benjamin H. Smith, *Atlas of Delaware County*, map no. 6).

19. Deed Book A, vol. 1, pt. 2, Chester County Records.

20. MJB, p. 37.

21. Painter, "Notes."

22. *Records of the Courts of Chester County*, 2:29, 67.

23. Painter, "Notes."

24. Letter to his Children, 1777, copy made by his son William now in the Bartram Papers (hereafter cited as BP), Historical Society of Pennsylvania. A copy made from this is in the Friends' Historical Library, Swarthmore College.

25. Thomas Woody, *Early Quaker Education in Pennsylvania*, p. 154.

26. Ibid., pp. 186–87.

27. Ibid., pp. 109, 192, 198.

28. JB to Alexander Catcot, 26 May 1742, MJB, p. 324; JB to Peter Collinson (hereafter cited as PC), 1 May 1764, MJB, p. 263; William Bartram's account of his father, quoted by Darlington, MJB, p. 38; Ann Leighton, *American Gardens in the Eighteenth Century*, pp. 43–44.

29. Painter, "Notes."

30. Smith, *Atlas of Delaware County*, map no. 6; Painter, "Notes."

31. Francis D. West, "The Mystery of the Death of William Bartram, Father of John Bartram the Botanist," *The Pennsylvania Genealogical Magazine* 20 (1957):253.

32. Ibid.

33. Deed Book A, Carteret County, North Carolina, pp. 18–20. This information was very kindly supplied by Mrs. David R. Taylor in response to a request made to the clerk of court for Carteret County.

34. Alonzo Thomas Dill, Jr., "Eighteenth Century New Bern," pt. 3, *North Carolina Historical Review* 22 (1945):293–319.

35. Last Will and Testament of William Bartram, Will Book C, Chester County, p. 335.

36. See note 31.

37. Ibid.

38. See note 34.

39. Henry J. Cadbury, ed., "John Farmer's First American Journey, 1711–1714," *Proceedings of the American Antiquarian Society* 53 (1943):82. Farmer visited North Carolina, where he was "cridittably informed that a friend differed with his brethren of a monthly Meeting in Pensilvania & from thence removed himself & his Family & som Estate heither & would not settle amongst ffriends here who desired his Company: but settled above 20 Miles of amongst very Wicked People for the sake of very good & cheep Land which they & hee forcably took from Indians. . . ." This, along with the rest of Farmer's remarks, seems to confirm the account given by William Bartram in his "Life and Character of John Bartram," the manuscript of which is in the American Philosophical Society library.

40. Ibid.

41. William L. Saunders, ed., *The Colonial Records of North Carolina,* 1:827.

42. Vincent H. Todd and Julius Goebel, eds., *Christoph von Graffenreid's Account of the Founding of New Bern.*

43. Joseph W. Barnwell, ed., "The Tuscarora Expedition," *South Carolina Historical and Genealogical Magazine* 9 (1908):28–54.

44. Will Book C, Chester County, p. 335.

45. See note 31.

46. The account of William Smith, surviving executor of the testament of William Bartram, presented to the Orphans' Court of Chester County. A copy is at the Chester County Historical Society. At Chambers' death, Stephen Jackson was appointed in his place.

47. Dorothy B. Lapp, transcriber, *"Enterys of the Orphans Court of Chester County, Pennsylvania 1716–1730, 1732–1734,"* pp. 12, 17, 20–21, 25.

48. Account of William Smith, see note 46; William Bartram's widow had married John Smith of Burlington, West Jersey, on 7 December 1715 (Painter, "Notes").

49. The quotation is from a note in the hand of Joseph Parker Norris in John F. Watson's manuscript at the Library Company of Philadelphia; Mary E. Williamson, "The Maris Family," *Bulletin of the Friends Historical Association* 19 (1930):17; Smith, *Delaware County,* p. 524.

50. Painter, "Notes."

51. Frank Willing Leach, "Old Philadelphia Families, 80 Bartram," *North American* (Philadelphia), 20 December 1908.

52. Account of William Smith; Francis D. West Manuscript, American Philosophical Society Library; Tax Assessment Records, Chester County Historical Society.

53. Painter, "Notes"; Leach, "Philadelphia Families"; West, "Manuscript."

54. Deed Book H2, Philadelphia County Records, p. 252.

55. Emily Read Cheston, *John Bartram, 1699–1777: His Garden and His House*, pp. 23, 26.

56. Copy of marriage certificate from Concord Monthly Meeting Certificate Book in the American Philosophical Society Library.

57. Smith, *Delaware County*, pp. 484, 525. Mendenhall had represented Chester County in the assembly in 1712. His wife was Ann, daughter of Robert Pennell of Chichester Meeting.

58. Concord Monthly Meeting Certificate Book, p. 67 and entry for 10 October 1729.

59. JB to Jared Eliot, 24 January 1757, BP 1:48.

60. Cheston, *Bartram*, pp. 26–27.

61. PC to JB, 14 December 1737, MJB, p. 103.

62. William Wynne, "Some Account of the Nursery Gardens and the State of Horticulture in the Neighborhood of Philadelphia," *Gardener's Magazine* 8 (1832):272–77.

63. M. G. J. de Crèvecoeur, *Letters from an American Farmer*, pp. 188–89.

64. Stevenson Whitcomb Fletcher, *Pennsylvania Agriculture and Country Life*, 1:156.

65. Ronald H. True, "Some Pre-Revolutionary Agricultural Correspondence," *Agricultural History* 12 (1938):111–12; Stevenson Whitcomb Fletcher, "John Bartram, Farmer-Botanist," mimeographed manuscript, p. 12, John Bartram Association Deposit, American Philosophical Society library.

66. Tax Assessment Records, Chester County Historical Society.

67. Deed Book #70, Philadelphia County Records, p. 144.

68. Deed Book H2, Philadelphia County Records, p. 257.

69. Patent from Thomas and Richard Penn, 26 January 1768.

70. John Bartram's will, Will Book R, Philadelphia County Records, p. 277.

71. Leach, "Philadelphia Families."

72. Bartram's letter to his children, 1758. Typescript of a copy made by one of Bartram's children, now among the Bartram Papers (1:76) in the Friends' Historical Library, Swarthmore College.

73. Ibid.

74. Ibid.

NOTES TO CHAPTER 2

1. Benjamin Franklin, *The Autobiography of Benjamin Franklin*, p. 75.

2. Benjamin Franklin, *The Papers of Benjamin Franklin*, ed. Leonard W. Labaree, 1:344n. In 1746 Breintnall's widow presented two folio volumes of these charming prints to the Library Company of Philadelphia. Breintnall had added notes to these, which makes them even more interesting, and a number of them refer to Bartram.

3. See John Fothergill, *Some Account of the Late Peter Collinson,* and R. Hingston Fox, *Dr. John Fothergill and His Friends.*

4. PC to JB, 16 January 1743/44, MJB, pp. 166–67.

5. "A Letter from John Bartram, M.D. to Peter Collinson, F.R.S. concerning A Cluster of small Teeth observed by him at the Root of each Fang or great Tooth in the Head of a Rattle-Snake, upon dissecting it," *Philosophical Transactions* (hereafter cited as *Phil. Trans.*) 41 (1740):358–59. Until Breintnall's death in March 1746 Collinson's letters were sent in his care.

6. Margery Purver, *The Royal Society: Concept and Creation.*

7. E. St. John Brooks, *Sir Hans Sloane: The Great Collector and His Circle.*

8. George Frederick Frick and Raymond Phineas Stearns, *Mark Catesby, the Colonial Audubon.*

9. PC to JB, 20 June 1734/35, MJB, p. 60.

10. Franklin, *Autobiography*, p. 87.

11. JB to PC, 6 December 1739, BP 2:7.

12. MJB, pp. 59–63.

13. Ibid.

14. PC to JB, 12 February 1734/35, MJB, p. 67.

15. PC to JB, 20 February 1734/35, MJB, p. 68.

16. PC to JB, 31 March 1734/35, BP 2:14.

17. PC to JB, 20 February 1734/35, MJB, p. 68.

18. PC to JB, 24 January 1734/35, MJB, pp. 63–64.

19. PC to JB, 19 June 1735, BP 2:18.

20. PC to JB, 12 February 1734/35, MJB, p. 66. Collinson's instructions are in BP 2:80.

21. PC to JB, 20 January 1736/37, MJB, pp. 82–83.

22. PC to JB, 25 February 1740/41, MJB, p. 140.

23. PC to JB, 1 June 1736, MJB, p. 77.

24. 7 June 1736, MJB, p. 80.

25. 20 December 1737, MJB, p. 109.

26. 26 January 1738/39, MJB, p. 124.

27. 25 February 1740/41, 3 February 1741/42, MJB, pp. 140, 148.

28. 16 May 1741, MJB, pp. 155–56. Darlington misdated this letter 1742. The references to Bartram's letter of 25 September 1740 (now in the Linnean Society of London) make a 1741 date more acceptable.

29. PC to JB, 19 June 1735, BP 2:18, 3 February 1735/36, BP 2:33, 20 September 1736, MJB, pp. 81–82; JB to PC, extract from letter of 27 February 1736/37, Royal Society of London archives, LBC 25, p. 118.

30. For a thorough account of Lord Petre's horticultural activities see Winifred Notman Prince, "John Bartram and Thorndon Park," *Garden Journal* 7 (1957):141–43, 152, 8 (1957):189–91.

31. Miles Hadfield, *Gardening in Britain*, p. 226.

32. 24 January, 13 March 1734/35, MJB, pp. 63, 69–70.

33. PC to JB, 12 March, MJB, p. 72. The list attached to this letter is in the Bartram Papers, dated 5 February 1735/36.

34. PC to JB, 1 June 1736, MJB, p. 77.

35. Maurice Bear Gordon, *Aesculapius Comes to the Colonies*, pp. 443–44; Francis R. Packard, *History of Medicine in the United States*, 1:274–81. Dr. Witt's medical diplomas for his apprentices attested to their proficiency both in medicine and "Astral Science."

36. JB to PC, late spring, 1740, BP 1:20:3.

37. PC to JB, 22 July 1740, MJB, p. 137.

38. PC to JB, 3 February 1735/36, MJB, p. 87.

39. 1 June 1736, MJB, p. 76.

40. Joseph Ewan and Nesta Ewan, *John Banister and His Natural History of Virginia, 1678–1692*, p. 213.

41. PC to JB, 20 March, 21 April 1735/36, MJB, pp. 74–75.

42. PC to JB, 28 August, MJB, p. 80.

NOTES TO CHAPTER 3

1. Logan to JB, MJB, pp. 307–8.

2. See Frederick B. Tolles, *James Logan and the Culture of Provincial America*, and Arthur Raistrick, *Quakers in Science and Industry*, pp. 260–61.

3. Logan to PC, 8 June 1736, from the Deborah Logan papers, quoted in *The Friend* (Philadelphia) 11 (4 August 1838):347.

4. PC to JB, 28 August 1736, MJB, pp. 80–81; JB to PC, May 1738, BP 1:14.

5. See note 3.

6. MJB, p. 307.

7. Logan to Linnaeus, 17 October 1738, Linnean Correspondence, Linnean Society of London.

8. MJB, p. 105.

9. 19 August 1737, Logan Papers, 10:67, Historical Society of Pennsylvania.

10. 14 December 1737, MJB, p. 106.

11. 12 February 1735/36, MJB, p. 67.

12. PC to Dr. J. J. Dillenius, 31 July 1736, Winifred Notman Prince, "John Bartram in the Cedar Swamps," *Notes and Documents* 81 (1957):186–88.

13. 20 September 1736, MJB, p. 82.

14. 26 April 1737, Royal Society of London archives, LBC 25, pp. 112–16.

15. Raymond Phineas Stearns, *Science in the British Colonies of America*, pp. 468–71.

16. 26 April 1737, Journal Book of the Royal Society, 16:333; MJB, p. 101.

17. May 1738, MJB, p. 119.

18. See "Additional Observations on the Cicada . . . By the late Mr. John Bartram. From a MS. in the possession of the Editor" [Dr. Benjamin Smith Barton], *Medical and Physical Journal* 1, pt. 1 (1804):56–59.

19. Ibid., 54:64–68.

20. 26 April 1737, Royal Society of London archives, LBC 25, pp. 112–16.
21. JB to PC, BP 1:18.
22. BP 2:24:1, 2:25.
23. PC to JB, 12 March 1735/36, MJB, pp. 72–73, 20 March 1735/36, MJB, p. 74.
24. See list of plants which PC referred to Dillenius. BP 2:75; JB to Dillenius, 1 August 1738, MJB, p. 308; JB to PC, May 1738, MJB, p. 119. The cave was probably Crystal Cave near Reading.
25. PC to JB, 14 December 1737, MJB, p. 104; Ernest Earnest, *John and William Bartram, Botanists and Explorers*, p. 45.
26. PC to JB, 20 May 1737, MJB, p. 98.
27. PC to JB, 14 March 1736/37, 12 August 1737, MJB, pp. 92, 99.
28. 20 May 1737, BP 2:75, 14 May 1736/37, MJB, p. 94.
29. PC to JB, MJB, p. 132. Darlington misdated this letter 1739. There are a number of references to martagons in PC's letters during the next several years, and it is difficult to be sure that he is referring to the same one each time.
30. 20 December 1737, MJB, p. 107.
31. MJB, pp. 119–20.
32. 20 September, BP 2:30.
33. 17 February, BP 2:34. Darlington omitted this portion of Collinson's letter and misdated it as 1737 rather than 1737/38, MJB, p. 88.
34. 20 December, MJB, p. 107.
35. 14 December 1737, MJB, p. 104.
36. May 1738, MJB, p. 119.
37. 11 November 1738, BP 1:19:5.
38. 7 February 1738/39, MJB, pp. 122–23, 126.
39. PC to JB, 14 December 1737, MJB, pp. 103, 105.
40. PC to JB, 14, 22 March 1736/37, MJB, pp. 91, 94.
41. 6 April 1738, MJB, p. 117.
42. PC to JB, 27 January 1737/38, MJB, p. 110.

NOTES TO CHAPTER 4

1. Bartram's account of this trip is contained in an incomplete and undated letter to Collinson written during the summer of 1738, BP 1:14:5.
2. Kearsley to PC, 16 July 1739, Royal Society of London archives, LBC 26, pp. 393–98.
3. The virtues ascribed to this plant are still remarkable today. The Lakeland Nursery catalogue for 1976 advertises that "Chinese Druggists get 10 times more than Gold for GINSENG. . . . For over 50 Centuries the Chinese have prized this Exotic 'Man Plant' for Strength, Virility, Rejuvenation and Longevity." Collectors in Indiana received $60 per pound in 1976 (*Richmond* [Virginia] *Times Dispatch*, 23 March 1976). Among the holdings of the Korean Unification Church in Norfolk, Virginia, is the Jen-

sen Ginseng Company "which imports a herbal tea made from the root of the ginseng plant" (ibid., 15 June 1977).

4. 25 November 1738, History of Science #1, Reel 8, frame 3480 (from the originals in the Royal Society of London archives), American Philosophical Society Library.

5. Bond to JB, 20 February 1738/39, MJB, p. 316.

6. 17 November 1739, Linnean Correspondence, Linnean Society of London.

7. PC to JB, 1, 24 February, MJB, pp. 125, 127.

8. JB to PC, 18 July 1739, BP 1:19:1.

9. Undated letter of JB to PC, apparently written in September 1738, BP 1:18.

10. Betsy C. Corner and Christopher C. Booth, eds., *Chain of Friendship; Selected Letters of Dr. John Fothergill of London*, pp. 46–47.

11. 17 February 1737/38, MJB, p. 89.

12. Ibid.

13. 24 December 1737, E. G. Swem, ed., *Brothers of the Spade. Correspondence of Peter Collinson of London, and of John Custis of Williamsburg, Virginia, 1734–1746*, pp. 50, 54.

14. The description of Bartram's trip that follows is taken, unless otherwise indicated, from his "Journal of a Trip to Maryland and Virginia," BP 1:14.

15. For more on Thomas, see Paul Wilstach, *Tidewater Maryland*, p. 277.

16. A short account of Richard Hall is in Francis Sims McGrath, *Pillars of Maryland*, p. 142.

17. Edmund Berkeley and Dorothy Smith Berkeley, *John Clayton, Pioneer of American Botany*.

18. JB to PC, 13 November 1758, Academy of Natural Sciences, Philadelphia.

19. JB to PC, 18 July 1739, BP 1:19.

20. Swem, *Brothers*, pp. 9–20.

21. Custis to PC, 12 August 1739, ibid., p. 61.

22. JB to Custis, 19 November 1738, BP 1:23. JB's description of Indian physic in Franklin's *Poor Richard*, 1741.

23. Stearns, *Science*, pp. 289–90.

24. Undated letter of JB to PC, apparently written in November 1739, BP 1:19; JB to PC, 6 December 1739, BP 2:7; and JB's description of Indian physic in Franklin's *Poor Richard*, 1741. See appendix 2.

25. Custis to PC, 18 July 1738, 12 August 1739, Swem, *Brothers*, pp. 55, 61.

26. For a good account of Byrd's scientific activities, see Stearns, *Science*, pp. 280–93.

27. William Byrd, *History of the Dividing Line Betwixt Virginia and North Carolina*, Introduction by William K. Boyd and Percy G. Adams, p. 272.

28. *Virginia Gazette*, April 1737.

29. Byrd to JB, 30 November 1738, BP 1:94, 23 March 1738/39, BP 1:17:4; JB to Byrd, November 1738, BP 1:14:10.

30. Swem, *Brothers*, p. 157.

31. JB to PC, 27 May 1743, MJB, p. 163.

32. BP 1:14.

NOTES TO CHAPTER 5

1. Conway Zirkle, "Plant Hybridization and Plant Breeding in Eighteenth-Century American Agriculture," *Agricultural History* 43 (1969): 25–38.

2. MJB, p. 118.

3. JB to PC, 9 December 1738, BP 1:17:3.

4. 26 July 1740, Linnean Society of London.

5. JB to PC, 29 April 1740, BP 1:18.

6. Spring of 1739, BP 1:17:4, quoted in Conway Zirkle, *Beginnings of Plant Hybridization*, p. 146. Zirkle noted that Darlington (MJB, p. 315) had omitted several of the sentences of this letter and commented that although he "had been a member of Congress for six years, he remained a man of the most delicate sensibilities, so delicate, in fact, that he omitted from Bartram's letter just those portions which describe the sexual parts of flowers and the hybridization" (p. 145).

7. MJB, p. 136.

8. 20 July, BP 1:49.

9. 2 October 1760, MJB, p. 225, 19 July 1761, BP 1:53. The part of this letter which referred to the double larkspur was omitted by Darlington, MJB, p. 228.

10. MJB, pp. 95–96.

11. JB to Dillenius, undated (early 1739), BP 1:23; Dillenius to JB, 26 April 1738, Historical Society of Pennsylvania.

12. JB to Dillenius, 1 August 1738, MJB, pp. 308–9.

13. Dillenius to JB, 22 June 1741, MJB, p. 310.

14. Dillenius to JB, 15 October 1740, MJB, pp. 309–10. Vernon collected in Maryland in 1698.

15. JB to Dillenius, 5 December 1739, BP 1:19:6.

16. JB to Catesby, 22 March 1740/41, BP 1:42:3.

17. MJB, p. 135.

18. 22 July 1740, BP 2:53:1–4, omitted in MJB, p. 136.

19. #434. JB presented this book to the Library Company on 17 April 1773. It is inscribed, "John Bartram His Booke 1742 sent by Doctor Dillenius professor at Oxford."

20. JB to Dillenius, undated letter, BP 1:23. Many of the plants in the Oxford garden listed by Dillenius (Sherard MSS 208) were undoubtedly grown from seed sent by JB, but Dillenius did not record the origin of many of these.

21. Bartram's notes, copied by Carlotta Herring-Brown "From the

Dillenius Collection Herbarium Library Oxford Eng," are now at the American Philosophical Society Library.

22. 12 April 1739, MJB, pp. 130–31.

23. 18 July 1739, BP 1:19:1.

24. PC to JB, 20 October 1740, MJB, p. 138.

25. December 1739, BP 1:20:6; PC to JB, 20 October 1740, MJB, p. 138.

26. Ibid.

27. Sir James Edward Smith, *A Selection of the Correspondence of Linnaeus and Other Naturalists,* 1:8, 12, 16.

28. 2 "Juny" 1746, MJB, p. 356.

29. The plants given his name are today called burweeds. They have been placed in a new genus, *Triumfetta,* one species of which retains *Bartramia* as a specific name. They are native to Florida, a region which Bartram had not then visited. See John Kunkel Small, *Manual of the Southeastern Flora,* pp. 841–42. The generic name *Bartramia* was later revived and applied to a genus of mosses.

30. See Bartram-Cressy correspondence 1739–41, in the Bartram Papers.

31. PC to JB, 2 September 1739, 10 June 1740, BP 2:51–52.

32. Mark Catesby, *The Natural History of Carolina, Florida and the Bahama Islands,* 2:71–73, 98.

33. MJB, pp. 319, 321.

34. Catesby to JB, 20 May 1740, MJB, pp. 319–20.

35. MJB, p. 321.

36. 20 May 1737, MJB, p. 96.

37. PC to JB, 6 April 1738, MJB, p. 117.

38. 25 February 1740/41, MJB, p. 141.

39. Catesby to JB, March 1741/42, MJB, p. 322.

40. JB to PC, 17 November 1742, BP 2:24:1, 2:25.

41. Catesby, *Natural History,* 2:101, 108, 111, 116, 117.

42. March 1741/42, MJB, p. 322.

43. 18 November 1742, BP 1:24.

44. Late spring, 1742, BP 1:29:3.

45. Ibid.

46. JB to PC, 6 July 1742, MJB, p. 158.

47. March 1741/42, MJB, p. 323.

48. JB to Catesby, late spring 1742, BP 1:29:3.

49. JB to PC, 21 June 1743, BP 1:15:1.

50. 2:104–5.

51. Ibid., p. iv.

52. 15 April 1746, MJB, pp. 323–24.

53. JB to Colden, 6 October 1746, Cadwallader Colden, *Letters and Papers of Cadwallader Colden* (hereafter referred to as LPCC), 3:270–72.

54. 3 March 1747, BP 2:73.

55. MJB, p. 302.

56. Ibid., pp. 302–3. JB's copy of Sir Hans' book is now in the Boston

Public Library. Both volumes bear the following inscription: "John Bartram his book   A present from Sir Hans Sloan 1742."

57. JB to PC, 6 July 1742, MJB, p. 158.

58. MJB, pp. 303–4.

59. Sloane MSS 4019, ff. 132–33, British Museum.

60. MJB, p. 163. The cup is now in the Rare Book Room of the University of Pennsylvania library, Philadelphia.

61. MJB, p. 305.

62. Letter of 8 December 1745, MJB, p. 306.

63. 23 November 1743, MJB, p. 304.

64. Autograph Collection of Physicians and Chemists, 4, Historical Society of Pennsylvania.

65. MJB, p. 153.

66. MJB, p. 159.

67. JB to Colhoun, 26 July 1739, BP 1:19:1; JB to PC, November 1739, BP 1:19; Colhoun to JB, 5 November 1739, BP 2:7.

NOTES TO CHAPTER 6

1. The account of this trip is contained in a letter from JB to PC, 25 September 1740, BP 1:42.

2. Franklin, *Autobiography*, p. 129.

3. 25 February 1740/41, MJB, p. 141.

4. 22 July 1741, BP 1:21:6.

5. 3 February 1741/42, BP 2:56. Darlington also included this letter but exercised that "sensitivity" noted by Zirkle in censoring the latter part of PC's comment.

6. PC to JB, 25 February 1740/41, MJB, pp. 139–41.

7. JB to PC, 22 July 1741, BP 1:21:6.

8. 5 March 1740/41, LPCC 2:208; Colden to PC, n.d., ibid., p. 211.

9. Stearns, *Science*, pp. 493–97. Colden practiced medicine for about ten years after moving to New York, according to Roy N. Lokken, professor of history, East Carolina University.

10. The account of this trip, except where noted, is in JB's letter to PC, 22 July 1741, BP 1:21:1–6.

11. John E. Stillwell, *Historical and Genealogical Miscellaney*, 3:25–31; *Dictionary of American Biography*.

12. JB to Bayard, n.d., but probably June 1741, BP 1:21.

13. JB to PC, 18 October 1741, BP 1:23.

14. Edgar M. Bacon, *The Hudson River*, pp. 486–88.

15. JB to Bayard, June 1741, BP 1:21.

16. Ibid.

17. Ibid.

18. JB to PC, n.d., but early fall 1741, BP 1:22:2.

19. JB to Bayard, June 1741, BP 1:21.

20. JB to PC, 18 October 1741, BP 1:23. The accounts of his next three trips are all contained in this letter.

21. 3 March, MJB, p. 152.
22. LPCC 2:247.
23. Prince, "John Bartram," *Garden Journal* 7 (1957):152.
24. British Museum Additional Manuscripts 28,726, ff. 64–65, 92–93.
25. Aylmer Bourke Lambert, "Notes Relating to Botany, Collected from the Manuscripts of the Late Peter Collinson," *Transactions of the Linnean Society* 10 (1811):13.
26. Prince, "John Bartram," *Garden Journal* 7 (1957):143, 8 (1957): 189; "Introduction of American Seeds into Great Britain by Peter Collinson," British Museum (Natural History).
27. MJB, p. 145.
28. Addressee unknown, 1742?, BP 1:29:3.
29. Summer of 1742, BP 1:29:4.
30. 17 November 1742, BP 2:24:1, 30 November 1743, BP 1:26.
31. 3 July 1742, MJB, p. 157.
32. Prince, "John Bartram," *Garden Journal* 8 (1957):191.
33. JB to PC, 24 July, 5 September 1742, MJB, pp. 160–61.
34. Colden to PC, 13 November 1742, LPCC 2:280.
35. JB to Colden, 25 September 1742, LPCC 2:274; JB to Clayton, 1 September 1744, BP 1:28.
36. JB to PC, 17 November 1742, BP 2:24:1.
37. JB to Clayton, 1 September 1744, BP 1:28.
38. JB to Dillenius, 14 November 1742, MJB, p. 311.
39. JB to Colden, 25 September 1742, LPCC 2:274, 16 January 1742/43, LPCC 3:4.
40. JB to PC, 24 July, 5 September 1742, MJB, pp. 159–61.
41. JB to Colden, 16 January 1742/43, LPCC 3:3, 6 March 1746/47, LPCC, 3:362.
42. JB to Colden, 23 October 1742, LPCC 2:274–77.
43. LPCC 3:23–24.

NOTES TO CHAPTER 7

1. LPCC 3:24.
2. John Bartram, Lewis Evans, and Conrad Weiser, *A Journey from Pennsylvania to Onondago in 1743*, Introduction by Whitfield J. Bell, Jr., p. 7; *Pennsylvania Gazette*, 1 September 1743.
3. Cadwallader Colden, *The History of the Five Indian Nations Depending on the Province of New-York in America*.
4. Bell, Introduction, *A Journey*, p. 9.
5. John Bartram, *Observations on the Inhabitants, Climate, Soil, Rivers, Productions, Animals, and other matters worthy of Notice, made by Mr. John Bartram in his Travels from Pensilvania to Onondago, Oswego and the Lake Ontario In Canada.* Unless otherwise indicated, the account that follows is based on Bartram's *Observations*.
6. Bell, *A Journey*, p. 107.
7. *Colonial Records of Pennsylvania 1683–1790*, 1st ser., 4:660–61.

8. Lewis Weston Dillwyn, *Hortus Collinsonianus – An Account of the Plants Cultivated by the Late Peter Collinson, Esq., F.R.S.*, p. 34.

9. Through a printer's error "Davis's Streights" appeared as "Daon's Streights" but has been changed here for clarity.

10. 17 September 1743, LPCC 7:339.

11. Undated, BP 1:44, in reply to PC's letter of 10 February 1757, MJB, pp. 212–13.

12. 1 September 1743.

13. Whitfield J. Bell, Jr. and Ralph L. Ketcham, "A Tribute to John Bartram, With a Note on Jacob Engelbrecht," *Pennsylvania Magazine of History and Biography* 83 (October, 1959):446–51.

14. JB to PC, 24 July 1744, MJB, p. 172.

15. 25 July 1744, MJB, p. 351.

16. Gronovius to Bartram, 26 June 1751, Helen A. Choate, "An Unpublished Letter by Gronovius," *Torreya* 16:117. The original letter is in the Smith College library. Some of the cargo was sold at Dieppe. De Jussieu acquired many of the botanical items, and only a few seeds eventually reached Gronovius. Bartram's letter to Sir Hans Sloane was forwarded to that gentleman by the French (Sloane to Bartram, 16 October 1745, Historical Society of Pennsylvania).

17. Poole to JB, 3 July 1750, BP 4:96.

18. JB to Gronovius, 24 January 1750/51, archives of the Hunt Institute for Botanical Documentation.

19. Jackson, a member of the Inner Temple, was renowned for the breadth of his knowledge in many fields. Dr. Samuel Johnson called him "the all-knowing," and Charles Lamb referred to him as "the omniscient Jackson" (Carl Van Doren, *Letters and Papers of Benjamin Franklin and Richard Jackson 1753–1785*, pp. 3, 1).

20. PC's copy with notes and corrections in the British Museum (Natural History).

21. 27 March 1750/51, Labaree, *Franklin*, 4:122.

22. 19 June 1751, University Library Erlangen.

23. Gronovius to JB, 26 June 1751, *Torreya* 16:118.

NOTES TO CHAPTER 8

1. N.d., BP 1:38.

2. Misdated 1739 by Darlington, MJB, p. 132.

3. Benjamin Franklin, *A Proposal for Promoting Useful Knowledge among the British Plantations in America*, reprinted in the *Pennsylvania Gazette*, 28 January 1768.

4. Franklin to Colden, 4 November 1743, LPCC 3:34.

5. JB to Colden, 29 April 1744, Gratz Collection, Case 7, Box 21, Historical Society of Pennsylvania.

6. Franklin to Colden, 5 April 1744, *Proceedings of the American Philosophical Society* 22 (1884–85):1.

7. Ibid.

8. 27 March 1744, Yale University library.
9. See note 4. Spencer, a physician trained at Edinburgh and London, was also known as a capable "Man-Midwife."
10. LPCC 3:65–66.
11. Ibid., pp. 93–94.
12. Ibid., p. 182.
13. Carl Van Doren, "The Beginnings of the American Philosophical Society," *Proceedings of the American Philosophical Society* 87 (1943):286.
14. LPCC 3:61.
15. Ibid., p. 160.
16. 17 April 1745, Linnean Correspondence 5, p. 484, Linnean Society of London.
17. Franklin to Colden, 15 August 1745, LPCC 3:143.
18. 7 April 1745, Boston Public Library.
19. Ibid.
20. JB to Colden, 4 October 1745, LPCC 3:158–60.
21. Gronovius to JB, 25 July 1744, MJB, pp. 350–51.
22. Ibid., p. 350; Gronovius to JB, 24 April 1745, American Philosophical Society Library.
23. Gronovius to JB, 25 July 1744, MJB, p. 351.
24. Gronovius to JB, 24 April 1745, American Philosophical Society Library.
25. Ibid.
26. Gronovius to JB, 2 "Juny" 1746, MJB, p. 355.
27. JB to Gronovius, 16 November 1745, American Philosophical Society Library.
28. JB to PC, 10 May 1762, MJB, p. 235.
29. JB to Mitchell, 3 June 1744, BP 1:27:4; Edmund Berkeley and Dorothy Smith Berkeley, *Doctor John Mitchell: The Man who Made the Map of North America*, pp. 1–29.
30. JB to Colden, 2 November 1744, LPCC 3:78–79.
31. Berkeley and Berkeley, *Mitchell*, pp. 54–62.
32. Ibid., pp. 47–53, 70–71.
33. Ibid., pp. 30–39; JB to Colden, 2 November 1744, LPCC 3:78–79.
34. JB to Colden, 2 November 1744, LPCC 3:78–79. Berkeley and Berkeley, *Mitchell*, pp. 65–71.
35. JB to Gronovius, 6 December 1745, MJB, p. 353.
36. For an account of Mitchell's life in England, see Berkeley and Berkeley, *Mitchell*.
37. JB to PC, 10 December 1745, BP 1:30:3.
38. October 1744, LPCC 3:94–95.
39. JB to Colden, 2 November 1744, ibid., pp. 78–79.
40. "Dissertatio Brevis de Principiis botanicorum . . . Conditorum . . . ," *Acta Physico-Medica Academae Caesarae . . . Ephemerides* 8 (1748):188–224.
41. JB to PC, March 1745, BP 1:29:2; JB to Colden, 7 April 1745, Boston Public Library, 15 July 1745, LPCC 3:132.
42. LPCC 3:129–32.

43. 6 October 1746, ibid., pp. 270–72.
44. Franklin to Colden, 10 July 1746, ibid., p. 226; Stearns, *Science*, p. 568.
45. Franklin, *Autobiography*, pp. 190–91.
46. 23 February 1747, Labaree, *Franklin*, 3:110.
47. 6 March 1746/47, LPCC 3:363.
48. Ibid., pp. 409–10, 414–15.
49. 30 January, BP 1:17:2. Incomplete in MJB, p. 180.

NOTES TO CHAPTER 9

1. Peter Kalm, *Peter Kalm's Travels in North America*, ed. Adolph B. Benson (hereafter cited as KT), 1:36.
2. KT 1:1.
3. Peter Kalm, *Kalm's Account of His Visit to England on His Way to America in 1748*, ed. Joseph Lucas.
4. KT 1:36–37.
5. KT 1:71–73.
6. KT 1:73–74.
7. KT 1:75–76.
8. KT 1:172–73.
9. KT 1:281.
10. Matti Kerkkonen, *Peter Kalm's North American Journey, Its Ecological Background and Results*, p. 94.
11. KT 2:739.
12. 8 August 1749, MJB, pp. 368–69.
13. Logan to PC, 28 February 1749/50, Labaree, *Franklin*, 3:468–70.
14. KT 1:63.
15. KT 1:xvii.
16. KT 1:62.
17. MJB, p. 371. The phrase "whom we are ready to tax with ingratitude" was omitted by Darlington. See original in BP 1:31:2.
18. 20 April, MJB, p. 377. J. R. Forster's English translation of Kalm's *Travels* was published in 1770–71. He presented a copy to the American Philosophical Society on 1 May 1772.
19. KT 1:61.
20. The bill is now in the American Philosophical Society Library.
21. Short, born in Scotland, moved to Sheffield, where he had a flourishing practice; 5 September 1751, *Pennsylvania Gazette*. It was reprinted in the summer of 1765, ibid., 13, 27 June, 4 July.
22. P. 287. This plant is also known as butter-and-eggs.
23. Stearns, *Science*, p. 590.
24. PC to JB, 13 February 1752/53, MJB, p. 191.
25. 10 March 1750, microfilm of Castle Dobbs Collection (at the University of North Carolina Library at Chapel Hill).
26. 5 May, Chicago Historical Society, 27 June, BP 3:100.
27. Dobbs to Collinson, 23 February 1749/50, Collinson Common

Place Book, p. 126, Linnean Society of London.

28. BP 3:101. The society had been founded in 1731 by Dobbs and others to promote the improvement of agriculture in Ireland. Alan R. Eager, librarian of the society, kindly sent the above extract. Surprisingly and unfortunately, the records of the society show no further communication to or from Bartram.

29. *Pennsylvania Gazette*, 21, 22 November 1744, 13 October 1748, 21, 28 February 1748/49.

30. 11 July, Labaree, *Franklin*, 4:6.

31. 18 July. Benjamin Smith Barton, "Memorandums Concerning the Earthquakes of North America," *Philadelphia Physical and Medical Journal* 1, pt. 1 (1804):65–67.

32. 1 August 1750, Historical Society of Pennsylvania.

33. 14 March 1752, New York Public Library. Bartram was quite capable of displaying the gift of descriptive eloquence for which his son William has been better known. This letter was quoted in *John and William Bartram's America*, ed. Helen Gere Cruikshank, and was mistakenly credited to the Historical Society of Pennsylvania.

34. V. A. Eyles, "The Extent of Geological Knowledge in the Eighteenth Century and the Methods by Which It Was Diffused," *Toward a History of Geology*, ed. Cecil J. Schneer, pp. 178–79. Also see George W. White, "Early American Geology," *The Scientific Monthly* 76 (1953):134–41. Not until 1742 was a geology course offered at the Jardin du Roi, and eleven years later one was established at Marischal College at the University of Aberdeen.

35. Richmond E. Myers, "Observations on Pennsylvania Geology and Minerals," *Proceedings of the Pennsylvania Academy of Science* 19 (1945):114.

36. Smith, *Linnaeus*, 2:174.

37. Extract of Bartram's letter made by Collinson, Linnean Society of London library.

38. Fothergill to JB, 22 February 1743/44, MJB, pp. 333–34.

39. 24 July 1744, MJB, pp. 337–38.

40. BP 4:16.

41. BP 1:30, incompletely quoted in MJB, pp. 338–39.

42. 4 October 1745, LPCC 3:158.

43. Mitchell to JB, 2 June 1747, MJB, p. 365.

44. 6 January 1746/47.

45. 7 November 1745, MJB, p. 329.

46. Ibid., JB to Colden, n.d., LPCC 3:179.

47. JB to Colden, 25 January 1745/46, Simon Gratz Autograph Collection, Historical Society of Pennsylvania.

48. Gronovius to Richard Richardson, 7 December 1739, Smith, *Linnaeus*, 2:189.

49. BP 4:43; JB to Gronovius, 30 November 1743, MJB, p. 349.

50. Gronovius to JB, 25 July 1744, MJB, pp. 349–50.

51. Colden to JB, 9 May 1746, MJB, p. 331. In his translation, Colden queried "Lakes of Canada," asking "is not this a mistake?"

52. 16 November 1745, Miscellaneous Manuscript Collection, American Philosophical Society library.

53. JB to Gronovius, 6 December 1745, MJB, pp. 352–53.

54. Gronovius to JB, 2 "Juny" 1746, MJB, p. 354.

55. Gronovius to JB, 26 June 1751, Smith College library (Helen A. Choate, ed., "An Unpublished Letter by Gronovius," *Torreya* 16:116–20).

56. J. F. Gronovius, *Index Suppellectilis Lapidae quam Collegit.* There is a copy of this rare book at the Library Company of Philadelphia. On the flyleaf is written "The Gift of Mr. John Bartram."

57. Björn Kurtén, *The Age of Dinosaurs*, pp. 176–77.

58. PC to JB, n.d. but probably 16 June 1751, MJB, p. 186.

59. "A Letter from Mr. John Bartram of Pensylvania to P. Collinson, Esq., F.R.S. in which there is a remarkable Conformity of Sentiments with the Author of some Physico-mechanical Conjectures on the Propagation of the shocks of Earthquakes (see p. 221) tho' it is impossible they could borrow one from another," *Gentleman's Magazine* 26 (1756):474.

60. 30 November 1752, MJB, pp. 359–60.

61. See note 59. The influence of the deluvialists, Dr. John Woodward and Bishop Thomas Burnet, was still strong.

62. 10 February 1756, MJB, p. 204.

63. JB to PC, 27 April 1755, BP 1:35:23.

64. JB to Garden, 14 March 1756, MJB, p. 393; Thomas B. Nolan, acting director of the Geological Survey, U.S. Department of the Interior, to Francis D. West, 1/17/55.

65. For the interesting rediscovery of this map among the Franklin Papers at the American Philosophical Society library, see the report of the committee on the library for 1973 (pp. 227–28).

66. William Wertenbaker, "Explorer" [Maurice Ewing], *New Yorker*, 18 November 1974, p. 60.

NOTES TO CHAPTER 10

1. JB to Alexander Catcott (1725–79), English clergyman and geologist, with whom he exchanged a few letters, 26 May 1742, MJB, p. 324.

2. JB to PC, 20 August 1753, MJB, p. 193.

3. JB's "Journal of Trip to Kattskills with Billy," BP 1:35:1–9. Unless otherwise indicated, references to this trip are from his journal.

4. Franklin to Colden, 25 October 1753, LPCC 4:143; Colden to Franklin, 19 November 1753, ibid., pp. 414–15.

5. This was near where the Catskill Mountain House was built many years later.

6. Years later Billy described this incident with interesting variations from his father's account: "Again, when in my youth, attending my father on a journey to the Catskill Mountains, in the government of New-York; having nearly ascended the peak of Giliad, being youthful and vigorous in the pursuit of botanical and novel objects, I had gained the summit of a steep rocky precipice, a-head of our guide, when, just entering a shady vale, I saw at the root of a small shrub, a singular and beautiful

appearance, which I remember to have instantly apprehended to be a large kind of Fungus which we call Jews ears, and was just drawing back my foot to kick it over, when at the instant, my father being near, cried out, a rattle snake my son, and jerked me back, which probably saved my life; I had never before seen this one, this was of the kind which our guide called a yellow one, it was very beautiful, speckled and clouded. My father plead for his life, but our guide was inexorable, saying he never spared the life of a rattle snake, and killed him; my father took his skin and fangs." William Bartram, *The Travels of William Bartram, Naturalist's Edition,* ed. Francis Harper, p. 169 (p. 270 in the original text).

7. William Martin Smallwood and Mabel S. C. Smallwood, *Natural History and the American Mind,* p. 89.

8. 25 (January 1755):82; BP 4:97.

9. See appendix 4.

10. 8 August 1763, BP 1:56:3.

11. PC to JB, 10 February 1760, BP 3:14.

12. 14 January 1754, Labaree, *Franklin,* 5:192.

13. Undated letter, MJB, p. 370.

14. *Philosophical Transactions* 48 (1754):499–503.

15. Pp. 188–93.

16. JB to PC, 22 January 1757, BP 1:45. Incomplete in MJB, pp. 211–12.

17. Ibid.

18. MJB, pp. 195–96.

19. MJB, p. 209.

20. London, 1751, p. 88.

21. 6 December 1766, MJB, p. 442.

22. Undated letter, JB to PC, BP 1:47. This letter evidently contained JB's letter of 16 December 1754 to J. F. Gronovius, now at the Linnean Society of London; David Colden to his mother, 10 September 1754, LPCC 9:142.

23. 13 February 1754, Labaree, *Franklin,* 5:197.

24. Edmund Berkeley and Dorothy Smith Berkeley, *Dr. Alexander Garden of Charles Town,* pp. 43–44.

25. Ibid., pp. 44–45.

26. 15 March 1755, Smith, *Linnaeus,* 1:286.

27. JB wrote on 12 October 1755, thanking Garden for a letter of 18 May, MJB, p. 390.

28. 19 July 1753, MJB, p. 193.

29. Thomas Harrison Montgomery, *A History of the University of Pennsylvania,* p. 532. Further references to the academy are from Montgomery unless otherwise indicated.

30. 27 April, MJB, p. 199.

31. 14 March 1756, MJB, p. 392.

32. 18 February 1756, MJB, p. 205.

33. *Gentleman's Magazine* 28 (1758):7–8, including remarks by Bartram.

34. PC to Linnaeus, 12 May 1756, Smith, *Linnaeus*, 1:39.
35. PC to JB, 28 May 1766, MJB, p. 280.
36. Oscar Theodore Barck, Jr., and Hugh Talmage Lefler, *Colonial America*, pp. 461–66.
37. JB to George Edwards, 27 January 1757, *Philadelphia Medical and Physical Journal* 1, part 2 (1805):18–19. The Indians' dogs fascinated the children. Their sharp-pointed ears convinced them that they were of the wolf breed.
38. JB to PC, 30 September 1763, MJB, p. 255.
39. MJB, pp. 198–99.
40. Franklin, *Autobiography*, pp. 167–72.
41. Ibid., pp. 174–75.
42. 10 July 1755, BP 1:34:2.
43. JB to PC, 18 October 1741, BP 1:23.
44. Albert Henry Smyth, *The Writings of Benjamin Franklin*, 2:282.
45. JB to PC, 28 September 1755, BP 1:35:27.
46. MJB, p. 372.
47. Smyth, *Franklin*, 3:60–61.
48. 20 September 1751 (?), MJB, p. 187.
49. Smyth, *Franklin*, 3:280.
50. Ibid., p. 281. Franklin was introducing not only Bartram but Francis Alison, vice provost of the academy. It is quite probable that he traveled north with the Bartrams, but this is not established.
51. JB to PC, 28 September 1755, MJB, p. 200; JB to Eliot, 24 January 1757, Yale University library.
52. JB to PC, n.d., BP 1:36.
53. JB to Philip Miller, 3 November 1756, BP 1:48.
54. JB to PC, 28 September 1755, MJB, p. 200.

NOTES TO CHAPTER 11

1. *Pennsylvania Gazette*, 20 November, 18, 25 December 1755, 1, 22 January, 19 February 1756.
2. 21 February 1756, MJB, p. 206.
3. 20 January 1756, MJB, p. 202.
4. PC to JB, 10 February 1756, MJB, p. 203.
5. JB to PC, 30 May 1756, MJB, p. 207.
6. *Pennsylvania Gazette*, 1 December 1748.
7. Ibid., 15 November 1750.
8. 25 September, MJB, p. 215.
9. PC to JB, 16 June 1751, MJB, pp. 184–85.
10. PC to JB, 22 September 1751, BP 3:7.
11. Hingston Fox, *John Fothergill*, pp. 172–73.
12. PC to JB, December 1751, BP 2:84.
13. PC to JB, n.d., BP 3:6. Darlington published part of this letter under the date of 13 February 1753 (MJB, pp. 190–92). It was almost cer-

tainly 1753/54 from references to JB's "dissertation on your Oaks and Hickories," about which he wrote on 20 August 1753 (MJB, p. 193): "I hope to send thee this fall. . . ."

14. MJB, p. 202.

15. Clipping in West Collection, Bartram Association papers, American Philosophical Society library.

16. 18 March 1757, BP 2:96. The incomplete letter in MJB, p. 214, does not mention Moses.

17. The Shoemaker family had emigrated from Germany in 1683, settling in Germantown. Samuel Shoemaker was a member of the Philadelphia Common Council (*Pennsylvania Magazine of History and Biography* 2 [1875]:35–36). His sister Sarah married Pennington (ibid. 25 [1911]:403n).

18. JB to PC, 29 July 1757, BP 1:44.

19. JB to PC, 11 November 1757, Academy of Natural Sciences, Philadelphia.

20. He may well have been one of the Darby children taught by a schoolmaster mentioned in the *Pennsylvania Gazette*, 13–20 June 1734: "A watchmaker who said he'd served his time in Va. was engaged by several Darby people to teach their children — ran around with [a] woman, got her pregnant, found in bed with her — forced to marry & took off presumably to N.Y. Public warned."

21. David L. Cowen, "A Store Mixt, Various, Universal," *The Journal of the Rutgers University Library* 25 (1961):5.

22. Harry B. Weiss and Grace M. Ziegler, *Thomas Say, Early American Naturalist*, pp. 19, 5–13.

23. Advertisement in the *Pennsylvania Gazette*, 20 May 1756.

24. Information kindly supplied by Dr. Whitfield J. Bell, Jr.

25. Leach, "Philadelphia Families," *North American.*

26. John Bartram's will, Will Book R, Philadelphia County, p. 277.

27. Leach, "Philadelphia Families."

28. JB to Garden, 14 March 1756, MJB, p. 392.

29. 23 (April 1753):200.

30. JB to PC, 8 July 1753, MJB, p. 194.

31. 20 August 1753, MJB, p. 193.

32. Descriptions of Native Trees, October 1753, BP 1:32:1, 1:41:1–14.

33. JB to Gronovius, 6 December 1753, West Collection, Bartram Association papers, American Philosophical Society library.

34. JB to Miller, 20 April 1755, MJB, p. 377.

35. See note 32.

36. PC to JB, 13 February 1753/54, MJB, pp. 189–90.

37. MJB, p. 196.

38. Ibid.

39. 16 December 1754, BP 1:35:17, incomplete in MJB, p. 197.

40. JB to PC, 16 December 1754, BP 1:47; *Gentleman's Magazine* 25, pp. 503–4, 550–51.

41. JB to Miller, 20 April 1755, MJB, p. 377.

42. PC to JB, 18 February 1756, MJB, p. 205.

43. 25 (September 1755):407–8.

44. 3 November, BP 1:48.

45. 29 July 1757, MJB, p. 402.

46. 11 November 1757, The Academy of Natural Sciences of Philadelphia, MS Coll. 15*.

47. JB to PC, 25 September 1757, MJB, p. 215.

48. JB to PC, 25 September 1757, BP 1:44:7.

49. The account that follows is based on "The Disownment of John Bartram," *Bulletin of the Friends Historical Association* 17 (1928):16–22.

50. 28 February–7 March, 14–21 March.

51. "Life and Character of the Chinese Philosopher Confucius in the hand Writing of John Bartram the Elder, the American Botanist Philosopher," MS, Gordon Lester Ford Collection, Pierpont Morgan Library.

52. BP 1:76, copy in the Friends' Historical Library, Swarthmore College.

53. Now in the library of the Earl of Derby at Knowsley Hall.

54. PC to JB, 6 April 1759, MJB, p. 218.

55. Garden to Colden, 4 November 1754, LPCC 4:471–73. Some twenty-two years after Bartram's death it was estimated that "there are 2,000 species of our native productions, contained in a space of six acres." Others have referred to six acres of garden. The figure of 2,000 would include some plants added by his sons after his death and may be exaggerated. On the other hand, it referred only to native plants, and Bartram had a very large number from abroad. (John William Harshberger, *The Botanists of Philadelphia*, p. 71.)

56. 3 May 1762, B.M. Add. MSS 21648, f. 129.

57. JB to Miller, 18 February 1759, John Bartram Association collection, American Philosophical Society library.

58. Kalm, *Kalm's Account*, p. 108.

59. JB to Miller, 20 April 1755, MJB, p. 376.

60. Ibid.

61. 28 August 1758, MJB, p. 389.

62. 18 February 1759, John Bartram Association collection, American Philosophical Society library.

63. Darlington thought that this was sent to Philip Miller rather than Collinson. See MJB, pp. 219, 383–88.

64. Ibid.

65. The following account comes from Bartram's partial journal of his trip, BP 1:54.

66. Fairfax Harrison, ed., "Mrs. Browne's Diary in Virginia and Maryland," *Virginia Magazine of History and Biography* 32 (1924):311–12n.

67. PC to JB, 29 May 1759, BP 2:49, 3 November 1759, MJB, p. 222.

68. *Pennsylvania Gazette*, 10 June 1762, 7 July 1763, 17 October 1765, 28 February 1760.

NOTES TO CHAPTER 12

1. Swem (*Brothers*, p. 137) and Ewan (*William Bartram*, p. 35) have both indicated that Bartram made this trip both ways on horseback. This is most improbable. He never mentioned collecting a plant between Philadelphia and Charles Town. Alexander Garden wrote to John Ellis (Smith, *Linnaeus*, 1:476) that Bartram "proposes to go to Cape Fear, and from thence home by land." He definitely went to Cape Fear from Charles Town by water (see his letter to Billy, June 1761, BP 1:39), and he borrowed a horse from his brother to ride home from there (letter to his brother William, n.d., BP 1:73).

2. Berkeley and Berkeley, *Garden*, p. 138.

3. Ibid., p. 152.

4. Elise Pinckney, *Thomas and Elizabeth Lamboll, Early Charleston Gardeners*, pp. 1–7; PC to JB, 22 May 1762, MJB, p. 236.

5. JB to PC, 22 May 1761, BP 1:53.

6. Mary Barbot Prior, "Letters of Martha Logan to John Bartram, 1760–1763," *South Carolina Historical Magazine* 59 (1958):38; Stearns, *Science*, p. 584.

7. JB to PC, 22 May 1761, BP 1:53.

8. PC to JB, 1 August 1761, MJB, pp. 230–31.

9. JB to PC, 10 May 1762, MJB, p. 235; Sarah Hopton to JB, 18 February 1762, BP 4:52.

10. Garden to John Ellis, 21 March 1760, Smith, *Linnaeus*, 1:476–78; JB to PC, 10 May 1762, BP 1:58.

11. JB to Billy, June 1761, BP 1:39.

12. Dobbs to JB, 13 December 1760, BP 3:102; Powell to JB, 10 March 1761, BP 4:99.

13. Francis D. West Papers, American Philosophical Society library; Saunders, *Colonial Records of North Carolina*, 22:271–72; Green to JB, 18 May 1761, BP 4:30.

14. Colonel Bartram's sister had died at Philadelphia about the time he went to Carolina (will of Elizabeth, dated 5 December 1732 and proved 5 May 1733, Chester County Wills).

15. Mary married Thomas Robeson and Sarah married Thomas Brown (Grimes, *North Carolina Wills and Inventories*, pp. 469–71). There is some uncertainty with regard to the stepdaughter. William Bartram wrote to John in 1761 (BP 1:73, n.d.) and referred to "My Son lw Anthony Gully." There is no evidence to suggest that William had any daughters other than Mary and Sarah or that either was ever married to Anthony Gully, ship captain and landowner. Elizabeth Locke Smith was a widow when she married William. A Bladen County will, witnessed by Elizabeth Bartram and Susanna Gully, suggests the existence of a stepdaughter, Susanna Smith. This supposition came to us from Mrs. Frank P. Hunter, Jr., a descendant of William's daughter, Mary Robeson.

16. JB to Billy, June (?) 1761, BP 1:39, 1 September 1761, New-York Historical Society; Colonel William Bartram to JB, n.d., BP 1:73.

17. There was no medical school in Philadelphia, but the Pennsylvania Hospital had been founded by Dr. Thomas Bond and Franklin in 1751. It was hoped that a medical school would eventually be started and associated with the hospital (Hingston Fox, *Fothergill*, p. 366).

18. Colonel William Bartram to JB, n.d., BP 1:75.

19. JB to PC, December 1744, MJB, p. 173.

20. Clayton to JB, 23 July 1760, MJB, pp. 406–7.

21. Clayton to JB, 30 August 1760, MJB, p. 408; Daniel B. Smith to William Darlington, MJB, p. 325n.

22. JB to PC, 30 September 1763, MJB, p. 254; Catesby, *Natural History*, 2:101.

23. JB to PC, 30 September 1763, MJB, p. 254; Clayton to JB, 30 August 1760, MJB, p. 408.

24. Berkeley and Berkeley, *Clayton*, pp. 128–38. Curious as it may seem, this quotation is from a letter written to Gronovius (10 September 1758, American Philosophical Society library), who was known by Collinson to have worked for years on a third part and to be considering a new edition. Yet Collinson made no comment whatever on this most unusual state of affairs.

25. PC to JB, 15 June 1763, BP 3:33; Clayton to JB, 1 September 1760, MJB, p. 408; Berkeley and Berkeley, *Clayton*, pp. 135–36, 212.

26. Berkeley and Berkeley, *Clayton*, pp. 83, 149; Clayton to JB, 25 February 1764, MJB, p. 411.

27. Clayton to JB, 23 February 1761, 23 July 1760, MJB, pp. 407–9.

28. JB made a note of plants "Sent Brother 1760" on the back of a letter dated 21 April 1760, which he had received from Nathaniel Powell, BP 4:98.

29. PC to JB, 15 September 1760, BP 3:17.

30. JB to PC, 22 May 1761, BP 1:53.

31. 17 September 1760, MJB, p. 58; JB to PC, 19 July 1761, MJB, p. 228.

32. Ellis to Garden, 8 April 1761, Smith, *Linnaeus*, 1:508.

33. JB to PC, 22 May 1761, BP 1:53.

34. JB to PC, 13 November 1758, Academy of Natural Sciences library; 24 June 1760, MJB, p. 224; JB to Miller, 18 February 1759, John Bartram Association papers, American Philosophical Society library.

35. JB to PC, 3 December 1762, BP 1:56:2, 1 May 1763, BP 1:59; PC to JB, 1 May 1763, BP 1:59.

36. JB to PC, 1 May 1764, BP 1:55, 8 August 1763, BP 1:56.

37. Charles R. Hildeburn, "Sir John St. Clair, Baronet," *Pennsylvania Magazine of History and Biography* 9 (1885):1–2, 12; *Pennsylvania Gazette*, 20 July 1758.

38. St. Clair to JB, 11 February 1761, BP 4:104.

39. Ibid.

40. St. Clair to JB, 27 February 1761, BP 4:105, 4 November 1761, BP 4:107.

41. Powell to JB, 10 March 1761, BP 4:99.

42. N.d., 1760, BP 1:73, n.d., probably April 1761, BP 1:75.

43. Billy to JB, 6, 20 May 1761, BP 1:68.

44. JB to PC, 22 May 1761, MJB, p. 227; Edwards to Billy, 15 November 1761, MJB, p. 420. Edwards had been grateful for the specimens sent to him by the Bartrams and in 1759 had sent John directions "for etching or engraving on copper plates, with aqua fortis." The specimens were included in Edwards' *Essays Upon Natural History, and other Miscellaneous Subjects*, published in 1770 (Ewan, *William Bartram*, p. 19).

45. BP 1:39.

46. Ibid.

47. MJB, pp. 412–13.

48. 6 July 1761, Royal Society of Arts archives, London.

49. Colonel William Bartram to JB, 5 August 1761, MJB, p. 415.

50. JB to Billy, 1 September 1761, New-York Historical Society library.

51. 14 August 1761, MJB, p. 232; JB to Eliot, n.d., Yale University library; "Specimens Sent by Captain Friends 1761," BP 4:107.

52. George Harrison Fisher, "Brigadier-general Henry Bouquet," *Pennsylvania Magazine of History and Biography* 3 (1879):121–43; Morton, *Colonial Virginia*, 2:739–40; PC to JB, 1 April 1762, MJB, pp. 233–34 and footnote.

53. John W. Jordan, ed., "Journal of James Kenny, 1761–1763," *Pennsylvania Magazine of History and Biography* 37 (1913):19–24. The account of Bartram's Fort Pitt visit is taken from Kenny's journal unless otherwise noted.

54. In Collinson's garden records, he noted: "Aristolochia scandens from the Ohio River; seed Collected by Bartram given Gordon who raised it in 1761. Called Aromatic Vine" (Dillwyn, *Hortus*, p. 4).

55. This road had been laid out for the Ohio Company by Nemolin, an Indian chief, under the direction of Thomas Cresap in 1750 (Emerson D. Fite and Archibald Freeman, *A Book of Old Maps Delineating American History*, p. 225).

56. JB to Eliot, n.d., but sometime in October 1761, Yale University library.

57. JB to Billy, 5 October–November? 1761, BP 1:51.

58. Bouquet to JB, 25 December 1761, Emmet 6266, New York Public Library, 3 February 1762, MJB, p. 425.

59. PC to JB, 5 October 1762, MJB, p. 241.

NOTES TO CHAPTER 13

1. JB to PC, 14 August 1761, MJB, p. 232.

2. Smallwood and Smallwood, *Natural History*, p. 89.

3. BP 3:37.

4. Norman G. Brett-James, *The Life of Peter Collinson*, pp. 51–54.

5. PC to JB, 25 February 1741/42, MJB, p. 141.

6. See note 4.

7. See appendix 6.
8. Ibid.
9. PC to JB, 1 April 1762, MJB, p. 233; JB to PC, n.d. but written in July 1762, BP 1:58:2. The nuts sent by Bouquet were probably of the Illinois hickory or pecan (*Carya olivaeformis* Nutt.).
10. JB to Billy, 27 December 1761, MJB, p. 421; Samuel Green to JB, 2 February 1762, BP 4:33.
11. Colonel William Bartram to JB, 11 June 1762, BP 1:77.
12. Barck and Lefler, *Colonial America*, p. 469.
13. PC to JB, 22 May 1762, MJB, p. 236; JB to PC, 3 December 1762, MJB, p. 242.
14. 3 December 1762, MJB, p. 243.
15. John Clayton and John Frederick Gronovius, *Flora Virginica*, pp. 3–4.
16. PC to JB, 25 July 1762, MJB, pp. 239–40.
17. 15 July 1762, MJB, p. 428.
18. James Wright to JB, 22 August 1762, B.M. Add. MSS 21,648, ff. 333–34, quoted by George Gaylord Simpson, "The Beginnings of Vertebrate Paleontology in North America," *Proceedings of the American Philosophical Society* 86 (1942):130–88.
19. 1 May 1763, BP 1:59, 3 December 1762, MJB, p. 243.
20. 27 December 1761, MJB, p. 420.
21. JB to PC, 10 May 1762, BP 1:58.
22. JB to PC, 13 January 1763, BP 1:66.
23. JB to PC, 29 August 1762, BP 1:56.
24. JB to "Moses or William Bartram at Cape Fear," 9 November 1762, MJB, pp. 422–23; Colonel William Bartram to JB, 18 May 1761, BP 1:69; Garden to JB, 15 February 1762, BP 2:4:1.
25. JB to Eliot, 1 December 1762, Yale University Library.
26. JB to Moses or Billy, 9 November 1761, MJB, pp. 422–23.
27. Ibid.; T. J. Kirkland and R. M. Kennedy, *Historic Camden*, p. 51; JB to Moses or Billy, 9 November 1762, MJB, p. 422.
28. JB to PC, 19 August 1764, BP 1:55:4.
29. PC to JB, 23 February 1763, MJB, p. 246.
30. JB to Moses or Billy, 9 November 1762, MJB, pp. 422–23; JB to PC, 8 August 1763, BP 1:56:3.
31. Daniel Solander identified from Bartram's specimens sent to Collinson "*Aesculus Hippocastanum* Linn., *Aesculus pavia* Linn., and *Aesculus media*," the last "not taken notice of by Dr. Linnaeus"; JB to PC, 13 January 1763, BP 1:66.
32. Ibid.; JB to Eliot, 1 December 1762, Yale University library.
33. JB to Moses or Billy, 9 November 1762, MJB, p. 423.
34. JB to PC, 13 January 1763, BP 1:66.
35. PC to JB, 23 February 1763, MJB, p. 246.
36. JB to Eliot, 30 January 1763, Yale University library.
37. PC to JB, 10 May 1763, BP 3:41. Daniel Carl Solander (1736–82), student of Linnaeus.
38. Dillwyn, *Hortus*, p. 18.

39. Billy to JB, 20 May 1761, BP 1:68; JB to Billy, June 1761, BP 1:39; PC to JB, 25 July 1762, MJB, p. 239.

40. JB to PC, 29 August 1762, BP 1:56; PC to JB, 5 October, 10 December 1762, MJB, pp. 241–44.

41. PC to JB, 11 March, 10 May, 8, 30 June 1763; JB to PC, 6 January, 1 May 1763; all in MJB, pp. 245–51.

42. PC to JB, 6 December 1763, MJB, p. 258; PC postscript on letter of Daniel Solander to JB, 17 April 1763, BP 4:103.

43, 30 June 1764, BP 3:53.

44. John Bartram, "Diary of A Journey Through the Carolinas, Georgia and Florida from July 1, 1765, to April 10, 1766," annotated by Francis Harper, *Transactions of the American Philosophical Society*, n.s. 33, pt. 1 (1942), p. 104.

45. 4 August 1763, MJB, p. 252.

46. 7 April 1763, MJB, p. 248.

47. JB to Eliot, 1 December 1762, Yale University library.

48. 2 June 1763, Smith, *Linnaeus*, 1:316.

49. William Logan was a lawyer and member of the governor's council, 1747–75; JB to Eliot, 30 January 1763, Yale University library.

50. JB to PC, 8 August 1763, BP 1:56.

51. Barck and Lefler, *Colonial America*, p. 491.

52. JB to PC, 23 October 1763, MJB, p. 255, 4 March 1764, MJB, p. 261.

53. JB to PC, 30 September, MJB, pp. 254–55.

54. JB to PC, 11 November 1763, 4 March 1764, PC to JB, 6 December 1763, MJB, pp. 256, 258, 262.

55. 1 June 1764, MJB, p. 264.

56. JB to PC, 23 September 1764, MJB, p. 266.

57. Samuel N. Rhoads, ed., *Botanica Neglecta: William Young, Jr.*, Preface; Garden to Ellis, 12 April, 25 July 1761, Smith, *Linnaeus*, 1:506, 512.

58. Johann David Schoef, *Travels in the Confederation, 1783–84*, trans. Alfred J. Morison, p. 37.

59. JB to PC, 23 September, 15 October 1764, MJB, pp. 266–67.

60. Franklin to PC, 24 September 1764, Labaree, *Franklin*, 9:352–53.

61. JB to Louisa Ulrica Drotting, Queen of Sweden, 23 September 1764, University of Uppsala library.

62. 15 October 1764, MJB, p. 267.

63. 24 September 1764, Labaree, *Franklin*, 11:353. It may have been that it was Young's Germanic origins which appealed to the queen.

64. Copy of undated letter in West deposit, Bartram Association papers, American Philosophical Society library.

65. John Brett Langstaff, *Doctor Bard of Hyde Park*, p. 71; Hope to JB, 4 November 1763, MJB, pp. 432–33. Bard, an apprentice of Dr. Kearsley, had practiced in Philadelphia until 1746, when he moved to New York. His son became one of the founders of the medical school connected with King's College and General Washington's physician after the revolution.

66. Langstaff, *Bard*, p. 77.
67. JB to Hope, 4 October 1764, MJB, pp. 433–34.
68. MJB, pp. 434–35.
69. Hope to JB, 23 March 1771, MJB, p. 435; PC to JB, 10 April, MJB, p. 287.
70. JB to PC, 22 November 1764, MJB, pp. 267–68.
71. Franklin to JB, 14 February 1765, Labaree, *Franklin*, 12:61–62.
72. Mrs. Franklin to her husband, 8 January 1765, ibid., pp. 15–16.
73. Leach, "Old Families," *North American*, and advertisements in the *Pennsylvania Gazette*.
74. JB to Archibald Bartram, 1761, MJB, pp. 416–18. De Crèvecoeur reported that JB told him that the gilt-framed coat-of-arms hanging in his hall had been brought from England (MJB, p. 49).

NOTES TO CHAPTER 14

1. The following account of Crèvecoeur's visit is taken from his *Letters*, Letter XI, "From Mr. IW-N AL-Z, a Russian Gentleman; describing the visit he paid at my request to Mr. John Bertram, the celebrated Pennsylvanian Botanist," pp. 182–97. At one time this account was thought to be fictional, but there can no longer be any question that Crèvecoeur himself did visit Bartram in the spring of 1765. Crèvecoeur referred to this visit in a letter to Bartram's sons, John and William, a few years later (Earnest, *John and William Bartram*, p. 14). Bartram also referred to his "Friend St. John" in a letter to Bernard de Jussieu, 25 April 1765, now at the Laboratoire de Phanérogamie, Muséum National d'Histoire Naturelle, Paris. We are indebted to J. Mercier who kindly sent us a copy of this letter. Although Crèvecoeur certainly exercised some literary license in recording his recollections of his visit, he gave the only lengthy contemporary description of the Bartram household extant. He mentioned Bartram's appointment as King's Botanist, but he learned of this after his visit. For an interesting account of Crèvecoeur's life, see Henry L. Bourdin, Ralph H. Gabriel, and Stanley T. Williams, *Sketches of Eighteenth Century America*, pp. 1–13.
2. JB to Bernard de Jussieu, 25 April 1765; see note 1.
3. This reference was presumably to Harvey, whose grave is at the bottom of Bartram's garden near the river (Cheston, *John Bartram*, p. 23).
4. 25 April 1765; see note 1. J. Mercier wrote us that the catalogue of their herbarium mentions many collections of Pennsylvania and Philadelphia in addition to those identified as Bartram specimens.
5. JB to Billy, 19 May 1765, MJB, p. 424.
6. Franklin to JB, 14 February 1765, Labaree, *Franklin*, 12:61–62.
7. JB to Billy, 19 May 1765, MJB, p. 424.
8. Ibid.
9. 11 April, 9, 23 May 1765.
10. MJB, pp. 268–69.
11. PC to JB, May [1765], MJB, pp. 269–70.

12. PC to JB, 13 November 1765, MJB, p. 273.

13. 1 June 1765, BP 4:58.

14. 15 July 1765, Smith, *Linnaeus*, 1:537–38.

15. 19 September 1765, MJB, p. 271.

16. JB to Billy, 7 June 1765, MJB, pp. 424–25; PC to JB, 19 September 1765, MJB, p. 271.

17. The following account, unless otherwise noted, is taken from Bartram's diary, edited by Harper.

18. Mrs. St. Julien Ravenel, *Charleston, the Place and the People*, pp. 158–59.

19. Moultrie later became lieutenant-governor of East Florida, where he lived for many years.

20. Garden to Ellis, 15 July 1765, Smith, *Linnaeus*, 1:536–38.

21. 19 September 1765, MJB, p. 271.

22. Garden to Ann Bartram, 29 August 1765, "Letters Colonial and Revolutionary," *Pennsylvania Magazine of History and Biography* 42 (1918):76–77.

23. MJB, p. 272.

NOTES TO CHAPTER 15

1. Unless otherwise noted, the account of Bartram's travels given in this chapter is based on his diary, edited by Harper.

2. JB to PC, 19 August 1764, MJB, p. 265.

3. MJB, pp. 425–26.

4. Bartram's description was "the first scientific account of these giant fossil oysters. It was not until nearly 70 years later that they were given the technical name of *Ostrea georgiana* by Conrad" (Harper, Bartram's "Diary," pp. 25, 65).

5. Ibid., p. 28.

6. Franklin, *Autobiography*, pp. 130–31.

7. *Travels through North and South Carolina, Georgia, East and West Florida*, 1792 Facsimile, Introduction by Gordon De Wolf, p. 466.

8. The river for which the plant was named is today spelled Altamaha. For an interesting account of the tree, see Charles F. Jenkins, "The Historical Background of Franklin's Tree," *Pennsylvania Magazine of History and Biography* 57 (1933):193–208.

9. Harper had made clear that Billy returned home in 1777, not 1778, as had been widely believed (William Bartram, *Travels*, p. 422).

10. This "is perhaps the earliest extant reference to the Ogeechee lime (*Nyssa ogeche*)" (Harper, Bartram's "Diary," p. 67).

11. Ibid., p. 33.

12. PC to JB, 28 December 1765, MJB, p. 274.

13. N.d., MJB, p. 400.

14. 12 February 1766, MJB, p. 399.

15. Isaac to his father, 15 August 1765, New-York Historical Society library.

16. PC to JB, 28 May 1766, MJB, pp. 279–80.

17. Billy gave an elaborate account of killing a large rattlesnake at the request of the Seminole Indians (Harper, *Travels*, pp. 164–65).

18. Many years later Billy wrote that his father "received his orders to serch for the Sources of the great River St. Juan." He did not indicate whether these orders came from Governor Grant or from England and he was frequently inaccurate ("Some Account of the Late Mr. John Bartram").

19. Barck and Lefler, *Colonial America*, p. 526.

NOTES TO CHAPTER 16

1. This account of the Bartrams' travels continues to be based on Bartram's diary, edited by Harper, except where otherwise noted.

2. If these were Kentucky coffee trees, *Gymnocladus dioica* (L.) Koch, called by Linnaeus *Guilandina dioica* in his *Species Plantarum* (1753), they were well south of their present-day range. They may well have been introduced by the Indians from the Mississippi valley, as suggested by Harper, Bartram's "Diary," p. 89. Although Dr. Yeats appears to have started this trip with the Bartrams, there is no further reference to him.

3. *Ximenia americana* L., also known as tallowwood,

4. Lamboll to JB, 16 February 1761, BP 4:60.

5. Charles L. Mowat, "The Tribulations of Denys Rolle," *Florida Historical Quarterly* 23 (1944):1–3; Lamboll to JB, 15 September 1764, MJB, p. 436.

6. *The Scots Magazine* 28 (1766):50.

7. Harper, *Travels of William Bartram*, p. 630.

8. This is thought to have been the first written report of the Florida wood rat, *Neotoma floridana floridana*, which was not fully described until George Ord did so in 1818 (Harper, Bartram's "Diary," p. 72).

9. Bartram later sent Collinson a description of this tree, with a drawing of the seed pod and some leaves. These were given to John Ellis, to whom one of two recognized species is now credited, *Illicium floridanum* Ellis, the star anise. Ellis recognized the plant as another species of the tree first reported by Kaempfer from Japan and was soon corresponding with Linnaeus and others about it. In December 1770 Ellis wrote to William Aiton concerning an attempt to grow the tree at Kew and called attention to Bartram's statement that it would stand severe frost. By 1774, Fothergill had "a good many plants of the *Illicium*" growing and was pleased by its "most grateful fragrance." (PC to Billy, 28 July 1767, MJB, p. 291; Ellis to Linnaeus, Smith, *Linnaeus*, 1:211, 242, 245, 252; Ellis' letter to Aiton was quoted in the notes of Carlotta Herring-Browne, now at the Historical Society of Pennsylvania; Fothergill to JB, 8 September 1774, MJB, p. 348.)

10. These taros (*Colocasia antiquorum* ?) from the Far East were thriving under cultivation and even escaping into the marshes.

11. JB to PC, June, 26 August 1766, MJB, pp. 281, 283.

12. JB to Billy, 5 April 1766, BP 1:62; Harper, Bartram's "Diary," p. 76.

13. Harper, Bartram's "Diary," p. 49; PC to JB, 28 May 1766, MJB, p. 279; JB to Billy, 5 April 1766, BP 1:62.

14. JB to Billy, 5 April 1766, BP 1:62.

15. Ibid.; JB to Billy, 9 April 1766, New-York Historical Society library.

16. JB to Billy, 5 April 1766, BP 1:62, 9 April 1766, New-York Historical Society library.

17. See note 16.

18. JB to Billy, 9 April 1766, New-York Historical Society library.

19. Ibid.; JB to PC, June 1766, MJB, p. 281.

20. JB to Billy, 3 July 1766, New-York Historical Society library.

21. Laurens to JB, 9 August 1766, MJB, pp. 438–42.

22. Laurens to Billy, 17 September 1766, University of Florida library.

23. PC to JB, 28 May 1766, MJB, p. 279; JB to PC, 26 August, 5 December 1766, MJB, pp. 283, 285.

24. *The Scots Magazine* 28 (1766):541; *The Gentleman's Magazine* 36 (1767):166–69.

25. PC to JB, 3 February 1767 (?), BP 3:80.

26. MJB, p. 291.

27. PC to JB, 19 September 1767, MJB, p. 293.

28. P. 202.

29. Pp. 173–74.

NOTES TO CHAPTER 17

1. JB to PC, June 1766, BP 1:49d; PC to JB, Jr., 20 March 1766, MJB, p. 275.

2. PC to JB, 26 March, 28 May 1766, MJB, pp. 276, 279.

3. JB to PC, June 1766, MJB, p. 281; PC to JB, 21 August 1766, MJB, p. 282; James Britten, *The Sloane Herbarium*, ed. J. E. Dandy, p. 89.

4. PC to JB, 10 April 1767, 28 May 1766, MJB, pp. 287, 279; JB to PC, 5 December 1766, MJB, p. 285.

5. 31 July, Thomas Penn Letterbook 3, p. 366, Historical Society of Pennsylvania library; Deed Book D36, Philadelphia County, p. 20.

6. Ibid. Isaac and Moses had purchased a nine-acre tract and other land jointly on 29 June and 21 July 1767 from the estate of Lloyd Zachary, possibly for the raising of medicinal plants (Deed Book D65, Philadelphia County, pp. 274–76).

7. Lamboll to Billy, 28 April 1767, Pinckney, *Lamboll*, p. 35; nothing is known about what disposition Billy had made of his slaves or the equipment that his father had bought, or about the destination of the ship or its wreck.

8. Pinckney, *Lamboll*, p. 35.

9. MJB, pp. 287–88.

10. MJB, pp. 288–91.

11. PC to JB, 25 December 1767, MJB, p. 296.

12. PC to JB, 29 February 1768, BP 3:75.

13. PC to Billy, 16 February 1768, MJB, pp. 296–97.
14. PC to JB, 17 February 1768, MJB, p. 298; *Gentleman's Magazine* 37 (1767):391–93.
15. PC to JB, 6 July 1768, MJB, p. 300.
16. PC to Billy, 19 July 1768, MJB, pp. 300–302.
17. 11 June 1762, MJB, p. 237.
18. PC to JB, 29 February 1768, BP 3:75.
19. N.d., Bennett to Dr. David van Royen, BPL 1900, University of Leiden library. Collinson referred to Bennett as "very curious and industrious in procuring seeds and plants from abroad." He moved his "extensive greenhouses" to Whitechapel when the machinery at the Shadwell water works was "deleterious" to them (Hadfield, *Gardening*, p. 227).
20. Wilfred Blunt, *The Art of Botanical Illustration*, p. 151.
21. PC to JB, 21 August 1766, MJB, p. 282.
22. PC to Colden, 25 February 1764, LPCC 6:290.
23. Dillwyn, *Hortus*, p. vii.
24. Franklin to JB, 9 January (with postscript of 28 January) 1769, Labaree, *Franklin*, 16:9–10.
25. JB to Franklin, 10 April 1769, ibid., pp. 109–11.
26. Gratz Collection (European Physicians), Case 12, Box 20, Historical Society of Pennsylvania library.
27. John Coakley Lettsom, *Memoirs of John Fothergill, M.D*, p. 41.
28. See note 26.
29. Fothergill to JB, 1 May 1769, MJB, p. 340.
30. JB to Fothergill, 26 November 1769, British Museum (Natural History).
31. Michael Collinson to JB, 1 March 1770, 28 June 1771, MJB, pp. 446–47, 449–50.
32. Fothergill to JB, 1 May 1769, MJB, p. 340, 13 January 1770, BP 4:19; JB to Fothergill, 10 June 1770, British Museum (Natural History).
33. JB to Fothergill, 26 November 1769, British Museum (Natural History).
34. Fothergill to JB, September 1772 (?), BP 4:18.
35. Fothergill to JB, 1 May 1769, MJB, pp. 339–40; JB to Fothergill, 12 August 1769, British Museum (Natural History). Fothergill had paid Purver "£1000 for the copyright and had it printed at his own expense" (Fox, *Fothergill*, p. 27).
36. Fothergill to JB, 19 March 1770, MJB, p. 343; JB to Fothergill, 26 November 1769, British Museum (Natural History).
37. Franklin to JB, 9 January 1769, MJB, p. 403; JB to Franklin, 10 April 1769, Labaree, *Franklin*, 16:109–11; Franklin to JB, 9 July 1769, MJB, p. 403.
38. 29 November 1769, Labaree, *Franklin*, 16:249–50; it is unfortunate that Collinson's copy was not published, for it was more detailed and completely frank. Bartram's rough copy at the Historical Society of Pennsylvania lacks the East Florida description.
39. JB to Franklin, 29 November 1769, Labaree, *Franklin*, 16:249.
40. MJB, p. 445.

41. Wrangel to JB, 2 July 1769, MJB, pp. 444–45.

42. Ibid.

43. Archives of the Linnean Society of London. See appendix 8 for extract from the letter.

44. Brooke Hindle, *The Pursuit of Science in Revolutionary America, 1735–1789*, pp. 119–21, 273.

45. Ibid., pp. 122–24, 128; for an interesting account of the rivalry between the two societies and their eventual union, see also pp. 129–40.

46. JB to Billy, 25 April 1771, B.C692.1, Collinson-Bartram Papers, American Philosophical Society library; JB to Billy, 21 July 1771, Z10–18, 1:159, College of Physicians of Philadelphia library.

47. JB to Wrangel, 6 July 1771, Royal Swedish Academy of Sciences.

48. Family Bible record of Colonel Bartram's death; JB to Billy, 25 April 1771 (see note 46); account book, Robeson Papers of Mary Bartram Robeson Hunter.

49. JB to Wrangel, 6 July 1771, Royal Swedish Academy of Sciences.

50. Will of James Bartram, Chester County Historical Society library.

51. Will of John Bartram, dated 17 January 1772, Will Book R, Philadelphia County, p. 277; JB to Billy, 21 July 1771, Z10–18, 1:159, College of Physicians of Philadelphia library; JB to Franklin, 29 April 1771, Franklin Papers, American Philosophical Society library.

52. 17 July 1771, Jared Sparks, *The Works of Benjamin Franklin*, 7:534–35.

53. 21 July 1773, MJB, p. 456.

54. Michael Collinson to JB, 15 August 1771, MJB, pp. 450–51, 8 January 1773, BP 3:82.

55. William Bartram's "Common Place Book and Original M.S. Notes of William Bartram circa 1760–1800, Philadelphia, Pa.," deposited in the library of the American Philosophical Society by Mrs. John A. Robinson, a direct descendant of John Bartram.

56. JB to Billy, 15 July 1772, photostat at the Historical Society of Pennsylvania library.

57. Fothergill to JB, undated (probably October 1772), MJB, pp. 343–46.

58. BP 4:23, 26.

59. Harper, William Bartram's *Travels*, pp. xix–xx.

60. 23 March, MJB, pp, 435–36.

61. JB to Franklin, 24 November 1770, Franklin Papers 3, 34, American Philosophical Society library.

62. Franklin to JB, 22 August 1772, Salford Public Libraries, Salford (England).

63. Franklin to JB, 17 October 1772, Haverford College library.

64. Franklin to JB, 10 February 1773, MJB, p. 405.

65. 7 April 1773, Gratz Collection, Historical Society of Pennsylvania library.

66. Lamboll to Billy, 9 November 1773, Pinckney, *Lamboll*, pp. 36–37.

67, Chalmers to Billy, 17 May 1774, MJB, pp. 464–65; Chalmers to JB, 12 July 1774, BP 4:104.

68. 8 September, MJB, pp. 347–48.

69. Freeman to JB, "12 mo. 18th 1774," and "7 mo. 15th, 1775," MJB, pp. 462–63.

70. 22 September 1774, MJB, pp. 459–60.

71. Franklin to JB, 27 May 1777, MJB, p. 406.

72. Loan made 11 August 1774, note now in the Rush MSS 34, p. 96, Library Company of Philadelphia deposit in the Historical Society of Pennsylvania; Dr. Rush to his wife, 14 April 1777, also in the Rush MSS.

73. 27 March 1775, BP 1:78.

74. Harper, William Bartram's *Travels*, p. 276.

75. Ibid., pp. 295–96.

76. Among the Bartram papers at the Historical Society of Pennsylvania are two copies of this, one incomplete, in John's handwriting, and the other, complete, in Billy's handwriting (BP 1:102).

77. MJB, pp. 43–44, based on "records of the American Philosophical Society."

78. West Manuscripts, John Bartram Association deposit, American Philosophical Society library.

79. Will Book R, Philadelphia County, p. 277.

NOTES TO CHAPTER 18

1. William Henry Dillingham, *Tribute to the Memory of Peter Collinson*, p. 14.

2. 3 November 1754, MJB, p. 197.

3. See bibliography.

4. *Studies on the Comparative Ethology of Digger Wasps of the Genus Bembix*, p. 18.

5. Harper, "Diary," pp. 16, 20.

6. 10 February 1756, MJB, p. 204.

7. JB to Colden, 7 April 1745, Boston Public Library.

8. JB to Linnaeus, n.d., Fall 1769, Linnean Society of London archives.

9. BP 1:35:17.

10. MJB, p. 199.

11. 12 October 1755, MJB, p. 392.

12. JB to PC, 30 June 1763, MJB, p. 251.

13. 25 March, MJB, p. 398.

14. For a very good account of Bartram's children and grandchildren, see Leach, "Philadelphia Families," *North American*.

15. Anonymous, "Trees and Pleasure Grounds in Pennsylvania," *The Horticulturist* 5 (1850):251–55.

16. Francois de Barbé-Marbois, *Our Revolutionary Forefathers: The Letters of the Marquis Francois de Barbé-Marbois*, p. 132.

17. The manuscript "Catalogue" is now in the archives of the Hunt Institute for Botanical Documentation. The printed catalogue of trees and

shrubs was referred to by Humphry Marshall in his *Arbustum Americanum.* This is probably the item (#467) listed by Anne-Marie Bidal in her *Inventoire des Archives du Muséum National d'Histoire Naturelle* (Paris, 1934) as "*Catalogue d'arbres, d'arbustes et de plantes qui croissent en Amerique et produisent des graines en maturité dans le jardin de John Bartram, près de Philadelphie . . .*" (1783), a single sheet imprint. We are indebted to J. Mercier, of the Laboratoire de Phanérogamie, Muséum National d'Histoire Naturelle, for sending us a copy.

18. William Parker Cutler and Julia Perkins Cutler, eds., *Life, Journals and Correspondence of the Rev. Manasseh Cutler, L.L.D.*, 1:272–74.

19. 17 January, Thomas Jefferson, *Thomas Jefferson's Garden Book*, ed. Edwin Morris Betts, pp. 109–10, 5 April 1802, pp. 279–80.

20. André Michaux, "Portions of the journal of André Michaux, botanist . . .," intro. and annotation by C. S. Sargent, *Proceedings of the American Philosophical Society* 26 (19 October 1888):57, 58, 68, 101, 103; Ulysses Prentiss Hedrick, *A History of Horticulture in America to 1860*, p. 16.

21. Joseph Ewan, "William Bartram's Hidden Role . . .," *Actes du XIe Congrès International d'Histoire des Sciences* 5 (1968):57.

22. Catalogue of the "Kingsessing Botanic Gardens" by John Bartram, Jr., pp. 6–7.

23. Cheston, *Bartram*, p. 24; Harshberger, *Botanists of Philadelphia*, pp. 69–71.

24. William Wynne, "Some Account of the Nursery Gardens and the State of Horticulture in the Neighborhood of Philadelphia," *Gardener's Magazine* (London) 8 (June 1832):272–73.

25. MJB, p. iv. When Carlotta Herring-Browne was in London, she found some notes on the recollections of John Jay Smith (1892) in the Friends' Reference Library. Smith noted that he had been looking for autographs and was given permission to check over the Bartram correspondence before Dr. Darlington "had conceived the happy idea of marketing its contents." The letters were "found in a little garret over the seed room, into which a stove pipe had for an age penetrated, smoking the paper terribly . . ." (West papers, American Philosophical Society library).

26. Harshberger, *Botanists of Philadelphia*, pp. 71–74.

27. Thomas Meehan, "John Bartram's Wood-shed," *Meehan's Monthly* 6 (1896):17; Meehan, *Ornamental Trees*, pp. 69, 127, 154.

28. Harshberger, *Botanists of Philadelphia*, pp. 74–75.

29. William Jay Youmans, *Pioneers of Science in America*, p. 39; "John Bartram," *Meehan's Monthly* 1 (1891):31.

30. Samuel N. Baxter, "Restoration of Plants in Bartram's Garden by the Fairmount Park Commission of Philadelphia," *Bartonia*, supp. to #12 (1931):40.

31. Cheston, *Bartram*, pp. 31–32.

32. Personal communication.

Literature Cited

I. IMPORTANT BARTRAM REPOSITORIES

Academy of Natural Sciences of Philadelphia
American Philosophical Society Library: Bartram Association Deposit, Bartram-Collinson Papers, Franklin Papers, Miscellaneous manuscripts and microfilms
British Museum (Natural History)
Historical Society of Pennsylvania: Bartram Papers, Maria Dickinson Collection, Dreer Collection, Simon Gratz Collection, Logan Papers, Thomas Penn Letter Books, and other manuscripts
New-York Historical Society: Bartram Folder
Royal Society of London Archives
Yale University Library: Jared Eliot Collection

II. OTHER MANUSCRIPT COLLECTIONS

Arnold Arboretum
Boston Public Library
British Museum Library
Chester County (Pennsylvania) Court Records
Chester County Historical Society
Chicago Historical Society
College of Physicians of Philadelphia
Erlangen-Nürnberg University: Jean Ambrose Beurer Papers
Friends House Library, London
Haverford College
Hunt Institute for Botanical Documentation
Knowsley Hall collection in the possession of the Earl of Derby
Library Company of Philadelphia
Lichfield (England) Joint Record Office
Linnean Society of London archives
Muséum National d'Histoire Naturelle, Paris

New York Public Library
Philadelphia County Court Records
Pierpont Morgan Library
Royal Society of Arts (London)
Royal Swedish Academy of Sciences
Salford (England) Public Library
Smith College Library
Swarthmore College, Friends Historical Library
University of Amsterdam
University of Florida
University of Leiden
University of Oxford: Sherardian Collection, Bodleian Library
University of Uppsala

III. Printed Materials

Alston, Charles. "On the Sexes of Plants." *Gentleman's Magazine* 24 (1754): 465–66.
American Philosophical Society. "Manuscript Minutes of its Meetings." *Proceedings of the American Philosophical Society* 22 (1884–85):1–711.
Anonymous. "The Disownment of John Bartram." *Bulletin of the Friends Historical Association* 17 (Spring 1928):16–22.
———."Letters Colonial and Revolutionary." *Pennsylvania Magazine of History and Biography* 42 (1918):76–77.
——— ("A Massachusetts Subscriber"). "Trees and Pleasure Grounds in Pennsylvania." *The Horticulturist* 5 (1850):251–55.
Bacon, Edgar Mayhew. *The Hudson River.* New York, 1902.
Barbé-Marbois, Francois Marquis de. *Our Revolutionary Forefathers, the Letters of Francois, Marquis de Barbé-Marbois.* New York, 1929.
Barck, Oscar Theodore, and Lefler, Hugh Talmage. *Colonial America.* New York, 1958.
Barnhart, John Hendley. "Bartram Bibliography." *Bartonia*, supplement to #12 (31 December 1931):51–67.
Barnwell, Joseph W., ed. "The Tuscarora Expedition." *South Carolina Historical and Genealogical Magazine* 9 (January 1908):28–54.
Bartram, John. "Additional Observations on the Cicada Septendecim. By the late Mr. John Bartram. From a MS. in the possession of the editor." Edited by B. S. Barton. *Medical and Physical Journal* 1, pt. 1 (1804):56–59.
———. "A Description of the Great Black Wasp, from Pensylvania, as communicated from Mr. John Bartram, to Mr. Peter Collinson, F.R.S." *Philosophical Transactions* 46 (1749):278–79.
———. "A further Account of the Libellae or May-flies, from Mr. John Bartram of Pensylvania, communicated by Mr. Peter Collinson, F.R.S." *Philosophical Transactions* 46 (1750):400–402.
———. "A Letter from John Bartram, M.D. to Peter Collinson, F.R.S. concerning a Cluster of small teeth observed by him at the Root of each

Fang or Great tooth in the Head of a Rattle-Snake, upon dissecting it." *Philosophical Transactions* 41 (1740):358–59.

———. "A Letter from Mr. John Bartram of Pensylvania, to P. Collinson, Esq., F.R.S. in which there is a remarkable Conformity of Sentiments with the Author of some Physico-mechanical Conjectures on the Propagation of the shocks of Earthquakes (see p. 221) tho' it is impossible they could borrow one from another." *Gentleman's Magazine* 26 (October 1756):474–75.

——— (with William Stork). *An Account of East-Florida with a Journal kept by John Bartram of Philadelphia, Botanist to His Majesty for the Floridas; upon a Journey from St. Augustine up the River St. John's.* London, 1766; 2d ed., 1767; 3d ed., including a plant list by John Ellis, 1769; 4th ed., 1774; reimpression by *Florida Mirror* (of 1767 ed.), 1881.

———. "An Account of some very curious Wasps' Nests made of Clay in Pensilvania; by Mr. John Bartram: Communicated by Mr. Peter Collinson, F.R.S." *Philosophical Transactions* 43 (1745):363–65.

———. "An extract of Mr. Wm. [*sic*] Bartram's observations in a journey up the River Savannah in Georgia, with his son, on discoveries." *Gentleman's Magazine* 37 (April 1767):166–68.

———. "Diary of a Journey Through the Carolinas, Georgia, and Florida from July 1, 1765, to April 10, 1766." Annotated by Francis Harper. *Transactions of the American Philosophical Society*, n.s. 33, pt. 1 (December 1942):1–120.

———. "Extract of a Letter from Dr. John Bartram, to Mr. Peter Collinson, F.R.S. containing some Observations Concerning the Salt-Marsh Muscle, the Oyster Banks, and the Fresh-Water Muscle of Pennsylvania." *Philosophical Transactions* 43 (1744):157–59.

———. "Extract of a Letter from Mr. John Bartram, of Philadelphia, to Benjamin Franklin, Ll.D. F.R.S. relating to a remarkable Aurora Borealis." *Philosophical Transactions* 52 (1762):97.

———. "Indian Physick." In Richard Saunders, *Poor Richard's Almanac*, Preface. Philadelphia, 1741.

———. Preface and Appendix to *Medicina Britannica*. 3d ed. by Thomas Short. Philadelphia, 1751. Reprinted, 1765.

———. "Memorandums concerning the Earthquakes of North America." Edited by B. S. Barton. *Medical and Physical Journal* 1, pt. 1 (1804):65–67.

———. "Native American or Indian Dogs." Edited by B. S. Barton. *Medical and Physical Journal* 1, pt. 2 (1805):18–19.

———. "Notices of the Epidemics of Pennsylvania and New-Jersey, in the Years 1746, 1747, 1748, and 1749." Edited by B. S. Barton. *Medical and Physical Journal* 1, pt. 1 (1804):3–5.

———. "Observations made by Mr. John Bartram, at Pensilvania, on the Yellowish Wasp of that Country: In a Letter to Mr. Peter Collinson, F.R.S." *Philosophical Transactions* 53 (1763):37–38.

———. *Observations on the Inhabitants, Climate, Soil, Rivers, Productions, and other Matters Worthy of Notice made in travels from Pensilvania* to Onondago, Oswego and the Lake Ontario in Canada, with account of Niagara by Peter Kalm.* London, 1751; reprint, with map and one plate added, Rochester, 1895; reprint in John Bartram, Lewis Evans, and Conrad Weiser, *A Journey from Pennsylvania to Onondago in 1743.* Introduction by Whitfield J. Bell, Jr. Barre, Massachusetts, 1973.

———. "Of the Great Black Wasp of Pennsylvania, communicated to the Royal Society, by Mr. P. Collinson, F.R.S., being an Extract of his Friend, Mr. John Bartram's Letter." *Gentleman's Magazine* 21 (February 1751):101.

———. Preface on red cedars. In Richard Saunders, *Poor Richard Improved.* Philadelphia, 1749.

———. "Some Observations on the Dragon-Fly or Libella of Pensilvania, Collected from Mr. John Bartram's Letters, Communicated by Peter Collinson, F.R.S." *Philosophical Transactions* 46 (1750):323–25.

———. "Some Remarks on Dr. Alston's Dissertation on the Sexes of Plants . . . by two celebrated botanists of North America, both dated June 10, 1755." *Gentleman's Magazine* 25 (September 1755):407–8.

———. *John and William Bartram's America.* Edited by Helen Gere Cruickshank. New York, 1957.

Bartram, John, Jr. *Catalogue of Trees, Shrubs and Herbaceous Plants Indigenous to the United States of America, Cultivated and Disposed of By John Bartram & Son at their Botanical Garden, Kingsess, near Philadelphia. . . .* Philadelphia, 1807.

Bartram, William. "Some Account of the Late Mr. John Bartram of Pennsylvania." *Medical and Physical Journal* 1, pt. 1 (1804):115–24.

———. "Travels in Georgia and Florida, 1773–74: A Report to Dr. John Fothergill." Edited by Francis Harper. *Transactions of the American Philosophical Society,* n.s. 33, pt. 2 (November 1943):123–242.

———. *The Travels of William Bartram, Naturalist's Edition.* Edited by Francis Harper. New Haven, 1958.

———. *Travels Through North and South Carolina, Georgia, East and West Florida.* Facsimile of the 1792 London edition. Introduction by Gordon De Wolf. Savannah, 1973.

Baxter, Samuel N. "Restoration of Plants in Bartram's Garden by the Fairmount Park Commission of Philadelphia." *Bartonia,* supp. to #12 (December 1931):38–50.

Bell, Whitfield J., Jr. "A Box of Old Bones: A Note on the Identification of the Mastodon, 1766–1806." *Proceedings of the American Philosophical Society* 93 (May 1949):169–77.

———, and Ketcham, Ralph L. "A Tribute to John Bartram, with a Note on Jacob Engelbrecht." *Pennsylvania Magazine of History and Biography* 83 (October 1959):446–51.

Berkeley, Edmund, and Berkeley, Dorothy Smith. *Dr. Alexander Garden of Charles Town.* Chapel Hill, 1969.

———. *Dr. John Mitchell: The Man who Made the Map of North America.* Chapel Hill, 1974.

———. *John Clayton: Pioneer of American Botany.* Chapel Hill, 1963.

Besse, Joseph. *A Collection of the Sufferings of the People Called Quakers.* 2 vols. London, 1753.

Bidal, Anne-Marie. *Inventoire des Archives du Muséum National d'Histoire Naturelle.* Paris, 1934.

Blunt, Wilfred. *The Art of Botanical Illustration.* London, 1955.

Bourdin, Henri L.; Gabriel, Ralph H.; and Williams, Stanley T. *Sketches of Eighteenth Century America.* New Haven, 1925.

Bowden, James. *The History of the Society of Friends in America.* 2 vols. London, 1850, 1854.

Brett-James, Norman G. *The Life of Peter Collinson.* London, n.d.

Britten, James. *The Sloane Herbarium.* Edited by J. E. Dandy. London, 1958.

Brooks, E. St. John. *Sir Hans Sloane: The Great Collector and His Circle.* London, 1954.

Browne, Mrs. "Mrs. Browne's Diary in Virginia and Maryland." Edited by Fairfax Harrison. *Virginia Magazine of History and Biography* 32 (October 1924):305–20.

Bunting, Morgan. "The Names of the Early Settlers of Darby Township, Chester County, Pennsylvania." *Pennsylvania Magazine of History and Biography* 24 (1900):182–86.

Byrd, William. *Histories of the Dividing Line Betwixt Virginia and North Carolina.* Introduction by William K. Boyd and Percy G. Adams. New York, 1967.

Catesby, Mark. *The Natural History of Carolina, Florida and the Bahama Islands.* 2 vols. London, 1729–47. Revised by Mr. [George] Edwards, of the Royal College of Physicians, London, 1771.

Chester County. *"Enterys" of The Orphans Court of Chester County, Pennsylvania 1716–1730, 1732–1734.* Transcribed by Dorothy Lapp. Danboro, Pa., 1973.

———. *Index to Chester County Wills and Intestate Records 1713–1850.* Transcribed by Bart Anderson, Dorothy B. Lapp, and Marwood Darlington. Danboro, Pa., 1970.

———. *Records of the Courts of Chester County, Pennsylvania 1681–1697.* Philadelphia, 1910.

———. *Records of the Courts of Chester County, Pennsylvania, 1697–1710.* Transcribed by Dorothy Lapp. Danboro, Pa., 1972.

Cheston, Emily Read. *John Bartram, 1699–1777: His Garden and His House.* 2d ed. Philadelphia, 1953.

Clayton, John, and Gronovius, John Frederick. *Flora Virginica.* Leiden, 1762.

Clokie, Hermia Newman. *An Account of the Herbaria of the Department of Botany in the University of Oxford.* Oxford, 1964.

Colden, Cadwallader. *Letters and Papers of Cadwallader Colden.* 8 vols. New York, 1920.

———. *The History of the Five Indian Nations Depending on the Province of New-York in America.* Part I, 1727; Part II, 1747. Ithaca, 1958.

Cowen, David L. "A Store Mixt, Various, Universal." *The Journal of the Rutgers University Library* 25 (December 1961):5.

Crèvecoeur, Michel Guillaume Jean de ("St. John, J. Hector"). *Letters from an American Farmer*. London, 1913, from the 1782 London ed.

Cutler, the Reverend Manasseh. *Life, Journals and Correspondence of Rev. Manasseh Cutler, L.L.D.* Edited by William Parker Cutler and Julia Perkins Cutler. 2 vols. Cincinnati, 1888.

Darlington, William, ed. *Memorials of John Bartram and Humphry Marshall*. Facsimile of the 1849 edition. Introduction by Joseph Ewan. New York, 1967.

Dictionary of American Biography.

Dill, Alonzo Thomas, Jr. "Eighteenth Century New Bern." Part 3. *North Carolina Historical Review* 22 (July 1945):293–319.

Dillenius, John Jac. *Historia Muscorum*. London, 1741.

Dillingham, William Henry. *Tribute to the Memory of Peter Collinson with some Notice of Dr. Darlington's Memorials of John Bartram and Humphry Marshall*. Philadelphia, 1851.

Dillwyn, Lewis Weston. *Hortus Collinsonianus—An Account of the Plants Cultivated by the Late Peter Collinson, Esq., F.R.S.* Swansea, 1843.

Earnest, Ernest. *John and William Bartram, Botanists and Explorers*. Philadelphia, 1940.

Edwards, George. *Essays upon Natural History and Other Miscellaneous Subjects*. London, 1770.

Evans, Howard E. *Studies on the Comparative Ethology of Digger Wasps of the Genus Bembix*. Ithaca, New York, 1957.

Ewan, Joseph. "Annals of 'The Most Wonderful Plant in the World' (Darwin)." *Sonderdruck aus Festschrift Für Claus Nissen*. Wiesbaden, 1973.

———. *William Bartram, Botanical and Zoological Drawings, 1756–1788*. Philadelphia, 1968.

———. "William Bartram's Hidden Role in the Beginnings of Natural History in the United States." *Actes du XIe Congrès International d'Histoire des Sciences* (Warsaw) 5 (1968):55–57.

———, and Ewan, Nesta. *John Banister and His Natural History of Virginia, 1678–1692*. Urbana, Illinois, 1970.

Eyles, W. A. "The Extent of Geological Knowledge in the Eighteenth Century and the Methods by Which It was Diffused." In *Towards a History of Geology*, edited by Cecil J. Schneer. Cambridge, Mass., 1969.

Farmer, John. "John Farmer's First American Journey, 1711–1714." Edited by Henry J. Cadbury. *Proceedings of the American Antiquarian Society* 53 (April 1943):78–95.

Fisher, George Harrison. "Brigadier-general Henry Bouquet." *Pennsylvania Magazine of History and Biography* 3 (1879):121–43.

Fite, Emerson D., and Freeman, Archibald. *A Book of Old Maps Delineating American History*. New York, 1969.

Fletcher, Stevenson Whitcomb. *Pennsylvania Agriculture and Country Life*. 2 vols. Harrisburg, 1950.

Fogg, John M., Jr. "A List of Bartram Trees and Shrubs." *Morris Arboretum Bulletin* 18 (December 1967):75–81.

Fothergill, John. *Chain of Friendship, Selected Letters of Dr. John Fothergill of London.* Edited by Betsy C. Corner and Christopher C. Booth. Cambridge, Mass., 1971.

———. *Some Account of the Late Peter Collinson.* London, 1770.

Fox, R. Hingston. *Dr. John Fothergill and His Friends.* London, 1919.

Franklin, Benjamin. "A Proposal for Promoting Useful Knowledge among the British Plantations in America." *Pennsylvania Gazette* (28 January 1768).

———. *Letters and Papers of Benjamin Franklin and Richard Jackson 1753–1785.* Edited by Carl Van Doren. Philadelphia, 1947.

———. *The Autobiography of Benjamin Franklin.* New York, 1955.

———. *The Papers of Benjamin Franklin.* Edited by Leonard W. Labaree. 20 vols. New Haven, 1959–.

———. *The Works of Benjamin Franklin.* Edited by Jared Sparks. 10 vols. Boston, 1856.

———. *The Writings of Benjamin Franklin.* Edited by Albert Henry Smyth. 10 vols. New York, 1907.

Frick, George Frederick, and Stearns, Raymond Phineas. *Mark Catesby, The Colonial Audubon.* Urbana, Illinois, 1961.

Gipson, Lawrence Henry. *Lewis Evans.* Philadelphia, 1939.

Gordon, Maurice Bear. *Aesculapius Comes to the Colonies.* Ventnor, N.J., 1949.

Gronovius, John Frederick. "An Unpublished Letter by Gronovius." Edited by Helen A. Choate. *Torreya* 16:116–20.

———. *Index Suppelactilis Lapidae quam collegit.* Leiden, 1750.

———, and Clayton, John. *Flora Virginica.* Leiden, 1762.

Hadfield, Miles. *Gardening in Britain.* London, 1960.

Harper, Francis. *See* Bartram, John, "Diary of a Journey"; Bartram, William, "Travels in Georgia and Florida" and *The Travels of William Bartram.*

Harshberger, John William. *The Botanists of Philadelphia and Their Work.* Philadelphia, 1899.

Harvey, John. *Early Horticultural Catalogues.* Bath, 1973.

Hedrick, U. P. *A History of Horticulture in America to 1860.* Oxford, 1950.

Hildeburn, Charles R. "Sir John St. Clair, Baronet." *Pennsylvania Magazine of History and Biography* 9 (January 1885):1–14.

Hindle, Brooke. *The Pursuit of Science in Revolutionary America, 1735–1789.* Chapel Hill, 1956.

Jackson, Joseph. *Encyclopedia of Philadelphia.* 3 vols. Harrisburg, 1932.

Jefferson, Thomas. *Thomas Jefferson's Garden Book.* Edited by Edwin Morris Betts. Philadelphia, 1944.

Jenkins, Charles F. "The Historical Background of Franklin's Tree." *Pennsylvania Magazine of History and Biography* 57 (1933):193–208.

Kalm, Peter. *Kalm's Account of His Visit to England on His Way to America in 1748.* Edited by Joseph Lucas. London, 1792.

———. *Peter Kalm's Travels in North America.* Edited by Adolph B. Benson. 2 vols. New York, 1937.

Kenny, James. "Journal of James Kenny, 1761–1763." Edited by John W. Jordan. *Pennsylvania Magazine of History and Biography* 37 (1913):19–24.

Kerkkonen, Matti. *Peter Kalm's North American Journey, Its Ideological Background and Results.* Helsinki, 1959.

Kirkland, T. J., and Kennedy, R. M. *Historic Camden.* Columbia, S.C., 1905.

Kremers and Urdang's *History of Pharmacy.* Revised by Glenn Sonnedecker. Philadelphia, 1963.

Kurtén, Björn. *The Age of Dinosaurs.* New York, 1968.

Lambert, Aylmer Bourke. "Notes Relating to Botany, Collected from the Manuscripts of the Late Peter Collinson." *Transactions of the Linnean Society* (London) 10 (1811).

Lamboll, Thomas. *Thomas and Elizabeth Lamboll: Early Charleston Gardeners.* Edited by Elise Pinckney. Charleston, S.C., 1969.

Langstaff, John Brett. *Doctor Bard of Hyde Park.* New York, 1942.

Leach, Frank Willing. "Old Philadelphia Families, 80 Bartram." *North American* (Philadelphia) 20 December 1908.

Leighton, Ann. *American Gardens in the Eighteenth Century.* Boston, 1976.

Lettsom, John Coakley. *Memoirs of John Fothergill, M.D.* London, 1786.

Linnaeus, Carolus. *A Selection of the Correspondence of Linnaeus and Other Naturalists.* Edited by James Edward Smith. 2 vols. London, 1821.

Logan, Martha. "Letters of Martha Logan to John Bartram, 1760–1763." Edited by Mary Barbot Prior. *South Carolina Historical Magazine* 59 (1958):38–46.

Marshall, Humphry. *Arbustum Americanum.* Philadelphia, 1785.

McGrath, Francis Sims. *Pillars of Maryland.* Richmond, 1950.

Meehan, Thomas. "John Bartram." *Meehan's Monthly* 1 (August 1891):31.

———. "John Bartram." *Meehan's Monthly* 3 (August 1893):126.

———."John Bartram's Wood-shed." *Meehan's Monthly* 9 (June 1899):96.

———. *The American Handbook of Ornamental Trees.* Philadelphia, 1853.

Michaux, André, "Portions of the journal of André Michaux, botanist . . . 1785–1796." Introduction and annotation by C. S. Sargent. *Proceedings of the American Philosophical Society* 26 (19 October 1888):1–145.

Miller, Philip. *The Gardener's Dictionary Containing the Methods of Cultivating and Improving the Kitchen, Flower, Fruit, and Pleasure Garden.* London, 1752.

Mitchell, John. "Dissertatio Brevis de Principiis botanicorum et zoologorum de que novo .,. . Generum plantarum recens conditorum. . . ." *Acta Physico-Medica Academae Caesare . . . Ephemerides* 8 (1748): 118–224.

———. *The Present State of Great Britain and North America.* London, 1767.

Montgomery, Thomas Harrison. *A History of the University of Pennsylvania.* Philadelphia, 1900.

Mowat, Charles L. "The Tribulations of Denys Rolle." *Florida Historical*

Quarterly 23 (July 1944):1–74.

Myers, Richmond E. "Observations on Pennsylvania Geology and Minerals." *Proceedings of the Pennsylvania Academy of Science* 19 (1945):114.

North Carolina. *The Colonial Records of North Carolina.* Edited by William L. Saunders. 30 vols. Raleigh, 1886.

Packard, Francis R. *History of Medicine in the United States.* 2 vols. Philadelphia, 1931.

Pennant, Thomas. *Arctic Zoology.* 2 vols. London, 1784.

Pennsylvania. *Colonial Records of Pennsylvania 1683–1790.* 16 vols. Philadelphia, 1852–53.

———. *Minutes of the Provincial Council of Pennsylvania, Colonial Records of Pennsylvania.* 1st ser. 16 vols. Harrisburg, 1851.

Pennsylvania Gazette, 1732–77.

Prince, Winifred Notman. "John Bartram and Thorndon Park." *Garden Journal* 7 (1957):141–43, 152, 8 (1957):189–91.

———."John Bartram in the Cedar Swamps." *Notes and Documents* 81 (January 1957):86–88.

Proceedings Centennial Anniversary Friends' Meeting House, Darby, Pennsylvania, 1805–1905. N.p., n.d.

Pursh, Frederick. *Flora Americae Septentrionales.* 2 vols. London, 1814.

Purver, Margery. *The Royal Society: Concept and Creation.* Cambridge, Mass., 1967.

Pyle, Howard. "Bartram and his garden." *Harper's New Monthly Magazine* 60 (February 1880):321–30.

Raistrick, Arthur. *Quakers in Science and Industry.* New York, 1968.

Ravenel, Mrs. St. Julien. *Charleston, The Place and the People.* New York, 1927.

Royal Society (London). *Philosophical Transactions.*

Schneer, Cecil J., ed. *Toward a History of Geology.* Cambridge, Mass., London, 1969.

Schoepf, Johann David. *Travels in the Confederation 1783–84.* Translated by Alfred J. Morrison. New York, 1968.

Simpson, George Gaylord. "The Beginnings of Vertebrate Paleontology in North America." *Proceedings of the American Philosophical Society* 86 (September 1942):130–88.

Small, John Kunkel. *Manual of the Southeastern Flora.* New York, 1933.

Smallwood, William Martin, and Smallwood, Mabel Sarah Coon. *Natural History and the American Mind.* New York, 1941.

Smith, Benjamin H. *Atlas of Delaware County Showing the Early Grants and Patents.* Philadelphia, 1880.

Smith, George. *History of Delaware County, Pennsylvania.* Philadelphia, 1862.

Stearns, Raymond Phineas. *Science in the British Colonies of America.* Urbana, Illinois, 1970.

Stillwell, John E. *Historical and Genealogical Miscellaney.* 5 vols. New York, 1916.

Swem, E. G. *Brothers of the Spade. Correspondence of Peter Collinson of*

London, and of John Custis of Williamsburg, Virginia, 1734–1746. Barre, Mass., 1957.

Tolles, Frederick B. *James Logan and the Culture of Provincial America.* Boston, 1957.

True, Rodney Howard. "John Bartram's Life and Botanical Explorations." *Bartonia,* supp. to #12 (December 1931):7–19.

————. "Some Pre-Revolutionary Agricultural Correspondence." *Agricultural History* 12 (April 1938):107–17.

Van Doren, Carl. "The Beginnings of the American Philosophical Society." *Proceedings of the American Philosophical Society* 87 (1943):277–89.

Von Graffenried, Christoph. *Christoph von Graffenried's Account of the Founding of New Bern.* Edited by Vincent H. Todd and Julius Goebel. Raleigh, N.C., 1920.

Weiss, Harry B., and Ziegler, Grace M., *Thomas Say, Early American Naturalist.* Springfield, Ill., 1931.

Wertenbaker, William. "Explorer" [Maurice Ewing]. "Profiles," *New Yorker,* 4, 11, 18 November 1974.

West, Francis D. "The Mystery of the Death of William Bartram, Father of John Bartram, the Botanist." *The Pennsylvania Genealogical Magazine* 20 (1957):253.

White, George W. "Early American Geology." *The Scientific Monthly,* March 1953, pp. 134–41.

Williams, Gabriel, and Williams, Stanley T. *Sketches of Eighteenth Century America.* New Haven, 1925.

Williamson, Mary E. "The Maris Family." *Bulletin of the Friends Historical Association* 19 (Spring 1930):17.

Wilstach, Paul. *Tidewater Maryland.* Indianapolis, 1931.

Woody, Thomas. *Early Quaker Education in Pennsylvania.* New York, 1920.

Wynne, William. "Some Account of the Nursery Gardens and the State of Horticulture in the Neighborhood of Philadelphia...." *Gardener's Magazine* (London) 8 (June 1832):272–77.

Youmans, William Jay. *Pioneers of Science in America.* New York, 1896.

Young, William, Jr. *Botanica Neglecta: William Young, Jr.* Edited by Samuel N. Rhoads. Philadelphia, 1916.

Youngken, Heber W. *A Textbook of Pharmacognosy.* Philadelphia, 1948.

Zirkle, Conway. "Plant Hybridization and Plant Breeding in Eighteenth-Century American Agriculture." *Agricultural History* 43 (January 1969):25–39.

————. *The Beginnings of Plant Hybridization.* Philadelphia, 1935.

Index

Acacia (*Robinia*), 213, 276
Aconite (*Aconitum*), 184
Alder (*Alnus rugosa*?), 149
Alfalfa (*Medicago sativa*), 11
Allegheny barberry, 210
Alligator (*Alligator mississipiensis*), 237, 256, 258, 259, 260
Alsine. *See* Chickweed
Alston, Dr. Charles, 53, 157, 175
American Philosophical Society, 112–20, 283, 296–97
Amsonia, 192, 209
Andromeda (*Arsenococcus*?), 252
Anise. *See* Star anise
Apothecary shop, 171, 185
Apple (*Malus*), 183, 210, 230
Arborvitae (*Thuja occidentalis*), 59
Argyll, Duke of, 120–21, 135, 203, 313
Aristolochia, 199
Arum, 277
Aster, 45, 183

Balm of gilead fir (*Abies balsamea*), 80, 81–82, 88, 89, 150
Banana (*Musa sapientum*), 259
Bard, Dr. John, 218, 350n65
Bard, Samuel, 218
Barley (*Hordeum*), 281
Bartram, Ann, daughter, 15, 219–20, 237, 292
Bartram, Ann Mendenhall, second wife, 10, 11, 15, 32, 123, 171–72, 194–95, 197–98, 208, 221, 234, 238, 250, 272–73, 292

Bartram, Benjamin, son, 15, 193, 208, 284, 292
Bartram, Elizabeth, grandmother, 1, 2, 6, 9, 210
Bartram, Elizabeth, half sister, 7–8
Bartram, Elizabeth (1734–35), daughter, 15
Bartram, Elizabeth, daughter, 15, 284, 292
Bartram, Elizabeth Smith, stepmother, 6–8
Bartram, Elizah Hunt, mother, 3–4, 327
Bartram, George, son-in-law, 219–20, 284
Bartram, Isaac, uncle, 2, 4, 6, 273
Bartram, Isaac, son, 9, 171, 185, 197, 204, 208, 250–51, 273, 283, 284, 291–92, 354n6
Bartram, James, brother, 1, 2, 4, 284
Bartram, James, son, 15, 171–72, 284, 291, 292
Bartram, John, grandfather, 1, 2, 3, 9, 305
Bartram, John, uncle, 2
Bartram, John, botanist: education of, 4–5, 35, 293; land owned by, 6, 7, 9–10, 13–15, 171–72, 273, 291–92; and Indians, 6–8, 13, 46, 79, 89–90, 91–109 passim, 128, 134, 160–61, 167–68, 184, 186, 198; children of, 9, 15–17, 148, 179–80, 290–91; houses of, 10–12, 180–81, 273, 284, 291–92, 301; farming practices of, 11–13, 164–65, 197, 224; garden of, 11, 180–82, 191–92, 223, 300–304, 345n55; publications of,

369

13, 21, 130, 131–33, 153–55, 175–76, 267–71, 306–8; and B. Franklin, 13, 51–52, 86–87, 109, 111, 112–20 passim, 146, 153, 157, 163–64, 168–69, 176–77, 205–6, 217–18, 219–20, 226, 246, 280–81, 284, 287; and land drainage, 11–13, 163–64, 223, 224; and conservation, 13, 285; philosophy of, 15–17, 178–80, 290–91; library of, 22, 36, 48, 65, 72–73, 75–76, 79, 140, 153, 158, 164, 183, 205, 291; and Sir Hans Sloane, 32, 72–75, 83, 292; remuneration of, 32–33, 46–49, 279, 285; pollen studies by, 37–38, 175–76; journals of, 45, 79, 83, 105, 110–11, 140, 155, 192, 201, 231, 234, 245, 250–51, 263, 267, 269–71, 274, 281; maps by, 45, 79, 144–45, 259, 263; and Mark Catesby, 51, 53, 68–72, 83, 174; and John Clayton, 54–55, 190–92, 205–6; experiments of, 61–65, 175–76; medical interests of, 56–57, 58, 65, 131–33, 237, 296, 306; and Dr. John F. Gronovius, 66, 67, 110–11, 118–19, 135–36, 138–41, 205–6; honors received by, 67–68, 73, 74–75, 227–28, 281–82, 283, 287, 304; drawings by, 79, 83, 180–81; and Philip Miller, 83, 174–75, 176, 182–83; and the American Philosophical Society, 112–20, 283, 296; and Dr. John Mitchell, 119–21, 135, 270–71; proposed publications of, 122–23, 172–75, 280–81; and Peter Kalm, 126–31; geological and paleontological interests of, 128–29, 136–47, 157, 158, 227, 233, 237, 238, 240–41, 261, 295–96, 319; ecological interests of, 128, 231, 282, 297; meteorological interests of, 129, 231, 234, 244, 250–51, 282; and evolution, 135–36, 295; five-guinea boxes of, 151–53, 202–4, 308–10; and bird migration, 155–56; and Dr. Alexander Garden, 157–58, 186–89, 227–28, 229–32, 234, 246, 250, 299–300; and Michael Collinson, 177, 277, 278–79, 284–85, 289; and Darby Meeting, 177–79, 323; and plant introduction, 183–84; and slaves, 184, 224–25, 264; and Thomas Lamboll, 187, 227, 229, 230–31, 234, 256, 263–64, 273, 274, 288; and nurserymen, 193, 203–4, 311–13; greenhouse of, 193–94, 223; and mammoths, 206–7, 214; and George III,

216–17, 219, 227–28, 236, 263, 269, 272, 277; and St. John de Crèvecoeur, 221–26, 351n1; and St. Johns River, 256–63; will of, 284, 291–92; death of, 291; evaluation of, 292–300; zoological contributions of, 294–95; botanical contributions of, 296–99, 320–22; customers of, 311–19
—trips to: Jerseys, 34, 38–39, 40, 79, 83, 177, 214; Pennsylvania, 44–45, 50–51, 77–79, 91–94, 193, 197, 198–201; Maryland, 47, 49; Virginia, 47, 49, 53–60, 144–45, 184–85; New York, 80–82, 84, 88–89, 91–111, 148–51, 156–57; Connecticut, 163–66; Carolinas, 186–92, 207–10, 228–37; Georgia, 237–46; Florida, 246–63
Bartram, John, Jr., son, 15, 184–85, 214, 272, 274–75, 284, 291–92, 301–2
Bartram, Mary, great-grandmother, 2, 305
Bartram, Mary, daughter, 15, 172, 284, 292
Bartram, Mary Maris, first wife, 9, 171
Bartram, Moses, son, 15, 41, 169–71, 185, 197, 204, 208, 269, 274–75, 283, 284, 285, 291, 292, 354n6
Bartram, Richard, great-grandfather, 1, 305
Bartram, Richard (1724–27), son, 9
Bartram, William, father, 2, 3–4, 5–7
Bartram, Col. William, half brother, 7–8, 184, 189–90, 195–96, 197, 204, 207, 208, 233–35, 284, 346n14
Bartram, William, son, 15, 152, 204–5, 212, 292, 301; trips with father, 148–51, 163–66, 228, 232–63, 341n6; drawings by, 158–60, 174, 234, 250–51, 263, 274–75, 278, 282, 285, 287, 288; career of, 159, 168–69, 190, 195–96, 204, 263–67, 273, 283–90; and Dr. John Fothergill, 275, 285, 287
Bartram, Dr. William, 190, 197–98, 204, 284
Bartram Association, 303–4
Bartramia, 67–68, 73, 304
Bay, 190, 195, 244, 245, 253, 255
Bear, 41, 43, 130, 155, 259, 260, 295
Bee, 25, 74, 256
Beech (*Fagus*), 231, 238
Beetle, 43
Belemnites, 142–43
Bellwort (*Uvularia*), 240
Bennett, William, 276

Bentinck, Margaret Cavendish. *See* Portland, Duchess of
Birch (*Betula*), 89, 127, 156, 174
Bird, 153–56, 158, 260–61, 287
Blackberry (*Rubus*), 183
Blackbird (Grackle? *Quiscalus quiscula*), 72
Bloodroot (*Sanguinaria canadensis*), 132
Bond, Dr. Phineas, 117, 138, 283
Bond, Dr. Thomas, 52–53, 115, 117, 136, 138, 283, 347n17
Boneset (*Eupatorium perfoliatum*), 133
Bonsalls, 3, 172, 284
Borer, 74
Bouncing bet (*Saponaria officinalis*), 183
Bouquet, Gen. Henry, 198–201, 204, 206, 213–14, 226, 228, 248
Braddock, Gen. Edward, 161–63, 194
Breintnall, Joseph, 18, 20, 22, 32, 109–10, 328n2
"Briony" (*Bryonia dioica*), 176
Buffalo (*Bison*), 100
Bullfrog (*Rana catesbeiana*), 28, 279–80
Burweed, 334n29
Bute, Earl of, 121–22, 135, 203, 217, 226, 275, 277, 314, 315
Butter-and-eggs, 339n22
Butterflies, 25
Buttonbush (*Cephalanthus*), 253
Byrd, Col. William, 57–59, 63–64

Cabbage tree (*Sabal palmetto*), 248, 260
Campion (*Lychnis*), 62–63, 64, 68, 139
Cardinal flower (*Lobelia cardinalis*), 45
Carolina allspice (*Calycanthus*), 209, 213
Carolina pea (*Dolichos*?), 254, 266
Cartlidge, Elizabeth Bartram, aunt, 3, 5, 49
Cassina (*Ilex vomitoria*), 242
Catalpa (*Pinckneya*?), 247
Caterpillars, 41, 43
Catesby, Mark, 21, 27–31, 51, 53, 58, 68–72, 83, 116, 118, 120, 126, 174, 191
Catskills, 25, 81–82, 88–89, 148–51, 156–57
Cedar, red (*Juniperus virginiana*), 13, 33, 38, 55, 83, 84
Cedar, white (*Chamaecyparis thyoides*), 38–39, 83, 134
Centaury (*Centaurea*), 160
Ceratiola ericoides, 209
Chalmers, Dr. Lionel, 285, 288
Chambers, Benjamin, great-uncle, 7, 8

Charlotia, 256, 258
Cherry, 66, 85, 89, 156
Chew, Dr. Samuel, 18–19
Chick-pea (*Cicer arietinum*), 281
Chickweed (*Stellaria*), 139, 183
Chiggerweed (*Asclepias tuberosa*), 132–33
Child, Capt. James, 170–71, 195
Chimney swift (*Chaetura pelagica*), 71, 88
Chinaberry tree (*Melia azedarach*), 195
Chinese tallow tree (*Sapium sebiferum* or *Stillingia sebifera*), 287
Chokecherry (*Padus*), 187
"Christophoriana" (*Actaea*), 96
Cinquefoil (*Potentilla*), 11, 127
Citron (*Citron medica*), 259
Clayton, John, 54–55, 65, 66, 67, 116, 119, 175, 190–92, 205–6, 276, 281
Claytonia, 67
Cliff swallow (*Petrochelidon pyrrhonota*), 88
Clover, red (*Trifolium pratense*), 11
Clover, white (*Trifolium repens*), 11
Cockspur thorn (*Crataegus crus-galli*), 85
Coffee. *See* Kentucky coffee tree
Colden, Dr. Cadwallader, 67, 80, 81, 88–89, 90, 91, 109, 114–17, 119, 120, 122, 124–25, 132, 149–50, 156–57, 254, 276
Coldenia, 68
Collinson, Michael, 177, 277, 278–79, 284–85, 289
Collinson, Peter, 22–23, 32–34, 53, 57, 61, 64–65, 67–68, 78, 112, 115, 120, 126, 133, 164, 172, 180, 187, 205, 250, 263; garden of, 18–19, 68–69, 275–76; and plant introduction, 18–19, 183–84; and Bartram's publications, 19, 21, 41, 110–11, 175–76, 268–70, 306–8; and Bartram's collections, 19, 22–24, 32–33, 43–47, 49, 51–53, 66, 83, 88–89, 151–53, 177, 192, 202–4, 211–13, 245; and the Royal Society, 19, 21, 39–43, 52; plant exchange with Bartram, 22–24, 32–33; and zoology, 25–32, 39–41; and Sir Hans Sloane, 26, 72–75; and the Lords Petre, 32, 43–46, 80, 83–86, 88, 213; gifts to Bartram, 32–33, 45, 53, 75–76, 156, 193; and Bartram payments, 32–33, 46–49, 279, 285; and James Logan, 35–37; and Linnaeus, 36, 67, 126, 191; and Bartram's jour-

nals, 45, 79, 83, 105, 110–11, 140, 155, 192, 201, 231, 234, 245, 250–51, 263, 267, 269–71, 274, 281; and geology, 136, 142, 206–7, 234–35; and William Bartram, 158–60, 168–69, 174, 274–75; and Moses Bartram, 169–70, 185, 269, 274; and Bartram's trees, 172–75; and "King's Botanist," 216–17, 226–28, 272; death of, 277

Colocasia (Nelumbo lutea?), 233, 274–75, 278, 279, 280. *See also* Taro

Coreopsis, 199

Cormorant *(Phalacrocorax)*, 71

Corn *(Zea mays)*, 11, 55, 61, 98, 99, 100, 101, 105, 165, 176, 258, 266, 268

Cotton *(Gossypium)*, 254, 258, 268

Crataegus, 85, 165

Cressy, Dr. J. Slingsby, 68

Crow *(Corvus)*, 71

Crow garlick *(Allium vineale)*, 183

Cucumber *(Cucumis sativus)*, 176, 258

Custis, John, 54, 55–57

Cyclamen, 193

Cypress *(Taxodium distichum)*, 238, 242, 246, 253, 266, 268

Dahoon holly *(Ilex cassine)*, 253

Daisy, ox-eye *(Chrysanthemum leucanthemum)*, 183

Dalibard, Thomas Francis, 153, 224, 314

Dandelion *(Taraxacum officinale)*, 183

Darby Meeting, 6, 177–79, 291, 323

Darlington, Dr. William, 302, 333n6

De Brahm, Gerard, 262, 273

De Crèvecoeur, St. John, 221–26, 301–2, 351

Deer *(Odocoileus)*, 26, 245, 256

De Jussieu, Antoine, 52–53, 224

De Jussieu, Bernard, 224, 226

Dewberry *(Rubus)*, 183

Dillenius, John Jacob, 39, 65–66

Dittany *(Cunila origanoides)*, 25

Dobbs, Gov. Arthur, 133–34, 189, 195, 211, 213, 234, 314

Dock *(Rumex)*, 183

Dog fennel *(Eupatorium capillifolium)*, 183

Dogwood *(Cornus)*, 33, 85, 231, 233

Dragonhead *(Dracocephalum* or *Moldavica)*, 200

Dublin Society, 114, 134, 314, 340n28

Ducks, 71, 261

Dudley, Paul, 39–40, 61

Ecology, 41–43, 297

Edwards, George, 153–55, 195, 348n44

Eel *(Anguilla rostrata)*, 98

Ehret, George, 159, 160, 175, 191, 276

Eliot, the Rev. Jared, 163–65, 208

Ellis, John, 192–93, 213, 215–16, 227, 270, 280, 287, 314, 353n9

Elm *(Ulmus)*, 32

Evans, Lewis, 92–109 passim, 119, 134

Farmer, John, 327n39

Fever tree *(Pinckneya pubens)*, 245

Fish, 72, 118, 141, 230, 242, 249, 258, 268

Flax *(Linum usitatissimum)*, 11

Flea, 92

Forts, 161–62, 198–200, 242, 243, 245–47, 250, 252, 253, 254, 256

Fossils, 25, 72, 79, 140–41, 142–43, 146, 206–7, 230, 231, 295, 319

Fothergill, Dr. John, 53, 54, 136–38, 275, 277–80, 285, 287, 288–89

Franklin, Benjamin, 283; and John Bartram, 13, 51–52, 86–87, 109, 111, 112–20, 146, 153, 157, 163–64, 168–69, 176–77, 205, 217–18, 219–20, 226, 246, 280–81, 284, 287, 314, 315; and the Junto, 22; and the *Pennsylvania Gazette*, 51–52, 86–87, 109, 179; and the Rev. George Whitefield, 77, 244; and Peter Collinson, 111, 205, 226; and the American Philosophical Society, 112–20; and Peter Kalm, 130; and his stove, 134; and Dr. Cadwallader Colden, 157; and the Philadelphia "Academy," 159; and the Indians, 160, 167; and General Braddock, 161–62; and the Rev. Jared Eliot, 163–64; and William Bartram, 168–69; and England, 176–77, 219, 226, 277, 280–81

Franklinia alatamaha, 245–46, 290, 301

Freeman, James, 278–79, 284–85, 287, 289

Fringed orchis *(Habenaria)*, 68

Fringe tree *(Chionanthus virginica)*, 276

Galphin, George, 240–43, 245

Garden, Dr. Alexander, 157–58, 186–89, 196, 209, 214, 215–16, 226, 227–28, 229–32, 234, 250, 263–64, 299–300

Gentian *(Gentiana)*, 45, 127

Geology, 141, 146–47, 227, 233, 237, 238, 240, 261, 319

George III, 216, 234–35, 236, 263, 269, 272, 275, 277, 315
Geranium (or *Pelargonium*), 193
Germander "blew" (*Teucrium*), 37
Ginseng (*Panax quinquefolium*), 51–53, 58–59, 96, 133, 163, 184, 240, 331n3
Goldenrod (*Solidago*), 25, 33, 45
Gordon, Lord Adam, 226, 258
Gordon, James, 193, 203, 204, 212–13, 216, 311–12
Grant, Gov. James, 227, 248, 251–53, 255, 262, 269
Grape (*Vitis*), 149, 196, 230, 231, 258
Green, Dr. Samuel, 189, 205
Gronovius, Dr. John F., 52, 55, 61–62, 66, 67, 110, 111, 116, 118–19, 135–36, 138–41, 158, 205–6
Gronovius, Laurens, 205–6
Groundhog (*Marmota monax*), 26, 70
Gully, Capt. Anthony, 195, 198, 346n15

Habersham, James, 237, 245
Hackberry (*Celtis occidentalis*), 34, 83
Halesia, 276
Hawk, 74
Hellebore, false (*Veratrum viride*), 66
Hemlock (*Tsuga*), 88
Henbit (*Lamium amplexicaule*), 183
Hercules'-club (*Aralia spinosa*), 55, 255
Hermit crab (*Pagurus*), 118
Herons, 71
Hibiscus, 274
Hickory (*Carya*), 88, 173, 204, 231, 233
Hill, Dr. John, 156, 216
Holly (*Ilex*), 39, 55, 193
Honeysuckle (*Lonicera*), 25, 68
Hope, Dr. John, 218–19, 287, 316
Hopton, Sarah, 187
Hopton, William, 231
Hornbeam (*Carpinus*), 231
Hornet (*Vespa*), 25, 43, 74
Horse balm (*Collinsonia canadensis*), 132; *C. tuberosa*, 238
Horse chestnut (*Aesculus*), 57, 170, 200, 207, 210, 349n31
Horse sugar (*Symplocos tinctoria*), 187
Hummingbird (*Archilochus colubris*), 25
Hunt, Elizabeth Chambers, 3
Hunt, James, 3

Indian physic (*Gillenia*), 56–57, 58, 306
Indian pinkroot (*Spigelia marylandica*), 238

Indians, North American: attacks by, 6–8, 160, 167–68, 177, 184, 214–15; customs of, 13, 79, 242, 258–59, 261–62; danger of, 46, 79, 186, 205; Five Nations of, 89, 90–109 passim; meetings with, 91–109 passim, 251–53; Delawares, 108; Susquehanahs, 108; pottery of, 128; treatment of, 134; Bartram's feelings for, 108–9, 160–61; war with, 160–63; relations with whites, 109, 161, 198–200; Cherokees, 186, 288, 289; Shawnees, 206; Creeks, 242, 289
Indian shot (*Canna indica*), 68
Indian turnip (*Arisaema*), 25
Indigo, 133, 230, 268
Insects, 25, 30, 31, 33, 39–43, 53, 73–74, 83, 117–18, 129, 153, 227, 274, 275, 287
Iris, 200

Jacea (*Centaurea jacea*), 200
Jackson, Richard, 110–11, 164
Jardin du Roi, 83, 340n34
John Bartram Association, 303–4
Judas tree (*Cercis canadensis*), 85
Jungstrom, Lars, 126–27, 129, 130

Kalm, Peter, 126–32
Kenny, James, 199–201
Kentucky coffee tree (*Gymnocladus dioica*), 204, 255, 353n2
Kew, 121, 217, 280, 317, 353n9
Kingsessing, 3, 10, 13, 158, 198, 246, 272, 281, 292, 302
Kite, 71

Lady's slipper (*Cypripedium*), 28, 34; yellow (*C. parviflorum*), 68
Lamboll, Thomas, 187, 227, 229, 230–31, 234, 256, 263–64, 273, 274, 288, 289
Lamb's quarter (*Chenopodium alba*), 183
Larch (*Larix*), 276
Larkspur (*Delphinium*), 64–65
Laurens, Col. Henry, 229, 231, 234, 263–67 passim
Leatherwood (*Dirca palustris*), 59
Library Company of Philadelphia, 22, 112
Lichen, 66
Lily (*Lilium*), 46, 68, 187, 253, 278
Lily-of-the-valley (*Maiathemum canadense*), 156, 192, 209

Lime: *Citrus aurantifolia*, 259; *Nyssa ogeche*, 247
Linden (*Tilia*), 231
Linnaea borealis var. *americana*, 127
Linnaeus, Dr. Carolus, 36–38, 61, 67, 116, 126, 130, 131, 157, 158, 183, 191, 213, 214, 282, 294, 320–22
Liverwort (*Porella*), 66
Lizard, 72. *See also* Salamander
Loblolly bay (*Gordonia lasianthus*), 253, 255, 272
Locust (*Magicicada septemdecem*), 39–42, 74
Logan, James, 35–38, 57, 61, 86, 120, 129–30
Logan, Martha, 187
Logan, William, 214, 350n49
Lotus. *See Colocasia*
Louse, 74
Lucerne. *See* Alfalfa
Lycopodium, 66, 89

Magnolia, 31, 53, 85, 97, 208, 213, 231, 255, 275–76
Maidenhair fern (*Adiantum*), 240
Mammoths, 206–7, 214, 295
Maple (*Acer*), 83, 88, 156, 310–11
Maps, 40, 44, 47, 93, 257
Marshall, Humphry, 192, 302, 357n17
Marsh hawk (*Circus cyaneus*), 159
Martagon (*Lilium superbum*), 46
Martin (*Progne subis?*), 88
Meadia. *See* Shooting star
Medicinal plants, 56–57, 58, 65, 131–33, 156, 171, 236
Medicinal springs, 137–38
Medlar (*Mespilus germanica*), 23
Melon (*Cucumis*), 176, 258
Microscope, 37
Miller, Philip, 22–23, 65, 83, 174–75, 176, 182–83, 317
Mimosa, 194, 212
Mitchell, Dr. John, 65, 119–22, 126, 135, 270–71, 315, 318
Mitrewort (*Mitella*), 240
Mohole, 146–47
Mole (*Scalopus?*), 88
Moose (*Alces americanus*), 26
Moss, 65, 66
Moultrie, Maj. John, Jr., 229–30, 352n19
Mountain ash (*Sorbus americana*), 89
Mountain laurel (*Kalmia latifolia*), 68–69

Mt. Hope, 258–59, 290
Mt. Royal, 259, 261–63
Mulberry, 238
Mullein (*Verbascum*), 183
Mussel (*Unio?*), 258–59
Myrtle (*Myrica*), 83, 98, 127, 231

Night hawk (*Chordeiles minor*), 71
Norfolk, Duke of, 83, 85, 88, 203, 317
Northumberland, Duke of, 203, 217, 226, 276, 317

Oak (*Quercus*), 41–42, 46–47, 83, 173, 174, 219, 230, 231, 237, 247, 252, 255, 258, 261, 268
Oat (*Avena sativa*), 11, 210, 281
Onondago, 93, 98–106
Onobrichis (*Psoralea canescens?*), 232–33
Opossum (*Didelphys virginiana*), 26
Opula (*Viburnum opula*), 150
Orange (*Citrus*), 194, 247, 255, 256, 259, 260, 261
Oswego, 81, 91, 93, 101–5, 130
Oswego tea (*Monarda didyma*), 104
Owl, 71
Oysters (*Ostrea*), 240, 249, 307–8, 352n4

Palmetto (*Sabal*), 247, 248, 252, 256, 268
Papaw (*Asimina triloba*), 51, 53
Passenger pigeon (*Ectopistes migratorius*), 43, 295
Peach (*Prunus persica*), 210
Pear (*Pyrus*), 183
Penn, Thomas, 273, 289, 317
Pennington, Edward, 171, 344n17
Persimmon (*Diospyros*), 127
Petre, 8th Baron, 32–33, 43–46, 53, 79–80, 83–86, 88, 317
Petre, 9th Baron, 213, 276–77, 317
Pheasant (*Phasianus colchicus*), 71
Pigweed (*Chenopodium?*), 183
Pine (*Pinus*), 85, 89, 119, 219, 231, 237, 247, 252, 258, 268, 313
Pineapple (*Ananas comosus*), 86, 194
Pitt, William, 205, 213, 215
Plant hybridization, 61–65
Plants introduced to the U.S., 23–24, 57, 82, 156–57, 183–84, 230
Plum (*Prunus*), 199
Pokeweed (*Phytolacca americana*), 90
Portland, Duchess of, 275
Potato (*Solanum tuberosa*), 268

Powell, Nathaniel, 151, 204, 312
Prickly pear (*Opuntia*), 133
Pumpkin (*Cucurbita*), 249, 254
Purple-berried bay (*Tamala borbonia*?), 255
Pyramid of Eden (*Swertia carolinensis*), 209

Ragweed (*Ambrosia*), 183
Randolph, Isham, 59–60
Randolph, William, 59
Raspberry (*Rubus*), 183, 192
Rattlesnake (*Crotalus*), 21, 26, 32, 50, 57, 92, 96, 106, 115, 149, 150, 185, 253–54, 285, 341, 353n17
Rattlesnake root (*Pronanthes*), 133
Redbird (*Richmondena cardinalis*), 25
Reeds (*Phragmites*?), 260
Reindeer moss (*Cladonia*), 66
Rhododendron, 27, 45, 69, 70, 213, 276
Rhubarb (*Rheum*), 287
Rice (*Oryza*), 229–30, 231, 237, 246–47, 258, 261, 263, 264, 266, 268, 287
Richmond, 2d Duke of, 33, 83, 88, 203, 276, 318
Rocket (*Hesperus*), 200
Rolle, Lord Denys, 256, 258, 261, 265
Rosemary (*Ceratiola ericoides*?), 209
Royal Academy of Sciences of Stockholm, 281–82
Royal Society of Arts, 196–97
Royal Society of London, 21, 26, 39, 41, 52, 53, 112–13, 114, 120, 130, 153, 156, 294
Ruffed grouse (*Bonasa umbellus*), 153–54

St. Augustine, 234, 238, 248–50, 251, 254, 259, 262–63, 273, 274
St. Clair, Sir John, 194–95, 318
St. Johns River, 255–63, 267–71, 281
St. John's-wort (*Hypericum*), 200
Salamander, 89
Salt-marsh mussel (*Mytilus*?), 306–8
Sassafras, 39, 83, 137
Saxifrage (*Micranthes*?), 259
Say, Thomas, 171, 185, 291
Scarlet sage (*Salvia*), 274
Scotch lovage (*Ligusticum scothicum*),149
Scotch thistle (*Onopordum acanthium*), 183
Sea mounts, 141, 143–44
Service tree (*Amelanchia*), 85

Sheep sorrel (*Rumex*), 183
Shells, 25, 72–73, 74, 81, 118, 143, 227, 240, 258–59, 261, 275
Shickellamy, 94–95, 100
Ship worm (*Teredo*), 75
Shoemaker, Samuel, 171, 344n17
Shooting star (*Dodecatheon meadia*), 29, 67–68, 70, 190–91
Silk industry, 238, 243
Silkworm (*Bombyx mori*), 238, 243
Silphium, 210
Skullcap (*Scutellaria*), 92
Skunk weed (*Symplocarpus*?), 25, 68
Slaves, 184, 224–25, 262–63, 264
Sloane, Sir Hans, 21, 26, 32, 52, 57, 58, 72–75, 83, 292
Smartweed (*Polygonum*), 259
Smith, Elizabeth Locke, 346n15
Smith, William, 6, 7, 8
Snail, 25, 155, 227, 258
Snake, 25, 53, 72, 117, 258, 260, 275, 287
Snakeroot, 20, 22; Seneca snakeroot (*Polygala senega*), 56, 58
Society of Gentlemen, 218–19, 287, 314
Solander, Dr. Daniel, 211, 349n37
Solomon's seal (*Polygonatum*), 22, 24, 240; false (*Smilacina*), 24
Spalding, James, 258, 259, 290
Spencer, Dr. Archibald, 115, 116, 124
Spider, 118
Spirea, 68
Spruce (*Picea*), 89, 276
Squash (*Cucurbita*), 89, 98, 99, 105, 176
Star anise (*Illicium floridanum*), 261, 353n9
Stork, Dr. William, 267–71
Strawberry (*Fragaria*), 194
Stuart, Col. John, 234, 251–53
Stuartia melachodendron, 276, 313
Succory or chicory (*Cichorium intybus*), 37
Sumac (*Rhus*), 30, 193–94; staghorn (*R. typhina*), 51
Sweet gum (*Liquidambar styraciflua*), 61–62, 83, 237, 255
Sweet shrub (*Calycanthus*), 213
Swertia carolinensis (Walt.) O. Ktze., 209

Tallowood (*Ximenia americana*), 353n3
Tanier or eddo (*Caladium colocasia*), 262
Taro (*Colocasia antiquorum*?), 353n10
Tea (*Camellia*), 192–93
Templeman, Peter, 196

Tennent, Dr. John, 56–57, 58, 306
Terrapins, 25
Tipitiwichet sensative (*Dionaea musci-pula*), 211–13
Toadflax (*Linaria linaria*), 132, 183, 184
Tobacco (*Nicotiana*), 55, 72, 98, 100, 210
Tomato (*Lycopersicon esculentum*), 254
Tortoise, 159–60
Tulip poplar (*Liriodendron tulipifera*), 83–84, 238
Tumble turd (*Scarabaeus?*), 74
Tupelo (*Nyssa*), 190, 237, 313
Turkey (*Meleagris gallopavo*), 245, 256
Turk's-cap lily, 46, 278
Turnip (*Brassica*), 287
Turtle, 26, 53, 72, 88, 159
Turtlehead (*Chelone glabra*), 192

Viburnum, 89
Von Graffenreid, Baron, 7–8

Walnut, black (*Juglans nigra*), 33
Wasp, 25, 30, 72, 118, 256, 294–95, 357
Water lettuce (*Pistia stratiotes*), 259
Watermelon (*Citrullus vulgaris*), 101
Water nummularia (*Jussiaea* or *Isnardia?*), 259

Weiser, Conrad, 89–90, 91–109 passim, 134, 167
Wheat (*Triticum aestivum*), 11, 165, 210
Whippoorwill (*Caprimulgus vociferus*), 71
Whitefield, the Rev. George, 77–78, 80, 159, 244–45
Wild ginger (*Asarum canadense*), 184
Wild lime (*Ximenia americana*), 255
Witt, Dr. Christopher, 32, 33–34, 63
Wolf (*Canis nubilis*), 260
Woodcock (*Philohela minor*), 71
Wood rat (*Neotoma floridana floridana*), 260
Wrangel, the Rev. Charles Magnus, 237, 282
Wright, James, 206
Wright, Gov. James, 237–38, 243
Wyly, Samuel, 208–9

Yam (*Dioscorea*), 266
Yew (*Taxus*), 210; dwarf yew (*T. canadensis*), 89
Young, William, Jr., 215–16, 217, 227, 272